Complete Ukrainian

Olena Bekh
and
James Dingley

First published in Great Britain in 1997 by Hodder Education. An Hachette UK company.

First published in the US in 1997 by Contemporary Books, a Division of the McGraw-Hill Companies.

This edition published in 2016 by John Murray Learning.

British Library Cataloguing in Publication Data: a catalogue record for this title is available from the British Library.

Library of Congress Catalog Card Number: on file.

Paperback ISBN: 9781444104134

12

The publisher has used its best endeavours to ensure that any website addresses referred to in this book are correct and active at the time of going to press. However, the publisher and the author have no responsibility for the websites and can make no guarantee that a site will remain live or that the content will remain relevant, decent or appropriate.

The publisher has made every effort to mark as such all words which it believes to be trademarks. The publisher should also like to make it clear that the presence of a word in the book, whether marked or unmarked, in no way affects its legal status as a trademark.

Every reasonable effort has been made by the publisher to trace the copyright holders of material in this book. Any errors or omissions should be notified in writing to the publisher, who will endeavour to rectify the situation for any reprints and future editions.

Typeset by Cenveo® Publisher Services.

Printed and bound in Great Britain by CPI Group (UK) Ltd., Croydon, CR0 4YY.

John Murray Learning policy is to use papers that are natural, renewable and recyclable products and made from wood grown in sustainable forests. The logging and manufacturing processes are expected to conform to the environmental regulations of the country of origin.

Carmelite House
50 Victoria Embankment
London EC4Y 0DZ
www.hodder.co.uk

Contents

Meet the authors

Can you really teach yourself Ukrainian? No, not really, not without help. You need a textbook and some good sound recordings to start with. And that is where our book, *Complete Ukrainian*, comes in. We have the ideal background to provide the kind of help that learners need, particularly when they are trying to pick up the basics without a teacher. Both of us have many years' language teaching experience on which to build in creating a textbook that would be fun to write and, we hope, fun for the learner to use.

Olena is a native speaker and, as such, is well placed to ensure that the language used in this book is accurate and up to date. She holds a doctorate in linguistics from the Taras Shevchenko National University in Kyiv and gained practical experience of teaching and pedagogical research in Ukraine, the United Kingdom and the United States of America and in publishing the results of her research on the syntax and semantics of the Ukrainian language. Subsequently she worked in international development, holding a senior position in the International Renaissance (Soros) Foundation in Ukraine. Since 2002 she has been working for the World Bank in Ukraine and dealing with human capital development, and education- and health-related programmes. Currently, she works as an education specialist in one of the agencies of the European Union supporting the development and implementation of effective reform policies for education, training and labour market systems in the EU partner countries. She is based in Italy.

Jim learnt Ukrainian the hard way, so he knows all too well the difficulties that learners will meet. Now retired, he taught Russian and other Slavonic languages at university level throughout his career. He still maintains a passionate academic interest in the complexities – linguistic, historical and cultural – of the borderland areas of Eastern Europe where Poland, Lithuania, Belarus and Ukraine meet and has had to acquire a working knowledge of some eight languages in order to keep up with research and communicate with scholars who share his passion. He holds the Commander's Cross of Merit of the Republic of Poland and the Francis Skaryna Medal of the Republic of Belarus.

Naturally, we expect you will want to ask the question 'Is there a lot of grammar to learn?' and we would be less than wholly truthful if we were to answer with a bland 'No, you don't need to worry about grammar to make yourself understood.' Try to think of grammar in two ways: as the glue that helps you put sentences together in such a way as to help other people understand what you say and help you – with practice – understand their replies, and as something like Lego bricks that you can move around to ask a question or change the meaning of what you want to say. We both share an enthusiasm for Ukrainian and are glad of the opportunity to be of help as you start out on your journey of discovery of this fascinating language and country with its rich history and cultural heritage. The journey may be hard at times, but the reward is worth it! We feel truly sorry that we can't be with you as tutors, helping you in your everyday job of learning the beautiful Ukrainian language that we love and enjoy speaking so much. However, from the theory and practice of language learning, we wanted to give you one last piece of advice.

> **LANGUAGE TIP**
> A few hours a week won't get you very far. You have to keep the pressure up on yourself to work as much as you can around the textbook. Try to read and write the language, listen to broadcasts, even learning about Ukraine from English-language websites will help. Mix different activities, repeat over and over again. Try to find Ukrainian native speakers. Above all – keep practising!

We also hope that the company of good friends you will meet in this book as you travel along will make this journey a pleasurable one.

Just trust us, we will guide you right through to the end of the book!

Shchaslí voyee doróhi! *Have a good trip!*

Olena Bekh
and
Jim Dingley

Only got a minute?

In this course, the authors help you to be able to deal with everyday practical situations in Ukraine – saying who you are, where you come from, buying food and drink in shops and restaurants, getting around, feeling unwell (or feeling great!) and many, many more. When you have completed the course, you will be able to cope well in all of them and also feel able to express your own ideas and opinions.

One of the first things that you will find out is that Ukrainian uses a different alphabet, one that has 33 letters. The alphabet is known as Cyrillic. Don't be scared: many of the letters are shared with the Latin alphabet; in the majority of cases Ukrainian words are pronounced as they are written – which is a great asset. There are no shortcuts to learning it, but by breaking the alphabet into digestible chunks – letters that resemble their equivalents in the Latin alphabet and have roughly the same sound value, letters that look familiar but actually stand for a different sound, letters that look completely unfamiliar – the authors have tried to make it as simple as possible. As another way of helping you learn the alphabet, the introductory chapter gives words in Cyrillic and the nearest equivalent English letters. There are very few sounds in Ukrainian that differ greatly from English; just don't forget to roll your 'r's!

The basic structures of the Ukrainian language are set out so that you can start using them straight away, without the need to struggle with the grammar first. With regular practice – repetition, writing the exercises and listening to the recordings – you will soon find that you are making real progress.

So: **Добри́день** *Dobrýden* 'Hello' and welcome to Ukrainian!

Only got five minutes?

A couple of things you need to know about Ukraine at the start:

The country is called simply 'Ukraine', not 'The Ukraine' (we don't talk about 'The Argentine' any more!) and the country's capital city is 'Kyiv', not 'Kiev' (just as Peking is now Beijing).

The Ukrainian language in the world

The journey of discovery on which you are about to embark will take you down a long and, at times, difficult path that can lead to several destinations. If all you need are the basics in order to communicate at a survival level as a tourist in Ukraine, then this book provides exactly what you need. If your aim is broader, perhaps to conduct business in Ukraine or to study there, then, by the time you reach the end of this book, you will have a solid foundation on which to build. The result will be greatly enhanced if you can combine various methods of study and practising the language alongside self-study based on *Complete Ukrainian*. The knowledge you gain will come in extremely handy if you want to know more about the country and its history and culture.

If the path of language learning sometimes seems full of difficulties and obstacles, so on occasion do the paths taken by languages themselves. Ukrainian has come a long way from the somewhat lowly status of a language used primarily by peasants to that of a written and spoken language of state used in all spheres of public life, through periods when it was banned, disparaged or ignored.

Ukrainian is today spoken by nearly 40 million people in Ukraine (out of a total population of some 46 million). There are also long-standing Ukrainian communities in countries neighbouring on Ukraine, e.g. Moldova (Ukrainian is one of the official languages in Transnistria), as well as in Poland, Romania, Serbia and Slovakia. In Western Europe, quite sizeable Ukrainian communities can be found in the UK and France. There are especially large and vibrant diaspora communities in the USA and Canada. In all, it is claimed that there are more than 20 million Ukrainians or persons of Ukrainian descent living outside Ukraine.

The Vistawide website (www.vistawide.com/languages/top_30_languages.htm) ranks it 25th out of the 30 most widely spoken languages of the world.

What is Ukrainian?

It is an Indo-European language, i.e. it belongs to the large 'umbrella' grouping that includes English, French and German, and a member of the Slavonic (Slavic) group, which means, further, that it is related to Czech, Serbian and, in particular, to Polish and Russian.

OK – WHAT DOES THAT MEAN FOR THE LEARNER?

If you already know something of one of the other Slavonic languages, you will have a good idea of what to expect. They are much closer together than, say, English (in origin a Germanic language) is to German or Swedish.

Even if you don't, mastering Ukrainian is perfectly doable. Just bear a few points in mind:

▶ First, stress. Not in the sense of anxiety, although that may be involved as well, but where to place most emphasis in a word. In English, 'record' with stress on the first syllable doesn't mean the same thing as 'record' with stress on the second syllable, so learners of English have the same problem, even if not to the same extent. You have to learn the stress position of every word in Ukrainian that has more than one syllable. Throughout this book the stressed vowel is marked with an acute accent (the mark that is occasionally put on the letter e in words like 'café').

▶ Second, words and the alphabet used to write them. The alphabet used by Ukrainian is called Cyrillic and it has 33 letters. Here are a few words to act as a sample of what is to come. Don't be too alarmed by the strange shape of some of the letters: e.g. **Д**, **Щ**, **Я**. With practice they will become second nature.

  It is difficult to think of any specifically Ukrainian words that have come into English, but quite a lot of international, and more recently English, words have found their way into Ukrainian, just as they have in many languages of the world. Here's a chance to have a first look at words written in the Ukrainian alphabet. In these examples, we first present the word in its Ukrainian spelling and then in the system of using English letters to correspond more or less to the sounds of the Ukrainian letters.

  You're on your first visit to Ukraine and you're standing outside what looks obviously like a beauty parlour. There are two words on the shop window. What do you think will happen if you point to one of the words and ask in sign language 'Can I have one of those, please?'

  Татý tatoo **Манікю́р** maneekyoór (say it out loud and roll your 'r'!)

  Other words might not be so obvious: what do you think an **автóбус** (awtóboos) might be? What might you be able to do in a **ресторáн** (restorán)? What information will a **бíзнес-катало́г** (béznes katalóh) give you?

▶ Third: case. Not medical or legal, but grammatical. In Ukrainian, 'London' is written, letter for letter, **Лóндон**. However, if you want to say that you live 'in London', **Лóндон** becomes **у Лóндоні** (ee). And there is a lot more of this.

  You really cannot do without learning the alphabet and the grammatical terminology, e.g. noun, verb, genitive case, that is so necessary when it comes to describing what is going on. It is all set out and explained in the most straightforward way possible.

WHAT DO I, THE LEARNER, GET OUT OF ALL THIS EFFORT?

For one thing, by the time you have completed this book you will have learnt something about the way a different language is built up. You may think that little everyday verbs like 'be' and 'have' are so common that they must turn up in equally straightforward form in every language. No, in fact, they don't, unfortunately. Asking an apparently simple question like 'How old are you?' may have pitfalls when the Ukrainian answer, literally translated, comes out as 'To me (are) 50 years'. Why the word 'are' is in parentheses is something that you will find out about!

There may be, in the more recent or distant past, some family connection with Ukraine. You may wish to explore a country still not on the main tourist trails. You don't need to leave your computer if you would like to visit the spa resorts of the **Карпáти** (*karpáty*) 'Carpathian mountains', the renewed baroque splendour of **Львів** (*l'veew*) 'Lviv' (sometimes still wrongly spelt in some sources by the Russian form of its name 'Lvov' used in the Soviet times and now rapidly being replaced by the Ukrainian spelling) and the ancient city of **Київ** (*kí yeew*) 'Kyiv' on the river **Дніпрó** (*dneepró*). You may have heard about this river under its other name, 'Dnieper'. If literature is your interest, this book will give you the basis on which to expand your vocabulary. You will get to hear a lot about a poet called **Шевчéнко** (*Shewchénko*), even if you never read his poetry.

There are vast resources in Ukrainian on the internet: TV, radio, tourist guides, blogs, movies, whole libraries of digital books. A fresh world opens up.

Only got ten minutes?

Right from the start: the country is called 'Ukraine', *not* 'The Ukraine' (just as the northern Indian state is known as Punjab) and the name of the capital city in Latin script is enshrined in Ukrainian law as 'Kyiv', not 'Kiev'. After all, Mumbai is no longer called 'Bombay'.

The Ukrainian language

Ukrainian is a member of the Slavonic or Slavic group of Indo-European Languages. It is normally assigned to the eastern group of Slavonic languages, which includes Belarusian and Russian, but it also shares many features with Polish. It can indeed be said that if you know one Slavonic language, you will have a headstart in learning any of the others.

English is also an Indo-European language, but in the Germanic group, meaning that its closest relatives are Dutch and Frisian, with German somewhat further removed, and languages such as Norwegian and Icelandic a long distance off on the family tree, although they, too, can be felt in the northern dialects of English in England and Scotland.

For writing, Ukrainian uses the Cyrillic alphabet consisting of 33 letters. The alphabet is associated with the 9th-century missionary activity of two Greek brothers, Saints Cyril and Methodius, among Slavs living in part of the old Roman province of Pannonia and in Moravia, now part of the Czech Republic, although it is almost certain that St Cyril did not actually devise the alphabet that bears his name himself.

The fact that the Ukrainian alphabet has 33 letters in comparison with the 26 of English does not mean that the language has more sounds. Several English sounds are written as two letters, e.g. 'ch' in 'church', 'sh' in 'ship'. The equivalent Ukrainian sounds are represented by one letter, respectively, **Ч** and **Ш**. There is a letter for the combination of 't' and 's' that you can hear at the end of the word 'cats' – **Ц**. There are words in Ukrainian that begin with this sound – **це́рква** (*tsérkva*) 'church'. (Here and elsewhere throughout this book the acute accent on any vowel marks where the stress in the word is to be placed. It is not part of the Ukrainian spelling system. The system of showing how the word is pronounced by using English letters is explained in the Introduction.) The unlikely (for English, at any rate) sound combination of 'sh' and 'ch' that can be heard in 'fresh cheese' has also just one letter: **Щ**, **щи́рий** (*shchí ryy*) 'sincere'. The 'y' sound in 'yet' followed by a vowel also gets a letter of its own: 'y' + 'a' = **Я**, 'y' + 'e' = **Є**, 'y' + 'ee' (as in 'feet') = **Ї**, 'y' + 'oo' (as in 'boot') = **Ю**.

There are two letters that deserve special mention: the first of these is **Ґ** 'g'. This letter had the privilege of being banned when Ukraine was part of the USSR and so has come to be associated very closely with the language of an independent Ukrainian state; people had to make do with **Г** for both 'g' and a sound very close to the English 'h' (except that you can't drop it in Ukrainian!).

The second letter, **ь**, the 'soft sign', has no sound of its own; it denotes that the consonant that stands before it is 'palatalized', pronounced with the tongue against the palate. One of the main features that distinguishes Ukrainian pronunciation from English is that several consonants have both 'hard' (not 'palatalized') and 'soft' ('palatalized') variants. (You can find more detail in the Introduction.)

There is, on the whole, a very good match between spelling and pronunciation in Ukrainian, i.e. none of the business in English of 'c' standing for 'k' in 'cup', for 's' in 'ceiling' and for 'ch' in 'concerto' or of 'oo' in 'foot' and 'loot'. The only letter that can represent two sounds is **в** (either 'v' or 'w') and even then there are guidelines that help in determining which of the two sounds the letter stands for in any particular instance.

As a Slavonic (Slavic) language Ukrainian may seem to have more grammar than English. Nouns have genders (masculine, feminine, neuter) and cases (seven of them). Adjectives must have the same gender, and be in the same case and number ('singular' or 'plural') as the noun which they accompany. Verbs, by the same token, are simpler than in English: they have only three tenses (compare English 'I go', 'I am going', 'I went', 'I have gone', 'I was going', etc.), although you should prepare yourself for a surprise that you do not find in English.

Both Ukrainian and English are classified as Indo-European languages, but, unfortunately, that is not of any real help when it comes to learning vocabulary. You may just about be able to see a connection between the words **молоко́** (*molokó*) and 'milk', but it is hard to believe that **хліб** (*khleeb*) 'bread' has the same origin as the English 'loaf'. A word of advice: as your vocabulary expands, try to note how words are constructed. They have a root, which gives the basic meaning, a suffix at the end, which may be a case form or could be saying 'this word is an adjective or adverb', there may be a prefix at the beginning of the word, which modifies the meaning of the root in some way. English can do this, too, although not to the same extent as Ukrainian, e.g. verb 'write', noun 'writer', verb with prefix 'underwrite'; or verb 'grow', noun with suffix 'growth', adjective with prefix and suffix 'overgrown'.

There are really very few words in English that have been taken from Ukrainian. Most of them are directly connected with Ukrainian realia, e.g. 'bandura', a folk instrument with 36 strings, and many of these words are found at all frequently only in the English of North America. We will come to why this should be so a little later.

The reverse procedure – English words being taken up by Ukrainian – is, however, much more in evidence. It is amusing to speculate how the name of an area of London on the south side of the river Thames, Vauxhall, where there were public pleasure gardens from the 17th to the 19th centuries, became **вокза́л** (*vokzál*) 'railway station'. Numerically far more important are what may be called 'international words'. For example, it should not be too difficult to guess where you are when you reach these stations on the Kyiv metro system (**Ки́ївський метрополіте́н** (*kí yeewskiy metropoleetén*)): **Політехні́чний Інститу́т** (*poleetekhnéechniyy eenstitóot*), **Університе́т** (*ooneeversitét*). Then there are the words that have been taken directly from English since independence: have a look at the name of the firm **По́рше Лі́зінг Украї́на** (*pórshe léezing ookrayééna*). **Try saying it out loud.**

Who speaks Ukrainian?

Ukrainian is spoken by over 40 million people in Ukraine and beyond. It is customary, when talking of Ukrainians outside Ukraine, to use the terms 'eastern diaspora', covering the countries of the former USSR, and 'western diaspora', i.e. Western Europe and North and South America. Do not forget, too, that there are quite large Ukrainian communities in several European countries that do not consist of émigrés – they have always been there: Moldova, Poland, Romania, Serbia, Slovakia.

A population that has been scattered far and wide is evidence of a complex history, something that you will be able to follow in Ukrainian when you have completed this book. In the meantime, here are just a few pointers.

The site on the river Dnipro (which you may know as 'Dnieper') now occupied by the city of Kyiv was settled many centuries ago, perhaps as long ago as the 5th century. Its importance as a river crossing point was undoubtedly due to the fact that two vital trade routes intersected here – one going north to south, between the Varangians (Norsemen) and the Greeks (Constantinople) and the other going east to west, between central Europe and central Asia and Baghdad. Eventually, Kyiv became the central city of a loose federation of princedoms known collectively as Kyiv Rus (rhyme it with 'goose'). Utterly destroyed by the Mongols in 1240, it began to regain some of its former glory only in the 15th century. By this time, the territories around Kyiv had been absorbed by the Grand Duchy of Lithuania (not to be confused with present-day Lithuania), only later, in 1569, to become part of the Kingdom of Poland and subsequently the Polish Commonwealth. This was the state that was divided at the end of the 18th century between the Russian Empire, the Austrian Empire and Prussia. Most Ukrainians became citizens of the Russian Empire, but there were many in the Austrian Empire. It was from here, more particularly from the region of Galicia (now in western Ukraine), that many Ukrainian peasants left in the 19th century, in search of a better life in Alberta, Canada, and elsewhere in North America. There were other emigrations, too, from the Russian Empire and after the revolutions of 1917 and the failure of the Ukrainian National Republic and after 1945. More recently, we have witnessed an economic migration, especially to the USA.

The different waves of emigration have done what they could to recreate Ukraine in their new homelands; they have built schools and churches, published newspapers and books and now create websites. They have sought, by all means possible, to keep their language and culture alive at times when it looked as though they might be crushed for good.

What can I do with Ukrainian once I have completed the book?

Apart from being a tourist in an as yet almost undiscovered country, there are many ways in which you can continue to develop your knowledge. You may live in an area in which there is an active Ukrainian community. The community may be centred around a church – Eastern Rite Catholic, Autocephalous Orthodox (another reason for learning Ukrainian is to discover what these terms mean and why they are so important in Ukrainian history) – and there may be language courses or classes on other aspects of Ukrainian culture and history. Even if there is no such community near where you live, there are plenty of resources on the web and search engines to help you find them.

You may wish to familiarize yourself with Ukrainian literature. This interest will inevitably bring you to **Тара́с Шевче́нко** (*tarás shevchénko*) (1814–1861), the Ukrainian national poet, and **Іва́н Франко́** (*eeván frankó*) (1856–1916). You can go back a little further in time to find out about Ivan Kotliarevsky (1769–1838), who in 1798 published the first modern Ukrainian book, a parody of Virgil's *Aeneid*; the heroes of the Trojan war are transformed into Zaporozhian Cossacks. (You will be able to use your knowledge of Ukrainian both to discover who exactly the Cossacks were, before they became the Russian Tsar's forces of law and order in the 19th century, and to find out what 'Zaporozhian' means.) There is a host of excellent writers of prose and poetry in the modern period. Volumes and volumes of folk literature of all kinds are waiting for you.

Perhaps at a more mundane level you will, with practice, be able to follow news and current affairs programmes on Ukrainian internet TV and radio stations and find out what people are blogging about in Ukrainian. In short, there is plenty that can be done!

Above all, try to speak whenever the opportunity arises. Even a few simple words will be greeted with joy and gratitude that you have taken the trouble to learn some words and sentences in the Ukrainian language.

Acknowledgements

Since its first publication this book has been through two editions: we are indeed grateful to all those who have used it in the process of self-study of the Ukrainian language. We were thrilled to learn that the book has been used by many of our colleagues for teaching Ukrainian in the classroom to groups and individual learners. During the preparation of this third, improved edition, we referred to as many reviews and comments from both professional language teachers and learners who used the book as we could find. We are particularly grateful to Dr Iryna Oliynyk and Ms Alina Pastukhova who have for more than 10 years been using the book for teaching foreign students in Ukraine. They took the time to provide us with excellent detailed comments, which have made a great contribution to the new edition. We would also like to express our gratitude to Professor Robert DeLossa and Dr Tatiana Nazarenko for their reviews of *Complete Ukrainian*, which can be found on the internet.

Credits

Front cover: © Jim Sugar/CORBIS

Back cover: © Jakub Semeniuk/iStockphoto.com, © Royalty-Free/Corbis, © agencyby/iStockphoto.com, © Andy Cook/iStockphoto.com, © Christopher Ewing/iStockphoto.com, © zebicho – Fotolia.com, © Geoffrey Holman/iStockphoto.com, © Photodisc/Getty Images, © James C. Pruitt/iStockphoto.com, © Mohamed Saber – Fotolia.com

Introduction

Ukraine is one of the new countries on the map of Europe, but the language and history of the people who live there can be traced back at least as far as the 10th century, when Kyiv (still better known as Kiev) was already a well-established meeting place of trade routes and nations. In Ukraine, it is possible to hear Bulgarian, Greek, Hungarian, Polish, Romanian, Rom, Russian and Yiddish. One language, however, unites all the people of Ukraine – Ukrainian, the sole official language of the Ukrainian state. Incidentally, Ukrainian forms of names of towns and rivers will be used throughout the book – hence Kyiv , L'viv , Odesa , Dnipro.

> **LANGUAGE TIP**
> It has taken several years since Ukraine became independent to achieve a standard form of spelling of place names in the Latin alphabet. '**Kyiv**' is the official form of the country's capital, but you will still often find the spelling '**Kiev**'.

There are many reasons for learning Ukrainian. Intellectual curiosity about the language and culture of a 'new' European people is certainly one. At a more immediately practical level, Ukraine is still waiting to be discovered as a tourist country. As Ukraine becomes stronger economically, the need will grow for foreign businessmen to have some idea of the language in order to do business there. Whatever the reason, we hope that you will enjoy the flavour of the Ukrainian language as much as you will enjoy the rich flavours of Ukrainian cooking.

How to use the book

The book is divided into 18 units. With one exception, each unit contains dialogues, grammar notes under the heading 'How the language works' and illustrative material to back up what you have learnt. Exercises of various types will give you a chance to test your knowledge.

We are convinced that the best way to learn Ukrainian is to acquire as soon as possible the ability to read, however slowly and painstakingly at first, dialogues and texts that we hope are both interesting and lively, even to the point of being far fetched! The recording provides an extra opportunity to hear the material and practise your own spoken Ukrainian. The first half of the book contains units that may seem to contain an alarming amount of grammar. Don't panic – it doesn't all need to be learnt at once! The information is there for continuous reference.

We hope to have succeeded in presenting the kind of Ukrainian that will be accepted and understood anywhere in Ukraine. Once you have completed the 18 units, you will have a solid foundation on which to develop your knowledge. Ukrainians will be delighted that you have taken the trouble to learn something of their language.

In *Complete Ukrainian*, you will meet a number of characters closely connected with Ukraine. Stephen Taylor is the director of Hermes Clothing. He is interested in business opportunities in Ukraine and has already started to learn Ukrainian. His friend, Taras Koval, an Englishman with a Ukrainian background, has been teaching him the language, and together they plan a trip to Ukraine that will combine business with pleasure. Taras is married to Vira from Ukraine. Before his trip to Ukraine Stephen makes a useful contact when he meets an English lawyer of Ukrainian extraction, Iuri Morozenko. Stephen's business contacts in Ukraine are Solomiia Maliarchuk, the director of a clothing company in Kyiv, and Ihor Stakhiv, the general manager of the company. You will also meet Ihor's wife Ol'ha and their three children, Natalka, Ostap and Olenka. Taras has a Ukrainian friend, Bohdan. During his trip around Ukraine Stephen meets his old friend, Andrew, an American journalist.

Pronunciation

Alphabet

You will first have to learn to recognize the Cyrillic alphabet, in which Ukrainian is written, and the sounds for which the letters stand. The Cyrillic alphabet has a long history and is closely linked to the spread of Orthodox Christianity. Other languages that use the Cyrillic alphabet are Belarusian, Russian and Serbian.

The Ukrainian alphabet has 33 letters in all.

The first group of letters includes those that are either identical or nearly so in both shape and sound, and those that are identical in shape to their English counterparts but represent an entirely different sound:

A [a]	K [k]	C [s]
B [v or w]	M [m]	T [t]
E [e]	O [o]	У [oo]
И [i]	P [r]	X [kh]
I [ee]	H [n]	

Letters and sounds

 TR 1, 01:15

in Ukrainian

Letters	English equivalent		Ukrainian words		
			Word	Transcription	Translation
Printed	Sound	Word			
A a	a	b<u>u</u>s	автомобíль	[awtomobíl']	*car*
B в	v/w*	<u>v</u>eal	вікнó	[veeknó]	*window*
		<u>w</u>ill	вчóра	[wchóra]	*yesterday*
			любóв	[l'oobów]	*love*
E e	e	<u>le</u>t	дéрево	[dérevo]	*tree*
И и	i	b<u>i</u>t	кнúга	[kníha]	*book*
I i	ee	<u>bea</u>t	квíтка	[kveétka]	*flower*
K к	k	<u>k</u>itten	кіт	[keet]	*cat*
M м	m	<u>m</u>ore	мóре	[móre]	*sea*
H н	n	<u>n</u>et	нéбо	[nébo]	*sky*
O o	o	p<u>o</u>t	олівéць	[oleevéts']	*pencil*

П п	p	s<u>p</u>it	папíр	[papeér]	*paper*
Р р	r	<u>r</u>oof	рýчка	[roóchka]	*pen*
С с	s	<u>s</u>ell	селó	[seló]	*village*
Т т	t	<u>t</u>art	тáто	[táto]	*daddy*
У у	oo/w*	t<u>oo</u>th	зуб	[zoob]	*tooth*
		<u>w</u>ill	учóра	[wchóra]	*yesterday*
Х х	kh	lo<u>ch</u>	хлóпчик	[khlópchik]	*boy*

*The letter **в** is pronounced [v] before a vowel, and [w] before a consonant or at the end of a word. Another example: the city of **Львів** in western Ukraine is pronounced [l'veew].

The letter **у** is pronounced [oo] between consonants, and [w] when it stands at the beginning of a word before a consonant.

You will find that the letters **в** and **у** can be interchanged in the same word (e.g. **вчóра** and **учóра** above) when they have the same pronounciation [w]. There are certain rules that govern whether you use **в** or **у**; they will be introduced later.

The remaining 20 letters all differ significantly from anything in the English alphabet:

Г [h]	Б [b]	Є [ye]	Ц [ts]
Ґ [g]	Ь [-]	З [z]	Ч [ch]
Д [d]	Ф [f]	Ї [yee]	Ш [sh]
Ж [zh]	Ю [yoo]	Й [y]	Щ [shch]
Л [l]			

Letters and sounds

 TR 1, 01:42

in Ukrainian			Ukrainian words		
Letters	English equivalent		Word	Transcription	Translation
Printed	Sound	Word			
Б б	b	<u>b</u>ush	брат	[brat]	*brother*
Г г	h	<u>h</u>ow	гáрний	[hárniy]	*beautiful*
Ґ ґ	g	<u>g</u>ang	ґáнок	[gánok]	*porch*
Д д	d	<u>d</u>o	друг	[drooh]	*friend*
Є є	ye	<u>ye</u>s	Єврóпа	[yewrópa]	*Europe*
Ж ж	zh	mea<u>s</u>ure	журналíст	[zhoornal'eést]	*journalist*

З з	z	<u>z</u>oo	зеле́ний	[zeléniy]	*green*
Ї ї	yee	<u>yea</u>st	ї́жа	[yeézha]	*food*
Й й	y	bo<u>y</u>	чо́рний	[chórniy]	*black*
Л л	l	<u>l</u>amp	ла́мпа	[lámpa]	*lamp*
Ф ф	f	<u>ph</u>oto	фо́то	[fóto]	*photograph*
Ц ц	ts	<u>ts</u>ar	це́рква	[tsérkva]	*church*
Ч ч	ch	<u>ch</u>ur<u>ch</u>	чолові́к	[cholovék]	*man, husband*
Ш ш	sh	<u>sh</u>ine	ша́пка	[shápka]	*hat*
Щ щ	shch	fre<u>sh</u> <u>ch</u>eese	кущ	[kooshch]	*bush*
Ь ь			низький́	[niz'kíy]	*low*
Ю ю	yoo	<u>you</u>th	юна́к	[yoonák]	*young man*
Я я	ya	<u>ya</u>rd	я́блуко	[yáblooko]	*apple*

Note on transcription: Letters within square brackets will always represent a transcription of the Ukrainian Cyrillic letters into the closest English equivalents that are given in this list. You will sometimes see combinations of letters in the transcription of Ukrainian words that represent quite a different sound from that which the same letters would stand for in an English word. The Ukrainian word **гай** [hay] means 'grove of trees'. The sequence [ay] has more or less the same sound as the letters 'ie' in 'lie' or 'y' in 'my'.

STRESS

The stressed part of the word will also be marked in transcription by an accent mark ['] over the vowel that bears the stress. Remember that the double letters [oo] and [ee] in transcription represent one sound. The stress mark will appear on the second letter, e.g. **ру́чка** [roóchka]. You have to learn the stress position of each new word in Ukrainian; there are no rules to help with this learning process, unfortunately!

CONSONANTS AND VOWELS

We can now divide the alphabet into **consonants**:

Бб, Вв, Гг, Ґґ, Дд, Жж, Зз, Йй, Кк, Лл, Мм, Нн, Пп, Рр, Сс, Тт, Фф, Хх, Цц, Чч, Шш, Щщ and **vowels:**

Аа, Ее, Єє, Ии, Іі, Її, Оо, Уу, Юю, Яя

Here is the complete Ukrainian alphabet, as it appears when printed:

Аа Бб Вв Гг Ґґ Дд Ее Єє Жж Зз Ии Іі Її Йй Кк Лл Мм Нн Оо
Пп Рр Сс Тт Уу Фф Хх Цц Чч Шш Щщ Ьь Юю Яя

And here is the complete alphabet, handwritten.

Аа	*Тт*	*Мм*	*Фф*
Бб	*Зз*	*Нн*	*Хх*
Вв	*Ии*	*Оо*	*Цц*
Гг	*Іі*	*Пп*	*Чч*
Ґґ	*Її*	*Рр*	*Шш*
Дд	*Йй*	*Сс*	*Щщ*
Ее	*Кк*	*Тт*	*Юю*
Єє	*Лл*	*Уу*	*Яя*

Notes

1 **The letter Щ stands for a combination of two sounds: Ш + Ч. Conversely, there are some combinations of two letters that actually stand for one sound:**

   ДЖ for the 'j' sound in 'jam', e.g. **я ходжу́** [ya khojoó] (*I go*);

   ДЗ for the 'dz' sound that can be heard at the end of the word 'buds', e.g. **дзе́ркало** [dzérkalo] (*mirror*).

2 You can see that several of the letters have exactly the same shape in both capital and small forms, e.g. Вв, Кк, Мм, Нн, Тт, in contrast to letters in the English alphabet that look like them, e.g. *Bb, Kk, Mm, Hh, Tt*. This similarity is preserved in some of the handwritten forms as well, for example:

PRINTED		HANDWRITTEN	
capital	small	capital	small
В	в	*В*	*в*
К	к	*К*	*к*
М	м	*М*	*м*
Н	н	*Н*	*н*
Т	т	*Т*	*т*

Examples: квíтка   *квітка*
                кіт   *кіт*
                вікнó   *вікно*

3 Look at the handwritten forms of the letters **Л, М, Я** when they are joined to preceding letters.

PRINTED		HANDWRITTEN	
capital	small	capital	small
Л	л	*л*	*л*
М	м	*М*	*м*
Я	я	*Я*	*я*

Here are some examples of these letters in various combinations; note the hook before the handwritten forms:

олівéць   *олівець*   земля́   *земля*
зелéний   *зелений*   лáмпа   *лампа*

Земля́ [zeml'á]   planet Earth
земля́ [zeml'á]   ground

You will see that the handwritten form of the letter **Л** has exactly the same height as the corresponding handwritten forms of **а, г, е, ж, и, м,** etc.

Make sure that you differentiate **M** and **T** in handwriting, e.g.:

PRINTED	HANDWRITTEN
мáма	*мама*
тáто	*тато*

LANGUAGE TIP
мáма [máma] *mum*

The 'soft sign'

As we said earlier, there are 33 letters in the Ukrainian alphabet. However, if you count the number of letters that represent consonants and vowels, you will find only 32. This is because there is one letter – **ь** – that has no sound value of its own, but which has a direct effect on the pronunciation of the consonant that stands before it.

CONSONANTS

Consonants can be pronounced either **hard** or **soft**. Take the Ukrainian letter **т**: if you pronounce it with the tip of your tongue against your top teeth, you produce the **hard** sound. If you try to pronounce the same sound with the tip of your tongue against the palate, you will automatically produce the soft sound. Try the same thing with some other Ukrainian consonants: **л, ц, н**. First, try to say the hard sound followed by the vowel **a**: **та – ла – ца – на**.

Now try the **soft** equivalent with the same vowel sound, but look at how we write them together: **тя – ля – ця – ня**.

тя – ля – ця – ня

The difference between hard and soft consonants can also occur at the end of words or in front of another consonant inside a word. Try to pronounce the vowel **a** before the hard consonants: **ат – ал – ац – ан**. Now look at how we write the soft equivalent; try to read the following sequences: **ать – аль – аць – ань**.

ать – аль – аць – ань

The letter **ь** is called the '**soft sign**'; it has no sound of its own, but is used to show that the consonant that stands before it is a soft one. The letter will be represented in transcription by an **inverted comma** [ʹ].

Just to make matters more complicated the soft sign normally appears as an ordinary apostrophe [ʹ] or as an acute accent [ʹ] or is omitted entirely when Ukrainian words (most frequently, placenames and personal names) are written in the Latin alphabet. The female first name **Ольга** will appear as [ólʹha] as a guide to understanding the Ukrainian letters in this chapter, but would normally be written as Olʹha, Olʹha or Olha. The city of **Львів** appears as [lʹveew] in our transcription system in this chapter, but normally looks like Lʹviv, Lʹviv or Lviv. In later units, when the transcription system is no longer being used, you will find Olʹha and Lʹviv.

Here are some examples of actual Ukrainian words:

день [den']	*day*	*день*
учи́тель [wchítel']	*teacher*	*учитель*
до́нька [dón'ka]	*daughter*	*донька*
низьки́й [niz'kíy]	*low*	*низький*

Note that the handwritten form of the soft sign looks something like the English 'b', but has a shorter downward stroke.

VOWELS

Let's look again at the vowel letters that denote sounds beginning with **й** [y]: **я** [ya], **ю** [yoo], **є** [ye], **ї** [yee]. When we read the letters in the alphabet, they denote two sounds: [y] followed by a vowel. This combination of sounds occurs very frequently in Ukrainian words:

я́блуко [yáblooko] *apple*	Євро́па [yewrópa] *Europe*
юна́к [yoonák] *young man*	їжа [yéézha] *food*

Three of these letters (**я, ю, є**) can also be used to show that a consonant occurring before them is to be pronounced soft, e.g. **тя** [t'a], **лю** [l'oo], **нє** [n'e]. As you can see, the [y] sound before the vowel [a, oo, e] disappears.

Now let's have some more practice:

яки́й [yakíy] *what kind of?*	любо́в [l'oobów] *love*
Ю́рій [yoóreey] *Yurii* (Ukrainian name)	цирк [tsirk] *circus*
ля́лька [l'ál'ka] *doll*	ла́мпа [lámpa] *lamp*

The letter **ï** is best described as lazy; it can only stand for the sounds [y] + [ee].

Let's go over this ground again. How do we know when to read the letters **я, ю, є** as two sounds when they occur inside a word and when to read them as one?

They are read as two sounds when they occur after a vowel, e.g. **поéзія** [poézeeya] (*poetry*), **ши́я** [shíya] (*neck*). We also read them as two sounds when between a consonant and one of the letters **я, ю, є, ï** you see an apostrophe ['] (not the reverse one ['] that we are using in the transcription to denote a soft consonant!). This denotes that the consonant is to be pronounced 'hard' with a following clear 'y' sound before the vowel. Here are some examples:

ім'я́ [eemyá]	*name*
здоро́в'я [zdoróvya]	*health*
прем'є́ра [premyéra]	*first night of a play*
інтерв'ю́ [eentervyoó]	*interview*

Now let's look at how these letters work together to form words. In Ukrainian, we say most words just as we write them and write them just as we say them. This phonetic principle in Ukrainian works most of the time.

Pronunciation exercises

Remember that the stress marks are intended as a guide to help you with pronunciation. They are not used in everyday printed texts and you do not need to write them except as a means of helping you memorize the position of the stress in each new word that you meet.

1 READING PRACTICE

a The first group of letters are close to their English counterparts in both shape and the sound that they represent.

A　　E　　З　　І　　К　　М　　О　　С　　Т

Аа	[a]	Ее	[e in let]
Зз	[z]	Іі	[ee]
Кк	[k]	Мм	[m]
Оо	[o]	Сс	[s]
Тт	[t]		

замо́к

міст

мі́сто

сім

кіт

b This second group contains letters some of which look like English letters but in fact represent different sounds.

В　　Д　　И　　Н　　Р　　У　　Х

Вв	[v, w]	Дд	[d]
Ии	[i]	Нн	[n]
Рр	[r]	Уу	[oo]
Хх	[kh]		

Ри́нок

рис

ка́ва

ві́сім

тури́ст

рука́

ніс

ву́хо

c This third group contains letters that are quite unlike anything in the English alphabet.

Б Г Ґ Є Ж Ї Й Л П Ф Ц Ч Ш Щ Ю Я

Бб	[b]	Гг	[h in how]
Ґґ	[g in gang]	Єє	[ye in yellow]
Жж	[zh]	Її	[yee]
Йй	[y]	Лл	[l]
Пп	[p]	Фф	[f]
Цц	[ts]	Чч	[ch]
Шш	[sh]	Щщ	[shch]
Юю	[yoo]	Яя	[ya]

You have now seen all the letters of the Ukrainian alphabet several times over! Here are some lists of words for you to practise. How many can you understand already? The first group is the easiest; the third group may require some guesswork.

d

бар	банк	факс	о́фіс	му́зика	таксі́
акто́р	метро́	ма́ма	ві́за	сестра́	те́ніс

e

бага́ж	бі́знес	бізнесме́н	балко́н
баскетбо́л	інфе́кція	клі́мат	телефо́н
гольф	план	калькуля́тор	фо́то
вокза́л	троле́йбус	лимо́н	шокола́д
журналі́ст	календа́р		

f

компа́нія	дире́ктор	ка́ртка	інститу́т
університе́т	папі́р	комп'ю́тер	Аме́рика
рестора́н	па́спорт	гара́ж	міні́стр
партне́р	адре́са	но́мер	аеропо́рт
докуме́нт	авто́бус	день	еконо́міка
іде́я	інтерв'ю́	коме́рція	америка́нець
креди́т	ла́мпа	ліфт	стоп
сигаре́та	молоко́	бана́н	суп
со́ус	вино́	соси́ска	верміше́ль

2 READING AND WRITING PRACTICE

a Now practise the handwritten forms of the Ukrainian alphabet. You have seen these words already.

Example: Друг [*Друг*]   Фо́то [*Фото*]

село́	ді́вчина	вікно́	ла́мпа
кущ	ля́лька	ґа́нок	папі́р
я́блуко	пое́зія	кіт	ї́жа
цирк	любо́в	кві́тка	де́рево
Ю́рій	мо́ре		

b Here are the names of some towns and rivers in Ukraine. Some you may have heard of, others may be completely new. Practise reading and writing the names.

i   towns and cities

Ки́їв	Льві́в	Оде́са	Я́лта
Полта́ва	У́жгород	Черка́си	Ха́рків
Черні́гів	Чорно́биль	Луцьк	Жито́мир
Ві́нниця	Терно́піль	Севасто́поль	Сімферо́поль

ii   rivers

Дніпро́	Буг	Доне́ць	Дні́стер

1 Добри́День! Як Ва́ше ім'я́?
Hello! What's your name?

In this unit you will learn:
- ▶ *How to introduce yourself*
- ▶ *How to introduce members of your family*
- ▶ *How to greet people*
- ▶ *How to identify objects (e.g. 'this is my house')*
- ▶ *How to ask simple questions using question words*
- ▶ *How to ask someone what their name is*

Діало́г 1 (*Dialogue 1*)

 TR 2, 00:09

Taras has invited Stephen to his home.

Тара́с	До́брий день, Сти́вене!* Про́шу захо́дити.
Сти́вен	Добри́день, Тара́се!* Як спра́ви?
Тара́с	Дя́кую, до́бре. А як ти?
Сти́вен	Дя́кую, непога́но.
Тара́с	Сіда́й, будь ла́ска.
Сти́вен	Ду́же дя́кую.

 TR 2, 00:37

до́брий день	*hello/how do you do?* (lit. *good day*)
добри́день	*hello/how do you do?*
про́шу захо́дити	*please come in* (lit. *[I] ask [you] to come in*)
як спра́ви?	*how are things?* (lit. *how things?*)
дя́кую	*thank you* (lit. *[I] thank*)
до́бре	*fine*
а як ти?	*and you?* (lit. *and how [are] you?*)
непога́но	*not bad*
сіда́й	*sit down*
будь ла́ска	*please*
ду́же дя́кую	*thank you very much* (lit. *very [much] [I] thank*)

> **LANGUAGE TIP**
> It is also very common to say **щи́ро дя́кую** (*thank you very much* (lit. *sincerely [I] thank*)).

---

* Special forms of the names **Сти́вен** and **Тара́с**, used when addressing people: see Unit 11.

Later that evening Taras shows Stephen a photograph of his family in Ukraine. **Мико́ла** is a Ukrainian male name; **Марі́я** and **Окса́на** are female ones.

Here is a picture of Taras' family with a friend.

Діало́г 2 (*Dialogue 2*)

 TR 2, 02:05

Тара́с	Це – мій брат. Його́ звуть Мико́ла. Він акто́р.
Сті́вен	А хто це?
Тара́с	Це – моя́ сестра́. Її́ ім'я́ Окса́на.
Сті́вен	Яка́ її́ профе́сія?
Тара́с	Вона́ музика́нт.
Сті́вен	А це твоя́ ма́ма?
Тара́с	Так. Її́ звуть Марі́я. Вона́ матема́тик.
Сті́вен	А то тако́ж твій брат?
Тара́с	Ні. То мій друг Е́ндрю.
Сті́вен	Він украї́нець?
Тара́с	Ні. Він не украї́нець. Він америка́нець.
Сті́вен	А його́ профе́сія?
Тара́с	Він журналі́ст. А це – я.

це	*this*
мій	*my*
його́ звуть	*his name is* (lit. *him [they] call*)
він	*he*
акто́р	*actor*
а	*and, but*
хто	*who*
моя́	*my*
сестра́	*sister*
її́	*her*
яка́	*what*
вона́	*she*
музика́нт	*musician*
твоя́	*your*
так	*yes*
її́ зву́ть	*her name is* (lit. *her [they] call*)
матема́тик	*mathematician*
то	*that*
тако́ж	*also, too, as well*
ні	*no*
не	*not*
Е́ндрю	*Andrew*
украї́нець	(lit.) *a Ukrainian man*
він украї́нець?	*is he Ukrainian?/a Ukrainian?*
америка́нець	(lit.) *an American*
профе́сія	*profession*

a Пра́вда чи непра́вда? (*True or false?*) Answer in Ukrainian

1 Це моя́ сестра́ Окса́на. Вона́ журналі́ст.

2 Це мій брат Мико́ла. Він акто́р.

3 Це моя́ ма́ма. Її́ ім'я́ Марі́я.

4 Це мій друг Е́ндрю. Він украї́нець.

b Answer the following questions in English

1 How does Stephen answer the question 'How are you?'

2 Who are the people on the photo?

3 What is the name of Taras' brother?

4 What is his mother's profession?

Як функціону́є мо́ва *How the language works*

1 'THE' AND 'A' IN UKRAINIAN

There are no definite ('the') or indefinite ('a') articles in Ukrainian.

> **LANGUAGE TIP**
> No 'the' or 'a' in Ukrainian? So how does the language differentiate sentences like 'Here is the book I was talking about' and 'Here is a book you might like to read'? The answer is quite simple – the difference will always be made clear by the context, the situation in which the word occurs. You will see how it works as you gain more experience in reading Ukrainian.

2 'IS' IN UKRAINIAN

As you can see from the sentences in the dialogue, you do not need a word for 'is' in sentences such as 'This is my brother. He is an actor.' There will be more about this in the next unit.

3 ASKING SIMPLE QUESTIONS

In Ukrainian, the words for the statement **він украї́нець** (*he is Ukrainian*) and the question **він украї́нець?** (*is he Ukrainian?*) occur in the same order. In print, the question is obviously marked by the question mark. In speech, the intonation makes all the difference. In a question, the voice rises and falls on the word that is important for the question:

Він украї́нець?   *Is he Ukrainian?*

Ukrainian makes frequent use of the little word **a** to introduce questions, e.g. from the dialogues **а ти?** (*and you?*), **а хто це?** (*and who's this?*), **а це твоя́ ма́ма?** (*is that your mother?*), **а то тако́ж твій брат?** (*and is that also your brother?*), **а його́ профе́сія?** (*and [what is] his profession?*).

It is used both to change the flow of the conversation and to seek new information. It can sometimes be translated into English as 'and' or 'so' at the beginning of the sentence.

It can also occur at the beginning of a statement, e.g. **а це я** (*and that's me*).

4 NOUNS

A noun is a word that refers to a person, e.g. boy – **хло́пчик**, sister – **сестра́**, journalist – **журналі́ст**; an object e.g. car – **автомобі́ль**, church – **це́рква**, photograph – **фо́то**; or abstract concept, e.g. day – **день**, love – **любо́в**, health – **здоро́в'я.**

5 GENDER

Look at the final letters of the words in these columns:

ві**н**	вон**á**	вон**ó**
сн**н**	д**óнькa**	не́б**о**
бр**ат**	сестр**á**	мóр**е**
цир**к**	лáмп**a**	вікн**ó**

The words **він**, **син**, **брат** are masculine in gender; **воná**, **дóнька**, **сестрá** are feminine. The nouns denote either male (**син**, **брат**) or female (**дóнька**, **сестрá**) human beings; the gender of the Ukrainian nouns therefore depends upon the sex of the person. **Не́бо**, **мóре** and **вікнó** all denote objects and are therefore neuter in gender. So what about **цирк** and **лáмпа**? After all they both denote objects, but have not been included in the list of neuter nouns.

> **LANGUAGE TIP**
> The issue here is that in Ukrainian gender is a grammatical principle that is not restricted to the sex distinctions of the natural world. Gender is assigned largely on the basis of the final letter of the noun in question.

If you look again at the gender list, you will see that masculine nouns end in a consonant, feminine nouns end in **-a** and neuter nouns end in **-o** or **-e**. 'Ending in a consonant' also covers those nouns that end in a consonant followed by the 'soft sign', e.g. **олівéць**. Feminine nouns can also end in **-я**, e.g. **ки́ця**.

The personal pronoun **він** can replace any noun of masculine gender and **вона** any noun of feminine gender; **воно** refers only to nouns of neuter gender.

Note: Some nouns ending in a soft consonant or **ч**, **ж**, **ш** are, in fact, feminine. Some nouns ending in **-я** are neuter. You have already seen one such neuter noun in this unit – **ім'я́** (name). When such problem nouns occur in the dialogues, the gender will be given in the wordlists: (m), (f), or (n).

6 ADJECTIVES

An adjective is a word used to describe a noun. Adjectives can denote the quality of an object (good, bad, beautiful, small, blue) or what the object is made of (wooden, woollen).

Adjectives change their form according to the gender of the noun they accompany. Look at the following examples:

Masculine	Feminine	Neuter
яки́й	**яка́?**	**яке́?**
га́рний буди́нок	га́рна ді́вчина	га́рне не́бо
зеле́ний олі́ве́ць	зеле́на ла́мпа	зеле́не по́ле
си́ній олі́ве́ць	си́ня ла́мпа	си́не не́бо

 по́ле   *field*
си́ній   *dark blue, navy*

You can see that masculine adjectives end in a vowel and a consonant (**ий** or **ій**), feminine adjectives in **а** or **я**, neuter adjectives in **е** or **є**. The adjective endings **ий** (m), **а** (f), and **е** (n) are called hard; the adjective endings **ій** (m), **я** (f), and **є** (n) are called soft. Two examples:

hard endings: добр**ий**, добр**а**, добр**е**

soft endings: си́н**ій**, си́н**я**, си́н**є**

As a rule, adjectives stand before the nouns they accompany, as in the sentence:

Це га́рна ді́вчина.   *This is a beautiful girl.*

The words **га́рна ді́вчина** (*a / the beautiful girl*) by themselves are only part of a sentence. See what happens when the adjective comes after the noun, e.g.

Ді́вчина га́рна.   *The girl is beautiful.*

7 PRONOUNS

Personal pronouns

A personal pronoun is a word that replaces a noun, for example:

This is my son. **He** is an actor.   Це мій син. **Він** актор.

This is my daughter. **She** is a musician.   Це моя́ до́нька. **Вона́** музика́нт.

Here are all the personal pronouns of Ukrainian. The first person pronouns refer to the speaker(s), the second person refers to the person(s) being spoken to, the third person refers to the person(s) or thing(s) being spoken about.

	Singular		Plural	
First person	я	*I*	ми	*we*
Second person	ти	*you*	ви	*you*
Third person	він	*he*		
	вона́	*she*	вони́	*they*
	воно́	*it*		

There is no distinction for gender in the third-person plural personal pronoun **вони́**.

Demonstrative pronouns

The words 'this', 'that' are called demonstrative pronouns. There will be more about these words in a later unit. For the time being simply note: **це** – 'this is', **то** – 'that is'.

Possessive pronouns

The possessive pronouns are:

мій *my, mine*	чий *whose*
твій *your, yours*	який *what kind of?*

You saw two examples involving the word **мій** in the dialogue:

мі**й** брат	*my brother*	мі**й** друг	*my friend*

You have already seen that the word for 'my' changes its form with feminine nouns:

мо**я** сестра́	*my sister*	мо**я** ма́ма	*my mother*

The word will also change its form with neuter nouns:

мо**є́** ім'я́	*my name*	мо**є́** село́	*my village*

The word for 'your' changes in the same way: **твій, твоя́, твоє́.** The question word 'whose?' also changes like this: **чий?, чия́?, чиє́?**

чий?	чия́?	чиє́?
мій брат	мо**я** сестра́	мо**є́** ім'я́

Чий це автомобі́ль?	*Whose car [is] this?*	Це мій	*It['s] mine.*
Чия́ то кни́га?	*Whose book [is] that?*	Не моя́	*[It's] not mine.*

Now look at the following examples:

мій автомобі́ль *my car*

Це мій автомобі́ль.	*This is my car.*	Автомобі́ль мій.	*The car is mine.*

As you can see, Ukrainian uses the same word **мій** for 'my' and 'mine'. The same applies to **твій**:

тво**є́** я́блуко *your apple*

Це тво**є́** я́блуко.	*This is your apple.*	Я́блуко тво**є́**.	*The apple is yours.*

LANGUAGE TIP

You – Ви or ти?

Use the personal pronoun **ти** when addressing one person whom you know well, e.g. a relative or a close friend (like the French *tu*). **Ви** is used when talking to several people or as a polite form of address to one person whom you do not know very well, e.g. in official situations, in talking to older persons, those who occupy a senior position, etc. In writing the pronoun **ви**, when used as a polite form of address to one person, has a capital letter: **Ви**. The corresponding possessive pronouns are **твій (твоя́, твоє́)** and **Ваш (Ва́ша, Ва́ше)**.

When meeting a Ukrainian for the first time, it is advisable to use **Ви** and **Ваш**.

---

8 CASE

Nouns, pronouns and adjectives change their endings for number and case. The case of a noun is determined by its function in the sentence. Nouns and pronouns are listed in wordlists and dictionaries in the nominative or 'naming' case. It most frequently occurs as the subject of a sentence or as the description of the subject, e.g. **Я – англі́єць, Окса́на – музика́нт,** where the personal pronoun and all the nouns are in the nominative case. Adjectives are listed in the form of the masculine nominative singular.

9 ASKING QUESTIONS WITH QUESTION WORDS *ХТО? ЩО?*

хто?	*who?*	що?	*what?*

We can make simple questions by adding question words:

Хто це?	*Who is this?*	Що то?	*What is that?*

10 HOW TO SAY WHAT YOUR NAME IS

Моє́ ім'я́ Тара́с.	*My (first) name is Taras.*
Моє́ прі́звище Кова́ль.	*My surname is Koval.*

It is possible to say the same thing in the following way:

Мене́ звуть Тара́с Кова́ль.   *My name is Taras Koval.*

звуть – *[they] call*

The words **Мене́ звуть** literally mean 'me [they] call'. Both Ukrainian phrases, **Моє́ ім'я́** and **Мене́ звуть,** are the equivalent of the English 'my name is'.

Моє́ ім'я́ . . .	Моє́ прі́звище . . .	Мене́ звуть . . .

11 HOW TO ASK WHAT SOMEONE'S NAME IS

a informal

Як твоє́ ім'я́? *What is your (first) name?* (lit. how [is] your name?)

Як твоє́ прі́звище? *What is your surname?*

Як тебе́ звуть? *What is your name (and surname)?*

b formal/polite

Як Ва́ше ім'я́?	Як Ва́ше прі́звище?	Як Вас звуть?

тебе́ (from **ти**)	*you*
вас (from **ви**)	*you*

Test yourself: Впра́ви (*exercises*)

1 **Read the dialogues again. Complete the table by putting a cross (+) in the right box:**

	журналі́ст	музика́нт	акто́р	матема́тик
Марі́я				
Éндрю				
Мико́ла				
Окса́на				

2 **Now answer a few questions following the examples:**

Хто це?	Це брат.	Хто то?	То сестра́.
Що це?	Це кві́тка.	Що то?	То вікно́.

(друг, учи́тель, ма́ма, хло́пчик, ля́лька, чолові́к, ла́мпа, де́рево, ді́вчинка, ґа́нок, мо́ре)

3 **Now some questions, saying 'yes' or 'no' in Ukrainian.**

Example: Це автомобі́ль? – Ні, це де́рево. (*No, it's a tree*):

a Це чолові́к? (*Yes, it's a . . .*)

b Це кни́га? (*Yes, it's a . . .*)

c То кві́тка? (*No, it's a doll.*)

d То ру́чка? (*No, it's a bush.*)

e Це хло́пчик? (*Yes, it's a . . .*)

f То це́рква? (*Yes, it's a . . .*)

g Це я́блуко? (*No, it's a pencil.*)

4 **a** **Name these people (choose their names from the list that follows).**

   b **Imagine that you are meeting these people. How would you ask each of them what their names and professions are. How might they reply?**

| **i** Окса́на Вели́чко | **iii** Е́ндрю Кро́сбі |
| **ii** Марі́я Кова́ль | **iv** Сті́вен Те́йлор |

5 Write out the following nouns in three columns, according to their gender. At the same time, check that you know what each one means:

| *Masculine* | *Feminine* | *Neuter* |
| **чолові́к** | **жі́нка** | **со́нце** |

со́нце, чолові́к, жі́нка, де́рево, ґа́нок, вікно́, кві́тка, кіт, не́бо, хло́пчик, кущ, автомобі́ль, буди́нок, ді́вчинка, я́блуко, юна́к, ї́жа, друг, кни́га, мо́ре, олівець, папі́р, ру́чка, фо́то, це́рква, ша́пка, ля́лька, цирк, ла́мпа, журналі́ст, сестра́

6 Choose the right form of the adjective to go with the nouns in the list that follows:

Example: **Брат висо́кий**

a Брат	(висо́кий, висо́ка, висо́ке)
b Кві́тка	(га́рний, га́рна, га́рне)
c Ру́чка	(мій, моя́, моє́)
d Я́блуко	(зеле́ний, зеле́на, зеле́не)
e Село́	(краси́вий, краси́ва, краси́ве)

вели́кий	*big, great, large*
краси́вий	*beautiful, handsome*
ціка́вий	*interesting*
те́плий	*warm*
висо́кий	*tall, high*
мале́нький	*little, small*
стіле́ць (m)	*chair*

7 Answer the following questions, using adjectives from the list.

Example: Яки́й це буди́нок? Це вели́кий буди́нок.

a Яке́ це я́блуко?	Це (*small*)
b Яка́ це кві́тка?	Це (*beautiful*)
c Яка́ це ша́пка?	Це (*warm*)
d Яке́ це де́рево?	Це (*tall, high*)
e Яка́ це кни́га?	Це (*interesting*)

8 **Now do the reverse! Form simple questions from these sentences:**

Example: Чий це стілéць? Це мій стілéць.

a _____? Це моя́ ля́лька.

b _____? Це мій олівéць.

c _____? Це моé я́блуко.

d _____? Це моя́ кни́га.

e _____? Це моé фóто.

f _____? Це мій кіт.

9 **Find the correct answer to the questions on the left from the list of answers on the right:**

a Це висóке дéрево? **i** Так, це гáрна дíвчина.

b Це гáрна дíвчина? **ii** Так, це тéпле мóре.

c Це тéпле мóре? **iii** Ні, це зелéний папíр.

d Це вели́кий буди́нок? **iv** Ні, це низьки́й кущ.

e Це чóрний папíр? **v** Ні, це малéнький буди́нок.

f Це висóкий кущ? **vi** Так, це висóке дéрево.

10 **a** **You are in Kyiv. At a reception, you are asked what your name is. What are the words that you are likely to hear? How will you respond?**

b **You are showing some photographs to a Ukrainian friend. Your friend asks if one of the people in the photo is your brother. What does s/he actually say? You reply that it is not your brother – it is a friend. How will you phrase your reply in Ukrainian?**

2 Дуже приємно з Вами познайомитися
Very nice to meet you

In this unit you will learn:

▶ *How to make a simple description of a room*
▶ *How to say you like something*
▶ *What to say when someone is introduced to you*
▶ *The names of some countries and nationalities*
▶ *Something about the plural*
▶ *How to count from 1 to 4*

Діало́г 1

 TR 3, 00:08

The next evening Taras again invites Stephen to his home to meet his wife and to discuss some business questions.

Тара́с	Приві́т, Сті́вене!
Сті́вен	До́брий ве́чір. Як життя́?
Тара́с	Норма́льно, дя́кую. Ві́ро, познайо́мся: це мій друг Сті́вен.
Сті́вен	Сті́вен Те́йлор.
Ві́ра	Ду́же приє́мно, Ві́ра. Перепро́шую, як Ва́ше прі́звище?
Сті́вен	Те́йлор. Я англі́єць.
Ві́ра	Ду́же ра́да з Ва́ми познайо́митися. Тара́се, запро́шуй дру́га до віта́льні.
Тара́с	Сті́вене, захо́дь, будь ла́ска. Про́шу сіда́ти.
Сті́вен	Дя́кую. Це ду́же га́рна, сві́тла кімна́та. Тут вели́кі ві́кна, м'які́, зручні́ ме́блі. Як тут за́тишно!
Тара́с	Ми ма́ємо не ду́же вели́кий буди́нок, але́ ми його́ ду́же лю́бимо.
Сті́вен	Ти ма́єш сад?
Тара́с	Так. Я ма́ю га́рний сад. Хо́чеш подиви́тися?
Сті́вен	О, це вели́кий сад. Мені́ ду́же подо́баються ці зеле́ні кущі́ та яскра́ві кві́ти. І тут такі́ висо́кі дере́ва. Вони́, ма́буть, ду́же старі́?
Тара́с	Так. Ти зна́єш, Сті́вене, сього́дні не ду́же те́плий день. Тут прохоло́дно. Ході́мо до кімна́ти.

V	привíт!	hi!
	вéчір	evening
	як спрáви?	how are things?
	спрáва	matter
	нормáльно	OK
	познайóмся: це мій друг	meet my friend. (lit. get acquainted: this is my friend)
	дýже приéмно	very nice to meet you
	перепрóшую	excuse me/I beg your pardon
	дýже рáда з Вáми познайóмитися	I am very pleased to meet you (lit. [I am] very glad with you to get acquainted)
	запрóшуй дрýга	invite [your] friend
	до вітáльні	to the living room
	вітáльня	living room
	захóдь	come in
	прóшу, сідáти	please sit down
	свíтла (m. nom. sg.: **свíтлий**)	bright (feminine form)
	кімнáта	room
	тут	here
	м'якí (m. nom. sg.: **м'якúй**)	soft (plural form)
	зручнí (m. nom. sg.: **зрýчнúй**)	comfortable (plural form)
	мéблі	furniture (plural form)
	зáтишно	[it is] cosy
	як тут зáтишно!	how cosy it is here (lit. 'how here [it is] cosy')
	ми мáємо	we have
	алé	but, however
	ми йогó дýже лю́бимо	we love it very much (lit. 'we it very much like')
	ти мáєш	you have
	сад	garden
	я мáю	I have
	хóчеш подивúтися?	[do you] want to have a look?
	менí (дýже) подóбаються	I like (very much)
	ці	these
	та	and
	яскрáві (m. nom. sg.: **яскрáвий**)	brightly coloured (plural form)
	такí (m. nom. sg.: **такúй**)	such (plural form)
	мáбуть	perhaps, maybe
	старí (m. nom. sg.: **старúй**)	old (plural form)
	знáєш	[you] know
	сьогóдні	today
	прохолóдно	[it is] cool, chilly
	ходíмо	let's go
	до кімнáти	to/into the room

This is one time when we really can say 'don't worry too much about the grammar'. The dialogues would be completely artificial if we left certain phrases until after we had explained the grammar! That is why in many cases we provide both English equivalents and a literal translation of what the Ukrainian says word by word. A good example of a grammatical point is **запро́шуй дру́га** *invite [your] friend*. The Ukrainian for *'friend'* is **друг,** so something is clearly going on. Exactly what you will find out later. For the time being, simply get to know the whole phrase. The same goes for the literal translations. These will give you an idea of how Ukrainian puts words together in sentences.

a Пра́вда чи непра́вда? Answer in Ukrainian

1 Сті́вен Те́йлор – украї́нець.   **2** Тут вели́кі ві́кна.

3 Тара́с ма́є га́рний сад.   **4** Сього́дні ду́же те́плий день.

b Answer the following questions in English

1 How does Taras introduce Stephen to Vira? Repeat the phrase.

2 Which room in Taras' house is very beautiful?

3 What do we know about the trees in Taras' garden?

4 Why do Taras and Stephen decide to go back into the house?

Як функціону́є мо́ва

Nouns, pronouns, adjectives and verbs in Ukrainian change their endings according to the role they play in each sentence. You have already seen how adjectives change their endings to 'agree with' the gender of the noun with which they occur.

1 'SINGULAR' AND 'PLURAL'

The endings also tell us about the **number** of the noun (and adjective, if there is one) in question; the singular number is used to refer to one person or object, the plural number to refer to more than one.

Some nouns in Ukrainian, like **ме́блі** in the dialogue, exist only in the plural form. Such words will be specifically marked in the wordlists.

The wordlist for the dialogues in this unit gives adjectives in the form in which they occur there but also in the form in which they occur in dictionaries.

2 HOW IS THE PLURAL FORMED?

In this unit, you have already seen several plural forms of nouns and adjectives:

зеле́ні кущі́   вели́кі ві́кн**а**

яскра́в**і** кві́т**и**   високі дере́в**а**

Most Ukrainian masculine and feminine nouns in the plural have one of the endings **и, і, ї**. Which one depends on the ending in the singular. Look at these examples:

кімна́т**и** (кімна́та)   учителі́ (учи́тель)

сад**и́** (сад)   гаї́ (гай)

кущі́ (кущ)   ши́ї (ши́я)

зе́мл**і** (земля́)

a Masculine and feminine nouns

▶ If the last consonant in the noun is hard, use **и** (**кімна́та, сад**).

▶ If the last consonant in the noun is soft (i.e. is followed by the 'soft sign' or the letters **я, ю**, or **є**, which show that the preceding consonant is soft) or one of the following letters **ж, ч, ш, щ, ц**, use **і** (**кущ, віта́льня, учи́тель**).

▶ If the last letter of the noun is **й** (**гай**) or **я** (**ши́я**) after a vowel, substitute **ї** for that letter.

Note: Two nouns that you have already met form their plurals in a somewhat irregular way. Make special note of:

друг – дру́з**і**   кві́тка – кві́т**и**

Some nouns lose a vowel when forming the nominative plural, e.g.:

англі́єць – англі́йці   буди́нок – буди́нки

стіле́ць – стільці́   ґа́нок – ґа́нки

олівець – олівці́   день – дні

Such words will always be indicated in the wordlists.

b Neuter nouns

Neuter nouns ending in **-о** in the singular always end in **-а** in the nominative plural. Those neuter nouns that have an **-е** ending in the singular change that ending to **а** or **я** (i.e.: **а** after a hard consonant, **я** after a soft consonant or **р**):

ві́кн**а** (вікно́)   се́л**а** (село́)

дере́в**а** (де́рево)   мор**я́** (мо́ре)

прі́звищ**а** (прі́звище**)**

The neuter noun **ім'я́** requires special attention. Its nominative plural is **імена́**.

3 MAKING ADJECTIVES PLURAL

The plural ending for both hard and soft adjectives is the same, irrespective of the gender of the following noun: **-і**

	hard		soft
м'яки́й	м'які́	си́ній	си́ні
га́рний	га́рні		
до́брий	до́брі		

4 'MY', 'YOUR', 'OUR' IN THE PLURAL

Here are the forms of the possessive pronouns 'my' and 'your':

мій, моя́, моє́	мої́
твій, твоя́, твоє́	твої́
ваш, ва́ша, ва́ше	ва́ші

Note: The forms of **наш** (*our*) are like those of **ваш**.

5 NUMBER AND NUMBERS

 TR 3, 01:34

Learning about the plural naturally leads into counting. The numbers 1–4 in Ukrainian are:

▶ **Оди́н** (*masculine*)/**одна́** (*feminine*)/**одне́** (*neuter*) is followed by the nominative singular:

оди́н стіле́ць	одна́ кімна́та	одне́ вікно́

▶ **Два** (*masculine and neuter*)/**дві** (*feminine*), **три**, **чоти́ри** followed by the nominative plural:

два стільці́/два вікна́/дві кімна́ти	три брати́	чоти́ри вікна́

Діало́г 2

 TR 3, 01:54

Now for a chance to check your knowledge so far.

A chance meeting in the street. Taras accidentally touches the handbag a woman who is walking towards him hand in hand with a tall man.

Тара́с	О! . . . Лі́до, яка́ зу́стріч! Ви́бач, будь ла́ска!
Лі́да	До́брий ве́чір, Тара́се! Познайо́мся: це мій чолові́к, Володи́мир.
Тара́с	Ду́же ра́дий познайо́митися. Тара́с.
Володи́мир	(*shakes Taras' hand*) Перепро́шую, як Ва́ше ім'я́?
Тара́с	Тара́с. Тара́с Кова́ль.
Володи́мир	Ду́же приє́мно.

Лі́да	Як твої́ спра́ви?
Тара́с	Непога́но. А як ви?
Лі́да	Ду́же до́бре. Сього́дні ду́же га́рний, те́плий день і ми гуля́ємо.
Тара́с	Ну, до́бре, щасли́во . . .
Лі́да	Тара́се . . . Слу́хай, подзвони́ коли́-небудь. Ось наш телефо́н. Ми запро́шуємо в го́сті.
Володи́мир	Так, подзвоні́ть неодмі́нно!
Тара́с	Чудо́во. Дя́кую.

V
зу́стріч (f)	*meeting*
яка́ зу́стріч!	*what a meeting!*
ви́бач, будь ла́ска	*please excuse me*
ми гуля́ємо	*we're out for a walk* (inf. **гуля́ти**)
щасли́во	*cheerio! good luck!*
слу́хай!	*listen!*
подзвони́ коли́-небудь	*phone [us] sometime* (inf. **подзвони́ти**)
ми запро́шуємо в го́сті	*we invite [you] to visit us*
подзвоні́ть неодмі́нно!	*phone [us] without fail!*

> **LANGUAGE TIP**
> The verb forms **сіда́й/сіда́йте, бува́й/бува́йте, зателефону́й/зателефону́йте, ви́бач/ви́бачте** are known as imperatives. They are used to give commands ('Come here!') or make requests ('Phone me later'). The forms with **-те** are plural, i.e. used when addressing more than one person, or as a polite form of address to one person (the difference between **ви** and **ти**).

6 WHAT IS A VERB?

Verbs denote an action ('Stephen *runs* quickly'; 'she *is reading* a book'), a mental process ('Taras *thinks* logically') or a state ('Vera is my sister'). They also denote when the action takes place. **Tense** means the time of the action to which the verb refers: **past, present** or **future.** Ukrainian verbs have separate forms for all three tenses. In this unit, you will learn the forms of the **present tense.**

7 THE VERB 'TO BE'

Це – мій брат Мико́ла.	*This is my brother Mykola.*
То – мій друг Е́ндрю.	*That is my friend Andrew.*

These sentences can also be expressed in a slightly different way:

| Це є мій брат Микóла. | This is my brother Mykola. |
| То є мій друг Éндрю. | That is my friend Andrew. |

The word є ('is' or 'are') is not compulsory – you can either use it or leave it out in sentences like this.

First person	**я є**	*I am*	**ми є**	*we are*
Second person	**ти є**	*you are*	**ви є**	*you are*
Third person	**він є**	*he is*		
	вонá є	*she is*	**вони́ є**	*they are*
	вонó є	*it is*		

8 THERE IS/THERE ARE

| Тут вели́кі ві́кна, м'які́, | Here there are large windows and |
| зру́чні мéблі. | soft, comfortable furniture. |

Sentences with 'there is'/'there are' in English usually denote the location of person or objects, e.g. 'there are two girls here', 'there is a letter on the table'. In Ukrainian, there is no equivalent phrase for 'there is'/'there are' and the location comes at the beginning of the sentence:

Тут висóкі дерéва.	There are tall trees here.
Тут вели́кі ві́кна.	There are large windows here.
У вітáльні м'які́, зручні мéблі.	There is soft, comfortable furniture in the living room.

9 IT IS

Тут зáтишно.	It is cosy here.
Сьогóдні прохолóдно.	It is chilly today.
Дýже приємно з Вáми познайóмитися.	It is very nice to meet you.

> **LANGUAGE TIP**
> Ukrainian does not use a word for 'it' in sentences like this where the pronoun 'it' does not seem to refer to a noun. After all, you cannot ask 'What is chilly today?' and expect to get a reasonable answer!

10 ADVERBS

An adverb describes how an action is performed, e.g. 'he can run *quickly*', 'Stephen speaks Ukrainian *well*'. Many adverbs in English end in *-ly*, e.g. neatly, beautifully, thoughtfully. In Ukrainian, adverbs can be formed from adjectives by replacing the **-ий** ending of the masculine nominative singular with **-o**, e.g.:

приє́мний	*pleasant*	приє́мно	*pleasantly*
га́рний	*beautiful*	га́рно	*beautifully*

A few adverbs end in **-e**, e.g.:

до́брий	*good*	до́бре	*well*

Words like **за́тишно** (*it is cosy*), **прохоло́дно** (*it is cool*) (see section 10 in this unit) are also adverbs in form and are formed from adjectives in exactly the same way:

До́бре, що Ви мій друг.	*It's great that you're my friend.*
Те́пло сього́дні.	*It's warm today.*

11 VERBS – THE DICTIONARY FORM

Every verb has a base form used for dictionaries called an infinitive. Most Ukrainian verbs have infinitives ending in **–ти**, for example:

захо́ди**ти**, сіда́**ти**.

The equivalent form in English is 'to come in', 'to sit down'.

Some special forms of the infinitive

You have also seen two infinitives (**познайо́митися, подиви́тися**) that are slightly different because they end in **-ся**.

See what a change in meaning it can make:

дозво́льте познайо́мити . . .	*let [me] introduce (somebody)*
дозво́льте познайо́митися	*let [me] introduce myself*

LANGUAGE TIP
дозво́льте *let [me]*

The suffix **-ся** can come after any personal form of the verb, as well as the infinitive, e.g.:

Мені́ подо́баються кві́ти.	*I like the flowers* (lit. the flowers please me).

There will be more about **-ся** in Unit 5.

Note: The infinitive of the verb 'to be' is **бу́ти**.

12 THE PRESENT TENSE OF VERBS

Ukrainian verbs are divided into two **conjugation** patterns. The word conjugation refers to the form of the personal endings. The significant feature of the first conjugation is the letter **-е** (after a consonant) or **-є** (after a vowel) in the second- and third-persons singular and the first- and second-persons plural. For example, the verb **ма́ти** (*to have*):

First person	я ма́**ю**		ми ма́**ємо**
Second person	ти ма́**єш**		ви ма́**єте**
Third person	він ма́**є**		
	вона́ ма́**є**		вони́ ма́**ють**
	воно́ ма́**є**		

Here are some first conjugation verbs in the present tense:

	зна́ти *(to know)*	сіда́ти *(to sit down)*	запро́шувати *(to invite)*	дя́кувати *(to thank)*
I	зна́**ю**	сіда́**ю**	запро́шу**ю**	дя́ку**ю**
you	зна́**єш**	сіда́**єш**	запро́шу**єш**	дя́ку**єш**
he/she/it	зна́**є**	сіда́**є**	запро́шу**є**	дя́ку**є**
we	зна́**ємо**	сіда́**ємо**	запро́шу**ємо**	дя́ку**ємо**
you	зна́**єте**	сіда́**єте**	запро́шу**єте**	дя́ку**єте**
they	зна́**ють**	сіда́**ють**	запро́шу**ють**	дя́ку**ють**

Verbs like **ма́ти**, **зна́ти** and **сіда́ти** are completely regular; you can deduce the forms of the present tense from the infinitive. However, you can see from the last two verbs that the infinitives contain a syllable (**-ва-**) which is not present in the other forms given here. **Перепро́шувати** (could be translated as 'to excuse oneself', 'to say sorry') has grammatical forms that change exactly like those of **запро́шувати** ('to invite, welcome someone'). This is why all verbs will be listed in the infinitive and the forms of the first- and second-persons singular when necessary, because from those forms all other forms of the present tense can be deduced.

13 A REMINDER – GIVING ORDERS AND MAKING REQUESTS

The verb forms **познайо́мся/познайо́мтесь**, **запро́шуй/запро́шуйте**, **заходь/заходьте**, **сіда́й/сіда́йте**, **зателефону́й/зателефону́йте** are called imperatives. They denote orders, requests or invitations: **заходь, будь ла́ска** (*come in, please*).

14 ASKING QUESTIONS WITHOUT QUESTION WORDS

Question words are words like 'who', 'what', 'whose', 'how' – **хто, що, чий, як**. Questions without a question word (Unit 1) are formed in writing simply by adding a question mark or by rising intonation in speech.

However, frequent use is made of a little word **чи** followed by the question itself:

Чи він англі́єць?	*Is he English?* (lit. [is] he [an] Englishman?)
Чи ти ма́єш сад?	*Do you have a garden?*
Чи ти хо́чеш подиви́тися?	*Do you want to have a look?*

15 HOW TO

a Greet people in Ukrainian

time of day	formal		informal
6:00–12:00	Доброго ра́нку!	*good morning*	Приві́т! *Hi!* (at any time)
12:00–18:00	До́брий день!	*good afternoon/ day*	
18:00–22:00	До́брий ве́чір!	*good evening*	

b Ask: How are things?

 TR 3, 02:53

▶ Questions

Як спра́ви?	*How are things?*
Як життя́?	*How's life?*
Як чолові́к/дружи́на?	*How's the husband/the wife?*
Як ді́ти?	*How are the children?*

TR 3, 03:20

▶ Possible replies

Дя́кую, . . .	*Thanks, . . .*
чудо́во	*great! fine!*
ду́же до́бре	*very good*
до́бре	*good*
непога́но	*not bad*
норма́льно	*OK*
так собі́	*so-so*
не ду́же до́бре	*not very good*
пога́но	*bad, rotten*
жахли́во	*absolutely awful*

c Introduce yourself and other people

Дозвóльте відрекомендувáтися:	Я – Стíвен.
Дозвóльте познайóмитися:	Менé звуть Стíвен.
	Моє́ ім'я́ Стíвен.
	Моє́ прíзвище Тéйлор.

In informal situations when addressing one person and introducing someone, you can say:

Познайóмся: це Стíвен.

When introducing yourself in a very informal situation, you can say:

Привíт! я Стíвен.   *Hi! I [am] Stephen.*

But be very sure. This way of introducing yourself is extremely casual!

When being introduced to someone for the first time you shake hands and say: **Дýже приє́мно** and name yourself, e.g. **Я Петрó Гнатю́к**, or **Дýже рáдий** (m)/**рáда** (f) **з вáми познайóмитися**.

Here are some phrases for introducing other people:

Дозвóльте предстáвити:	Це Джон.
Дозвóльте відрекомендувáти:	Це мій друг Джим.
Дозвóльте познайóмити:	Це моя́ пóдруга Марíя.
Познайóмтеся:	Це Марíя.

d Say: Here is . . .

Ось телефóн.	Ось наш будúнок.
Ось мій автомобíль.	Ось моя́ машúна.

e Identify some countries and nationalities

 TR 3, 04:15

краї́на (country)	націонáльність (*nationality*)	
	(*m*)	(*f*)
Украї́на (*Ukraine*)	украї́не**ць**	украї́н**ка**
Амéрика (*America*)	америкáне**ць**	америкáн**ка**
Німéччина (*Germany*)	німе**ць**	німке́**ня**
Канáда (*Canada*)	канáде**ць**	канáд**ка**
Росíя (*Russia*)	росія́**нин**	росія́**нка**
Áнглія (*England/Great Britain*)	англі**є́ць**	англí**йка**
Фрáнція (*France*)	францý**з**	французе́**нка**
Ітáлія (*Italy*)	італі**є́ць**	італí**йка**

Іспа́нія (Spain)	іспа́н**ець**	іспа́**нка**
Австра́лія (Australia)	австралі́**єць**	австралі́**йка**
Япо́нія (Japan)	япо́н**ець**	япо́н**ка**

Note:

▶ The word for 'foreigner': **інозе́мець** (m), **інозе́мка** (f).

▶ All the masculine nouns in the list ending in **-ець** or **-єць** lose their final vowel when forming the nominative plural, e.g.:

іспа́н**ець**	іспа́**нці**	япо́н**ець**	япо́**нці**
англі́**єць**	англі́**йці**	італі́**єць**	італі́**йці**

▶ The nominative plural of **росія́нин** is exceptional: **росія́ни**.

? Test yourself: Впра́ви

1 **Add the necessary pronoun, ти or ви:**

   a . . . сіда́єш.

   b . . . ма́єте сад?

   c . . . зна́єш Сті́вена?

Then, make the **ви** form in those sentences where there are **ти** forms now and vice versa.

2 **You are acting as interpreter between a visitor who does not speak Ukrainian and your Ukrainian host who does not speak English. Put the visitor's remarks into Ukrainian and the host's replies into English:**

Example

Visitor	*This is a bright room.* **Це сві́тла кімна́та**.
Host	**Так, кімна́та ду́же сві́тла**. *Yes, the room is very bright.*
Visitor	*What room is that?*
Host	Там віта́льня.
Visitor	*It's very cosy!*
Host	Так, тут м'які́, зручні́ ме́блі.
Visitor	*Is this your garden? It's big!*
Host	Так, це мій сад. Він ду́же га́рний.

3 **Put the infinitives in brackets into the correct form required by the personal pronoun in each sentence:**

   a Я (**ма́ти**) зручни́й буди́нок.   **b** Він (**сіда́ти**) в крі́сло.

   c Ми (**запро́шувати**) до віта́льні.   **d** Ти (**зна́ти**), де Тара́с?

> **LANGUAGE TIP**
> In Ukrainian, you sit down into an armchair – **в крі́сло**.

4 **Make complete sentences out of the following words:**

   a друг, це, мій.   **d** віта́льні, запро́шуємо, до.

   b англі́йка, вона́.   **e** Марі́я, кана́дка.

   c ма́є, буди́нок, вели́кий, він.

5 **Answer the following questions in Ukrainian with 'yes' or 'no' as required, using the words in brackets as a guide:**

Example: Чи Сті́вен америка́нець? (*Englishman*) Ні, він англі́єць.

   a Чи це віта́льня? (*living room*) . . .

   b Чи це Ві́ра? (*Oksana*) . . .

c Чи тут вели́кі ві́кна? (*little windows*) . . .

d Чи це Ваш брат Мико́ла? (*my friend Andrew*) . . .

6 Identify the nationality in each of the following sentences according to the example:

Example: *Peter comes from England*. Він англі́єць.

a *This musician comes from Germany*. Він . . . .

b *My wife comes from Italy*. Вона́ . . . .

c *This is a journalist from Spain*. Він . . . .

d *You come from Russia*. Ти . . . .

e *I am from Ukraine*. Я . . . .

f *This person is from Australia*. Вона́ . . . .

7 Give Ukrainian equivalents of the English phrases in the following dialogue:

Тара́с	Приві́т!
Сті́вен	*Hello! Please come in.*
Тара́с	Як спра́ви?
Сті́вен	*Thank you, fine. And you?*
Тара́с	Дя́кую, непога́но.
Сті́вен	*Please sit down.*
Тара́с	Дя́кую. Як тут за́тишно.

8 Complete the following dialogue by translating the English words in brackets into Ukrainian:

Оле́г	Добри́день, як (*life*)?
Мико́ла	(*OK*), дя́кую. А як ти?
Оле́г	(*Absolutely awful*). Познайо́мся, (*this is my wife*) Тетя́на. Тетя́но, це мій (*friend*).
Тетя́на	(*Very*) приє́мно (*with you*) познайо́митися. (*I beg your pardon*), як Ва́ше (*first name*)?
Мико́ла	Мико́ла.
Оле́г	(*Please sit down*).
Мико́ла	(*Thank you*).
Тетя́на	Ви украї́нець?
Мико́ла	Ні, я італі́єць, (*my mother is Ukrainian*). Її́ звуть Марі́я. (*Your house is very beautiful*.) Як тут (*cosy*).
Оле́г	(*Yes*), цей буди́нок (*is very old*), але́ (*comfortable*). (*We have*) зру́чні, сві́тлі (*rooms*), га́рний (*garden*).

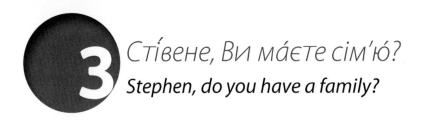

3 Стíвене, Ви мáєте сім'ю?

Stephen, do you have a family?

In this unit you will learn:
▶ *How to offer things*
▶ *How to say please and thanks*
▶ *How to talk about your family*
▶ *How to say goodbye*

Діалóг 1

TR 4, 00:07

Same evening in Taras' house in London. Conversation over coffee.

Тарáс	Ти хóчеш пи́ти чай чи кáву?
Стíвен	Кáву, будь лáска.
Вíра	Цу́кор?
Стíвен	Ні, дя́кую.
Тарáс	Я пам'ятáю, ти не лю́биш цу́кру. Бери́, будь лáска, тíстечка, їж пéчиво.
Вíра	*(offers cakes)* Прóшу, пригощáйтеся.
Стíвен	Дя́кую. О, це ду́же смáчно. Я люблю́ тíстечка.
Тарáс	Чи тобí нали́ти ще кáви?
Стíвен	Так, прóшу. Ду́же дóбра кáва.

хóчеш (inf.: **хотíти**; 1st person **хóчу**)	*you want*
пи́ти (**п'ю, п'єш**)	*to drink*
чай	*tea*
чи	*(here:) or*
кáву (nom.: **кáва**)	*coffee*
цу́кор	*sugar*
пам'ятáю (inf.: **пам'ятáти**)	*I remember*
ти не лю́биш цу́кру	*You don't like sugar*
бери́ (inf.: **брáти; беру́, берéш**)	*take!*
тíстечка (sg.: **тíстечко**)	*(fancy) cakes*
їж (inf.: **їсти**; present tense: **їм, їси́, їсть; їмó, їстé, їдя́ть**)	*eat!*

пе́чиво	biscuits
пригоща́йтеся (inf.: **пригоща́тися**)	help yourself!
сма́чно	[it is] tasty
Чи тобі́ нали́ти ще ка́ви?	Shall [I] pour you out some more coffee?

Як функціону́є мо́ва

1 MORE ORDERS AND REQUESTS

This dialogue introduces more imperative forms. The form of the imperative depends on the pronoun that would be used when speaking to that person, **ти** or **ви**. Here are both forms of the imperatives that you have seen so far:

ти (singular – informal)	**ви** (plural or formal singular)
бер-**и́**	бер-**і́ть**
їж	їж-**те**
запро́шу-**й**	запро́шу-**й**-те
захо́**дь**	захо́**дь**-те
знайо́**м**-ся	знайо́**м**-те-ся
подзвон-**и́**	подзвон-**і́**-ть
пригоща́-**й**-ся	пригоща́-**й**-те-ся

Note: The hyphens are there to help you see how the words are built up. The rules for forming the imperative are given in Unit 18. All new imperative forms occurring in the texts will be given in the wordlists.

LANGUAGE TIP

What follows is the beginning of an exploration of the case system of nouns and adjectives in Ukrainian. We advise you not to try to learn the endings by heart at this stage. Instead, use the following information as a point of reference to which you can return as often as you need. With practice and repetition, you will soon become familiar with the whole concept of 'case' and the way in which nouns and adjectives change.

The object of a sentence (accusative case)

The accusative case is primarily used as the case of the direct object, i.e. the form for the word that is at the 'receiving end' of the action of the subject:

Запро́шуй **дру́га**.	Ти не лю́биш **цу́кру**.
Ти ма́єш **сад**?	Бери́ **ті́стечка**.
Ти хо́чеш пи́ти **чай**?	Їж **пе́чиво**.
Ти хо́чеш пи́ти **ка́ву**?	Я люблю́ **ті́стечка**.

The masculine singular nouns **сад** and **чай** do not change their form; in other words, their accusative singular form is exactly the same as the 'dictionary form', the nominative singular. The same is true of the neuter singular noun **пе́чиво**; the accusative neuter plural noun **ті́стечка** is also identical to the nominative plural.

However, three nouns have changed in form:

Запро́шуй дру́г**а**.   *Invite [your] friend.*
(nom. sg.: друг)

Ти хо́чеш пи́ти ка́в**у**?   *Do you want to drink coffee?*
(nom. sg.: ка́ва)

Ти не лю́биш цу́кр**у**.   *You don't like sugar.*
(nom. sg.: цукор)

Ка́ва is a feminine noun; all feminine nouns ending in **-a** in the nominative singular change the **-a** to **-y** in the accusative singular. **Друг** and **цу́кор**, however, are both masculine singular nouns and yet they behave differently from the other masculine nouns in the list.

1 ANIMACY

We need to look at the meaning of the word **друг**, 'friend', i.e. a male human being. The idea of animacy is of great importance in Ukrainian grammar. When it comes to forming the accusative singular, masculine nouns in the singular are divided into animate and inanimate. Animate nouns cover all the animal kingdom, including male human beings; in the accusative singular, they add **-a** to the form of the nominative singular. Masculine nouns referring to objects and abstract concepts are all inanimate. Animacy is also important in the plural of feminine nouns denoting human beings and animals.

2 ENDINGS OF THE ACCUSATIVE CASE – NOUNS

The following tables will give you an overview of the endings for the nominative and accusative cases in both the singular and plural.

a Masculine inanimate nouns

Nom. s.	па́спорт	буди́нок	олівець́
Acc. s.	па́спорт	буди́нок	олівець́
Nom pl.	паспорти́	буди́нки	олівці́
Acc. pl.	паспорти́	буди́нки	олівці́

b Masculine animate nouns

Nom. s.	брат	друг	учи́тель	англі́єць	росія́нин
Acc. s.	бра́т**а**	дру́г**а**	учи́тел**я**	англі́йц**я**	росія́нин**а**
Nom pl.	брати́	дру́зі	учителі́	англі́йці	росія́ни
Acc. pl.	брат**і́в**	дру́з**ів**	учител**і́в**	англі́йц**ів**	росія́н

c Feminine inanimate nouns

Nom. s.	кни́га	ву́лиця	зу́стріч
Acc. s.	кни́г**у**	ву́лиц**ю**	зу́стріч
Nom pl.	кни́ги	ву́лиці	зу́стрічі
Acc. pl.	кни́ги	ву́лиці	зу́стрічі

d Feminine animate nouns

Nom. s.	сестра́	япо́нка	англі́йка	ки́ця
Acc. s.	сестр**у́**	япо́нк**у**	англі́йк**у**	ки́ц**ю**
Nom pl.	се́стри	япо́нки	англі́йки	ки́ці
Acc. pl.	сест**е́р**	япо́н**ок**	англі́й**ок**	киц**ь**

e Neuter nouns

Nom. s.	де́рево	прі́звище	мо́ре	життя́	ім'я́
Acc. s.	де́рево	прі́звище	мо́ре	життя́	ім'я́
Nom pl.	дере́ва	прі́звища	моря́	життя́	імена́
Acc. pl.	дере́ва	прі́звища	моря́	життя́	імена́

Notes:

▸ All inanimate nouns of whatever gender share endings for the nominative and accusative cases in the plural.

▸ Masculine and feminine animate nouns in the plural have different endings for the accusative case. In fact, it would be more accurate to say that feminine nouns in this case have no endings at all! The **-а** that marks the nominative singular ending of a feminine noun is dropped; in the case of **сестра́**, **япо́нка** and **англі́йка**, this would lead to a cluster of consonants at the end of the word. In such circumstances, a vowel is inserted between the consonants: **-о-** or occasionally **-е-**.

▸ Masculine animate nouns have a quite different ending in the accusative plural: **-ів**. Nouns like **росія́нин** behave somewhat differently; the nominative plural form is shorter and the accusative plural has no ending at all, like feminine nouns.

▸ Proper names (words like **Ю́рій**) are also nouns and have case endings. Of course, they are animate (**Я зна́ю Тара́са**). **Мико́ла**, although a male name, ends in **-а** and so declines like a feminine noun – hence **Я зна́ю Мико́лу**.

(Revise the sections on hardness and softness of consonants in the Introduction and section (2) in Unit 2.)

3 THE ACCUSATIVE CASE – PERSONAL PRONOUNS

	Nom.	Acc.	Nom.	Acc.
First person	я	мене́	ми	нас
Second person	ти	тебе́	ви	вас
Third person (m)	він	його́		
(f)	вона́	її	вони́	їх
(n)	воно́	його́		

Reminder: the third-person pronouns make no gender distinction in the plural.

4 ENDINGS OF THE ACCUSATIVE CASE – ADJECTIVES

The tables that follow give the endings of both the nominative and accusative cases.

a With animate nouns

Hard endings

	Nom. s.	Acc. s.	Nom. pl.	Acc. pl
M.	добрий	добр**ого**	добрі	добр**их**
F.	добра	добр**у**	добрі	добр**их**

Soft endings

	Nom. s.	Acc. s.	Nom. pl.	Acc. pl
M.	синій	син**ього**	сині	син**іх**
F.	синя	син**ю**	сині	син**іх**

b With inanimate nouns

Hard endings

	Nom. s.	Acc. s.	Nom. pl.	Acc. pl
M.	добрий	добр**ий**	добрі	добр**і**
F.	добра	добр**у**	добрі	добр**і**
N.	добре	добр**е**	добрі	добр**і**

Soft endings

	Nom. s.	Acc. s.	Nom. pl.	Acc. pl
M.	синій	сині**й**	сині	син**і**
F.	синя	син**ю**	сині	син**і**
N.	синє	син**є**	сині	син**і**

Діало́г 2

 TR 4, 00:50

The conversation over coffee and cakes continues.

Ві́ра	Сті́вене, Ви ма́єте сім'ю́?
Сті́вен	Я неодру́жений. У ме́не є батьки́ в Шотла́ндії. Ма́ма пенсіоне́рка, а та́то працю́є в ба́нку. Ще я ма́ю бабу́сю. А Ва́ші батьки́ у Великобрита́нії?
Ві́ра	Ні. Вони́ в Украї́ні. Ма́ма й та́то живу́ть у Черні́гові, а ті́тка в Ки́єві.
Сті́вен	Я ще не ду́же до́бре зна́ю украї́нські міста́. Перепро́шую, чи Ви не зна́єте, котра́ годи́на?
Ві́ра	Дев'я́та. Ви поспіша́єте?
Сті́вен	Так, тро́шки. Я вже ма́ю йти́ додо́му. Ду́же дя́кую за гости́нність.
Тара́с	Прихо́дь іще́.
Сті́вен	До поба́чення!
Ві́ра	На все до́бре!
Тара́с	Па!

(не)одру́жений		*(un)married*
Я ма́ю		*I have* [you can also use **у ме́не є** here]
батьки́		*parents*
в Шотла́ндії (nom.: **Шотла́ндія**)		*in Scotland*
пенсіоне́рка		*pensioner* (f)
працю́є (inf.: **працюва́ти**)		*works*
в ба́нку (nom.: **банк**)		*in a bank*
ще (here:)		*also, as well*
бабу́сю (nom.: **бабу́ся**)		*granny*
живу́ть (inf.: **жи́ти; живу́, живе́ш**)		*[they] live*
в Черні́гові (nom.: **Черні́гів**)		*in Chernihiv*
ті́тка		*aunt*
в Ки́єві (nom.: **Ки́їв**)		*in Kyiv*
міста́ (nom.: **мі́сто**)		*towns*
котра́ годи́на?		*what time is it?* (lit. which hour?)
дев'я́та (m. nom. sg.: **дев'я́тий**)		*nine o'clock* (lit. ninth)
Ви поспіша́єте? (inf.: **поспіша́ти**)		*are you in a hurry?*
тро́шки		*a little*
ма́ю (inf.: **ма́ти**)		*(here:) have to, must, should*
іти́ (here: **йти́** after a word ending in a vowel) **(іду́, іде́ш)**		*to go*
додо́му		*home*
дя́кую за гости́нність		*thanks* (lit. *I thank*) *for the hospitality*
прихо́дь іще́! (**іще́ = ще** after a word ending in a consonant)		*come again!*
до поба́чення		*goodbye*
на все до́бре		*all the best*
па		*bye-bye*

Here are some questions on both dialogues.

a Пра́вда чи непра́вда? Answer in Ukrainian

   1 Сті́вен лю́бить ті́стечка.

   2 Тара́с і Ві́ра живу́ть у Полта́ві.

   3 Сті́вен до́бре зна́є украї́нські міста́.

   4 Ві́ра поспіша́є додо́му.

b Answer the following questions in English

   1 What kind of drink does Stephen choose?

   2 Is Stephen married?

   3 Where do Vira's parents live?

   4 At what time does Stephen have to go home?

Як функціонýє мóва

2 PREPOSITIONS

A preposition is a word that, together with the endings of nouns, pronouns and adjectives, helps to relate words to one another in a sentence. Examples of English prepositions are 'about', 'into', 'for'.

So far you have seen the Ukrainian prepositions **з** and **до: я дýже рáдий з Вáми познайóмитися** (*I am very pleased to get acquainted with you*); **запрóшуй до вітáльні** (*invite (him) into the living room*); **ходíмо до кімнáти** (*let's go to the room*), but for the time being just learn the whole phrase, because different cases are involved.

Here are some prepositions that are followed by a noun or pronoun in the accusative case:

a у/в (*to, into*)

Оксáна сідáє в автомобíль. Oksana gets (lit. sits down) into the car.

(*on*) (*with days of the week*)

Я не працюю в субóту. I don't work on Saturday.

> **LANGUAGE TIP**
>
> *Note:* the preposition **у/в** is followed by a different case in some phrases in the dialogue; it has a different meaning there (*in*) and is followed by a different case (the locative) that will be dealt with later. For the time being learn the phrases in which this case occurs, e.g. **в Шотлáндії, в бáнку**.

b на (*to*)

Я йдý на робóту. I am going to work.

Я ї́ду на вокзáл. I am travelling to the station.

The difference in usage (with the accusative case) between the prepositions **у/в** and **на** in the meaning 'to' is best left to experience! Just note the phrases where each preposition occurs.

c про (*about*)

Я знáю про фíрму "Гéрмес- I know about the Hermes
Клóзінг" Clothing firm.

d за (*for,* after **дя́кую**)

Дя́кую за квíти. Thanks for the flowers.

V **субóта** Saturday
робóта work
вокзáл station

3 ANOTHER USE FOR *ЧИ*

You have already seen that **чи** introduces a question without a question word (as in **Чи він англíєць?**). It can also be used to mean 'or', as in **Він англíєць чи українець?**

4 HAVING AND HAVING TO

у мéне є   *I have*

Stephen uses both ways of saying 'to have' in Ukrainian in the space of a few lines. You saw the verb **мáти** in the previous unit; it corresponds exactly in form to the English verb.

The other construction (**у мéне є**) is a very common way of expressing possession. It will be explained in detail in Unit 5. For now, compare the two ways in which Stephen can say that he has a granny:

Я мáю бабýсю   *(accusative case – granny is the object)*

У мéне є бабýся   *(nominative case – granny is the subject)*

In the phrase **мáю йтѝ додóму**, we see a form of the verb **мáти** followed by an infinitive in the sense of '**I have to** go home'.

5 *КИ́ЇВ* AND *ЧЕРНÍГІВ*

The capital city of Ukraine is called **Ки́їв**, but when we are actually in Kyiv, we are **у Ки́єві**. Similarly with **Чернíгів** – when there, we are **у Чернíгові**. This **alternation of vowels** (**і** with **о** or **е**, **ї** with **є**) within words is an important feature of Ukrainian.

You have already seen that **мій** and **твій** change to **моя́/твоя́**, **моє́/твоє́**, **мої́/твої́**.

The words in which this alternation occurs will be specially marked in the wordlists in the following way: (alt. **і/о**), (alt. **і/е**) or (alt. **ї/є**). There will be more on this in Unit 12.

6 START TO TALK ABOUT YOUR FAMILY!

 TR 4, 01:50

First, a few new words.

роди́на	*(extended) family (i.e. not only you, your husband/wife and children, but grandchildren, grandparents, aunts, uncles, etc.)*
дідýсь	*granddad*
замíжня	*married (a woman to a man)*

(Note: because of the meaning, this adjective is always in the feminine gender! Note also that it has a soft ending.)

дя́дько (m)	*uncle*
дити́на (pl.: дíти)	*child*
онýк	*grandson*
онýчка	*granddaughter*
племíнник	*nephew*
племíнниця	*niece*
дружи́на	*wife*
жíнка	*woman, wife (colloquial)*

Now for some sample sentences:

Чи Ви ма́єте сім'ю́?

Так, я ма́ю дружи́ну (чолові́ка), си́на й до́ньку.

Ні, я неодру́жений (незамі́жня).

Чи у Вас є ді́ти?

У ме́не є син/до́нька.

У ме́не є сини́/три до́ньки

Чи у те́бе є діду́сь?

Так. Він ду́же стари́й. А ще я ма́ю бабу́сю.

Де живе́ твоя́ роди́на?

У ме́не є батьки́ в Шотла́ндії. Ма́ма пенсіоне́рка, а та́то
    працю́є в ба́нку.

7 HOW TO OFFER THINGS AND WHAT TO SAY IN REPLY

a Formal:

Ви хо́чете чай чи ка́ву?   Про́шу, ка́ву.

Бері́ть, будь ла́ска, тісте́чка.   Дя́кую.

Ї́жте, будь ла́ска, пе́чиво.   Дя́кую, я не хо́чу.

Вам нали́ти ще ка́ви?   Так, про́шу.

b Informal:

Вам ка́ви чи ча́ю?   Ча́ю, будь ла́ска.

Ка́ва?   Так, про́шу.

Чай?   Ні, ка́ва.

Цу́кор?   Ні, дя́кую.

Будь ла́ска, бери́ тісте́чка.

Їж пе́чиво.

Ще ка́ви?

> **LANGUAGE TIP**
>
> Instead of using a complete sentence when offering someone something (**Ви хо́чете чай чи ка́ву?** *Do you want tea or coffee?*), people often drop the verb (**Вам ча́ю чи ка́ви?** lit. *For you some tea or coffee?* Don't worry that the words for tea and coffee have changed their form; here, we use the genitive case, covered in Unit 4).

8 PLEASE AND THANKS

Always use a polite **Про́шу!** or **Будь ла́ска!** (*please*) when making a request and follow up with **Дя́кую** (*thank you*). When you thank somebody for something, you will hear **Про́шу!** in response. You should do the same when someone thanks you.

9 IT'S TIME TO SAY GOODBYE

 TR 4, 02:52

До поба́чення!	*Goodbye*

(the most commonly used phrase: lit. until next meeting)

До зу́стрічі!	*See you!*
До ве́чора!	*See you tonight!*
До за́втра!	*See you tomorrow!*
Щасли́во!	*Good luck! Cheerio!*

Some very informal phrases:

Бува́й (to one person)/ Бува́йте (plural)	*Bye for now!*
Па!	*Bye-bye*

Test yourself: Впра́ви

1 Divide the following sentences into two columns:

   i where **ма́ти** means 'to have';

   ii where **ма́ти** means 'to have to', 'must'

     a Я ма́ю сад.

     b Я ма́ю йти́.

     c Він ма́є поспіша́ти.

     d Ти ма́єш ка́ву.

     e Ти ма́єш чита́ти кни́гу.

     f Ти ма́єш телефо́н.

2 Insert the correct form of one of the following verbs: ї́сти, пи́ти, бра́ти, жи́ти according to the sense:

     a Сті́вен ... ті́стечка.

     b Ти ... ка́ву?

     c Він ... у Ки́єві.

     d Ми ... чай.

   (*Note*: the forms can be worked out from the information in the wordlist.)

3 Complete the sentences by putting the words in the right-hand column into the accusative case:

Тара́с зна́є

     дівчина

     кни́га

     мі́сто

     англі́єць

     украї́нець

4 Here are some dialogues to be reconstructed entirely in Ukrainian:

TR 4, 03:52

   a Reply to the questions in Ukrainian:

Host	Ти хо́чеш чай чи ка́ву?
You	Coffee, please.
Host	Вам нали́ти ще ка́ви?
You	Yes, please.
Host	Цу́кор?
You	No, thanks.
Host	Бери́, будь ла́ска, ті́стечка.
You	Thanks very much, I like cakes.
Host	Про́шу.
You	Thank you. It's very tasty.
Host	Тобі́ ще ка́ви?
You	Yes, please. It's very good coffee.

b Provide your part of this dialogue in Ukrainian:

You	Excuse me, what's the time?
Host	Дев'я́та.
You	Thanks.
Host	Ви поспіша́єте?
You	Yes. I am in a great hurry. I have to go home.
Host	До зу́стрічі.
You	Many thanks for your hospitality. Goodbye.

5 Complete the sentences, using the correct endings of the accusative case:

			M	N	F
a	Я ї́ду	на	(вокза́л)	(мо́ре)	(робо́та)
b	Я чита́ю	про	(бі́знес)	(життя́)	(сім'я́)
c	Я зна́ю		(Ки́їв)	(мі́сто)	(Украї́на)
d	Я ма́ю		(автомобі́ль)	(я́блуко)	(кни́га)
e	Я ма́ю		(дя́дько)		(ті́тка)

6 Talk about your family! У Вас є сім'я́?

Try a variety of answers, using the phrase **У ме́не є**:

a I have a brother and two sisters.

b I have three grandsons.

c I have a husband/wife.

Now use the phrase **Я ма́ю**:

d I have a husband/wife.

e I have a grandson.

f I have my parents in Scotland.

"Алло́! Я телефону́ю з Ло́ндона . . ."
'Hello! I am calling from London . . .'

In this unit you will learn:
- ▶ *How to make a telephone conversation*
- ▶ *How to say what is possible and what is necessary*
- ▶ *Something about Ukrainian surnames*
- ▶ *How to count from 5 to 10*

Діало́г

TR 5, 00:06

Stephen is on the phone to his Ukrainian partners. Here is his conversation.

Сті́вен	Алло́? До́брий день.
Секрета́рка	Добри́день.
Сті́вен	Це Вас турбу́є Стівен Те́йлор.
Секрета́рка	Перепро́шую?
Сті́вен	Моє́ прі́звище Те́йлор. Чи мо́жна попроси́ти до телефо́ну па́ні Маля́рчу́к?
Секрета́рка	Одну́ хвили́ночку, па́не Те́йлор.
Сті́вен	Дя́кую.
(Pause)	
Маля́рчу́к	Алло́, я слу́хаю.
Сті́вен	Па́ні Маля́рчу́к, це телефону́є Сті́вен Те́йлор з фі́рми "Ге́рмес Кло́зінг".
Маля́рчу́к	О, до́брий день, Сті́вене. Ду́же ра́да. Де Ви за́раз? Зві́дки Ви телефону́єте?
Сті́вен	Я телефону́ю з А́нглії, з Ло́ндона. Ма́ю до Вас спра́ву.
Маля́рчу́к	Слу́хаю Вас.
Сті́вен	Я хо́чу відві́дати Ки́їв та і́нші міста́ Украї́ни. Я не ма́ю бага́то ча́су, але хо́чу побу́ти кі́лька днів у Льво́ві. Чи Ви мо́жете замо́вити для ме́не готе́ль?
Маля́рчу́к	З приє́мністю. Сті́вене, Вам тре́ба офіці́йне запро́шення?
Сті́вен	Ду́маю, так.
Маля́рчу́к	Нема́є пробле́м. Ви ма́єте квито́к на літа́к до Ки́єва?

Стівен	Так, я вже́ замо́вив квито́к на Украї́нські авіалі́нії.
	Я ма́ю оде́ржати ві́зу за три дні. Дя́кую за допомо́гу.
	Я ду́же ра́дий Вас чу́ти.
Маля́рчу́к	Дя́кую за дзвіно́к.
Стівен	До поба́чення.
Маля́рчу́к	До зу́стрічі.

(*Note*: from now on words will be given in their dictionary form, i.e. nominative singular for nouns, nominative masculine singular for adjectives, infinitive for verbs (plus first- and second-persons singular where these forms cannot be deduced from the infinitive). In this unit only, the forms in which the words occur in the dialogue will be added in parentheses.)

телефонува́ти (here: **телефону́ю**)	*to telephone*
з (preposition + gen.)	*from*
алло́	*hello (at the start of a telephone conversation)*
турбува́ти (here: **турбу́є**)	*to trouble*
це Вас турбу́є Сті́вен Те́йлор	*this is Stephen Taylor troubling you*
мо́жна	*[it is] possible*
попроси́ти	*to ask for, to request*
па́ні	*Mrs*
одну́ хвили́ночку!	*just a moment!*
хвили́на	*moment, minute*
пан	*Mr (the form* **па́не** *is used when addressing someone)*
слу́хати (here: **слу́хаю**)	*to listen*
це телефону́є Сті́вен Те́йлор	*this is Stephen Taylor phoning*
де?	*where?*
зві́дки?	*from where?*
відві́дати	*to visit*
бага́то (+ gen.)	*much, a lot of*
час	*time*
побу́ти	*to spend some time*
кі́лька (+ gen.)	*a few, several*
Львів (here: **у Льво́ві**)	*L'viv (alt.* **і/о**)
замо́вити	*to order, to book, to make a reservation*
готе́ль (m)	*hotel*
приє́мність (f)	*pleasure*
з приє́мністю	*with pleasure*
пробле́ма	*problem*
нема́є пробле́м	*no problem! (lit. there are no problems)*

тре́ба	*[it is] necessary*
офіці́йний (here: **офіці́йне**)	*official*
запро́шення (n)	*invitation*
ду́маю, так	*I think so (lit. I think yes)*
літа́к	*plane*
квито́к *на літа́к до Ки́єва*	*ticket **for** the plane **to** Kyiv*
вже	*already*
я вже́ замо́вив квито́к	*I have already ordered the ticket*
авіалі́нії (pl.)	*airlines*
оде́ржати	*to get, receive*
ві́за (here: **ві́зу**)	*visa*
за три дні	*in three days' time*
допомо́га (here: **допомо́гу**)	*help, assistance*
чу́ти	*to hear*
дзвіно́к	*(telephone) call*

a Пра́вда чи непра́вда?

1 Сті́вен телефону́є з Ки́єва.

2 Сті́вен уже́ замо́вив квито́к на літа́к.

3 Він тако́ж уже́ ма́є ві́зу.

4 Сті́вен хо́че відві́дати Ки́їв.

b Да́йте ві́дповідь на ці запита́ння англі́йською мо́вою (Answer these questions in English)

1 Who is the person Stephen is phoning?

2 Does Stephen have a lot of time for his visit?

3 Does Stephen need a letter of invitation for his forthcoming visit?

4 How does Stephen intend to travel to Ukraine?

Як функціону́є мо́ва

1 THE GENITIVE CASE
Calling Kyiv from London

The dialogue contains phrases involving two prepositions that are followed by the **genitive case**:

Мо́жна попроси́ти па́ні	*Is it possible to ask Mrs Maliarchuk*
Маля́рчу́к до телефо́ну?	*[to come] to the telephone?*

(You have already seen phrases with **до** and the genitive meaning 'to', 'into' in Unit 2.)

Я телефону́ю з А́нглії,	*I am phoning from England,*
з Ло́ндона.	*from London.*

The genitive case is used after several prepositions which will be listed later. It is also used after words denoting an unspecified quantity, e.g.:

▶ бага́то (*much, many, a lot of*)   бага́то книг   *a lot of books*
▶ ма́ло (*little, few, not much, not many*)   ма́ло ча́су   *little time*
▶ кі́лька/де́кілька (*several, a few*)   кілька днів   *a few days*
▶ and in the plural after the numerals 5–10.

Related to this is the use of the genitive case in a partitive sense, e.g.:

нали́ти ка́в**и**, ча́**ю**   *to pour out some coffee, tea*

нали́ти бага́то ка́в**и**, ча́**ю**,   *to pour out a lot of coffee, tea*

The genitive case sometimes corresponds to the English -'s/-s' ending, e.g.:

Це сестра́ Сті́вена.   *This is Stephen's sister.*

2 ENDINGS OF THE GENITIVE CASE – NOUNS

Masculine nouns (animate and inanimate)

Nom. s.	па́спорт	буди́нок	олівце́ц	телефо́н
Gen. s.	па́спорт**а**	буди́нк**у**	олівц**я́**	телефо́н**у**
Nom pl.	паспорти́	буди́нки	олівці́	телефо́ни
Gen. pl.	паспорт**і́в**	буди́нк**ів**	олівц**і́в**	телефо́н**ів**

Nom. s.	брат	хло́пчик	друг	учи́тель	англі́єць
Gen. s.	бра́т**а**	хло́пчик**а**	дру́г**а**	учи́тел**я**	англі́йц**я**
Nom pl.	брати́	хло́пчики	дру́зі	учителі́	англі́йці
Gen. pl.	брат**і́в**	хло́пчик**ів**	дру́з**ів**	учител**і́в**	англі́йц**ів**

Feminine nouns (animate and inanimate)

Nom. s.	кни́га	ву́лиця	сестра́	компа́нія	зу́стріч
Gen. s.	кни́г**и**	ву́лиц**і**	сестр**и́**	компа́ні**ї**	зу́стріч**і**
Nom pl.	кни́ги	ву́лиці	се́стри	компа́нії	зу́стрічі
Gen. pl.	кни**г**	ву́лиц**ь**	сест**е́р**	компа́н**ій**	зу́стріч**ей**

Neuter nouns

Nom. s.	де́рево	прі́звище	мо́ре	життя́	ім'я́
Gen. s.	де́рев**а**	прі́звищ**а**	мо́р**я**	життя́	і́м**ені**
Nom pl.	дере́ва	прі́звища	моря́	життя́	імена́
Gen. pl.	дере́в	прі́звищ	мор**і́в**	житті́**в**	іме́**н**

Notes:

a Masculine

There are two possible endings, **-а** (**-я**) or **-у** (**-ю**). The rules for determining which ending can be attached to which noun are complex. The vocabulary at the back of the book provides information on the correct genitive singular ending for all masculine nouns that occur in this book.

b Feminine

There is no ending at all in the genitive plural, except in the case of nouns like **зу́стріч** (which end in a consonant in the nominative singular), where the ending is -**ей**.

c Neuter

Neuter nouns that have a nominative singular ending in -**е** or -**я** have the same genitive plural endings as masculine nouns. Neuter nouns with a nominative singular ending in -**о** (and some in -**е** like **прі́звище**) are like feminine nouns in that they have no ending at all in the genitive plural.

3 ADJECTIVES – GENITIVE CASE

Hard endings

	Nom. s.	Gen. s.	Nom. pl.	Gen. pl.
M.	до́брий	до́бр**ого**	до́брі	до́бр**их**
F.	до́бра	до́бр**ої**	до́брі	до́бр**их**
N.	до́бре	до́бр**ого**	до́брі	до́бр**их**

Soft endings

	Nom. s.	Gen. s	Nom. pl.	Gen. pl
M.				
F.	си́ній	си́нь**ого**	си́ні	си́н**іх**
N.	си́ня	си́нь**ої**	си́ні	си́н**іх**
	си́нє	си́нь**ого**	си́ні	си́н**іх**

4 PERSONAL PRONOUNS – GENITIVE CASE

	S.	Pl.
First person	мене́	нас
Second person	тебе́	вас
Third person (m)	його́	
(f)	її	їх
(n)	його́	

44

Notes:

▶ There is a stress shift in **мене́, тебе́** when they are preceded by a preposition: **до ме́не, до те́бе**.

▶ When the third-person pronouns are preceded by a preposition they change their form: **до ньо́го, у не́ї, до ни́х**. There is also a stress shift in the singular forms.

5 POSSESSIVE PRONOUNS – GENITIVE CASE

Here are the genitive endings:

	Nom. s.	Gen. s.	Nom. pl.	Gen. pl
M.	мій	мого́	мої́	мої́х
F.	моя́	моє́ї	мої́	мої́х
N.	моє́	мого́	мої́	мої́х

Твій has the same endings as **мій**.

	Nom. s.	Gen. s.	Nom. pl.	Gen. pl
M.	наш	на́шого	на́ші	на́ших
F.	на́ша	на́шої	на́ші	на́ших
N.	на́ше	на́шого	на́ші	на́ших

Ваш has the same endings as **наш**.

Refer back to the table of personal pronouns given earlier. The genitive forms of the third-person pronouns, both singular and plural, also fulfil the function of possessive pronouns, e.g.:

його́ сестра́	*his sister*	його́ життя́	*his life*
його́ друг	*his friend*	його́ батьки́	*his parents*

As you can see, the word **його́** remains the same, irrespective of the gender or number of the accompanying noun. The same is true of **її́** (*her*) and **їх** (*their*).

Note: **Його́** and **її́** can also mean 'its' when referring to an inanimate masculine/neuter or feminine noun.

Впра́ва

Here is a description of Stephen's office; it contains a lot of words in the genitive case. Can you spot them all? Check the vocabulary at the back of the book for the meaning of new words. Read the text and then answer the questions on it.

Це кабінéт Стíвена. Стíвен Тéйлор – дирéктор велúкої компáнії "Гéрмес-Клóзінг", якá продаé мóдний óдяг. Кабінéт Стíвена велúкий і свíтлий. Там багáто книг і мáло мéблів: одúн стіл, однé крíсло, чотúри стільцí. Стíвен мáє кíлька украïнсько-англíйських та áнгло-украïнських словникíв, тому́ що він чáсто рóбить перéклади з англíйської мóви на украïнську. Стíвен мáє комп'ю́тер, калькуля́тор, телефóн, автовідповідáч, телевíзор і настíльну лáмпу. На столí лежúть пáпка для пóшти; там є дéкілька діловúх листíв, а такóж привáтний лист із Кúєва від дру́га. На столí такóж стоïть фóто мáми Стíвена та йогó сестрú. На стінí – велúкий календáр з Украïни.

a Прáвда чи непрáвда?

1 Стíвен – дирéктор компáнії, якá продаé мéблі.

2 Стíвен чáсто рóбить перéклади з англíйської мóви на украïнську.

3 На столí лежúть я́блуко.

4 У кабінéті Стíвена (*in Stephen's office*) є багáто мéблів.

b Дáйте вíдповідь на ці запитáння англíйською мóвою

1 How many armchairs are there in Stephen's office?

2 Why does he need the Ukrainian dictionaries?

3 Who is the private letter from?

4 What is hanging on the wall?

6 PREPOSITIONS WITH THE GENITIVE CASE

до *to/till*   до Кúєва (*direction – to Kyiv*)

до мíста (*to town*)

до обíду (*time – 'till lunch'*)

Note: **Я мáю телефонувáти до ньóго.** *I have to phone him.*

пíсля	*after*	пíсля обíду
з	*from*	з Кúєва, з Амéрики (*direction, e.g. a letter from America*)
		з дру́гої годúни (*time – 'from two o'clock'*)

від	from	від бра́та (*a sender, e.g. a letter from my brother*)
		від Оде́си (*distance, e.g. two hundred kilometres from Odesa*)
		ліво́руч/право́руч від метро́ (*to the left/right of*)
без	without	без я́блук, без ка́ви
для	for	для бра́та, для дружи́ни
бі́ля	by, next to	бі́ля телефо́ну

Note: **до** (+ genitive), **у/в** (+ accusative), **з – від** (+ genitive).

Compare the following sentences:

Я ї́ду в університе́т.	*I am going to the university.* (I work there, am a student)
Я ї́ду з університе́ту.	*I am going* (coming) *from the university.* (I was there for a specific purpose)
Я ї́ду до університе́ту.	(1) *I am going to the university.* (i.e. same meaning as в університе́т)
	(2) *I am going as far as the university.* (but I'm not going to enter the building – perhaps Університе́т is the name of a bus stop or metro station)
Я ї́ду від університе́ту.	*I am going* (coming) *from the university.* (from outside the building or from the bus stop or metro station with that name)

The preposition **з** can also take the form **із** or **зі** if:

i the word it follows ends with more than one consonant or:

ii the word before which it stands begins with more than one consonant.

| лист із Ки́єва від дру́га | *a letter from Kyiv from my friend, i.e. a letter from my friend in Kyiv* |

7 NUMBERS 5–10

 TR 5, 02:42

Число́	Скі́льки?	Котри́й?
5	п'ять	п'я́тий
6	шість	шо́стий
7	сім	сьо́мий
8	ві́сім	во́сьмий
9	де́в'ять	дев'я́тий
10	де́сять	деся́тий

The numerals answering the question word **скі́льки?** (*how many?*) (i.e. one, two, three, etc.) are called cardinal numerals. Those which answer the question **котри́й?** (*which one?*) (i.e. first, second, third, etc.) are called ordinal numerals.

The ordinal numerals 1st–4th are as follows:

1st – **пе́рший**   *2nd* – **дру́гий**

3rd – **тре́тій** (soft endings!)   *4th* – **четве́ртий**

8 VERBS – SECOND CONJUGATION

The second conjugation differs from the first in certain endings:

	S.	Pl.
1	-ю/-у	-имо*
2	-иш*	-ите*
3	-ить*	-ять/-ать

говори́ти (*to speak*)		**стоя́ти** (*to stand*)	
1	говорю́	гово́римо	стою́	стоїмо́
2	гово́риш	гово́рите	стоїш	стоїте́
3	гово́рить	гово́рять	стоїть	стоя́ть

Look at the forms of the first-person singular and the third-person plural of the following verbs:

люби́ти (*to love*)		**роби́ти**	
1	люблю́	лю́бимо	роблю́	ро́бимо
2	лю́биш	лю́бите	ро́биш	ро́бите
3	лю́бить	лю́блять	ро́бить	ро́блять

and at the first-person singular of **леті́ти** (*to fly*):

---

* **И** is replaced by **ї** after a vowel or apostrophe.

я лечу́	ми летимо́
ти лети́ш	ви летите́
він	
вона лети́ть	вони летя́ть
воно	

Such changes will be noted in the wordlists in the following way:

люби́ти (люблю́, лю́биш, . . . лю́блять)

лети́ти (лечу́, лети́ш)

LANGUAGE TIP

On the basis of this information, it is possible to deduce all the other forms of the present tense of virtually any Ukrainian verb.

9 IS IT POSSIBLE?

Чи мо́жна попроси́ти до	[Is it] possible to ask
телефо́ну па́ні Маля́рчу́к?	Mrs Maliarchuk [to come] to the telephone?

This is the best way of asking for someone on the phone. It also introduces the useful word **мо́жна**, which literally means 'it is possible/permitted/feasible':

Чи мо́жна захо́дити до кімна́ти?	May I/we come into the room?
Чи мо́жна лети́ти до Полта́ви?	Can/may I/we fly to Poltava? (Is it possible to . . . ?)
Чи мо́жна зателефонува́ти до Ки́єва?	Can/may I/we phone Kyiv?
Чи мо́жна подиви́тися по́шту?	Can/may I/we have a look at the mail?
(Так,) мо́жна.	Yes, you can/may.
(Ні,) не мо́жна.	No, you can't/may not.

10 IS IT NECESSARY?

Вам тре́ба офіці́йне запро́шення?	Do you need an official invitation? (lit. is an official invitation necessary for you?)
Чи тре́ба захо́дити?	Do I/we need to come in?
Чи тре́ба лети́ти до Полта́ви?	Do I/we have to fly to Poltava? (is it necessary to . . . ?)

Чи потрíбно зателефонувáти до Ки́єва?	*Do I/we have to phone Kyiv?*
Чи потрíбно подиви́тися пóшту?	*Must I/we have a look at the mail?*
(Так,) потрíбно.	*Yes, you must/have to/it is necessary.*
(Так,) трéба.	*Yes, you must/have to/it is necessary.*
(Ні,) не потрíбно.	*No, you don't have to/it isn't necessary.*
(Ні,) не трéба.	*No, you don't have to/it isn't necessary.*

LANGUAGE TIP

Here we have a new form (**вам**) of the pronoun **ви**, which we need in this construction. You have already seen it in the phrase **Вам чáю чи кáви?** earlier in this unit. It is the form of the **dative case** and will be explained more fully in Unit 6. For the time being, simply learn the whole phrase.

The word **трéба** is colloquial; a more formal equivalent is **потрíбно**. **Трéба** could be replaced in all the preceding examples by **потрíбно** with no change at all in meaning.

---

11 MRS MALIARCHUK – SOMETHING ON SURNAMES IN UKRAINIAN

Grammatically speaking, the verb **попроси́ти** is followed by the **accusative** case. The word **пáні** (*Mrs*) never changes and the surname Maliarchuk, although it ends in a consonant, does not change either because it here refers to a woman. Asking for Mr Maliarchuk would be a different matter altogether: **Чи мóжна попроси́ти пáна Малярчукá?**

12 MINUTES AND MOMENTS

Хвили́на is a minute consisting of 60 seconds. The suffix that the receptionist adds, **-очка**, is sometimes called a diminutive suffix.

LANGUAGE TIP

Obviously, there is no such thing as a small minute, so 'moment' is the most appropriate translation. She could also have said **однý хвили́нку** with no difference in meaning, except perhaps that **хвили́ночка** has a greater 'feelgood factor'. The intention presumably is to make Stephen hope that he really will not have to wait too long! Ukrainians make a great deal of use of such suffixes to colour their speech. Attention will be drawn to them whenever they occur in future dialogues.

Incidentally, she uses the **accusative** case because of the imperative **чекáйте!** (*wait!* – infinitive **чекáти**) that she assumes will be supplied by the hearer.

13 HOW TO JOIN SIMPLE SENTENCES TOGETHER

And, an', 'n'

The use of the Ukrainian words for 'and' **і**, **й**, **та**, depends on the sounds that surround them.

a   **і** is used when the preceding word ends and/or the following word starts with a consonant (including those in **я**, **ю**, **є**, **ї**), e.g.:

Óфіс Стíвена велúкий і свíтлий. Там багáто книг і мáло мéблів.

b   **й** occurs between vowels/or after a vowel and before a consonant, e.g.:

Мáма **й** тáто в Полтáві; Украïна **й** Áнглія

c   **та** is used in order to avoid a cluster of two **і** sounds between words, e.g.:

зелéні кущí **та** яскрáві квíти; Кúїв **та** íнші містá.

In formal situations, **а такóж** can also be translated as 'and':

Там є дéкілька діловúх листíв, **а такóж** привáтний лист із Кúєва.

'Which' and 'that'

In the dialogue and text, you have seen phrases such as:

Стíвен Тéйлор – дирéктор велúкої компáнії, **якá** продаé мóдний óдяг.

Чудóво, **що** ви телефонýєте.

The words **якá** and **що** join the two parts of the phrase that are separated in writing by a comma. You have already seen **якá** before (**якúй**, **якá**, **якé**; **якí**: *what kind of? which?*). It also functions as a **relative pronoun** in Ukrainian. It would be possible to say in English 'Stephen Taylor is the director of a large company. The company makes fashionable clothing.' However, it is more convenient to avoid a repetition of the word 'company' and make one sentence by using the relative pronoun 'that' or 'which'. The pronoun is called 'relative' because it relates back to an item already mentioned. The form of **якúй** preserves the gender of the noun to which it refers (here the noun **компáнія** is feminine).

Що, when it joins two parts of a sentence, is the equivalent of English 'that' in sentences like 'He said that he would come tomorrow.'

> **LANGUAGE TIP**
> The word 'that' is sometimes omitted in English sentences: 'It's good you're phoning', 'it's great you called'. It is much more unusual to omit **що** in Ukrainian.

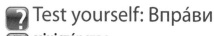

Test yourself: Впра́ви

міністе́рство	*ministry*
парла́мент	*parliament*
о́зеро	*lake*
дискéта	*floppy disk*

1 **Complete the table, putting the noun in brackets into the correct form of the genitive singular (or plural, after the words бага́то, ма́ло, скі́льки, п'ять):**

	M	N	F
до	(брат)	(мі́сто)	(Амéрика)
з	(вокза́л)	(мі́сто)	(робо́та)
пі́сля	(обі́д)	(прі́звище)	(розмо́ва)
без	(цу́кор)	(вікно́)	(сестра́)
для	(друг)	(міністе́рство)	(маши́на)
бі́ля	(банк)	(дéрево)	(ла́мпа)
буди́нок	(парла́мент)	(міністе́рство)	(фі́рма)
ча́шка	(чай)	(молоко́)	(ка́ва)
бага́то (ма́ло, скі́льки?)	(словни́к)	(о́зеро)	(спра́ва)

2 **Insert the correct form of the Ukrainian word for 'and' (і, й, та) in the following sentences:**

   a   Сті́вен ма́є комп'ю́тер . . . калькуля́тор.

   b   На столі́ є ла́мпа . . . автовідповіда́ч.

   c   В о́фісі є стіл, стільці́ . . . і́нші мéблі.

3 **Insert the necessary preposition (від, до, пі́сля, без, для, у/в) in the following sentences:**

   a   . . . обі́ду я ї́ду . . . дру́га.

   b   Я ї́ду . . . квитка́.

   c   Чолові́к сіда́є . . . маши́ну.

   d   Я працю́ю . . . понеді́лка.

   e   Це лист із Ки́єва . . . ма́ми.

   f   Я ма́ю дискéти . . . комп'ю́тера.

4 **Using information from this unit and the previous one, say some things about yourself in Ukrainian:**

I live in London. This is my office. The office is large and bright, it has very comfortable furniture. I am the director of a big company. I want to visit Kyiv and other cities of Ukraine. I have already ordered my ticket on Ukrainian Airlines.

I am not married but I have a large family. I have parents in Scotland, five brothers and four sisters. I also have lots of friends.

5 **Complete the dialogue by translating the English phrases into Ukrainian:**

A	Алло́, слу́хаю.
B	*Good afternoon. This is (your name) speaking.*
	Мо́жна попроси́ти до телефо́ну (*the name of the person to whom you wish to speak*)?
A	*Just a moment, please. I'm sorry, who is speaking?*
B	Це (*your name*).
A	Дя́кую.

5 Нам тре́ба замо́вити но́мер у готе́лі
We need to book a room in a hotel

In this unit you will learn:
▶ *How to find your way around*
▶ *More about numbers*
▶ *How to say that you have (or don't have) something*
▶ *How to book a hotel room*
▶ *How to change money*
▶ *How to count from 11 to 1,000,000*

Діало́г 1

TR 6, 00:08

Solomiia Oleksandrivna Maliarchuk and Ihor Ivanovych Stakhiv, the Kyiv firm "Moda".

Маля́рчу́к	Íгоре Іва́новичу, ми ма́ємо замо́вити готе́ль для Сті́вена Те́йлора.
Ста́хів	Коли́ він прибува́є?
Маля́рчу́к	Два́дцять дев'я́того ли́пня, у четве́р.
Ста́хів	Гара́зд. Яки́й но́мер замо́вити? І на скілько́х?
Маля́рчу́к	Він про́сить два но́мери "люкс" – для ньо́го і для його́ дру́га.
Ста́хів	Нема́є пробле́м. На скі́льки днів?
Маля́рчу́к	На сім, до п'я́того се́рпня. Пі́сля Ки́єва він плану́є відві́дати Львів. На жа́ль, він не ма́є ча́су до́вго там бу́ти.
Ста́хів	Соломі́є Олександрі́вно, на скі́льки днів замо́вити готе́ль у Льво́ві?
Маля́рчу́к	На два дні, на шо́сте й сьо́ме се́рпня.
Ста́хів	Тако́ж, на двох, так?
Маля́рчу́к	Так. До ре́чі, Íгоре Іва́новичу, Сті́вен ціка́виться, чи мо́жна в Украї́ні розрахо́вуватися за това́ри креди́тною ка́рткою, че́ком чи готі́вкою. У Вас є но́мер його́ фа́ксу?
Ста́хів	Так.
Маля́рчу́к	Да́йте йому́, будь ла́ска, фа́ксом усю́ інформа́цію щодо фіна́нсів і повідо́мте нови́й курс обмі́ну валю́ти.
Ста́хів	До́бре.

коли́	*when*
прибува́ти	*to arrive*
два́дцять дев'я́того ли́пня, у четве́р	**on** *the twenty ninth of July,* **on** *Thursday*
ли́пень	*July*
гара́зд	*OK*
яки́й но́мер замо́вити?	*what kind of room [should I] book?*
на скількóх?	*for how many people?*
проси́ти (прошу́, про́сиш)	*to ask for*
він про́сить два но́мери	*he's asking* **for** *two rooms*
но́мер	*hotel room*
люкс	*de-luxe hotel room or suite*
на скі́льки днів [замо́вити готе́ль]?	*for how many days [should I book the hotel?]*
на сім [днів]	*for seven days*
до п'я́того се́рпня	**to** *the fifth of August*
на два дні, на шо́сте й сьо́ме се́рпня	*for two days, the sixth and seventh of August*
се́рпень	*August*
на двох	*for two people*
до ре́чі	*incidentally*
ціка́витися	*(here:) to wonder (lit. to be interested)*
розрахо́вуватися	*to pay, settle up*
това́р	*goods*
креди́тна ка́ртка	*credit card*
креди́тною ка́рткою	*with a credit card, by credit card*
чек	*cheque*
че́ком	*by cheque*
готі́вка	*cash*
готі́вкою	*with cash*
да́ти (here: **да́йте** - imperative)	*to give*
фа́ксом	*by fax*
уве́сь (here: **усю́**)	*all*
інфо́рмація	*information*
щó́до (+ gen.)	*as for, as far as . . . is/are concerned*
фіна́нси	*finances*
повідо́мити (here: **повідо́мте** - imperative)	*to inform*
нови́й	*new*
курс	*exchange rate, course*
о́бмін	*exchange*
валю́та	*currency*

a Пра́вда чи непра́вда?

1 Сті́вен прибува́є до Ки́єва 29 ли́пня.

2 Íгор Іва́нович ма́є замо́вити но́мер у готе́лі з два́дцять во́сьмого ли́пня до четве́ртого се́рпня.

3 Сті́вен про́сить оди́н но́мер "люкс".

4 Пі́сля Ки́єва Малярчу́к плану́є відві́дати Львів.

b Да́йте ві́дповіді на ці запита́ння англі́йською мо́вою

1 On what day of the week does Stephen arrive in Kyiv?

2 Who is going to accompany Stephen on his trip to Ukraine?

3 For how many days does Stephen need to book a hotel room in L'viv?

4 What kind of information is going to be sent to Stephen by fax?

Як функціону́є мо́ва

1 EXPRESSING POSSESSION

In Unit 3, Stephen says **У ме́не є батьки́ в Шотла́ндії** and **Я ма́ю бабу́сю**. In the space of a few lines he uses both ways of saying 'I have' in Ukrainian. The verb **ма́ти** is entirely regular, but the other expression is also very common and must be explained in some detail:

> У Сті́вена (gen.) є словники́   *Stephen has dictionaries* (lit. in
> (nom. pl.).   *Stephen's possession there are*
>   *dictionaries*).

The possessor goes into the genitive case after the preposition **у/в**, and the possession(s) into the nominative case.

We could say about Stephen:

> **У Сті́вена** на робо́ті є   *Stephen has several dictionaries*
> де́кілька словникі́в.   *at work.*

2 NEGATIVE EXPRESSIONS

The genitive case is used after negated verbs, i.e. verbs preceded by the word **не**, e.g.:

Сті́вен **ма́є** комп'ю́тер.	Сті́вен **не ма́є** комп'ю́тера.
Я **п'ю** ка́ву.	Він **не п'є** ка́ви.

Нема́є meaning 'there is/are no' is always written as one word, e.g.:

нема́є пробле́м	*there are no problems*
(contrast: є пробле́ма!	*there's a problem*)

and what (or who) there isn't goes into the genitive case. Another example:

Ста́хів тут?   *Is Stakhiv here?*

Ні, **його́/Ста́хова** тут нема́є.   *No, he/Stakhiv isn't here.*

The words **не ма́є** are written separately when they mean 'doesn't have'.

Possession		Non-possession	
Gen.	Nom.	Gen.	Gen.
у ме́не є	креди́тн**а** ка́ртк**а**	у ме́не нема́є	креди́тної ка́ртк**и**
Nom.	Acc.	Nom.	Gen.
я ма́ю	креди́тн**у** ка́ртк**у**	я не ма́ю	креди́тної ка́ртк**и**

3 SAYING 'YES, I HAVE' AND 'NO, I DON'T'

У Вас є но́мер його́ фа́ксу?

Так. *Yes.*	Ні. *No.*
Так, є. *Yes, I have.*	Ні, нема́є. *No, I don't.*
Так, у ме́не є но́мер його́ фа́ксу. *Yes, I've got his fax number.*	Ні, у ме́не нема́є но́мера його́ фа́ксу. *No, I haven't got his fax number.*

Чи Ви ма́єте но́мер його́ фа́ксу?

Так. *Yes.*	Ні. *No.*
Так, ма́ю. *Yes, [I] have.*	Ні, не ма́ю. *No, I haven't.*
Так, я ма́ю но́мер його́ фа́ксу. *Yes, I've got his fax number.*	Ні, я не ма́ю но́мера його́ фа́ксу. *No, I haven't got his fax number.*

4 NUMERALS – 11 UPWARDS

TR 6, 01:20

Число́:	Скі́льки?	Котри́й?
11	одина́дцять	одина́дцятий
12	двана́дцять	двана́дцятий
13	трина́дцять	трина́дцятий
14	чотирна́дцять	чотирна́дцятий
15	п'ятна́дцять	п'ятна́дцятий
16	шістна́дцять	шістна́дцятий
17	сімна́дцять	сімна́дцятий

18	вісімна́дцять	вісімна́дцятий
19	дев'ятна́дцять	дев'ятна́дцятий
20	два́дцять	двадця́тий
21 . . .	два́дцять оди́н	два́дцять пе́рший
30	три́дцять	тридця́тий
40	со́рок	сороко́вий
50	п'ятдеся́т	п'ятдеся́тий
60	шістдеся́т	шістдеся́тий
70	сімдеся́т	сімдеся́тий
80	вісімдеся́т	вісімдеся́тий
90	дев'яно́сто	дев'яно́стий
100	сто	со́тий
101 . . .	сто оди́н	сто пе́рший
200	дві́сті	двохсо́тий
300	три́ста	трьохсо́тий
400	чоти́риста	чотирьохсо́тий
500	п'ятсо́т	п'ятисо́тий
600	шістсо́т	шестисо́тий
700	сімсо́т	семисо́тий
800	вісімсо́т	восьмисо́тий
900	дев'ятсо́т	дев'ятисо́тий
1 000	ти́сяча	ти́сячний
2 000	дві ти́сячі	двохти́сячний
5 000	п'ять ти́сяч	п'ятити́сячний
1 000 000	мільйо́н	мільйо́нний
1 000 000 000	мілья́рд	мілья́рдний

Note on pronunciation: The words for 11–19, 20 and 30 all contain -**дцять**; in pronunciation the **д** is omitted, e.g. **два́(д)цять**. In the words for 16, 50 and 60 the letter **т** between consonants is also omitted in pronunciation, e.g. **шіс(т)на́дцять**.

LANGUAGE TIP

A reminder on agreement

Оди́н (одна́, одне́) is always followed by the nominative singular, however big the number, e.g.:

    ти́сяча одна́ ніч   *a thousand and one nights*

Два (дві), три and **чоти́ри** are always followed by the nominative plural, e.g.:

    сорок три листи́   *forty-three letters*

Діало́г 2

TR 6, 04:06

A conversation on a Kyiv street.

Вона́	Рома́не, ході́мо до рестора́ну. Я ду́же хо́чу ї́сти.
Він	Так, це ду́же до́бра ду́мка. Чека́й, я лише́ ма́ю поміня́ти гро́ші.
Вона́	Тобі́ бага́то тре́ба поміня́ти?
Він	До́ларів п'ятдеся́т, я ду́маю. Ти не зна́єш, яки́й сього́дні курс?
Вона́	Не зна́ю. Тре́ба запита́ти. Он пункт обмі́ну.
Він	Ході́мо. (To the cashier in the bureau de change) Ви міня́єте до́лари?
Каси́р	Скі́льки вам потрі́бно поміня́ти?
Він	П'ятдеся́т. У вас є гри́вні?
Каси́р	Так. Де ва́ші до́лари?
Він	Ось, про́шу.
Каси́р	(counts out the money and passes the hryvni across the counter) Будь ла́ска. Ось квита́нція.
Він	Ну що, ході́мо обі́дати?
Вона́	Так. Я стра́шно хо́чу ї́сти.

Рома́н	*Roman* (a common Ukrainian male name)
я ду́же хо́чу ї́сти	*I am very hungry* (lit. I very much want to eat)
ду́мка	*idea, thought*
я лише́ ма́ю поміня́ти гро́ші	*I just have to change [some] money*
гро́ші (pl., no sg., gen.: **грошей**)	*money*
до́ларів п'ятдеся́т	*about fifty dollars*

> **LANGUAGE TIP**
> The inversion of the numeral and the noun makes the amount approximate.

тре́ба запита́ти	*You'll have to ask*
пункт обмі́ну	*bureau de change*
каси́р	*cashier*
квита́нція	*receipt*
ну що!	*so alright, then!*
обі́дати	*to have lunch*
стра́шно	*terribly*

5 TRY NOT TO GET STRESSED ABOUT STRESS

You have already seen that it is impossible to predict which syllable in a Ukrainian word will be stressed. There have also been examples of nouns that change the position of their stress in different cases. It is beyond the scope of this book to go into detail on all the ways in which stress position can change; you will find that, with practice, it is possible to get to grips with stress!

There are, however, some stress problems that need special attention. The word **копі́йка** has nom. pl. **копі́йки́**, gen. pl. **копі́йо́к**. Look what happens when these forms are preceded by a numeral: **дві копі́йки**, **п'ять копі́йок**.

6 VERBS THAT END IN -*СЯ*

Here are some phrases that you saw in Unit 2:

Ду́же ра́да з Ва́ми познайо́мити**ся**.

Дозво́льте познайо́мити: **це** Джон.

Дозво́льте відрекомендува́ти**ся**: я – Джон.

Дозво́льте відрекомендува́ти: **це** Джон.

The additional letters **-ся** form the **reflexive suffix**, meaning that the subject of the verb (usually a person) does the action to himself/herself, e.g.:

пригоща́йся	*help yourself*

Compare:

Я не хо́чу турбува́**ти** дру́га.	*I don't want to worry my friend.*
Я не хо́чу турбува́**тися про** дру́га.	*I don't want to worry [myself] about my friend.*
Я **вмива́ю/одяга́ю** си́на.	*I am washing my son/getting my son dressed.*
Я **вмива́юся/одяга́юся**.	*I am getting washed/getting dressed.*

In later units, you will see that the addition of **-ся** gives the meaning 'each other' to some verbs, e.g. **ба́чити** (*to see*) – **ба́читися** (*to see each other*).

Here is the full present tense of both **турбува́ти** and **турбува́тися**:

турбува́ти		турбува́тися	
S.	Pl.	S.	Pl.
1. турбу́ю	турбу́ємо	1. турбу́юся	турбу́ємося
2. турбу́єш	турбу́єте	2. турбу́єшся	турбу́єтеся
3. турбу́є	турбу́ють	3. турбу́ється	турбу́ються

Note the ending of the third-person singular; **all** first conjugation verbs add **-ть** before **-ся**.

Note on pronunciation: The second-person singular ending **-шся** is pronounced [s's'a]; the third-person singular ending **-ться** is pronounced [ts'ts'a].

The addition of the reflexive suffix **-ся** can make the difference between a **transitive** and an **intransitive** verb. A transitive verb is one that has an object, e.g. 'I **opened** the door'. An intransitive verb has no object, e.g. 'the door **opened**':

Я **спини́в** автомобі́ль. *I stopped the car.* (transitive)

Автомобі́ль **спини́вся**. *The car stopped.* (intransitive)

There are verbs ending in **-ся** which:

either **a**   do not exist without it, e.g. **подо́батися** (*to please*), **смія́тися** (*to laugh*)

or **b**   have a completely different meaning when it is added, e.g. **розрахо́вуватися** (*to settle up*), **розрахо́вувати** (*to reckon, take account of, rely on someone*), **народи́ти** (*to give birth*), **народи́тися** (*to be born*).

7 NAMES IN UKRAINIAN

● **INSIGHT**

Ukrainians have three names: surname, first name and patronymic (which tells us the first name of the person's father). This is the usual order in official documents.

a   The surname (**прі́звище**), common to all members of the immediate family, e.g. **Кова́ль**, **Моро́з**. Surnames like these that end in a consonant have the same form for men and women. They decline when they refer to a man, e.g. (from the dialogue) (**Петра́**) **Маля́рчука́**, but not when they refer to a woman (**Соломі́ї**) **Маля́рчук**. By tradition, a woman may change her surname to that of her husband on marriage.

b   The first name (**ім'я́**), given by the parents to the child after birth. Ukrainian has a wealth of 'unofficial' forms of 'official' names, e.g.:

Марі́я: Марі́чка, Марі́йка, Мару́ся, Мару́сенька

Петро́: Пе́трик, Петру́сь

These familiar forms are extremely informal and should therefore never be used in official situations and documents or in combination with the patronymic.

c The patronymic (**ім'я по батькові**) is formed from the father's name by means of a variety of different suffixes, e.g.:

-ович-, -евич- (*male*):	Тарáс Петрó**вич** Ковáль
	Íгор Івáно**вич** Стáхів
-івн-(а) (*female*):	Оксáна Петрí**вна** Ковáль
-ївн-(а)	Тетя́на Андрí**ївна** Григорéнко

Like all proper names, patronymics decline; bear in mind that they are adjectives.

Solomiia Maliarchuk addresses her colleague Ihor Stakhiv in the **vocative case: Íгоре Івáновичу!** using his first name **Íгор** and his patronymic **Івáнович**. We now know that his father was called **Івáн**. In turn he addresses her as **Соломíє Олексáндрівно** (first name **Соломíя**, patronymic **Олексáндрівна**); Solomiia's father was **Олексáндр**.

This is the polite way of addressing Ukrainians in a formal situation. The endings of the vocative case are dealt with in detail in Unit 11.

8 ANOTHER USE FOR *ТАК*

You already know **так** as 'yes'. Ihor Stakhiv uses the word in the question **Такóж, на двох, так?** to mean '[It's] also for two, isn't it?' This is the so-called 'tag question' e.g.:

Вíра украї́нка, так?   *Vira is a Ukrainian, isn't she?*

The first part of such sentences should be pronounced like a statement, with question intonation only on the final word, **так**.

9 ANOTHER USE FOR *ЧИ*

Стíвен цікáвиться, **чи** мóжна в Украї́ні розрахувáтися за товáри кредúтною кáрткою.

*Stephen wonders **if/whether** it is possible to pay for goods in Ukraine with a credit card.*

You have already seen **чи** introduce questions without a question word or meaning 'or'. Here we see it being used to introduce what is called an indirect question. The direct question would have looked like this:

Stephen wonders: 'Is it possible to pay for goods, etc.?'

де?	where?	куди́?	where to? (whither?)	зві́дки?	where from? (whence?)
ось	here is ...	сюди́	to here (hither)	зві́дси	from here (hence)
он	[over] there is	туди́	to there (thither)	зві́дти	from there (thence)
тут	here	вперéд	to the front, forwards	спéреду	from the front
там	there				
правóруч	on the right				
лівóруч	on the left	назáд	to the rear, back(wards)	ззáду	from behind
попéреду	in front				
позáду	behind	прямо	straight		
далéко	far off	додóму	home(wards)		
бли́зько	near				
ви́соко	high				
ни́зько	low				
вдóма/удóма	at home				

LANGUAGE TIP

Words like 'whither, whence, etc.' have a decidedly quaint feel in English. The Ukrainian equivalents, however, are in everyday use, e.g.:

Де ти живéш?	**Where** do you live?
Куди́ ти йдéш?	**Where** are you going?
Зві́дки ти?	**Where** are you **from**?

 Test yourself : Впра́ви

1 Make phrases using the numerals and nouns, following the example:

При́клад: бага́то ти́сяч, ма́ло гро́шей, оди́н до́лар

> **LANGUAGE TIP**
> **при́клад** *example*

1 (Оди́н)	(гри́вня, до́лар, ти́сяча)
4 (Чоти́ри)	(гри́вня, до́лар, ти́сяча)
5 (П'ять)	(гри́вня, до́лар, ти́сяча)
22 (Два́дцять два)	(гри́вня, до́лар, ти́сяча)
78 (Сімдеся́т ві́сім)	(гри́вня, до́лар, ти́сяча)
200 (Дві́сті)	(гри́вня, до́лар, ти́сяча)
312 (Три́ста двана́дцять)	(гри́вня, до́лар, ти́сяча)
645 (Шістсо́т со́рок п'ять)	(гри́вня, до́лар, ти́сяча)
бага́то	(гро́ші, валю́та, гри́вня, до́лар, ти́сяча)
ма́ло	(гро́ші, валю́та, гри́вня, до́лар, ти́сяча)
тро́хи	(гро́ші, валю́та, гри́вня, до́лар, ти́сяча)

2 Make the following sentences negative (if they are positive) or positive (if they are negative):

> **LANGUAGE TIP**
> **помічни́ик** *assistant*

a Я ма́ю маши́ну.

b У ме́не нема́є са́ду.

c Ві́ра ма́є ті́стечко.

d У дире́ктора нема́є помічника́.

e Фі́рма ма́є літа́к.

f У те́бе нема́є квитка́?

3 Construct sentences using both ways of saying that the subject of the sentence doesn't have something, according to the example:

При́клад: Петро́ не (ма́ти) (брат).

Петро́ не ма́є бра́та.

У Петра́ нема́є бра́та.

a Ти не (ма́ти) (кни́га)?

b Вони́ не (ма́ти) (паспорти́).

c Я не (ма́ти) (сад).

d Ви не (ма́ти) (сад).

e Ві́ра не (ма́ти) (сестра́).

f Се́стри не (ма́ти) (гро́ші).

g Сті́вен іще́ не (ма́ти) (ві́за).

4 Turn your part of this dialogue into Ukrainian:

You	I need to book a room.
Hotel	На коли́?
You	For today.
Hotel	На скількóх?
You	For two people.
Hotel	На скі́льки днів?
You	For four.

5 Can you tell your wheres from your whithers? What words in the list are likely to be found in answers to the following question words?

Приклад: Де?   Там.

Де?

Зві́дки?

Куди́?

> впере́д, там, зві́дти, сюди́,
> спе́реду, ось, наза́д, зві́дси,
> тут, туди́

6 Some situations in which to practise your Ukrainian:

a in the hotel

You are at the check-in desk. Tell the clerk that you:

i *want a single room (a room for one)*

ii *for a week, or maybe two*

iii *don't have much money*

iv *need to change dollars into (на + acc) Ukrainian money*

b   walking along a Kyiv street with a Ukrainian friend. You suddenly say:

i   *let's go to a restaurant, I'm terribly hungry – but*

ii   *unfortunately I don't have any Ukrainian money.*

Your friend replies:

c   **i**   *There's a bureau de change up ahead, how much do you want to change?*

ii   *You want to change about twenty-five dollars.*

Який в Україні клімат?

What's the climate like in Ukraine?

In this unit you will learn:

▸ *How to say you are sorry*
▸ *How to say what you like*
▸ *How to say how old you are*
▸ *How to talk about the weather*
▸ *How to talk about events in the past*
▸ *How to use some time expressions*

Діалóг 1

TR 7, 00:07

In a pub near the Ukrainian Embassy.

Стíвен	Вúбачте, будь лáска . . . Я бáчу, що Ви читáєте украïнську газéту. Ви знáєте украïнську мóву?
Морозéнко	Так, я украïнець, алé я народúвся і живý в Лóндоні.
Стíвен	Пробáчте менí мою цікáвість . . . Менí дýже подóбається украïнська мóва. Я вивчáю ïï вжé два рóки. Менí допомагáє мій прúятель.
Морозéнко	Як дóбре! Напéвно, Ви вжé бувáли в Украïнí?
Стíвен	На жáль, ще ні. Я вивчáю мóву тут, у Лóндоні. Алé я збирáюся ïхати туди, тому що я мáю комерцíйні інтерéси.
Морозéнко	То Ви бізнесмéн?
Стíвен	Так, моя фíрма рóбить жінóчий і чоловíчий óдяг. Менí трéба відвíдати моïх украïнських партнéрів.
Морозéнко	Я бажáю Вам ýспіху! Ви ще такúй молодúй.
Стíвен	Це Вам здається. Менí вжé трúдцять п'ять рóків.
Морозéнко	Ось Вам моя візúтна кáртка. Менé звуть Юрíй Морозéнко. Я юрúст і чáсто бувáю в Украïнí. Якщó я мóжу Вам допомогтú, прошý менí подзвонúти. Я працюю щодня з дев'ятоï до п'ятоï годúни.
Стíвен	Дякую. *(Hands over his business card)* У Вас такé цікáве прíзвище: Морозéнко . . .
Морозéнко	Так, дýже "холóдне" . . . *(laughs).*
Стíвен	Алé морóз і хóлод це крáще, ніж цей жахлúвий дощ сьогóдні . . .

ви́бачте (inf: **ви́бачити**)		*pardon me*
ба́чу (inf: **ба́чити**)		*I see*
чита́єте (inf: **чита́ти**)		*you read*
газе́та		*newspaper*
розумі́єте (inf. **розумі́ти**)		*you understand, you see*
ме́шкаю (inf. **ме́шкати**)		*I live*
проба́чте (inf. **проба́чити**)		*pardon me*
допомага́є (inf: **допомага́ти**)		*[he] helps*
напе́вно		*for sure*
бува́ли (inf: **бува́ти**) **в . . .**		*have [you] been to …*
напе́вно, Ви вже́ бува́ли в Украї́ні		*you have probably already been to Ukraine*
збира́юся (inf: **збира́тися**)		*I am planning …*
комерці́йний		*commercial*
інтере́с		*interest*
бізнесме́н		*businessman*
жіно́чий		*female*
чолові́чий		*male*
жіно́чий і чолові́чий о́дяг		*women's and men's clothing*
бажа́ю (inf: **бажа́ти**)		*I wish*
у́спіх		*success*
молоди́й		*young*
здає́ться (3rd sg. of inf: **здава́тися**)		*it seems*
Це Вам здає́ться		*It just seems so to you*
візи́тна ка́ртка		*business card*
юри́ст		*lawyer*
щодня́		*every day*
якщо́		*if*
inf: **допомогти́**		*to help*
ра́нку		*of the morning* (dictionary form: **ра́нок** *morning*)
ве́чора		*of the evening* (dictionary form: **ве́чір** *evening*)
моро́з		*frost*
хо́лод		*cold*
кра́ще		*better*
ніж		*than*
жахли́вий		*terrible*
дощ		*rain*

Як функціонує мова

1 GIVING THINGS TO PEOPLE – THE DATIVE CASE

This case is used to denote the indirect object of a verb. English typically either has no special form, or uses the preposition 'to' or 'for', e.g.:

*Give **me** some money.*	*Give some money **to the man**.*
*I bought **my daughter** a horse.*	*I bought a horse **for my daughter**.*

You have already seen several instances of the dative case in Ukrainian:

Дя́кую **Вам** за допомо́гу.	*Thank **you** for [your] help.*
Проба́чте **мені́** мою́ ціка́вість.	*Forgive **me** my curiosity.*
Мені́ допомага́є мій при́ятель.	*My friend is helping **me**.*
Я бажа́ю **Вам** у́спіху.	*I wish **you** success.*
Ось **Вам** моя́ візи́тна ка́ртка.	*Here is my business card **for you**.*
Про́шу **мені́** подзвони́ти.	*Please give **me** a call.*
Телефону́йте **мені́**.	*Telephone **me**.*

The person you thank (**дя́кувати**), forgive (**проба́чити, ви́бачити**), wish something to (**бажа́ти**), help (**допомага́ти**), telephone (**зателефонува́ти**) is in the dative case.

> **LANGUAGE TIP**
> A reminder: you can also **телефонува́ти до** + someone in the genitive case – the meaning is exactly the same: **телефону́йте до ме́не/телефону́йте мені́**.

The dative case can also be used:

▶ with words denoting need, necessity

Сті́вене, **Вам тре́ба** офіці́йне запро́шення?	*Stephen, **do you need** an official invitation? (lit. Stephen, is an official invitation necessary **for you**?)*
Мені́ потрі́бно офо́рмити ві́зу для пої́здки в Украї́ну.	*I **need** to obtain a visa for the trip to Ukraine. (lit. It is necessary **for me** to obtain a visa for the trip to Ukraine.)*
Мені́ тре́ба відві́дати мої́х украї́нських партне́рів.	*I **need** to visit my Ukrainian partners. (lit. It is necessary **for me** to visit my Ukrainian partners.)*

▶ with a variety of 'impersonal expressions'

In English, such sentences often contain the pronoun 'it', e.g. It seems to me, it was very pleasant for me:

Це Вам здає́ться.	*That's just how **it seems to you**.*
Хо́лодно.	*It is cold.*
Мені́ хо́лодно.	***I am** cold* (lit. it is cold **for me**).

And some examples that you will encounter in the second part of the dialogue:

| **Мені́** пощасти́ло, що я Вас зустрі́в. | ***It is fortunate for me** that I met you.* |
| **Мені́** було́ приє́мно з Ва́ми познайо́митися. | *It was pleasant **for me** to make your acquaintance.* |

▶ with **подо́батися** (*to please*)

| Сті́венові подо́бається украї́нська мо́ва. | *Stephen likes Ukrainian.* (lit. the Ukrainian language is pleasing **to Stephen**.) |

In English, what you like is the **object**. In Ukrainian, what you like is the **subject.** Here is another example:

| Вам подо́баються ці кві́ти? | *Do you like these flowers?* (lit. do these flowers please you?) |

The subject of the Ukrainian sentence is **кві́ти**, a plural noun; therefore the verb has a plural ending, **подо́баються**.

▶ to give your age

Мені́ три́дцять п'ять ро́ків.	***I am** thirty-five.*
Окса́ні чоти́ри ро́ки.	***Oksana is** four.*
Скі́льки **Вам** ро́ків?	*How old **are you**?*

2 DATIVE CASE – NOUN ENDINGS

a Masculine nouns

Nom. s.	брат	друг	буди́нок
Dat. s.	бра́т**ові/у**	дру́г**ові/у**	буди́нк**у***
Nom. pl.	брати́	дру́зі	буди́нки
Dat. pl.	брат**а́м**	дру́з**ям**	буди́нк**ам**
Nom. s.	учи́тель	олівє́ць	англіє́ць
Dat. s.	учи́тел**еві/ю**	олівц**ю́***	англійц**еві/ю**
Nom. pl.	учителі́	олівці́	англі́йці
Dat. pl.	учител**я́м**	олівц**я́м**	англійц**ям**

---

* However, the ending **-ові** (**-еві/-єві**) is used very infrequently with nouns denoting inanimate objects.

The two types of ending for masculine nouns in the dative singular, **-ові (-еві/-єві), -у (-ю),** are interchangeable. The ending **-еві** is 'soft'; **-єві** occurs when the nominative ends in **-й**, e.g. **Олексíй** (man's name) – **Олексíєві**.

b Feminine nouns

Nom. s.	сестрá	вýлиця	компáнія	кни́га	зýстріч
Dat. s.	сестрí	вýлиці	компáніï	кни́зі	зýстрічі
Nom. pl.	сéстри	вýлиці	компáнії	кни́ги	зýстрічі
Dat. pl.	сéстрам	вýлицям	компáніям	кни́гам	зýстрічам

c Neuter nouns

Nom. s.	дéрево	мóре	прíзвище	життя́	ім'я́
Dat. s.	дéреву	мóрю	прíзвищу	життю́	ímені
Nom. pl.	дерéва	моря́	прíзвища	життя́	іменá
Dat. pl.	дерéвам	моря́м	прíзвищам	життя́м	іменáм

Note what happens in the dative singular to feminine nouns containing **г**, **к**, **х** before the final **-а**, e.g. **пóдруга, квíтка, мýха** (*fly*). Before the ending of the dative singular, **-і**, those consonants change:

г		**з**(і)	пóдру**г**а –	пóдру**з**і
к	+ і =	**ц**(і)	кáрт**к**а –	кáрт**ц**і
х		**с**(і)	мý**х**а –	мý**с**і

These changes are called 'consonant alternations'. They will be marked in the wordlists and the glossary. English has something similar in 'knife – knives', where the 'f' changes to 'v' and the plural ending 's' is pronounced 'z'.

3 ADJECTIVES – DATIVE CASE

Hard endings

	Nom. s.	Dat. s.	Nom. pl.	Dat. pl.
M.	дóбрий	дóбр**ому**	дóбрі	дóбр**им**
F.	дóбра	дóбр**ій**	дóбрі	дóбр**им**
N.	дóбре	дóбр**ому**	дóбрі	дóбр**им**

Soft endings

	Nom. s.	Dat. s.	Nom. pl.	Dat. pl.
M.	си́ній	си́нь**ому**	си́ні	си́н**ім**
F.	си́ня	си́н**ій**	си́ні	си́н**ім**
N.	си́нє	си́нь**ому**	си́ні	си́н**ім**

4 POSSESSIVE PRONOUNS – DATIVE CASE

	Nom. s.	Dat. s.	Nom. pl.	Dat. pl.
M.	мій	моє́му	мої́	мої́м
F.	моя́	мої́й	мої́	мої́м
N.	моє́	моє́му	мої́	мої́м

Твій has the same endings as **мій**.

	Nom. s.	Dat. s.	Nom. pl.	Dat. pl.
M.	наш	на́шому	на́ші	на́шим
F.	на́ша	на́шій	на́ші	на́шим
N.	на́ше	на́шому	на́ші	на́шим

Ваш has the same endings as **наш**.

5 PERSONAL PRONOUNS – DATIVE CASE

	S.	Pl.
First person	мені́	нам
Second person	тобі́	вам
Third person (m), (n)	йому́	
(f)	їй	їм

Діало́г 2

 TR 7, 01:57

Stephen and Yurii Morozenko talk about the weather in Ukraine.

Сті́вен	До ре́чі, мене́ ду́же ціка́вить пого́да в Украї́ні. Там те́пло зара́з?
Морозе́нко	Влі́тку жа́рко, мо́же бу́ти плюс три́дцять гра́дусів.
Сті́вен	За Це́льсієм?
Морозе́нко	Так. А взи́мку в Украї́ні за́вжди ду́же хо́лодно.
Сті́вен	Моро́з? (laughs)
Морозе́нко	Так, моро́з, ві́тер, сніг.
Сті́вен	Жахли́во. Коли́ мені́ хо́лодно, я не мо́жу працюва́ти.
Морозе́нко	Чому́? Украї́нці ма́ють те́плий о́дяг.
Сті́вен	Ду́же вдя́чний Вам за ціка́ву розмо́ву. Мені́ пощасти́ло, що я Вас зустрі́в.
Морозе́нко	Мені́ тако́ж ду́же приє́мно з Ва́ми познайо́митися. Телефону́йте мені́, якщо́ ма́єте ві́льний час.
Сті́вен	Неодмі́нно. До поба́чення, па́не Морозе́нко.
Морозе́нко	До зу́стрічі.

V	цікáвити	to interest
	погóда	weather
	влíтку	in summer
	жáрко	it is hot
	мóже бýти	maybe, perhaps
	плюс	plus
	грáдус	degree
	за Цéльсієм	centigrade
	узи́мку	in winter
	зáвжди	always
	хóлодно	[it is] cold
	вíтер	wind
	снíг	snow
	чомý?	why?
	вдя́чний	grateful
	менí пощасти́ло	I was fortunate
	зустрíти (here: **зустрíв**)	to meet
	Менí пощасти́ло, що я Вас зустрíв	It was lucky for me that I met you
	вíльний	free

a Прáвда чи непрáвда?

1 Морозéнко читáє англíйську газéту.

2 Стíвен вивчáє украї́нську мóву в Лóндоні.

3 Стíвена дýже цікáвить погóда в Іспáнії.

4 Взи́мку в Украї́ні дýже тéпло.

b Дáйте вíдповіді на ці запитáння англíйською мóвою

1 For how long has Stephen been learning Ukrainian?

2 What does Morozenko give to Stephen?

3 What is Morozenko's job?

4 Does Stephen like cold weather?

6 VERBS – TALKING ABOUT EVENTS IN THE PAST

It is very easy to form the past tense of verbs in Ukrainian. The important points to bear in mind are the **gender** and **number** of the subject. Here are some examples of the past tense that you have already seen:

Я замóвив квитóк.	**I have ordered** the ticket.
Чудóво, що **Ви зателефонувáли**.	[It's] great that **you phoned**.

Я народи́вся в Ло́ндоні.   *I was born* in London.

Мені́ дуже **пощасти́ло**, що **я**   *It was* very fortunate for me that

Вас **зустрі́в**.   *I met* you.

English has a variety of forms that can be grouped together as 'past tense': I have come, I came, I was coming, I had come. Ukrainian has no distinctions of this kind, relying almost entirely on context.

> **LANGUAGE TIP**
> The '**Я**' in the above examples is a male. A woman would say **Я замо́вила/народи́лася/зустрі́ла**.

How to form the past tense

Let's take as our example the sentence **Я замо́вив квито́к**. The past tense, **замо́вив**, ends in a hard consonant (**-в**) and is derived from the infinitive **замо́ви-ти**. By looking at the examples of the past tense in the plural just given, it is easy to make the plural form **Ви замо́вили**.

The ending **-в** denotes a masculine singular ending. It changes to **-л** to form the feminine and neuter singular endings (**-ла**, **-ло**) and the plural ending for all genders (**-ли**).

замо́вити			
S.			**Pl.**
M	F	N	
я, ти, він	я, ти, вона́	воно́	ми, ви (Ви), вони́
замо́ви**в**	замо́ви**ла**	замо́ви**ло**	замо́ви**ли**

Here are some examples of the past tense of verbs that you already know that are not quite so straightforward:

могти́ (to be able)   міг (m), могла́ (f), могло́ (n)   могли́ (pl)

і́сти (to eat)   їв (m), ї́ла (f), ї́ло (n)   ї́ли (pl)

*іти́ (to go)   ішо́в (m), ішла́ (f), ішло́ (n)   ішли́ (pl)

7 TIME PHRASES

a Котра́ годи́на? What's the time?

You have already met the phrase **Котра́ годи́на**? It literally means '*Which hour [is it]*'? There the reply was **Дев'я́та** (*nine o'clock:* lit. 'the ninth [hour]'). **Дев'я́та** is an adjective; it is in the feminine form because it agress with **годи́на**, even though that word is not necessarily used.

---

* Remember that the first letter **і** changes to **й** after a word ending in a vowel, e.g. **вона́ йшла́**.

In this dialogue, Lawyer Morozenko says **Я працю́ю щодня́ з дев'я́тої до п'я́тої годи́ни** (*I work every day from 9am to 5pm*, lit. *from the ninth [hour] of the morning to the fifth hour of the evening*), using the prepositions **з** (*from*) and **до** (*to*) followed by the genitive case.

> **LANGUAGE TIP**
> The 24-hour clock is most frequently used in timetables and official announcements, e.g. on railway and bus stations, and on radio and TV. In everyday, informal speech, words like **ра́нку** 'in the morning' and **ве́чора** 'in the evening' are used.

A polite way of asking what the time is or, indeed, any question:

Перепро́шую, чи Ви **не** зна́єте, котра́ годи́на?	*Excuse me, could you please tell me the time?*

b I've been doing something for ages and am still doing it

Я вивча́ю украї́нську мо́ву вже́ два ро́ки.	*I have been learning Ukrainian for two years [already].*

Stephen has been learning Ukrainian for a long time and he's still learning. Ukrainian uses the **present** tense (**вивча́ю**); English uses the perfect continuous tense (*has been learning*):

The English time phrase has a preposition 'for'; the equivalent phrase in Ukrainian is simply **два ро́ки** with no preposition:

Я живу́ в Ки́єві вже́ **два мі́сяці**.	*I have been living in Kyiv **for** two months [already].*
Скажі́ть, будь ла́ска, є пи́во? Я його́ ду́же люблю́.	*Tell me please, is [there] [any] beer? I like it a lot.*
Ні, його́ нема́є вже́ 5 днів. Але́ є ду́же до́бре вино́.	*No, there hasn't been [any] [for] five days. But [there] is [some] very good wine.*

c Every minute of every hour of every day . . .

Lawyer Morozenko goes to his office every day. He says **щодня́** (i.e. **що + день** in the genitive case) in Ukrainian. Many time words are built up in this way, e.g. **що + рік** gives **щоро́ку** (*every year*), **що + субо́та** produces **щосубо́ти** (*every Saturday*) and so on.

d Last week, next year, etc.

The genitive case is also used for these time expressions:

мину́лого ти́жня	*last week*
насту́пного ти́жня	*next week*
мину́лого четверга́	*last Thursday*
насту́пного четверга́	*next Thursday*
мину́лого ро́ку	*last year*
насту́пного ро́ку	*next year*

The seasons of the year

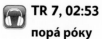

TR 7, 02:53

пора́ ро́ку   *season*

лі́то   весна́

о́сінь   зима́

▶ **зима́**		*winter*	взи́мку	*in winter*
	гру́день (gen.: гру́дня)	*December*		
	сі́чень (gen.: сі́чня)	*January*		
	лю́тий (gen.: лю́того)	*February*		
▶ **весна́**		*spring*	навесні́	*in spring*
	бе́резень (gen.: бе́резня)	*March*		
	кві́тень (gen.: кві́тня)	*April*		
	тра́вень (gen.: тра́вня)	*May*		
▶ **лі́то**		*summer*	влі́тку	*in summer*
	че́рвень (gen.: че́рвня)	*June*		
	ли́пень (gen.: ли́пня)	*July*		
	се́рпень (gen.: се́рпня)	*August*		
▶ **о́сінь**	(f) (alt. **i/e**)	*autumn*	восени́	*in autumn*
	ве́ресень (gen.: ве́ресня)	*September*		
	жо́втень (gen.: жо́втня)	*October*		
	листопа́д	*November*		

Note: The names of the months are spelt with a small letter in Ukrainian, not with a capital letter as in English. They are all **masculine** in gender.

● **INSIGHT**

The names of the Ukrainian months tell us more than their English Latin-based counterparts, e.g.:

Лю́тий (*February*) is indeed a 'cruel' month – this is what the adjective also means. You get out your **серп** (*sickle*) in **се́рпень** (*August*) to reap the harvest and the leaves fall in **листопа́д** (lit. *leaf-fall, November*).

? Test yourself: Впра́ви

1 a One of Taras' friends in Kyiv is gossiping about his neighbours. Here is some of the information he gives. However, some of it is wrong. Compare this information with the table and fill in the 'true' or 'false' boxes:

Це мої́ сусі́ди: Олексі́й Дми́трович, воді́й, йому́ – три́дцять чоти́ри ро́ки; Людми́ла Андрі́ївна, офіціа́нтка, їй – два́дцять оди́н рік; Петро́ Іва́нович, слю́сар, йому́ – со́рок вісім ро́ків; Мико́ла Григо́рович, учи́тель, йому́ – п'ятдеся́т шість ро́ків; Зо́я Анато́ліївна, пенсіоне́рка, їй – шістдеся́т два ро́ки; Окса́на Миха́йлівна, фотомоде́ль, їй – два́дцять вісім ро́ків.

V сусі́д (m) — *neighbour* (f: **сусі́дка**)
воді́й — *driver*
слю́сар — *plumber*
офіціа́нтка (f) — *waitress* (m: **офіціа́нт**)
фотомоде́ль — *model*

	True	**False**
i The teacher is 56.		
ii The waitress is 28.		
iii The model is 21.		
iv The plumber is 46.		
v The pensioner is 62.		
vi The driver is 37.		

b Now summarize the information given in the table in Ukrainian, giving the name and patronymic of each person in the correct case.

При́клад: Зо́ї Анато́ліївні шістдеся́т два ро́ки.

2 Put the words in brackets into the correct form of the dative singular:

a Майкл пи́ше лист (Джон).

b Це подару́нок (дружи́на).

c Тара́с телефону́є (дире́ктор).

d (Ната́лка) 30 ро́ків.

e (Оле́г) подо́бається му́зика.

f (Тетя́на) 24 роки́.

g (Андрі́й) ду́же ма́рко.

h (Катери́на) тре́ба ма́ти фотоапара́т.

i (Вади́м) потрі́бна маши́на.

j (Вона́) мо́жна подарува́ти кві́ти.

V	подару́нок	*present*
	подарува́ти (подару́ю, подару́єш)	*to give as a present*

3 Write out the following sentences in full, putting the words in brackets into the correct form:

		who?	what?	to whom? (if any)
a	Студе́нт	(писа́ти)	(лист – in pl.)	(учи́тель)
b	Мико́ла	(писа́ти)	(кни́га)	_____
c	Я	(писа́ти)	(ім'я́)	_____
d	Ми	(писа́ти)	(прі́звище – in pl.)	_____
e	Вони́	(писа́ти)	(факс)	(партне́р – in pl.)

4 Find the answers to the following questions from the right-hand column:

a Скі́льки Вам ро́ків?

i Взи́мку в Украї́ні хо́лодно.

b Чи хо́лодно взи́мку в Украї́ні?

ii Мені́ не подо́бається те́плий клі́мат.

c Вам подо́бається те́плий клі́мат?

iii Так, влі́тку там жа́рко.

d Чи влі́тку там жа́рко?

iv Мені́ вже́ 35 ро́ків.

5 Read the dialogues in Units 5 and 6 once again. Try turning the following sentences into Ukrainian:

a We have to book a hotel room.

b I am planning to visit France.

c We require two de-luxe rooms.

d I am a businessman and often visit Ukraine.

e I have no information on the finances.

f My friend was reading a Ukrainian newspaper.

g We've already been to Ukraine.

h Our firm makes cars.

6 Which of the Ukrainian sentences that you have just written answer the following questions?

a Яку́ газе́ту чита́в мій друг?

b Що ро́бить на́ша фі́рма?

c Хто плану́є відві́дати Фра́нцію?

d Чи я ча́сто бува́ю в Украї́ні?

TR 7, 03:50

7 Read the following weather forecast from the newspaper *Вечі́рній Ки́їв* and answer the questions:

ПОГО́ДА

Сього́дні со́нце зі́йде о 7 годи́ні 26 хвили́н, за́йде о 16 годи́ні 3 хвили́ни. Трива́лість дня 8 годи́н 37 хвили́н.

Як повідо́мили в Украї́нському гідрометце́нтрі ореспонде́нтові "Вечі́рнього Ки́єва", за́втра в Ки́єві хма́рно з проя́сненнями, уночі́ без о́падів, удень невели́кий дощ, ві́тер за́хідний, 7–12 ме́трів на секу́нду. Температу́ра вночі́ від 3 гра́дусів моро́зу до 3 гра́дусів тепла́, удень 3–8 гра́дусів тепла́.

зійти́	(here:) *to rise*
зайти́	(here:) *to set*
со́нце зі́йде	*the sun will rise*
о 7 годи́ні 26 хвили́н	*at 7.26am*
со́нце за́йде	*the sun will set*
трива́лість (f)	*length, duration*
кореспонде́нт	*correspondent*
гідрометце́нтр	*meteorological centre*
в Украї́нському гідрометце́нтрі	*in the Ukrainian met centre*
хма́рно	*cloudy*
проя́снення (n)	(here:) *clear period*
з проя́сненнями	*with clear periods*
уночі́, вночі́ *	*at night*
о́пади (pl.)	*precipitation*
уде́нь, вдень *	*during the day*
за́хідний	*western*
ві́тер за́хідний	*wind from the west*
7 ме́трів на секу́нду	*seven metres per second*

a What season do you think it is?

b How long is the day going to be?

c Is it going to rain at night or during the day?

d What is the temperature going to be during the day?

---

* Note the different spellings: see unit for an explanation.

7 Я ма́ю пла́ни розвива́ти торгі́влю з Украї́ною

I have plans to develop trade with Ukraine

In this unit you will learn:

▶ *How to answer the question* **де?** *(where?)*
▶ *How to play sports and musical instruments in Ukrainian*
▶ *More about telling the time*
▶ *More about saying what you like doing*
▶ *Some special features of Ukrainian verbs*

Діало́г

 TR 8

Stephen gives an interview to the Ukrainian newspaper "Kyiv Panorama".

Кореспонде́нт	Шано́вний па́не Те́йлор! Скажі́ть, будь ла́ска, яка́ мета́ Ва́шого майбу́тнього візи́ту до Украї́ни?
Сті́вен	Я ї́ду до ціє́ї краї́ни для переговóрів про ство́рення спі́льного підприє́мства. Я ма́ю зу́стрічі з украї́нськими бізнесме́нами, а тако́ж у Міністе́рстві торгі́влі, на Украї́нській бі́ржі, у Націона́льному ба́нку Украї́ни. Мій бі́знес – це виробни́цтво та про́даж мо́дного о́дягу.
Кореспонде́нт	Ще одне́ запита́ння. Скажі́ть, будь ла́ска, де Ви навчи́лися так до́бре розмовля́ти украї́нською мо́вою?
Сті́вен	Я вивча́ю її́ в Ло́ндоні. Я ма́ю серйо́зні пла́ни розвива́ти торгі́влю з Украї́ною і хо́чу зна́ти її́ мо́ву, розумі́ти свої́х коле́г у Ки́єві та Льво́ві без переклада́ча. Украї́нська мо́ва ду́же га́рна. Я ча́сто слу́хаю ра́діо, чита́ю украї́нські газе́ти й журна́ли. Мені́ тако́ж допомага́є мій друг, він украї́нець.
Кореспонде́нт	Розкажі́ть про Ва́ші смаки́.
Сті́вен	Я люблю́ му́зику, гра́ю на гіта́рі. Люблю́ спорт, гра́ю в те́ніс, гольф, волейбо́л. Мені́ тако́ж подо́бається смачна́ ї́жа і, звича́йно, га́рний, мо́дний о́дяг.
Кореспонде́нт	Ви ма́єте сім'ю́?
Сті́вен	Я неодру́жений.
Кореспонде́нт	Бажа́ю Вам приє́мної пої́здки й у́спіху в коме́рції.
Сті́вен	Ду́же дя́кую.
Кореспонде́нт	Дя́кую Вам за ціка́ву ро́зповідь.

V	**розвива́ти**	*to develop*
	торгі́вля з Украї́ною	*trade with Ukraine*
	шано́вний	*esteemed*
	мета́	*aim, purpose*
	майбу́тній (here: **майбу́тнього**)	*future (adj.)*
	візи́т (here: **візи́ту**)	*visit*
	краї́на (here: **краї́ни**)	*country*
	перегово́ри (here: **перегово́рів**)	*talks*
	ство́рення (n)	*creation*
	спі́льний (here: **спі́льного**)	*joint (adj.)*
	підприє́мство (here: **підприє́мства**)	*enterprise*
	спі́льне підприє́мство	*joint venture*
	з украї́нськими бізнесме́нами	*with Ukrainian businessmen*
	бі́ржа	*stock exchange*
	націона́льний (here: **націона́льному**)	*national*
	виробни́цтво	*production*
	про́даж	*sale*
	навчи́тися (here: **навчи́лися**)	*to learn*
	розмовля́ти украї́нською мо́вою	*to speak [in] Ukrainian [language]*
	серйо́зний (here: **серйо́зні**)	*serious*
	план	*plan*
	свій (here: **своїх**)	*(here:) my*
	коле́га (here: **коле́г**)	*colleague*
	переклада́ч (here: **переклада́ча**)	*interpreter, translator*
	слу́хати (here: **слу́хаю**)	*to listen [to]*
	журна́л (here: **журна́ли**)	*journal*
	розказа́ти (here imperative: **розкажі́ть**)	*to tell*
	сма́к (here: **смаки́**)	*taste*
	гра́ти	*to play*
	гра́ти в (+ acc.)	*to play games and sports*
	гра́ти на (+ loc.)	*to play musical instruments*
	гіта́ра (here: **гіта́рі**)	*guitar*
	спорт	*sport*
	те́ніс	*tennis*
	гольф	*golf*
	волейбо́л	*volleyball*
	смачни́й (here: **смачна́**)	*tasty*
	звича́йно	*of course*
	приє́мний (here: **приє́мної**)	*pleasant*
	коме́рція (here: **коме́рції**)	*commerce*
	ро́зповідь (f)	*account, narrative*

a Пра́вда чи непра́вда?

1 Сті́вен ма́є зу́стрічі з украї́нськими бізнесме́нами.

2 Сті́вен хо́че розвива́ти спорт в Украї́ні.

3 Сті́вен любить гра́ти на гіта́рі.

4 Кореспонде́нт бажа́є Сті́венові приє́мної пої́здки.

b Да́йте ві́дповіді на ці запита́ння англі́йською мо́вою

1 Which bank does Stephen intend to visit in Ukraine?

2 Why does Stephen often listen to the radio?

3 Who is helping Stephen learn Ukrainian?

4 What kind of clothes does Stephen like?

Як функціону́є мо́ва

1 ANOTHER POSSESSIVE PRONOUN

The dialogue in this unit introduces another possessive pronoun – **свій**, **своя́**, **своє́**, **свої́**. This word has a special 'reflexive' usage, which means that it will always 'refer back' to the subject of the sentence:

Я хо́чу розумі́ти **свої́х** колє́г у Ки́єві.	*I want to understand **my** colleagues in Kyiv.*

and:

Він не розумі́є **свої́х** колє́г.	***He** doesn't understand **his** colleagues.*

In other words, **свій** can mean 'my', 'your', 'his', 'her', 'its', 'our', 'their', according to context.

Свій declines exactly like **мій** and **твій**.

2 NOUNS – LOCATIVE CASE

The locative case is used to answer the question **де?** (*where?*) and **коли́?** (*when?*) in certain time expressions. There are several examples in the dialogue and the commentary. Here are tables giving the endings in the singular and plural for nouns and adjectives. This case never occurs without a preposition.

3 LOCATIVE CASE – NOUN ENDINGS

a Masculine nouns

Nom. s.	па́спорт	олівє́ць	буди́нок
Loc. s. (у/в, на +)	па́спорт**і**	олівц**і́**	буди́нк**у**
Nom pl.	паспорти́	буди́нки	олівці́
Loc. pl. (у/в, на +)	паспорт**а́х**	буди́нк**ах**	олівц**я́х**

84

Nom. s.	брат	друг	учитель	англі́єць
Loc. s. (у/в, на +)	бра́т**ові**	дру́г**ові**	учи́тел**еві**	англі́йц**еві**
Nom pl.	брати́	дру́зі	учителі́	англі́йці
Loc. pl. (у/в, на +)	брат**а́х**	дру́з**ях**	учител**я́х**	англі́йц**ях**

b Feminine nouns

Nom. s.	сестра́	ву́лиця	компа́нія	кни́га	зу́стріч
Loc. s. (у/в, на +)	сестрі́	ву́лиц**і**	компа́нії	кни́**зі**	зу́стрі**чі**
Nom pl.	се́стри	ву́лиці	компа́нії	кни́ги	зу́стрічі
Loc. pl. (у/в, на +)	се́стр**ах**	ву́лиц**ях**	компа́ні**ях**	кни́г**ах**	зу́стрі**чах**

c Neuter nouns

Nom. s.	де́рево	мо́ре	прі́звище	життя́	ім'я́
Loc. s. (у/в, на +)	де́рев**і**	мо́р**і**	прі́звищ**і**	життı́	і́м**ені**
Nom pl.	дере́ва	моря́	прі́звища	життя́	імена́
Loc. pl. (у/в, на +)	дере́в**ах**	мор**я́х**	прі́звищ**ах**	життı́**х**	імен**а́х**

> **LANGUAGE TIP**
>
> ▶ The masculine singular ending **-ові/-еві/-єві** is used predominantly with nouns denoting human beings.
>
> ▶ The masculine singular ending **-у** occurs after the suffixes **-к, -ак,-ик, -ок,** e.g. **у буди́нку** and in some other short nouns, e.g. **у ба́нку, у па́рку, у снігу́, у саду́, у гаю́**.
>
> ▶ Before the ending of the locative singular **-і**, the consonants **к, г, х** change in the following way: **к – ц; г – з; х – с**. Note that the consonant **-к** changes to **-ц** only when the locative ending is -і; when the locative ending is **-у** there is no change, e.g. **у ро́ці (рік), на бе́резі (бе́рег), на по́версі (по́верх), на по́друзі (по́друга), у кни́зі (кни́га), у руці́ (рука́)**.

4 ADJECTIVES – LOCATIVE CASE

Hard endings

	Nom. s.	Loc. s.	Nom. pl.	Loc. pl.
M.	до́брий	до́бр**ому**	до́брі	до́бр**их**
F.	до́бра	до́бр**ій**	до́брі	до́бр**их**
N.	до́бре	до́бр**ому**	до́брі	до́бр**их**

Soft endings

	Nom. s.	Loc. s.	Nom. pl.	Loc. pl.
M.	си́ній	си́нь**ому**	си́ні	си́н**іх**
F.	си́ня	си́н**ій**	си́ні	си́н**іх**
N.	си́нє	си́нь**ому**	си́ні	си́н**іх**

5 POSSESSIVE PRONOUNS – LOCATIVE CASE

	Nom. s.	Loc. s.	Nom. pl.	Loc. pl.
M.	мій	мо**є́му**	мої́	мо**ї́х**
F.	моя́	мо**ї́й**	мої́	мо**ї́х**
N.	моє́	мо**є́му**	мої́	мо**ї́х**

Твій and **свій** have the same endings as **мій**.

	Nom. s.	Loc. s.	Nom. pl.	Loc. pl.
M.	наш	на́ш**ому**	на́ші	на́ш**их**
F.	на́ша	на́ш**ій**	на́ші	на́ш**их**
N.	на́ше	на́ш**ому**	на́ші	на́ш**их**

Ваш has the same endings as **наш**.

6 PERSONAL PRONOUNS – LOCATIVE CASE

	S.	P.
First person	мені́	нас
Second person	тобі́	вас
Third person (m), (n)	ньо́му	
(f)	ній	них

Note: As the locative case occurs only with prepositions, the third-person pronouns always have the prefixed **н-** attached.

7 PREPOSITIONS WITH LOCATIVE CASE

у/в	in/at	у готéлі, у пáрку
		на брáтові, на учи́телеві
		в Одéсі, у мíсті
		у містáх
на	on/at	на робóті, на вýлиці,
		на дрýгому пóверсі

When to use у or в

The Ukrainian preposition meaning 'in' has two forms:

▶ **у**, used at the beginning of a sentence or after a break within a sentence (represented in writing by a comma):

| **У** Ки́єві є багáто цікáвих будíнків. | There are lots of interesting buildings in Kyiv. |
| Я вивчáю мóву тут, **у** Лóндоні. | I am studying the language here in London. |

▶ **в**, used after a word ending in a vowel:

| Я живý **в** Лóндоні. | I live in London. |
| Я чáсто бувáю **в** Украї́ні. | I am often in Ukraine. |

The same rules apply to **у/в** when it is used with the accusative or genitive case.

8 TIME PHRASES AND THE LOCATIVE CASE

a Years and months (see also Unit 8):

у ти́сяча дев'ятсóт дев'янóсто шóстому рóці	in 1996
у ли́пні	in July
у вéресні	in September
у листопáді	in November

Contrast **у** + accusative case for the days of the week, e.g. **у четвéр** (on Thursday etc.)

b At what time?

Use the preposition **о** (or **об** before a vowel):

о котрíй годи́ні?	at what time? (lit. at which hour?)
о пéршій	at one (lit. at the first)
об одинáдцятій годи́ні	at eleven

9 A SPECIAL USE FOR THE PREPOSITION *HA* AND THE LOCATIVE CASE

Що на ньо́му?	*What is he wearing?*
На Сті́венові мо́дний костю́м.	*Stephen is wearing a fashionable suit.*
На ньо́му бі́лий піджа́к.	*He is wearing a white jacket.*
…черво́не пальто́	*…a red coat*

> **LANGUAGE TIP**
>
> The verb **носи́ти (ношу́, но́сиш)**, which you will meet later with the meaning 'to carry', is also used to denote 'wearing', but with the additional meaning that the item in question is worn regularly:
>
> **Чи Сті́вен но́сить окуля́ри?**   *Does Stephen wear glasses?*

10 VERBAL ASPECT

Verbal aspect is to do with the way in which an action is viewed. Ukrainian verbs have two aspects: **imperfective** and **perfective**.

Imperfective

The imperfective aspect denotes that something is happening right now, was happening or will be happening at a particular moment, e.g.:

Сті́вен за́раз **телефону́є** до Ки́єва.	*Stephen **is phoning** Kyiv at the moment.*
Він **чита́в** украї́нську газе́ту.	*He **was reading** a Ukrainian newspaper.*
Вона́ **смія́лася**.	*She **was laughing.***

It can also denote an action that is repeated or is regular:

Сті́вен щоти́жня **телефону́є** до Ки́єва.	*Stephen **phones** Kyiv every week.*
Він щодня́ **чита́в** украї́нські газе́ти.	*He **read** (used to read) Ukrainian newspapers every day.*

The imperfective future is introduced in Unit 8.

Perfective

The perfective aspect denotes that the action has already commenced or has been completed in the past or will have been completed in the future, e.g.:

Вона засмія́лася.	*She burst out laughing.*
Добре, що ти зателефонува́в.	*It's good that you phoned (made this call).*

Perfective verbs cannot, therefore, have a present tense, as the present tense is used for actions that are either in progress now or are repeated.

The use of the perfective future will be looked at in Unit 9. There is no difference between imperfective and perfective verbs in the formation of the past tense.

11 HOW ARE ASPECTS FORMED?

Unfortunately, no rules can be given. Here are a few examples:

Group 1:	*Imperfective*	*Perfective*
	пи́ти	**ви́**пити
	смі́я́тися	**за**смі́я́тися
	диви́тися	**по**диви́тися
	чита́ти	**про**чита́ти
	ї́сти	**з'**ї́сти
	роби́ти	**з**роби́ти

Group 1 contains perfective verbs that have been formed from imperfective verbs by the addition of a **prefix**.

Group 2:	да**ва́**ти	да́ти
	прода**ва́**ти	прода́ти
	запро́шу**ва**ти	запроси́ти
	купу**ва́**ти	купи́ти

Group 2 contains imperfective verbs that are formed by means of the **suffixes -ва** or **-ува/-юва**.

Group 3:	вивч**а́**ти	ви́вч**и**ти
	замов**ля́**ти	замо́в**и**ти

Group 3 contrasts imperfective verbs with **-а** (or **-я** after a soft consonant) and perfective verbs with **-и**. Some other changes, e.g. as in **замовля́ти–замо́вити**, or shifts in stress position, may be involved.

Some verbs in Groups 2 and 3 also display **consonant alternations**, e.g.:

запро́**ш**увати, запро**си́**ти   замов**ля́**ти, замо́**ви**ти.

There will be more about consonant alternations in Unit 12.

Group 4:	допомага́ти	допомогти́
	зустріча́ти(ся)	зустрі́ти(ся)
	сіда́ти	сі́сти
	бра́ти	взя́ти
	захо́дити	зайти́

7 *Я ма́ю пла́ни розвива́ти торгі́влю з Украї́ною* **I have plans to develop trade with Ukraine**   89

Group 4 contains verbs that form their imperfective and perfective aspects in ways that are difficult to categorize; indeed, on occasion (e.g. **бра́ти**), the perfective is formed from a completely different word.

From now on the aspect of all new verbs will be marked in the wordlists as impf. (imperfective) or pf. (perfective).

Aspect and verbal prefixes

Let us look at some of the ways in which prefixes, such as those in Group 1, can affect meaning.

If we add the prefix **по-** to the verb **проси́ти** (*to ask for something*) we get the perfective equivalent, with no real change in meaning other than the stress placed on the completion of the action. However, if we add the prefix **за-** to the same verb, the new perfective verb has a completely different meaning: **запроси́ти** (*to invite*), from which, in turn, a new imperfective is formed: **запро́шувати**. Adding the prefix **пере-** to the same verb produces the verb 'to apologize' – **перепроси́ти, перепро́шувати**.

To some of the verbs in these groups, the prefix **по-** can give the meaning of 'doing a little bit of the action', e.g.:

працюва́ти	*to work*
попрацюва́ти	*to do a bit of work*

Aspect in the past tense

It is useful to consider the whole context that determines the use of either the imperfective or the perfective aspect of the verb in the past tense, e.g.:

Я пив ка́ву might occur in the following situations:

I was drinking coffee, but everyone else was drinking tea.

I was drinking coffee all through the meeting.

I drank (used to drink) coffee every day, but now I can't because of the state of my health.

whereas the likely situations for **я ви́пив ка́ву** are:

I drank up (finished drinking) my/the coffee, got up and left for work.

I have finished my coffee – look, there isn't any left.

? Test yourself: Впра́ви

1 **Put the words in brackets into the locative case, according to the example:**

При́клад: Мико́ла гуля́є в (парк). Мико́ла гуля́є в **па́рку**.

a На (кореспонде́нт) мо́дний костю́м.

b Мо́жна поміня́ти гро́ші в (Націона́льний банк).

c Я влі́тку був у (Ло́ндон).

d Ми живемо́ у (Львів).

e Музика́нт гра́є на (гіта́ра).

2 **Certain consonants change in the locative case. Give either the locative case form or the nominative case form, according to the information given:**

При́клад: Нога́ – но . . .   Нога́ – нозі́

          Р . . . – ро́ці   рік – ро́ці

a кни́га – кни . . .   **e** ка́рт . . . – ка́ртці

b по́дру . . . – подру́зі   **f** пої́здка – пої́зд . . .

c жі́нка – жін . . .   **g** му́ха – му . . .

d ля́ль . . . – ля́льці   **h** ру́ч . . . – ру́чці

3 **Insert the correct form of the preposition у/в in the following sentences:**

a У/в ме́не є батьки́ у/в Шотла́ндії.

b Та́то працю́є у/в ба́нку.

c Я незаба́ром ї́ду у/в Украї́ну.

d Словни́к у/в кабіне́ті.

e На скі́льки днів замо́вити готе́ль у/в Льво́ві?

f У/в вас є но́мер його́ фа́ксу?

g Ті́тка живе́ у/в Черні́гові.

4 **Complete the following sentences by adding the correct verb from the list:**

a Велосипе́д ду́же зру́чний. На ньо́му мо́жна (. . .).

b Мені́ подо́баються кни́ги. Їх мо́жна (. . .).

c Моя́ ма́ма ро́бить смачні́ ті́стечка. Я люблю́ їх (. . .).

d Моя́ сестра́ лю́бить бале́т, але́ вона́ не вмі́є (. . .).

e Мій друг купи́в гіта́ру. Він хо́че навчи́тися на ній (. . .).

> **тацюва́ти, ї́здити, гра́ти,**
> **ї́сти, чита́ти**

5 **Complete the following sentences by translating the English words and phrases into Ukrainian:**

a Стівен (*is phoning*) Київ зáраз.

b Ві́ра (*phones Kyiv*) щоти́жня.

c І́гор (*was reading*) газéту "Вечі́рній Ки́їв" (*yesterday*) увéчері.

d Оксáна (*used to read*) англі́йські кни́ги (*every day*).

6 **Get ready to give personal information about yourself. Try answering the following questions:**

a Скі́льки Вам рóків?

b У якóму рóці Ви народи́лися?

c У якóму мі́сяці Ви народи́лися?

d У які́й краї́ні Ви народи́лися?

e У якóму мі́сті Ви народи́лися?

f Де Ви тепéр мéшкаєте?

g Чи Ви вжé були́ в Украї́ні?

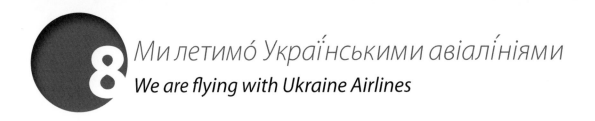

8 Ми летимо́ Украї́нськими авіалі́ніями
We are flying with Ukraine Airlines

In this unit you will learn:

▶ *How to express agreement*
▶ *How to talk about events that will be happening in the future*
▶ *How to talk about means of travel*
▶ *How to tell the time by the clock*

Діало́г 1

 TR 9, 00:08

A meeting with Bohdan Riznyk on a London street.

Богда́н	Тара́се, яко́го числа́ ти лети́ш до Украї́ни?
Тара́с	Два́дцять дев'я́того ли́пня, о пів на пе́ршу дня. Бу́ду відліта́ти з аеропо́рту Га́твік.
Богда́н	Яки́й це день?
Тара́с	Четве́р.
Богда́н	Ти леті́тимеш літако́м Австрі́йських авіалі́ній з переса́дкою у Ві́дні?
Тара́с	Ні, не че́рез Ві́день. Є прями́й рейс Украї́нських міжнаро́дних авіалі́ній "Ло́ндон – Ки́їв". Тому́ я бу́ду леті́ти Украї́нськими без зупи́нки. Ми летимо́ вдвох із мої́м дру́гом Сті́веном Те́йлором.
Богда́н	Я мо́жу відвезти́ вас своє́ю маши́ною до аеропо́рту, якщо́ тре́ба.
Тара́с	Дя́кую, нас відвезе́ Ві́ра.

число́	*number* (here: *date*)
Яко́го числа́ ти лети́ш до Украї́ни?	*On what date are you flying to Ukraine?*
Два́дцять дев'я́того ли́пня	*On the 29th of July*
пів	*half*
о пів на пе́ршу дня	*at half past twelve in the afternoon*
відліта́ти (imp.)	*to fly off*
аеропо́рт	*airport*
Га́твік	*Gatwick*
Яки́й це день?	*What day is that?*

літа́к	aircraft, plane
австрі́йський	Austrian
переса́дка	change (of transport)
Ві́день (m) (gen.: **Ві́дня**)	Vienna
Ти леті́тимеш літако́м Австрі́йських авіалі́ній з переса́дкою в Ві́дні?	Will you be flying with an Austrian Airlines plane, changing in Vienna?
че́рез (+ acc.)	(here:) via
прями́й	straight, direct
рейс	journey, flight
є прями́й рейс	there is a direct flight
міжнаро́дний	international
тому́	therefore
зупи́нка	stop
зру́чно	convenient
вдвох	the two of us together
відвезти́ (відвезу́, відвезе́ш) (pf.)	to take (away)
маши́на	car (colloquial)
Я мо́жу відвезти́ вас свое́ю маши́ною до аеропо́рту, якщо́ тре́ба	I can drive you to the airport in my car, if necessary

Як функціону́є мо́ва

1 VERBS – FUTURE TENSE (IMPERFECTIVE ASPECT)

The imperfective future tense is used to describe actions that will be taking place at some time in the future. There are two ways of forming this tense, both of which have exactly the same meaning. You may choose whichever form you find the easier, but you should be able to recognize both.

Type 1

This tense form comprises two words, just as in the English 'I **will read** the paper'. You will remember that the verb **бу́ти** (to be) has only one form (**є**) in the present tense. The future tense forms of this verb have first conjugation endings:

		S.	Pl.
	1	бу́ду	бу́демо
	2	бу́деш	бу́дете
	3	бу́де	бу́дуть

By combining these forms with the imperfective infinitive, you obtain the imperfective future, e.g.:

Я бу́ду працюва́ти за́втра.　　*I will be working* tomorrow.

Я бу́ду ї́хати до Льво́ва.　　*I will be going* to L'viv.

Type 2

The other form of the imperfective future is obtained by adding the suffix **-м** and the corresponding personal endings, also of the first conjugation, to the imperfective infinitive, e.g.:

	S.	Pl.
1	ї́хатиму	ї́хатимемо
2	ї́хатимеш	ї́хатимете
3	ї́хатиме	ї́хатимуть

In the dialogue, we find the following expressions:

a　**Бу́ду відліта́ти** з аеропо́рту Га́твік.

b　**Я бу́ду леті́ти** Украї́нськими без зупи́нки.

c　Ти **леті́тимеш** літако́м Австрі́йських авіалі́ній?

d　Ми **летимо́** вдвох з мої́м дру́гом Сті́веном Те́йлором.

e　Яко́го числа́ ти **лети́ш** до Украї́ни?

Taras and Bohdan could have changed their future around with no change in meaning:

Я леті́тиму Украї́нськими без зупи́нки.

Ти бу́деш леті́ти літако́м Австрі́йських авіалі́ній?

We can translate sentences (**d**) and (**e**) as:

I am flying together with my friend Stephen Taylor.

On what date **are you flying** to Ukraine?

The present tense in English corresponds exactly to the present tense in Ukrainian here. In both languages, it is possible to use verbs in the present tense with future meaning when something has been definitely decided.

2 THE INSTRUMENTAL CASE

The instrumental case is used to denote the means by which something is done; in English, this idea is most often expressed with the prepositions 'by' or 'with'. It is therefore particularly common with words meaning various forms of transport, e.g.:

Я лечу́ до Ві́дня літако́м　　*I am flying to Vienna **by a plane***
Австрі́йських авіалі́ній.　　　　*of Austrian Airlines.*

Я лечу́ до Ві́дня　　　　　　*I am flying to Vienna **by/with***
Австрі́йськ**ими** авіалі́ні**ями**.　　***Austrian Airlines**.*

| Він їде поїзд**ом** до Ки́єва. | He is going to Kyiv **by train.** |
| Вони́ їдуть автóбус**ом** до робóти. | They are going to work **by bus.** |

Note: Ukraine has underground railways (**метрó**) in two major cities: Kyiv and Kharkiv. The word **метрó** is neuter and indeclinable; it cannot, therefore, have an instrumental ending. Instead, you travel **на метрó** (*by underground*).

▶ By extension, the instrumental case is used with words like **вýлиця, плóща, мíсто**:

| Я хóчу погуля́ти вýлицями Ки́єва. | I want to take a walk **through** the streets of Kyiv. |
| Ми йдемó Хреща́тиком. | We are walking along Khreshchatyk Street. |

▶ The instrumental case is also used to refer to job descriptions, e.g. **Ким працю́є Стíвен?** (lit. As who does Stephen work?) (**Ким** is the instrumental form of **Хто**):

| Стíвен працю́є дирéктор**ом**. | He is the director (lit. Stephen works as the director). |

▶ It is also used after certain verbs, e.g. **ціка́витися** (to be interested in), **займа́тися**, which literally means 'to deal with', 'to be busy with', **опікува́тися**, 'to patronize':

Íгор дýже ціка́виться мýзик**ою**.	Ihor is very interested in music.
Моï знайóмі бýдуть займа́тися квитк**а́ми**.	My acquaintances will deal with the tickets.
Я займа́юся тéніс**ом**.	I go in for tennis.

▶ Where being and becoming are involved: the instrumental case is used after the verbs **бýти** (*to be*) and **става́ти (стаю́, стає́ш)** (*to become*):

| Коли́ я був хлóпчиком, менí подóбалося ïздити на велосипéді. | When I was a boy, I liked riding a bike. |
| Чéрез дéсять рокíв я бýду дирéктор**ом** фíрми. | In ten years' time I'll be director of the firm. |

LANGUAGE TIP

The instrumental case is also used in a special phrase involving a plural personal pronoun, most frequently **ми,** and the preposition **з:**

| **Ми летимó вдвох із моïм дрýгом.** | My friend and I are flying together. (lit. We are flying the two of us together with my friend.) |

Later in the dialogue we have:

Ми зі Стівеном бу́демо у Льво́ві.   *Stephen and I will be in L'viv.*

The verbs in these sentences are in the first-person plural form because the subject is **ми**.

3 INSTRUMENTAL CASE – NOUN ENDINGS

a Masculine nouns

Nom. s.	па́спорт	буди́нок	оліве́ць	телефо́н
Inst. s.	па́спорт**ом**	буди́нк**ом**	олівц**е́м**	телефо́н**ом**
Nom. pl.	паспорти́	буди́нки	олівці́	телефо́ни
Inst. pl.	паспорт**а́ми**	буди́нк**ами**	олівц**я́ми**	телефо́н**ами**

Nom. s.	брат	хло́пчик	друг	учи́тель	англі́єць
Inst. s.	бра́т**ом**	хло́пчик**ом**	дру́г**ом**	учи́тел**ем**	англійц**ем**
Nom. pl.	брати́	хло́пчики	дру́зі	учителі́	англі́йці
Inst. pl.	брат**а́ми**	хло́пчик**ами**	дру́з**ями**	учител**я́ми**	англійц**я́ми**

Nom. s.	трамва́й
Inst. s.	трамва́**єм**
Nom. pl.	трамва́ї
Inst. pl.	трамва́**ями**

b Feminine nouns

Nom. s.	кни́га	ву́лиця	сестра́	компа́нія	зу́стріч
Inst. s.	кни́г**ою**	ву́лиц**ею**	сестр**о́ю**	компа́ні**єю**	зу́стріч**чю**
Nom. pl.	кни́ги	ву́лиці	се́стри	компа́нії	зу́стрічі
Inst. pl.	кни́г**ами**	ву́лиц**ями**	сестр**а́ми**	компа́ні**ями**	зу́стріч**ами**

c Neuter nouns

Nom. s.	де́рево	прі́звище	мо́ре	життя́	ім'я́
Inst. s.	де́рев**ом**	прі́звищ**ем**	мо́р**ем**	життя́**м**	і́мен**ем**
Nom. pl.	дере́ва	прі́звища	моря́	життя́	імена́
Inst. pl.	дере́в**ами**	прі́звищ**ами**	мор**я́ми**	життя́**ми**	імен**а́ми**

The singular ending to watch out for is **-ю** on feminine nouns ending in a consonant, e.g. **зу́стріч**. The consonant preceding the ending of the instrumental singular is doubled, **зу́стріччю**, unless the noun ends in **-сть**, e.g. **приє́мність; з приє́мністю** (*with pleasure*).

4 ADJECTIVES – INSTRUMENTAL CASE

Hard adjectives

	Nom. s.	Inst. s.	Nom. pl.	Inst. pl.
M.	до́брий	до́бр**им**	до́брі	до́бр**ими**
F.	до́бра	до́бр**ою**	до́брі	до́бр**ими**
N.	до́бре	до́бр**им**	до́брі	до́бр**ими**

Soft adjectives

	Nom. s.	Inst. s.	Nom. pl.	Inst. pl.
M.	си́ній	си́н**ім**	си́ні	си́н**іми**
F.	си́ня	си́н**ьою**	си́ні	си́н**іми**
N.	си́нє	си́н**ім**	си́ні	си́н**іми**

5 POSSESSIVE PRONOUNS – INSTRUMENTAL CASE

	Nom. s.	Inst. s.	Nom. pl.	Inst. pl.
M.	мій	мо**ї́м**	мої́	мо**ї́ми**
F.	моя́	мо**є́ю**	мої́	мо**ї́ми**
N.	моє́	мо**ї́м**	мої́	мо**ї́ми**

Твій and **свій** have the same endings as **мій**.

	Nom. s.	Inst. s.	Nom. pl.	Inst. pl.
M.	наш	на́ш**им**	на́ші	на́ш**ими**
F.	на́ша	на́ш**ою**	на́ші	на́ш**ими**
N.	на́ше	на́ш**им**	на́ші	на́ш**ими**

Ваш has the same endings as **наш**.

6 PERSONAL PRONOUNS – INSTRUMENTAL CASE

		S.	Pl.
1		мно́ю	на́ми
2		тобо́ю	ва́ми
3	(m)	ним	
	(f)	не́ю	ни́ми
	(n)	ним	

7 PREPOSITIONS WITH INSTRUMENTAL CASE

з	*with*	з цу́кр**ом**, з молок**о́м**
за	*behind/beyond/on the other side of*	за стол**о́м**, за стін**о́ю**
пе́ред	*in front of*	пе́ред буди́нк**ом**
	just before in time expressions	пе́ред обі́д**ом** *(immediately before dinner)*
над	*over/above*	над крі́сл**ом**
під	*under/below*	під стол**а́ми**
між	*between*	між мо́рем і лі́**сом**

Note: the preposition **з** can also take the form **із** or **зі** in the same circumstances as when it means 'from' and is followed by the genitive case. See Unit 4.

Діало́г 2

 TR 9, 01:05

Bohdan and Taras continue their conversation.

Богда́н	Якщо́ не секре́т, ким працю́є твій при́ятель? Мені́ знайо́ме його́ ім'я́.
Тара́с	Сті́вен – дире́ктор компа́нії "Ге́рмес-Кло́зінг". Для ньо́го це пе́рша ділова́ пої́здка в Украї́ну. А я і́ду у відпу́стку. Хо́чу зустрі́тися з дру́зями, а тако́ж показа́ти Сті́венові Украї́ну. Він ніко́ли там не був. Ми бу́демо подорожува́ти пої́здом, паропла́вом, можли́во, автомобі́лем. Я вже́ домо́вився зі знайо́мими про допомо́гу з житло́м, вони́ займа́тимуться тако́ж на́шими квитка́ми. Ми бу́демо там два ти́жні.
Богда́н	Ти вже́ зна́єш свою́ адре́су в Украї́ні?
Тара́с	Я одра́зу пі́сля приї́зду напишу́ тобі́ листі́вку з на́шою адре́сою.
Богда́н	Чудо́во. Я незаба́ром, можли́во, і́хатиму до Льво́ва.
Тара́с	Ми зі Сті́веном бу́демо у Льво́ві шо́стого-сьо́мого се́рпня.
Богда́н	То побачимося з ва́ми шо́стого се́рпня на пло́щі Ри́нок?
Тара́с	О шо́стій ве́чора!
Богда́н	Зго́да! Шо́стого о шо́стій. Пе́ред апте́кою, бі́ля вхо́ду. Не забу́дь.
Тара́с	Я ніко́ли нічо́го не забува́ю. Ну, бува́й здоро́вий. До зу́стрічі!
Богда́н	Щасли́вої доро́ги! М'яко́ї поса́дки . . .

секре́т	secret
знайо́мий	familiar (as adj.); acquaintance (as noun)
Мені́ знайо́ме його́ ім'я́	His name is familiar to me
відпу́стка	holiday
показа́ти (покажу́, пока́жеш) (pf.)	to show
ніко́ли	never
подорожува́ти (-у́ю, -у́єш) (impf.)	to travel
по́їзд	train
паропла́в	steamer
можли́во	possibly, perhaps
домо́витися (домо́влюся, домо́вишся, . . . домо́вляться) (pf.)	to agree, arrange with
житло́	dwelling (here: *place to stay*)
адре́са	address
одра́зу	at once
прии́зд	arrival
написа́ти (напишу́, напи́шеш) (pf.)	to write
листі́вка	postcard
незаба́ром	soon
Я незаба́ром, можли́во, ї́хатиму до Льво́ва	I might soon be going to L'viv
поба́читися (pf.)	to see one another
пло́ща	square
ри́нок	market
То поба́чимося з ва́ми шо́стого се́рпня?	So we'll see each other on the sixth of August, right?
о шо́стій ве́чора	at six in the evening
шо́стого о шо́стій	on the sixth at six
зго́да	agreement
Зго́да!	OK! That's agreed!
апте́ка	chemist's shop
вхід (gen. вхо́ду)	entrance (alt. **i/o**)
забу́ти (забу́ду, забу́деш) (pf.)	to forget
не забу́дь!	don't forget!
нічо́го (gen. of **ніщо́**)	nothing
забува́ти (imp.)	to forget
бува́й здоро́вий	cheerio! (lit. *be healthy*)
доро́га (gen. pl.: **дорі́г**)	road, journey, way (alt. **i/o**)
поса́дка	landing

a Пра́вда чи непра́вда?

1 Тара́с і Сті́вен летя́ть в Украї́ну ре́йсом Украї́нських Авіалі́ній.

2 Богда́н відвезе́ Сті́вена і Тара́са до аеропо́рту.

3 Тара́с зна́є свою́ адре́су в Украї́ні.

4 Богда́н і Тара́с бу́дуть шо́стого се́рпня у Льво́ві на пло́щі Ри́нок.

b Да́йте ві́дповідь на ці запита́ння англі́йською мо́вою

1 Do Ukrainian Airlines have a direct flight to Kyiv?

2 How many times has Stephen been to Ukraine before?

3 What kind of transport will Taras and Stephen use when travelling around Ukraine?

4 At what time will Taras meet Bohdan in L'viv?

8 MORE TIME PHRASES

For (in the past)

Compare the use of the tenses in Ukrainian and English. Ukrainian uses the **imperfective** aspect in the following situations:

Я **працю́ю** тут **два роки́** (present tense).	*I have been working here for two years [and still work here].*
Я **працюва́в** тут **два роки́** (past tense).	*I worked here for two years.*

The Ukrainian sentences have no preposition in the time phrase.

In

Я ї́ду до Пари́жа **за** два ти́жні.	*I am going to Paris in two weeks (in two weeks' time).*
Я лечу́ до Пра́ги **че́рез** па́ру днів.	*I am flying to Prague in a few days.*

Ukrainian uses either of the prepositions **за** and **че́рез** and the accusative case.

9 GOING ON HOLIDAY AND BEING ON HOLIDAY

Тара́с ї́де **у** відпу́стку (acc.) до Украї́ни.	*Taras is going on holiday to Ukraine.*
Він бу́де **у** відпу́стці (loc.) в Украї́ні.	*[When he gets to his destination] he will be on holiday in Ukraine.*

10 'I DON'T NEVER FORGET NOTHING'

Pile on the negation in Ukrainian!

Він **ніко́ли** там **не** був.	*He has **never** been there.*
Я **ніко́ли нічо́го не** забуваю.	*I don't ever forget anything.*

11 MORE ON ORDINAL NUMERALS

Ordinal numerals (i.e. first, second, third . . ., etc.) decline like adjectives and, like adjectives, agree with the noun to which they relate.

Ordinal numerals consisting of more than one part, e.g. **сто шо́стий** (*one hundred and sixth*), are called compound ordinal numerals. Only the final element declines and all the component elements are written separately. Years are ordinal numbers in Ukrainian, i.e. 2010 is 'the two thousand tenth year':

	2010 рік
Nom. and acc.	дві ти́сячі десят**ий** рік
Gen.	дві ти́сячі десят**ого** ро́к**у**
Dat.	дві ти́сячі десят**ому** ро́к**у**
Loc.	у дві ти́сячі десят**ому** ро́**ці**
Instr.	дві ти́сячі десят**им** рок**ом**

12 IT'S TIME TO CHECK YOUR ENGAGEMENTS DIARY!

понеді́лок (gen.: **понеді́лка**)	*Monday*
вівто́рок (gen.: **вівто́рка**)	*Tuesday*
середа́	*Wednesday*
четве́р (gen.: **четверга́**)	*Thursday*
п'я́тниця	*Friday*
субо́та	*Saturday*
неді́ля	*Sunday*

Time expressions

Day

ура́нці/вра́нці	*in the morning*
уде́нь/вдень	*during the day/afternoon*
уве́чері/вве́чері	*in the evening*
уночі́/вночі́	*at night*
позавчо́ра	*the day before yesterday*

учо́ра/вчо́ра	*yesterday*
сього́дні	*today*
за́втра	*tomorrow*
післяза́втра	*the day after tomorrow*

Year, month, date

Яки́й за́раз рік? Дві ти́сячі шо́стий.

The ordinal numeral **шо́стий** is masculine because the word **рік** is understood from the context.

Яки́й за́раз мі́сяць? Ли́пень.

Яки́й сього́дні день ти́жня? Четве́р.

Яке́ сього́дні число́? Чотирна́дцяте. Чотирна́дцяте (*nom.*) ли́пня (*gen.*)

The ordinal numeral **чотирна́дцяте** is neuter because the word **число́** is understood from the context.

Яко́го числа́ . . .? (*On what date . . .?*)

Чотирна́дцят**ого** (*gen.*) ли́пн**я** (*gen.*)

Чотирна́дцят**ого** (*gen.*) ли́пн**я** (*gen.*) дві ти́сячі шо́ст**ого** (*gen.*)
ро́ку (*gen.*).

The **genitive** case of the ordinal numeral is used to express the date **on** which something occurs. No preposition is used.

This morning, etc.

Сього́дні вра́нці	*this morning* (lit. today in the morning)
учо́ра вдень	*yesterday afternoon* (lit. yesterday in the afternoon)
за́втра вве́чері	*tomorrow evening* (lit. tomorrow in the evening)
о 10-й ра́нку (*gen.*)	*at ten in the morning*
о 9-й ве́чора (*gen.*)	*at nine in the evening*

What time of day is it?

 TR 9, 02:49

годи́нник	*watch, clock*
доба́	*24 hours (i.e. whole day and night together)*

104

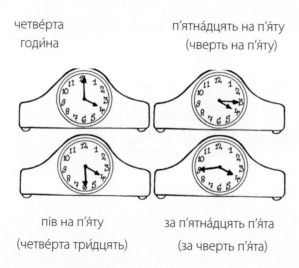

четве́рта
годи́на

п'ятна́дцять на п'яту
(чверть на п'яту)

пів на п'яту
(четве́рта три́дцять)

за п'ятна́дцять п'ята
(за чверть п'ята)

Котра́ годи́на

Remember: **котра́ годи́на**? literally means 'which hour [is it]?' The answer therefore contains the **ordinal** number for the hour in the feminine form:

4.00 **Четве́рта (годи́на)**   (lit. the fourth)

4.15 **П'ятна́дцять (хвили́н)**

     на п'яту (acc.)   (lit. fifteen minutes into the fifth)

     Чверть на п'яту (acc.)   (lit. a quarter into the fifth)

4.30 **Четве́рта три́дцять**

     Пів на п'яту (acc.)   (lit. half into the fifth)

4.45 **За п'ятна́дцять п'ята**

     За чверть п'ята

LANGUAGE TIP

Here, a sensible literal translation is scarcely possible. It may be helpful to think of **за** meaning 'within' in these time expressions, i.e. within fifteen [minutes] [it will be] [the] fifth [hour].

 чверть (f)   *quarter*

       пів   *half*

ра́нок

день

ве́чір

ніч

V	ра́нок	*morning*
	день	*afternoon*
	ве́чір	*evening*
	ніч	*night*

13 EXPRESSING AGREEMENT

Зустрі́ньмося (*let's meet*) на пло́щі Ри́нок.	*Let's meet on Market Square.*
Зго́да!	*OK!*
Львів – ду́же га́рне мі́сто.	*L'viv is a very fine city.*
Абсолю́тно зго́ден з Ва́ми.	*I agree with you entirely.*

Зго́да is a colloquial way of expressing agreement with a suggestion or proposal. A slightly more formal way of agreeing with someone is to say:

Я зго́ден (m)/зго́дна (f) з Ва́ми.

The plural form is **зго́дні**.

When you come to an agreement with someone, you could say:

Домо́вилися! (always plural and past tense, lit. [we] have agreed!)

До́бре	*fine!*
Гара́зд	*OK!*
Чудо́во	*great!*

? Test yourself: Впра́ви

1 **Write out the following sentences, using the correct form of the verb (positive or negative):**

a Він ніко́ли там (був/не був).

b Я ніко́ли (не літа́в/літа́в) літако́м.

c Степа́н ніко́ли (говори́в/не говори́в) бага́то.

d Цей чолові́к ніко́ли (не відліта́в/відліта́в) з Бори́споля.

> **LANGUAGE TIP**
> **Бори́спіль** (gen.: **Бори́споля**) = Boryspil (the name of Kyiv international airport) (alt. **i/o**)

2 **Give both imperfective future forms of the verb писа́ти:**

Я	бу́ду писа́ти,	писа́тиму
ти	_____	_____
він	_____	_____
ми	_____	_____
ви	_____	_____
вони	_____	_____

3 **Make sentences by putting the verb in brackets into the correct form of the imperfective future:**

Я	літако́м (леті́ти)
ти	у саду́ (працюва́ти)
він	спо́ртом (займа́тися)
ми	у Льво́ві (жи́ти)
ви	гро́ші (міня́ти)
вони́	на ву́лиці (чека́ти)

4 **Construct sentences by putting the verbs and nouns in brackets into the correct form:**

Я	(леті́ти)	(літа́к).
Ти	(ї́хати)	(авто́бус).
Він	(гуля́ти)	(ву́лиця).
Ми	(леті́ти)	(літа́к – in pl.).
Ви	(гуля́ти)	(ву́лиця – in pl.).
Вони	(ї́хати)	(авто́бус – in pl.).

5 **Complete the Ukrainian sentences by translating the English phrases in brackets:**

a Вона́ працю́є *(as the director's assistant)*.

b Мій дя́дько був *(a mathematician)*.

c Іре́на була́ *(John's wife) (for three years)*.

d У Ю́рія бу́де зу́стріч *(with English businessmen)*
(at 5 o'clock).

6 **Read the following extract from Solomiia's busy schedule and answer the questions that follow.**

Note how Solomiia gives instructions to herself by using the infinitive form of the verb:

понеді́лок	26 ли́пня	10.00	*Зу́стріч з юри́стом*
		11.30	*банк*
		12.15	*міністе́рство торгі́влі (не забу́ти докуме́нти!)*
		19.00	*те́ніс*
вівто́рок	27 ли́пня	10.30	*ле́кція в університе́ті*
		11.45	*фа́брика*
		13.00	*обі́д у рестора́ні "Дніпро́"*
		16.00	*зателефонува́ти до Полта́ви*
середа́	28 ли́пня	14.45	*Украї́нська бі́ржа*
			да́ти факс до Манче́стера
		19.00	*те́ніс*
четве́р	29 ли́пня		*зателефонува́ти до Іва́но-Франкі́вська*
			повідо́мити Мико́лі Фе́доровичу про квитки́
		22.00	*зустрі́ти С. Те́йлора (Ста́хів?)*
п'я́тниця	30 ли́пня		*замо́вити маши́ну на 10.00*
		14.30	*зайти́ до мілі́ції (гара́ж) розрахува́тися за телефо́н*
		19.00	*те́ніс*
субо́та	31 ли́пня		*вра́нці – зателефонува́ти Урсу́лі про концерт*
		19.30	*концерт (пала́ц "Украї́на")*
неді́ля	1 се́рпня		*на да́чу*

міліція — *police*
гара́ж — *garage*
да́ча — *summer house*

a Who is Solomiia meeting at 10am on Monday 26 July?

b What note does she make about her visit to the Ministry of Trade on that day?

c Where does she have to be at 11.45 on Tuesday?

d On what day and at what time does she have to phone Ivano-Frankivs'k?

e What does she have to inform Mykola Fedorovych about?

f What two things does she have to do on Friday after her visit to the police?

g Who is she going to phone on Saturday, and about what?

h When is Stephen due to arrive in Kyiv?

ПАСАЖИРСЬКИЙ КВИТОК ТА БАГАЖНА КВИТАНЦІЯ
PASSENGER TICKET AND BAGGAGE CHECK

566 4200 007 360 3
СК

ISSUED BY
Air Ukraine International
252135 Україна, Київ-135, Проспект Перемоги 14
Prospect Peremogy 14, 252135 Kyiv-135, Ukraine

Ваш па́спорт, будь ла́ска
Your passport, please

In this unit you will learn:

▸ *How to go through passport and customs control*
▸ *More about describing events in the future*
▸ *About verbs denoting motion in Ukrainian*

Діало́г 1

 TR 10, 00:06

In Boryspil Airport, Kyiv.

Тара́с	Ну, Сті́вене, з м'яки́м призе́мленням! За́раз пройдемо́ па́спортний і ми́тний контро́ль і пі́демо оде́ржувати наш бага́ж.
Passport control:	
Сті́вен	Добри́день.
Прикордо́нник	Добри́день. Ваш па́спорт, будь ла́ска. Па́не Те́йлор, у Вас службо́ва поїздка?
Сті́вен	Так.
Прикордо́нник	Скі́льки Ви плану́єте пробу́ти в Украї́ні?
Сті́вен	Кі́лька ти́жнів.
Прикордо́нник	Дя́кую. Ось Ваш па́спорт. (to Taras) Будь ла́ска, Ва́ші докуме́нти. Дя́кую. Па́не Кова́ль, яка́ мета́ Ва́шого приї́зду?
Тара́с	Я приї́хав на відпочи́нок.

призе́млення (n)	*landing*
з м'яки́м призе́мленням	*congratulations on a soft landing*
пройти́ (пройду́, про́йдеш) (pf.)	*to pass through*
за́раз про́йдемо [через] па́спортний і ми́тний контро́ль	*we'll just pass through passport and customs control*
піти́ (піду́, пі́деш) (pf.)	*to go*
пі́демо оде́ржувати наш бага́ж	*we'll go to fetch our luggage*
прикордо́нник	*frontier guard*

110

службо́ва поїздка	official trip
скі́льки?	how much? (here: how long?)
пробу́ти (пробу́ду, пробу́деш) (pf.)	to spend time
докуме́нт	document
приї́зд	(here:) visit
яка́ мета́ Ва́шого приї́зду	what is the purpose of your visit?
приї́хати (приї́ду, приї́деш) (pf.)	to come
я приї́хав на відпочи́нок	I've come for a holiday

Як функціону́є мо́ва

LANGUAGE TIP

Yet more stress!

You have now seen both **про́шу** and **прошу́**. Both words are the first-person singular form of **проси́ти** (*to ask*), but they are used in different contexts. **Про́шу** can be used in exactly the same circumstances as **будь ла́ска** (*please, you're welcome*), when offering something, when someone says **дя́кую** to you or in an invitation: **про́шу, захо́дьте** (*come in, please*). **Прошу́** is used to mean 'I ask for', 'I request'.

1 VERBS – PERFECTIVE FUTURE
Future tense (perfective aspect)

The perfective future is used to express the idea that an action will be performed and completed, e.g.:

Ми **про́йдемо** па́спортний контро́ль, а по́тім **пі́демо** оде́ржувати бага́ж.

We **shall pass** through passport control and **go** to collect our baggage.

The perfective future is formed with exactly the same personal endings as the present tense of imperfective verbs. Contrast the following forms:

читати		прочитати	
Imperfective, present tense		Perfective, future tense	
1 чита́ю	чита́ємо	прочита́ю	прочита́ємо
2 чита́єш	чита́єте	прочита́єш	прочита́єте
3 чита́є	чита́ють	прочита́є	прочита́ють

The perfective future points to the completion of the action, whereas the imperfective future stresses the performance of the action itself:

Я **прочита́ю** газе́ту і піду́ *I shall read the paper and go to*
на робо́ту. *work. (with the implication that I won't set off for work until I have finished reading the paper)*

Сього́дні на робо́ті я **бу́ду** *I'm going to read the paper at*
чита́ти/чита́тиму газе́ту. *work today. (with the emphasis on what I am going to be doing)*

2 VERBS OF MOTION

іти́ (impf.), **піти́** (pf.) (*to go (on foot)*), **пройти́** (pf.) (*to pass through*):

	іти́*	піти́	пройти́
Past tense			
M	ішо́в*	пішо́в	пройшо́в
F	ішлі́а*	пішла́	пройшла́
N	ішло́*	пішло́	пройшло́
Pl. (all genders)	ішли́*	пішли́	пройшли́

Verbs of motion cover such actions as going, riding, walking, running, swimming, flying, climbing, carrying. English makes a distinction between an action that is carried out regularly:

Every day I go to work.

and one that denotes a habitual feature, e.g.:

Fish **swim**. Birds **fly**.

and between an action being carried out at the moment of speech:

I **am going** to work.

and an action in progress in the past or future:

I **was going** (was on my way) to work, when I met an old friend.

Ukrainian makes a similar distinction, although in a more drastic way. But first here is another dialogue for you to practise your Ukrainian.

---

* All these forms can appear as **йти** etc. when they follow a word that ends in a vowel, e.g. **я йшо́в** (*I was going*) or when there is a prefix, e.g. **про + ішов = пройшо́в.**

Діало́г 2

 TR 10, 00:53

In the customs hall, after they have collected their luggage.

Працівни́ця ми́тниці	Ваш па́спорт, будь ла́ска. Ви запо́внили деклара́цію?
Тара́с	Так. Ось, про́шу.
Працівни́ця ми́тниці	Ви ма́єте предме́ти, заборо́нені до вве́зення? Збро́ю, наркоти́чні речови́ни?
Тара́с	Ні.
Працівни́ця ми́тниці	Поста́вте свої́ валі́зи на транспорте́р. Дя́кую. Ось Ва́ші докуме́нти. (*To Stephen*) До́брий день. Про́шу, па́спорт.
Сті́вен	Ось па́спорт і деклара́ція.
Працівни́ця ми́тниці	Яку́ Ви ма́єте інозе́мну валю́ту?
Сті́вен	Америка́нські до́лари. Су́му вка́зано в деклара́ції.
Працівни́ця ми́тниці	У Вас є украї́нські гро́ші?
Сті́вен	Ні. У ме́не нема́є украї́нських гро́шей.
Працівни́ця ми́тниці	Дя́кую. Мо́жете забра́ти свої́ докуме́нти й ре́чі. Всьо́го найкра́щого!

V

ми́тниця	*customs*
працівни́ця ми́тниці	*(female) customs officer*
деклара́ція	*declaration (customs declaration form)*
предме́т	*item, object*
заборо́нений	*prohibited, forbidden*
вве́зення (n)	*import*
предме́ти, заборо́нені до вве́зення	*items [that are] prohibited for import*
збро́я (sg.)	*weapons*
наркоти́чний	*narcotic*
речовина́	*substance*
поста́вити (поста́влю, поста́виш, . . . поста́влять) (pf.)	*to place*
поста́вте	*(second-person plural imperative form)*
валі́за	*suitcase*
транспорте́р	*conveyor*
інозе́мний	*foreign*
су́ма	*sum*

вказа́ти (вкажу́, вка́жеш) (pf.)	to indicate, point out
су́му вка́зано в деклара́ції	the sum is indicated on the customs declaration form
річ (f) (gen.: ре́чі)	thing (alt. i/e)
найкра́щий	best
всього́ найкра́щого!	all the best!

(a) Пра́вда чи непра́вда?

1 Стівен приї́хав на відпочи́нок.

2 Тара́с не ма́є предме́тів, заборо́нених до вве́зення.

3 Стівен не запо́внив деклара́цію.

4 У Стівена нема́є украї́нських гро́шей.

(b) Да́йте ві́дповіді на ці запита́ння англі́йською мо́вою

1 What do Stephen and Taras do immediately after their arrival in Kyiv airport?

2 What type of document does Stephen show the frontier guard?

3 What is prohibited for import into Ukraine?

4 What kind of foreign currency does Stephen have on arrival in Ukraine?

3 VERBS OF MOTION (*CONTINUED*)

Multi-directional

The verbs **ходи́ти**[*], **ї́здити**[*], **літа́ти**, **бі́гати**, **вози́ти**[*] and **води́ти**[*] all denote:

▶ the motion itself (e.g. 'I like running')

▶ performing the action, but with no particular direction begin specified (e.g. 'Every morning I run in the park')

▶ performing the action **there** and **back** (e.g. 'Last year I flew to Paris').

These verbs will therefore be called **multi-directional**.

Uni-directional

By contrast, the corresponding verbs **іти́**[*], **ї́хати**[*], **леті́ти**[*], **бі́гти**[*], **везти́**[*] and **вести́**[*] all denote:

▶ [in the present tense] performing the action in a particular direction now or at a specified time in the future (e.g. 'I am going to work')

▶ [in the past tense] being in process of performing the action at some time in the past (e.g. 'I was driving along when . . .').

These verbs will therefore be called **uni-directional**.

> **LANGUAGE TIP**
> Check the present and past tense forms of the verbs marked with an asterisk in the vocabulary at the back of the book – some of them are somewhat unpredictable!

Because both multi-directional and uni-directional verbs have present tense forms, they are **imperfective**.

Verbs of motion with prefixes

In this unit, we saw **пройти́**, **піти́** and **приї́хати**. They were all listed as perfective. The rule is:

When a prefix is added to a uni-directional verb of motion, such as those given in section 2, the verb thus created is **perfective**. When a prefix is added to a multi-directional verb of motion, such as those given in section 1, the verb thus created is **imperfective**. (A modification to the second part of this rule will be dealt with in Unit 11.)

Adding the prefix **по-** to **іти** gives **піти́**. **Піти́** and **пої́хати** are the perfective counterparts of **іти** and **ї́хати** – both verbs literally mean 'to set off'.

The addition of a prefix to **ї́здити** causes a change in the structure of the word, e.g. **приїжджа́ти**. The addition of a prefix ending in a consonant (e.g. **в**) requires the addition of the apostrophe: **в'їжджа́ти**. There are alternative forms, e.g. **приї́зди́ти** and **в'ї́зди́ти** with exactly the same meaning.

4 SHORT-FORM ADJECTIVES

With two exceptions, all the adjectives that you have met so far are **long-form** adjectives. That means that they have a full ending in the masculine nominative singular, e.g. **бі́лий**, **молоди́й**, **міжнаро́дний**. The first exception is **зго́ден**, as in **Я зго́ден з Ва́ми** (*I agree with you*). All the other endings are like those of ordinary adjectives, e.g.:

Я зго́дна (f) з Ва́ми.

Ми зго́дні (pl.) з Ва́ми.

Adjectives like **зго́ден** are called **short-form** adjectives. They are differentiated from long-form adjectives only by the ending – or rather lack of one! – in the masculine singular.

There are five other useful short-form adjectives that you should know:

пе́вен	*certain, sure* (other forms: **пе́вна**, **пе́вне**; **пе́вні**)
пови́нен	*obliged* (other forms: **пови́нна**, **пови́нне**; **пови́нні**)
ко́жен	*each, every* (other forms: **ко́жна**, **ко́жне**; **ко́жні**)
жо́ден	*none, no* (*kind of*) (other forms: **жо́дна**, **жо́дне**; **жо́дні**)
потрі́бен	*necessary* (other forms: **потрі́бна**, **потрі́бне**; **потрі́бні**)

Here are some more examples of usage:

Стівен **пови́нен** нам за́раз зателефонува́ти.	Stephen **is supposed** to ring us at any moment.
Ти **пе́вен**, що він зателефону́є?	Are you **sure** that he will ring?
Я працю́ю **ко́жен день**.	I work **every day**.

? Test yourself: Впра́ви

1 Identify the case of each adjective form in the following table:

Singular					
висо́кий	висо́кий	висо́кого	висо́кому	висо́кому	висо́ким
чо́рна	чо́рну	чо́рної	чо́рній	чо́рній	чо́рною
Plural					
висо́кі	висо́кі	висо́ких	висо́ких	висо́ким	висо́кими
чо́рні	чо́рних	чо́рних	чо́рних	чо́рним	чо́рними

2 Choose the most appropriate adjective from the list on the right to form phrases with the nouns in the left-hand column. Change the adjective endings when necessary:

Nouns	*Adjectives*
не́бо	до́вгий
трава́	важки́й
лимо́н	си́льний
чолові́к	жо́втий
ка́мінь	зеле́ний
доро́га	блаки́тний

3 Put the verb into the correct form of the present tense:

іти́ – ходи́ти

a І́гор (…) на робо́ту щодня́.

b І́гор (…) до теа́тру сього́дні.

ї́хати – ї́здити

c Богда́н за́втра (…) до Льво́ва.

d Богда́н за́вжди (…) до батькі́в авто́бусом.

4 Insert the missing verbs in the necessary form from the list that follows:

a Я (…) до те́бе че́рез де́сять хвили́н і (…) кни́гу. *(on foot)*

b Ма́ма вчо́ра (…) з робо́ти о 9 годи́ні ве́чора і (…) ті́стечка. *(on foot)*

c Моя́ по́друга ча́сто (…) на маши́ні й (…) ді́тям пе́чиво.

d Ро́берт (…) по́їздом за́втра вра́нці й (…) докуме́нти.

> прийти́, прихо́дити,
> проно́сити, пронести́,
> приї́хати, приїжджа́ти,
> привезти́, приво́зити.

9 *Ваш па́спорт, будь ла́ска Your passport, please*　　**117**

5 Translate your part in the dialogue into Ukrainian:

Прикордонник	Ва́ші докуме́нти, будь ла́ска.
You	*Here is my passport, ticket and customs declaration form.*
Прикордонник	Яка́ мета́ Ва́шої поʼʒ́дки?
You	*I've come for a holiday.*
Прикордонник	Ви ма́єте предме́ти, заборо́нені до вве́зення?
You	*I don't know what is prohibited.*
Прикордонник	Яку́ валю́ту Ви ма́єте?
You	*200 American dollars, 135 pounds.*
Прикордонник	У Вас є украї́нські гри́вні?
You	*No, I don't have any Ukrainian money.*

6 Taras phones Vira at home. How much of this dialogue can you understand without referring to the list of new words?

Тара́с	Алло́, Ві́рочко? Це я. Я вже́ в Ки́єві.
Ві́ра	Ну, як доро́га?
Тара́с	Долеті́ли норма́льно.
Ві́ра	Стоми́лися?
Тара́с	Тро́хи.
Ві́ра	Вас зустрі́ли?
Тара́с	Нас зустрі́в представни́к фі́рми "Мо́да".
Ві́ра	Але́ ж ви з ним не були́ знайо́мі . . .
Тара́с	У ньо́го в рука́х була́ табли́чка з на́шими прі́звищами, тому́ ми ле́гко знайшли́ оди́н о́дного.
Ві́ра	А як було́ з тра́нспортом?
Тара́с	Наш нови́й знайо́мий мав маши́ну. Це було́ ду́же зру́чно.
Ві́ра	Чудо́во.
Тара́с	Ми що́йно посели́лися в готе́лі. У нас зі Сті́веном два "лю́кси". Там є телеві́зор, холоди́льник. Все гара́зд.
Ві́ра	Сього́дні вам тре́ба до́бре відпочи́ти з доро́ги, про́сто погуля́ти ву́лицями.
Тара́с	Ми ще ніде́ не були́ і нічого не ба́чили. Але́ ми пі́демо че́рез годи́ну. Адже́ Сті́вен ще ніко́ли не був у Ки́єві.

V **Ві́рочка**	*Virochka, an affectionate form of Vira*
ну, як доро́га?	*so how was the journey?*
долеті́ти (долечу́, долети́ш) (pf.)	*to arrive (by plane)*
стоми́тися (стомлю́ся, сто́мишся, . . . сто́мляться) (pf.)	*to get tired*
Стоми́лися?	*Are [you] tired?*
Вас зустрі́ли?	*Were you met? (lit. did [they] meet you?)*
представни́к фі́рми "Мо́да"	*representative of the firm 'Moda'*
табли́чка	*board, notice*
тому́	*therefore*
ле́гко	*easily*
знайти́ (знайду́, зна́йдеш) (pf.) (past tense: **знайшо́в, знайшла́ знайшли́**)	*to find*
оди́н о́дного	*each other*
що́йно	*just*
посели́тися (pf.)	*to settle in*
відпочи́ти (-чи́ну, -чи́неш) (pf.)	*to have a rest*
погуля́ти (pf.)	*to go for a walk*
ніде́	*nowhere*
ми ще ніде́ не були́	*we haven't been anywhere yet*
адже́	*after all*

Я покажу́ вам буди́нок
I'll show you the building

In this unit you will learn:

▶ *How to describe the interior of a house or flat*
▶ *How to read the small ads in a newspaper*
▶ *How to become familiar with Ukrainians*
▶ *How to talk about your knowledge of foreign languages*

Текст

TR 11, 00:06

At the summer cottage. Taras tells the story.

Учо́ра в на́с був напру́жений день, а пі́сля робо́ти Іго́р Іва́нович запропонува́в пої́хати до ньо́го в го́сті. Він сказа́в: "Дружи́на бу́де ду́же ра́да познайо́митися з ва́ми. Вона́ готу́є щось ду́же смачне́ на вече́рю і чека́є нас о пів на сьо́му." Ми не запере́чували, бо були́ сто́млені й голо́дні.

Іго́р Іва́нович ма́є суча́сний двоповерхо́вий буди́нок. Навко́ло буди́нку – стари́й фрукто́вий сад. Уве́чері там ду́же ти́хо і па́хне кві́тами. Ве́чір був чудо́вий. Ста́хів поста́вив маши́ну в гара́ж, а по́тім ми зайшли́ в буди́нок. Две́рі відчини́ла його́ дружи́на, молода́ й ду́же вродли́ва жі́нка на ім'я́ О́льга. Вона́ так і сказа́ла під час знайо́мства: "Ду́же приє́мно познайо́митися. Я – О́льга." Я запита́в: "А по-ба́тькові?" Вона́ засмія́лася і відповіла́: "Про́сто О́льга." Ста́хів тако́ж запропонува́в перейти́ на "ти", і ми погоди́лися. Іго́р познайо́мив нас тако́ж із ді́тьми.

Їх у ньо́го тро́є: ста́рший син Оста́п, сере́дня до́нька Ната́лка й моло́дша до́нька Оле́нка. По́тім Іго́р запропонува́в: "Я покажу́ вам буди́нок." На пе́ршому по́версі – ку́хня, комо́ра й вели́ка віта́льня. На дру́гий по́верх веду́ть дерев'я́ні схі́дці, які́ госпо́дар буди́нку зроби́в сам. Нагорі́ є три спа́льні, кабіне́т Іго́ря, дитя́ча кімна́та, туале́т і ва́нна кімна́та.

Пі́сля вече́рі ми всі ходи́ли на прогу́лянку до рі́ки, сиді́ли над водо́ю, розмовля́ли, а Сті́вен, Іго́р і Оста́п на́віть попла́вали, тому́ що вода́ була́ ду́же те́пла й чи́ста.

Додо́му ми поверну́лися ду́же пі́зно, але́ в чудо́вому на́строї.

V у нас був	*we had*
напру́жений	*busy*
запропонува́ти (-у́ю, -у́єш) (pf.)	*to propose, suggest*
поḯхати (поḯду, поḯдеш) (pf.)	*to go*
гість (gen.: **го́сті**) (m)	*guest (alt. **i/o**)*
він запропонува́в поḯхати до ньо́го в го́сті	*he suggested going to visit him*
готува́ти (готу́ю, готу́єш) (impf.)	*to cook*
щось	*something*
щось ду́же смачне́	*something very tasty*
вече́ря	*supper*
готува́ти на вече́рю (acc.)	*to cook [something] for supper*
чека́ти (impf.)	*to wait*
запере́чувати (-ую, -уєш) (pf.)	*to object*
сто́млений	*tired*
голо́дний	*hungry*
суча́сний	*modern*
двоповерхо́вий	*two-storey*
навко́ло (preposition followed by gen.)	*around*
фрукто́вий	*fruit (adj.)*
фрукто́вий сад	*orchard*
ти́хий	*quiet, peaceful*
уве́чері там ду́же ти́хо	*in the evening it is very peaceful there*
па́хнути (3rd person sg. па́хне) (impf.)	*to smell*
там па́хне кві́тами	*there is a smell/it smells of flowers there*
зайти́(зайду́, за́йдеш) (pl. past tense: **зайшли́**) (pf.)	*to enter*
ми зайшли́ в буди́нок	*we entered the house*
две́рі (always pl.)	*door*
відчини́ти (pf.)	*to open*
вродли́вий	*beautiful, handsome*
вродли́ва жі́нка на ім'я́ О́льга	*a beautiful woman named Ol'ha/Ol'ha by name*
вона́ так і сказа́ла	*she simply said*
під ча́с (+ gen.)	*during*
знайо́мство	*acquaintance*
під ча́с знайо́мства	*while introducing each other/being introduced*
відповісти́ (f sg. past tense: **відповіла́**) (pf.)	*to answer*

про́сто	simply, just
перейти́ (pf.) на "ти"	lit. to go over to "ти"
погоди́тися (погóджуся, погóдишся) (pf.)	to agree
ста́рший	elder, eldest
Остáп	Ostap
серéдній	middle
Натáлка (affectionate form of Натáля)	Natalka
молóдший	younger, youngest
Олéнка (affectionate form of Олéна)	Olenka
ку́хня	kitchen
комóра	storeroom
дерев'я́ний	wooden
схíдці (pl.)	staircase
на дру́гий пóверх веду́ть дерев'я́ні схíдці	a wooden staircase leads up to the first floor
господáр	master of the house
зроби́ти (зроблю́, зрóбиш, . . . зрóблять) (pf.)	to make
сам	(here:) himself
нагорí	upstairs
спáльня	bedroom
дитя́чий	children's (adj.)
дитя́ча кімнáта	children's room
туалéт	toilet
вáнна кімнáта	bathroom
прогу́лянка	walk
рікá	river
ходи́ти на прогу́лянку до ріки́	to go for a walk to the river
ми сидíли над водóю	we sat by the water
нáвіть	even
поплáвати (pf.)	to have a swim
чи́стий	clean, pure
поверну́тися (поверну́ся, повéрнешся) (pf.)	to return
пíзно	late
нáстрій	mood (alt. **i/o**)
в чудóвому нáстрої	in a wonderful mood

READER'S ENCYCLOPEDIA® OF EASTERN EUROPEAN LITERATURE

Edited by
Robert B. Pynsent

With the Assistance of
S. I. Kanikova

HarperCollins*Publishers*

Bramborski serbski casnik (Brandenburg Sorbian newspaper), in which the literary element was small.

Throughout the 19th century and well into the 20th, verse always prevailed over prose. Upper Sorbian literature was led by BART-ĆIŠINSKI and the first discussion on Sorbian versification was conducted between him and Křesćan Bohuwěr Pful in *Łužica* in 1883. The leading Lower Sorbian poet at this time was KOSYK. However, in Upper Sorbian literature at least, the importance of prose was growing. The most interesting prose writers in the 1920s and 1930s were Jakub Lorenc-Zalěski (1874–1939) and Romuald Domaška (1869–1945). Writing for the theatre was also on the increase, though theatrical performances were still entirely the work of amateurs.

There is a blank space in Sorbian literary history between the banning of Sorbian publications by the Nazis in 1937 and the appearance in 1952 of BRĚZAN's *Kak stara Jančowa z wyšnosću wojowaše* (How old Mrs Janč fought with the authorities). This was the beginning of Socialist Realism. The Sorbs were now given unprecedented opportunities to develop their literature, so long as they respected certain ideological limits. *Łužica* (suppressed in 1937) was revived as *Rozhlad* (Survey) in 1950. The establishment of the Domowina (Homeland) publishing house in 1958 made possible the publication of hundreds of Sorbian books with state subsidies. The novel, a genre unknown to Sorbian literature before 1937, made its entry in the form of Kurt Krjeńc's (1907–78) *Jan. Roman pytaceho člowjeka* (Jan. A novel of a searching man, 1955), to be followed by BRĚZAN's trilogy and further prose works of substance by Marja Kubašec (1890–1976), KOCH and others. At the same time, the state-supported, professional Sorbian theatre blossomed, while the poets, led by LORENC, demonstrated the vitality of Sorbian verse. There were, of course, qualms about the political compliance induced by state subsidies and the air was cleared when the German Democratic Republic gave up the ghost in 1990.

•Robert Elsie (Ed.), *An Anthology of Sorbian Poetry from the Sixteenth Century to the Present Day* (London, Boston, 1990).

G. Stone, *The Smallest Slavonic Nation. The Sorbs of Lusatia* (London, 1972), pp. 41–89.

GCS

UKRAINIAN

Even before the Christianisation of Kievan Rus´ (988), service books were being translated into Church Slavonic from W and S Slavic sources. During the reign of Volodymyr ([Vladimir] 978–1015) and especially that of his son Yaroslav (1019–54) much was done to spread literature translated from Byzantine sources. The oldest extant book is the *Ostromir Gospel* (1056–57) (see BIBLE), though there were many other liturgical and devotional books, translations of the lives of the saints and of sermons. Some apocrypha also circulated in Ukraine and historical works (*The Jewish Wars* of Josephus) were translated in Kiev. Much of this literature was didactic in nature, but there were also some romances and adventure stories (e.g. a version of the ALEXANDER ROMANCE).

The original literature of Kievan Rus´, written in Church Slavonic, developed slowly, based on Byzantine models, and reached its zenith in the period from the

a Пра́вда чи непра́вда?

1 Тара́с і Сті́вен були́ сто́млені й голо́дні.

2 Íгор Іва́нович ма́є стари́й двоповерхо́вий буди́нок.

3 Дружи́ну Ста́хова звуть Оле́нка.

4 Ку́хня й комо́ра – на пе́ршому по́версі.

b Да́йте ві́дповіді на ці запита́ння англі́йською мо́вою

1 Who opened the door when the guests arrived?

2 How many daughters does Stakhiv have?

3 What did people do after the meal?

4 When did Taras and Stephen get back home?

● INSIGHT

Becoming familiar

The proposal **перейти́ на ти** (to go over to **"ти"**) is not made lightly in Ukrainian. It means that you are no longer regarded as a stranger, but are accepted as a friend. Taras is right to be concerned about Ol'ha's **ім'я́по-ба́тькові**, her patronymic, knowing that one of the polite forms of address in Ukrainian requires the first name and patronymic to be used together. The fact that Ol'ha herself proposes being on first-name terms is significant; it would not have been correct for Stephen to make the first move.

Як функціону́є мо́ва

1 WE HAD A BUSY DAY

We have already seen two ways of saying 'I have' in Ukrainian:

Я ма́ю бра́та/У ме́не є брат.	*I have a brother.*

In the second of these sentences, the verb is a form of **бу́ти** (*to be*) and so in the past tense ('I had', etc.), we find past tense forms of **бу́ти**:

У нас **був** напру́жений день.	*We **had** a busy day.*

Some more examples:

В Оста́па **є** гро́ші.	*Ostap **has** money.*
В Оста́па **були́** гро́ші.	*Ostap **had** money.*
У те́бе **є** маши́на?	*Do you have a car?*
У те́бе **була́** маши́на?	*Did you have a car?*

Now let's look at what happens when we make these sentences negative:

В Остáпа **немáє** грóш**ей.**   *Ostap has no money.*

В Остáпа **не булó** грóш**ей.**   *Ostap had no money.*

Note: the past tense of **немáє** is **не булó**.

In the future tense, the sentence will look like this:

В Остáпа **не бýде** грóш**ей.**   *Ostap won't have any money.*

2 IT SMELLS OF FLOWERS

The Ukrainian phrase has a verb – **пáхнути** (*to give off a scent*) – and the noun denoting what there is a smell of in the **instrumental** case:

Пáхне квíтами.   *There is a smell of flowers.*

Note: in this type of sentence, the verb has no subject; therefore, in the past tense, the verb has the **neuter** singular form:

Пáхло квíтами.   *There was a smell of flowers.*

3 COUNTING PEOPLE – COLLECTIVE NUMERALS

When counting humans, Ukrainian uses a special set of numerals, called **collective,** that are followed by nouns in the **genitive plural**, e.g.:

2	**двóє** брáтів	(compare:	два	готéлі)
3	**трóє** брáтів	(compare:	три	готéлі)
4	чéтв**еро** брáтів	(compare:	чотúри	готéлі)
5	п'ят**еро** брáтів	(compare:	п'ять	готéлів)
6	шéст**еро** брáтів	(compare:	шість	готéлів)
7	сéм**еро** брáтів	(compare:	сім	готéлів)
8	вóсьм**еро** брáтів	(compare:	вíсім	готéлів)
9	дéв'ят**еро** брáтів	(compare:	дéв'ять	готéлів)
10	дéсят**еро** брáтів	(compare:	дéсять	готéлів)

In actual practice, only the first few collective numerals are in regular use. Even so people frequently use the ordinary cardinal numerals with nouns denoting human beings, e.g. **два брáти**:

У ньóго **трóє дітéй.**   *He has **three children**.*

Їх у ньóго **трóє.**   *He has **three of them**.*

Нас булó **чéтверо.**   *There were **four of us**.*

Collective numerals are also used with nouns that have no singular form, e.g.

У кімнáті двóє **дверéй.**   *There are two **doors** in the room.*

Summer houses

The idea of a **дáча** can range from a humble old cottage on one floor to a newly built palatial mansion. The common element is that the **дáча** is a second home; the first home is in the city. Stakhiv's cottage is clearly impressive. It is a **двоповерхóвий будúнок** – a two-storey building, with rooms **на пéршому пóверсі** (on the **ground** floor) and **на дрýгому пóверсі** (on the **first** floor).

Beware! When you are told that the flat or office you are looking for is **на четвéртому пóверсі** in Ukrainian, remember that it is on the **third** floor in English!

Реклáмні оголóшення

Наймý квартúру в цéнтрі	*Flat sought to rent in the centre* (lit. I will rent a flat in the centre)
Здаю двокімнáтну (квартúру) з телефóном у цéнтрі	*Two-roomed (flat) with telephone to let in the centre* (lit. I am letting. . .)
Здам кв-ру (свою) без посерéдників	*(Own) flat to let – no agents* (lit. I will let (my own) flat without intermediaries)
Термінóво потрíбна квартúра з телефóном недалéко від метрó	*Flat with telephone near metro urgently needed*
Продаéться трикімнáтна квартúра (недóрого)	*Three-roomed flat for sale (not dear)* (lit. is being sold)
Продаю́ться мéблі імпортного виробнúцтва	*Imported furniture for sale*

V

оголóшення (n)	*advertisement, notice (in a newspaper), small ad*
посерéдник	*intermediary*
термінóвий	*urgent (adv:* **термінóво** *urgently)*
продавáтися	*to be sold*
квартúра	*flat*
однокімнáтна квартúра	*one-roomed flat*
дво-/трикімнáтна квартúра	*two-/three-roomed flat*
наймáти (impf.) (квартúру)	*to rent (a flat)*
здавáти (здаю́, здаéш) (impf.) (квартúру)	*to let (a flat)*

Here are the **perfective future** forms of these two verbs:

найня́ти (perf. infinitive)		**зда́ти** (perf. infinitive)	
найму́	на́ймемо	здам	здамо́
на́ймеш	на́ймете	здаси́	здасте́
на́йме	на́ймуть	здасть	здаду́ть

● **INSIGHT**

How to find the address you need

Most Ukrainians, at least in the towns, live in flats. They will give their address in the following way:

Вул. Франка́, буд. 16, кв. 115.

Or, more simply:

Франка́ 16/115.

Here **буд.** stands for **буди́нок** (block (of flats)) and **кв**. stands for **кварти́ра** (flat), so the address is: flat 115, no. 16 Franko Street. When streets are named after people, the person goes into the genitive case, e.g. **ву́лиця Франка́** (Franko Street). The actual blocks of flats can be very large, so number 16 could well extend a long way. In order to find the right flat easily, it is also important to know which staircase it is on; for this you will need to know the number of the **під'ї́зд**. By each **під'ї́зд** there will be a notice saying which flats can be found on that particular staircase. In these security-conscious days, you should also know the number of the **код** (code) that will open the door to the staircase.

4 TALKING ABOUT YOUR KNOWLEDGE OF LANGUAGES

 TR 11, 02:34

	зна́ю		know
Я	розумі́ю	I	understand
	вивча́ю		am learning
	украї́нську мо́ву		Ukrainian

LANGUAGE TIP
розумі́ти to understand

Я хо́чу зна́ти украї́нську мо́ву.	I want to know Ukrainian.
Я хо́чу вивча́ти украї́нську мо́ву.	I want to learn Ukrainian.
Я хо́чу розумі́ти украї́нську мо́ву.	I want to understand Ukrainian.

вільно

дóбре   розмовля́ю

Я не ду́же дóбре   українськ**ою**

     погáно   говорю́   мóв**ою** (inst.)

     не   володíю

Ви говóрите украї́нською мóвою?

Ви розмовля́єте украї́нською мóвою?

Ви розумі́єте украї́нську мóву? (acc.)

Перепрóшую, що Ви сказáли?

Я не розумі́ю.

Я не зрозумі́в.

Повторі́ть, будь лáска.

Перекладі́ть англі́йськ**ою** мóв**ою**.

Говорі́ть, будь лáска, повíльно.

V	**володíти (-íю, -íєш)** (+ inst.)	*to possess* (here:) *know well*
	вíльно	(here:) *fluently*
	зрозумíти (зрозумíю, зрозумíєш) (pf.)	*to understand*
	повтори́ти (pf.) (imperative: **повторі́ть**)	*to repeat*
	переклáсти (переклад́у, перекладéш) (pf.) (imperative: **перекладí́ть**)	*to translate*
	перекладí́ть з украї́нської мóви на англі́йську	*translate from Ukrainian into English*
	повíльно	*slowly*

❓ Test yourself: Впра́ви

1 Construct sentences according to the example:

Приклад: Я . . . (хотíти, зна́ти, італíйська, мóва).

Я хóчу зна́ти італíйську мóву.

a Я . . . (могти́, розмовля́ти, францу́зький, мóва).

Я . . . (хотíти, розмовля́ти, німéцький, мóва).

Я . . . (могти́, розумíти, цей, текст).

Я . . . (хотíти, зна́ти, цей, слóво).

b Він . . . (могти́, розмовля́ти, францу́зький, мóва).

Він . . . (хотíти, розмовля́ти, німéцький, мóва).

Вона́ . . . (могти́, розумíти, цей, текст).

Вона́ . . . (хотíти, зна́ти, цей, слóво).

c Ви . . . (могти́, розмовля́ти, францу́зький, мóва).

Ми . . . (хотíти, розмовля́ти, німéцький, мóва).

Ви . . . (могти́, розумíти, цей, текст).

Ми . . . (хотíти, зна́ти, цей, слóво).

d (Я) . . . (трéба, розмовля́ти, францу́зький, мóва).

(Ти) . . . (трéба, розмовля́ти, німéцький, мóва).

(Ми) . . . (трéба, розумíти, цей, текст).

(Ви) . . . (трéба, зна́ти, цей, слóво).

2 A friend of yours has asked you to help him write a letter to some Ukrainians he knows about his plans for the summer. He speaks a little Ukrainian but is afraid of making grammatical mistakes. Help him put the words into the correct form:

Дороги́й (Іва́н)!

Сьогóдні (п'ятна́дцять) (тра́вень) (1997) (рік). (Два́дцять) (ли́пень), у (середа́), (я/менé/менí) ї́ду в (Украї́на) і бу́ду відпочива́ти на (Чóрний) (мóре). (Я/менé/менí) хóчу замóвити (нóмер) у га́рному (готéль) для себé й своє́ї (дружи́на). Бíля (готéль) – чудóвий (парк), пéред (готéль) – (мóре), за (готéль) – (гóри). (Наш) (нóмер) на (трéтій) (пóверх) з (телевíзор), (холоди́льник), (телефóн), (душ). Про цей (план) (я/менé/менí) говори́в із (дружи́на). (Вона́/ї́ї/їй) (він/йогó/йомý) ду́же подóбається. (Вона́/ї́ї/їй) пропонýє ї́хати (пóїзд) з Ки́єва. (Квитки́) (ми/нас/нам) замóвили вчóра. Мóжна такóж летíти (літа́к), алé (квитки́) кóштують дóрого. З (Ки́їв) до (Одéса) трéба ї́хати (пóїзд) 14 (годи́на): (1) (ніч) і (1) (ра́нок). (Ми/нас/нам) хóчемо взя́ти СВ*, щоб ї́хати з (комфóрт). (Мій) (дружи́на) ду́же лю́бить ї́здити (пóїзд): сидíти в (купé), пи́ти (чай), диви́тися у (вікнó), ти́хо розмовля́ти абó чита́ти (кни́га) й не пам'ята́ти про (робóта) й (усí) (спра́ви), які́ трéба булó роби́ти у (Ки́їв). Потíм (ми/нас/нам) ма́ємо зроби́ти (переса́дка) в (Одéса) на електри́чка та ї́хати півгоди́ни до (мíсце) від почи́нку. В (Одéса) влíтку ду́же жа́рко. (Ми/нас/нам) замовля́ємо (нóмер) у (готéль) на

(двоє/двох/двом) на (два/дві) (ти́ждень). Пі́сля (Оде́са) ми ї́демо до (друг). (Він/його́/йому́) живе́ в (Херсо́н). (Я/мене́/мені́) ма́ю (лист) від (друг), де (він/його́/йому́) пи́ше, що хо́че (я/мене́/мені́) ба́чити. (Ми/нас/нам) із (дружи́на) ма́ємо ще (два/дві) (ти́ждень) й хо́чемо пої́хати до (Херсо́н) (зо) (ли́пень) на 14 (день). (Ви/вас/вам) подо́баються (наш) (пла́ни) на (лі́то)?

До (зу́стріч),

Рі́чард.

15 (тра́вень) 1997 р., Ло́ндон

*СВ [esvé] (спа́льний ваго́н) – *sleeping car*

3 Complete the following table:

	стіле́ць	підло́га	лі́жко	коридо́р (in plural)	поли́ця (in plural)	дзе́ркало (in plural)
Nom.						
Acc.						
Gen.						
Dat.						
Loc.						
Inst.						

4 Write in full the present and both future tenses of the following imperfective verbs:

a пи́ти

b писа́ти

c ї́сти

5 Write out in full the past tenses of the following verbs:

a чита́ти

b іти́

c леті́ти

6 Write out the following sentences, putting the words in brackets into the correct form:

a Що (лежа́ти – *past tense*) на (стіл)?

На (він) (лежа́ти – *past tense*) па́пка.

b Що ви (пи́ти – *present tense*) вра́нці?

Я (пи́ти – *present tense*) (ка́ва). Я (вона́) ду́же люблю́.

c З (хто) ви (розмовля́ти – *past tense*)?

Я (розмовля́ти – *past tense*) з (нови́й дире́ктор). Ви (знати) (він)?

7 Which room is which? Base your answer on the information given below (check any unfamiliar words in the vocabulary):

a Це гáрна, свíтла кімнáта. Тут стоя́ть: канáпа, журнáльний стóлик, два крíсла, телевíзор. На підлóзі лежи́ть ки́лим, на стіні́ ви́сить вели́ке дзéркало.

b У ціє́ї кімнáти є стіл, чоти́ри стільці́, гáзова плитá, холоди́льник.

c Це невели́ка кімнáта. Тут стої́ть письмóвий стіл, зручнé крíсло, ви́сить багáто поли́ць із книжкáми. На столí – комп'ю́тер, ди́скити, телефóн, факс, рýчки, олівцí, кíлька пáпок із докумéнтами.

8 Flat hunting: your friend has seen several flats and wants to buy one of them. He gives you a description of all four and a plan of the flat that he likes most of all. Find the flat that matches his plan (check unfamiliar words in the vocabulary):

Flat no. 1: У кварти́рі 3 кімнáти, вели́ка кýхня, вáнна, туалéт, невели́кий балкóн, коридóр 9 квадрáтних мéтрів.

Flat no. 2: Це двокімнáтна кварти́ра з кýхнею й хóлом. Вітáльня (20 мéтрів) з вели́ким балкóном. Вáнна й туалéт окрéмо, є комóра (3 мéтри). У спáльні тáкож малéнький балкóн.

Flat no. 3: Трикімнáтна кварти́ра на дрýгому пóверсі, кýхня (10 мéтрів) з вели́кою комóрою, алé немá балкóна, вáнна й туалéт малéнькі. Дýже вели́ка вітáльня, а дві íнші кімнáти – малéнькі (13 і 16 мéтрів).

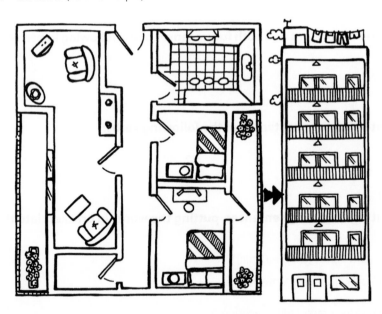

Flat no. 4: Трикімнáтна кварти́ра, трéтій пóверх шестиповерхóвого буди́нку. Вели́кий хол, кýхня 13 квадрáтних мéтрів, вітáльня 25 мéтрів і ще дві окрéмі кімнáти, два балкóни, комóра.

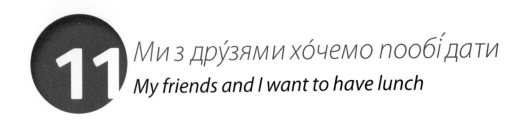

11 Ми з дру́зями хо́чемо пообі́дати
My friends and I want to have lunch

In this unit you will learn:
▶ *How to address people using the vocative case*
▶ *How to order a meal in a restaurant*
▶ *How to make sense of a menu and identify certain Ukrainian dishes*

Діало́г 1

 TR 12, 00:07

In the 'Ukraina' restaurant.

Тара́с	До́брий день! У вас є ві́льні сто́лики? Ми з дру́зями хо́чемо пообі́дати. Нас бу́де тро́є. Вони́ за́раз підійду́ть.
Офіціа́нтка	Так, про́шу. Де ви хо́чете сиді́ти?
Тара́с	Я ду́маю, бі́ля вікна́, пода́лі.
Офіціа́нтка	Про́шу, сіда́йте. Ось меню́.
(Stephen appears, accompanied by a young lady)	
Сті́вен	Тара́се, ти вже тут! Я хо́чу тебе́ познайо́мити із Соломі́єю.
Тара́с	Бо́же мій! Соломі́є! Я не знав, що це ти! Тре́ба було́ здогада́тися, адже́ в те́бе таке́ рідкісне ім'я́! Сті́вене, ми з Соломі́єю знайо́мі ма́йже сто ро́ків!
Соломі́я	Не перебі́льшуй! Я ще не така́ стара́ . . . Сті́вене, Ви ба́чите яки́й тісни́й світ! Ми з Тара́сом були́ дру́зями дити́нства, на́ші батьки́ товаришува́ли.
Сті́вен	А я збира́вся Вас офіці́йно предста́вити своє́му дру́гові . . . Яки́й дивови́жний ви́падок!

V **пообі́дати** (pf.)	*to have some lunch*
підійти́ (підійду́, підійдеш) (pf.)	*to come [closer]*
пода́лі	*a bit further off*
меню́ (n, indecl.)	*menu*
здогада́тися (pf.)	*to guess*
тре́ба було́ здогада́тися	*[I] should have guessed*
рідкісний	*rare, unusual*
адже́ в те́бе таке́ рідкісне ім'я́	*after all, you have such a rare name!*
ма́йже	*almost, nearly*

132

перебільшувати (-ую, -уєш) (impf.)	to exaggerate
Я ще не така стара́	I'm not that old yet!
тісни́й	narrow, tight
світ	world
ви ба́чите, яки́й тісни́й світ	you see how small the world is
дити́нство	childhood
Ми з Тара́сом були́ дру́зями дити́нства	Taras and I were childhood friends
товаришува́ти (-у́ю, -у́єш) (impf.)	to be friends
дивови́жний	strange
ви́падок (gen.: ви́падку)	chance, occurrence

Як функціону́є мо́ва

1 NOUNS

Addressing people – the vocative case

You have already seen several examples of the special forms of names used when addressing people:

| Тара́се! | Сті́вене! | Ігоре Іва́новичу! |
| Тетя́но! | Соломі́є | Олекса́ндрівно! |

Here is a summary of the endings for names already introduced:

Masculine

a *First names**

| Nom s. | Іва́н | Петро́ | Васи́ль | Сергі́й | Мико́ла |
| Voc. | Іва́не! | Петре́! | Васи́лю! | Сергі́ю! | Мико́ло! |

b *Patronymics*

| Nom s. | Іва́нович |
| Voc. | Іва́новичу! |

Feminine

a *First names***

| Nom s. | О́льга | Ната́ля | Марі́я |
| Voc. | О́льго! | Ната́лю! | Марі́є! |

b *Patronymics*

| Nom s. | Олекса́ндрівна |
| Voc. | Олекса́ндрівно! |

---

* Masculine: **-е** after a hard consonant or if the name ends in **-о; -ю** after a soft consonant or vowel; **-о** if the name ends in **-а**.

** Feminine: **-о** after a hard consonant; **-ю** after a soft consonant; **-є** after a vowel.

Notes on the vocative endings

You have also seen that the word for *Mr* (**пан**) has a vocative form **пáне!**, e.g. **пáне Тéйлор!** (The equivalent word for *Mrs* (**пáні**) has no separate vocative form.) *God* (**Бог**) can be addressed as **Бóже!**

In theory, it is possible to form the vocative case from every masculine and feminine noun in Ukrainian. You could, if you wished, address your car as **маши́но**.

There are no special vocative case endings in the plural and none at all in adjectives and pronouns. Likewise, surnames do not have vocative forms.

● INSIGHT

Foreigners will most often be addressed with **пан/пáні** followed by the first name or surname. This form of address is also perfectly acceptable when talking to Ukrainians, especially if you cannot remember the first name and patronymic! You can also address people using their academic or professional title, e.g. **Пáне профéсоре! Пáне дирéкторе!**

2 I SHOULD HAVE GUESSED

(For constructions with **трéба** and the dative case, see Unit 6.)

Note how the meaning changes from the present to the past tense:

Менí трéба відвíдати своїх українських партнéрів.	*I have to visit my Ukrainian partners.*
Менí трéба булó відвíдати своїх українських партнéрів.	*I should have visited my Ukrainian partners.* (with the implication that I didn't)

Діалóг 2

 TR 12, 01:20

Our friends order their meal.

Офіціáнтка	Перепрóшую, що Ви бýдете замовля́ти?
Тарáс	Ви́бачте, ми зáраз ви́рішимо. Óтже, товари́ство, що бýдемо їсти?
Стíвен	З холóдних закýсок я берý ікрý й овочéвий салáт.
Тарáс	Соломíє? . . .
Соломíя	Я бýду осетри́ну і салáт "Вечíрній".
Тарáс	А для мéне, прóшу, м'яснé асортí й маринóвані гриби́.
Офіціáнтка	Бýдете замовля́ти пéршу стрáву?

Стівен	Я бу́ду борщ.
Соломі́я	Я не хо́чу.
Тара́с	Я візьму́ осетро́ву соля́нку.
Офіціа́нтка	Дру́гі стра́ви?
Стівен	А що ви порекоменду́єте?
Офіціа́нтка	У нас ду́же смачне́ філе́ з гриба́ми, варе́ники, котле́та по-ки́ївськи.
Стівен	О, так, я візьму́ котле́ту по-ки́ївськи. Я її́ ду́же люблю́.
Тара́с	Я візьму́ варе́ники з карто́плею. А ти, Соломі́є?
Соломі́я	Я тако́ж бу́ду котле́ту по-ки́ївськи.
Тара́с	Дру́зі, що бу́демо пи́ти?
Стівен	У вас є кри́мське вино́?
Офіціа́нтка	Так, "Каберне́", "Муска́т", "Масса́ндра".
Тара́с	Чудо́во, пля́шку "Муска́ту", будь ла́ска.

V

о́тже	so, well then
товари́ство	(here:) people! folks!
заку́ска	hors d'oeuvres
ікра́	caviare
овоче́вий	vegetable (adj.)
сала́т	salad
осетри́на	sturgeon
м'ясне́ ассорті́ (n, indecl.)	assorted cold meats
марино́ваний	marinated
стра́ва	dish, course
борщ	borshch [a soup]
соля́нка	solyanka [a soup]
осетро́ва соля́нка	solyanka with sturgeon
філе́ (n, indecl.)	fillet
варе́ник	varenyk
котле́та	cutlet
по-ки́ївськи	Kyiv-style, à la Kyiv
карто́пля	potato[es]
кри́мський	Crimean
пля́шка	bottle

3 ADVERBS – KYIV-STYLE

по-ки́ївськи	Kyiv-style, à la Kyiv

A whole range of similar adverbs can be formed from adjectives denoting place and countries:

по-англі́йськи	in the English manner
по-украї́нськи	in the Ukrainian manner

Діалóг 3

TR 12, 02:46

During lunch.

Стíвен	О, дýже смáчно.
Тарáс	Я люблю́ тут обíдати. Соломíйко, розкажú, що в тébe нового.
Соломíя	Новúн мáло. Як зáвжди, багáто працю́ю. Розлучúлася з чоловíком, поміня́ла квартúру, купúла собáку.
Тарáс	Бóже, і це "мáло новúн"?
Соломíя	Це все відбулóся за тí рокú, колú ми не бáчилися. А як ти? Як Вíра?
Тарáс	О, все гарáзд. Вíра пúше дисертáцію, багáто працю́є в бібліотéках.
Соломíя	А ти приíхав у службóвих спрáвах чи на відпочúнок?
Тарáс	Прóсто скýчив за Украḯною, а такóж булó приéмно склáсти компáнію Стíвенові. Мýшу сказáти, що тобí дýже пощастúло з партнéром. Стíвен – ас у своḯй спрáві.
Соломíя	Я це вже зрозумíла. З ним дýже цікáво співпрацюва́ти.
Стíвен	Дя́кую. Сподівáюся на ýспіх нáшої спíльної спрáви.
Тарáс	*(To the waitress)* Мóжна попросúти рахýнок? Дя́кую.

розкажú, що в тébe нового	*tell [us] what's new with you*
новинá	*news item*
новúни (pl.)	*news*
розлучúтися (**з** + inst.) (pf.)	*to get divorced from*
це все	*all of this*
відбýтися (pf.)	*to happen*
за (preposition followed by acc.)	(here:) *during, over (in a time expression)*
це все відбулóся за тí рокú, колú ми не бáчилися	*this all happened over the* (lit. *those*) *years that* (lit. *when*) *we haven't seen each other*
бібліотéка	*library*
скýчити (**за** + inst.) (impf.)	*to long for, feel nostalgic about, miss*
склáсти (складý, складéш) (past tense: **склав, склáла, склáли**) (pf.)	*to put together, form*
склáсти компáнію (+ dat.)	*to be company [for someone]*
мýсити (мýшу, мýсиш) (impf.)	*must, to have to*
ас	*ace*

136

співпрацюва́ти (-у́ю, -у́єш) (**з** + inst.)	*to collaborate [with]*
сподіва́тися (impf.) (**на** + acc.)	*to hope [for]*
раху́нок	*bill*
попроси́ти раху́нок	*to ask for the bill*

4 WHAT'S NEW WITH YOU?

The basic construction is **що** followed by the adjective in the neuter genitive singular form (**ново́го** from **нове́**), e.g.:

Що в газе́ті ціка́вого?	*Is there anything interesting in the newspaper? (lit. what's interesting in the paper?)*

The construction **в те́бе**, involving the preposition **в/у** and the genitive case, is exactly the same as **у/в ме́не є** (*I have*).

The negative answer would be:

Нічо́го ново́го нема́є.	*There's nothing new.*

5 DURING

це все відбуло́ся за ті роки́ . . .	*all this happened during the years . . .*

The preposition **за** followed by the accusative case denotes the period of time over which certain things have been achieved, i.e. in this instance, Solomiia is now divorced and lives in a different flat with a dog.

Contrast the meaning of **за** with **під час**:

під час обі́ду ми розмовля́ли	*during lunch we chatted*

i.e. we chatted at the same time as eating lunch; the actions are simultaneous.

6 ASKING AND ASKING FOR
This is an opportunity for some revision!

Мо́жна попроси́ти раху́нок?	*May I ask for the bill?*

Проси́ти (impf.)/**попроси́ти** (pf.) means to ask **for** something; it is followed by a noun in the accusative case without a preposition. 'Asking' when a question is involved is **пита́ти** (impf.)/**запита́ти** (pf.) or **спита́ти** (pf.). There is no difference in meaning between the two perfective verbs:

Запита́й Сті́вена, чи він лю́бить украї́нський борщ.	*Ask Stephen if he likes Ukrainian borshch.*

Діалóг 4

Plans for tomorrow.

Тарáс	До рéчі, Соломíйко, ти зáвтра не дýже зáйнята? Я зáвтра повинен з'їздити за мíсто, а у Стívена вíльний день. Чи ти мóжеш побýти його гíдом?
Соломíя	З приємнíстю. Я мóжу показáти Вам Ки́їв.
Стívен	Я не хóчу завдавáти Вам турбóт. Якщó Ви зáйняті . . .
Соломíя	О, це дрібни́ці. А крім тóго, я теж мáю прáво на відпочи́нок.
Тарáс	Чудóво. Домóвилися.
Соломíя	Стívене, ми мóжемо зустрíтися біля Óперного теáтру об 11-й годи́ні дня і підемо на екскýрсію. Ви не заблукáєте?
Стívен	Сподівáюся, що ні.

зáйнятий	*busy*
з'їздити (з'їжджу, з'їздиш) (pf.)	*to make a trip*
за (preposition + acc.)	(here:) *beyond*
з'їздити за мíсто	*to make a trip out of town*
чи ти не мóжеш побýти його гíдом?	lit. *can you not be his guide for a bit?*
приємнíсть (gen.: **приємності**) (f)	*pleasure* (alt. **o/i**)
завдавáти (завдаю, завдаєш) (impf.)	(here:) *to cause*
турбóта	*trouble*
завдавáти турбóти (pl.) (+ dat.)	*to cause [someone] trouble*
дрібни́ця	*trifle, small matter*
це дрібни́ці	*it's nothing!*
крім (preposition followed by gen.)	*apart from*
теж	*also*
прáво (**на** + acc.)	*right [to]*
екскýрсія	*excursion*
піти на екскýрсію	*to go on an excursion*
заблукáти (pf.)	*to get lost*
сподівáюся, що ні	*I hope not*

а Прáвда чи непрáвда

1 Соломíя і Тарáс – дрýзі дити́нства.

2 Стívен лю́бить їсти котлéту по-ки́ївськи.

3 Тарáс замовля́є в ресторáні пля́шку шампáнського.

4 Соломíя нещодáвно купи́ла чóрного котá.

b Да́йте ві́дповіді на ці запита́ння англі́йською мо́вою

1 What kind of salad did Stephen order?

2 Is Solomiia a vegetarian?

3 What did Taras tell Solomiia about his wife's work?

4 Did Stephen ask Solomiia to be his guide at the weekend?

7 MORE ON PREFIXES WITH VERBS OF MOTION

The prefix **з-/с-** can be added to verbs of motion from the multi-directional group (revise verbs of motion in Unit 9) to produce perfective verbs meaning 'to go somewhere quickly and return'. That is why we can translate **з'ї́здити** as 'to make a trip'. Another example:

У нас горі́лки нема́є.	*We've no vodka. I'll [or someone*
Тре́ба збі́гати в магази́н.	*will] have to run down to*
	the shop.

8 EATING IN UKRAINE

Here is the order of a typical Ukrainian meal. First come the **холо́дні заку́ски** (cold hors d'oeuvres: mainly cold meats and fish) and **сала́ти** (salads). This is followed by the **пе́рша стра́ва** (or **пе́рше**) (first course: soup) and the **дру́га стра́ва** (or **дру́ге**) (second course: meat or fish in various forms with vegetables, pasta, rice or potatoes):

Що ви бу́дете замовля́ти	*What are you going to*
на пе́рше?	*order **for** first course?*
На дру́ге я бу́ду філе́.	*I'll take fillet for second course.*

Ordering a sweet is not very common. But if you like a sweet at the end of a meal, you will look for 'something sweet' or 'dessert' on the menu: **соло́дке** (neuter form of the adjective **соло́дкий** 'sweet') or **десе́рт**.

Read through this selection from the menu from the restaurant 'Ukraina', which is right in the centre of Kyiv, on the corner of **бульва́р Шевче́нка** (Shevchenko Boulevard) and **Пу́шкінська ву́лиця** (Pushkin Street) and use the material in it for later exercises.

Холо́дні заку́ски	*Cold hors d'oeuvres*
Ри́бні	**Fish**
Печі́нка тріско́ва	*Cod liver*
Креве́тки під майоне́зом	*Prawns in mayonnaise*
Оселе́дець із цибу́лею	*Herring with onion*
Шпро́ти	*Sprats*
Овоче́ві	**Vegetables**
Гриби́ марино́вані	*Pickled mushrooms*

Помідóри фарширóвані	*Stuffed tomatoes*
Огіркú свíжі	*Fresh cucumbers*
Пéрець болгáрський натурáльний	*Fresh Bulgarian sweet peppers*

М'яснí — **Meat**

Язúк відварнúй	*Boiled tongue*
Ковбасá	*Salami*

Гарячі закýски — **Hot hors d'oeuvres**

Голубцí овочéві	*Cabbage rolls stuffed with vegetables*
Дирунú з картóплі	*Potato pancakes*

Пéрші стрáви — **First course**

Борщ украïнський з пампушкáми	*Ukrainian borshch with garlic buns*
Юшка грибнá	*Mushroom yooshka*
Солянка осетрóва	*Sturgeon solyanka*

Дрýгі страви — **Second course**

Свинúна з гарнíром	*Pork with garnish*
Біфштéкс смáжений з гарнíром	*Fried steak with garnish*
Варéники з картóплею і грибáми	*Varenyky with potato and mushrooms*
Омлéт із 3-х яéць	*Omelette made with three eggs*

Солóдкі стрáви — **Sweet dishes**

Морóзиво: з горíхом з шоколáдом	Ice cream: *with nuts with chocolate*

Напоï — **Beverages**

Алкогóльні	*Alcoholic*
Горíлка Украïнська з пéрцем	*Vodka: Ukrainian with pepper*
Коньяк Ай-Пéтрі:	*Cognac Ai-Petri*
Вúна натурáльні' Кагóр Кабернé	*Table wines: Kagor Cabernet*

Шампа́нські ви́на:		Sparkling wines:	
Украї́нське напівсухе́		Ukrainian semi-dry	
Украї́нське напівсоло́дке		Ukrainian semi-sweet	
"Гранд Дюше́с"		'Grande Duchesse'	

Гаря́чі напої / Hot beverages

Чай	з цу́кром	Tea	with sugar
	з ме́дом		with honey
	з лимо́ном		with lemon
Ка́ва	чо́рна	Coffee	black
	з цу́кром		with sugar
	з молоко́м		with milk

Холо́дні напої, со́ки / Cold beverages, juices

Ка́ва з моро́зивом	Coffee with ice cream
Сік я́блучний	Apple juice
Сік апельси́новий	Orange juice

● INSIGHT

It is, of course, quite impossible to find an exact English equivalent for many of the names of Ukrainian dishes. **Варе́ники** are very similar to ravioli, stuffed with meat or vegetables. **Деруни́** are made from grated potato and served with sour cream (**зі смета́ною**). **Борщ** is a soup made primarily from beetroot with the addition of tomatoes, potatoes, cabbage and other vegetables. **Соля́нка** has a sourish taste; it can have either a fish or meat base. **Ю́шка** is another word for a kind of soup.

напі́й (gen.: **напо́ю**)	drink, beverage (alt. **o/i**)
сік (gen.: **со́ку**)	juice (alt. **o/i**)
сніда́нок (gen.: **сніда́нку**)	breakfast
обі́д	lunch
підвечі́рок (gen.: **підвечі́рку**)	tea (meal)
вече́ря	supper

? Test yourself : Впра́ви

1 Put the correct form of the preposition з/зі/із in the gap:

Приклад: Він . . . мно́ю   Він зі мно́ю

ча́шка . . . сто́лу

две́рі . . . кімна́ти

стіле́ць . . . ку́хні

телефонува́ти . . . кабіне́ту

квито́к . . . ста́нції

2 Compile a Ukrainian menu out of the dishes listed, putting them into the correct columns:

заку́ски	перші стра́ви	дру́гі стра́ви	напо́ї

гриби́ мариио́вані, борщ украї́нський з пампушка́ми, горі́лка украї́нська з пе́рцем, ковбаса́, ю́шка грибна́,

конья́к "Ай-Пе́трі", шампа́нське напівсухе́, ка́ва з молоко́м, соля́нка осетро́ва, голубці́ овоче́ві, варе́ники

з м'я́сом, омле́т із 3-х яє́ць.

3 You are with a Ukrainian friend Vasyl in the 'Ukraina' restaurant. You know what his likes and dislikes are. Look again at the menu and then answer the questions in Ukrainian:

Васи́ль лю́бить стра́ви з грибі́в, варе́ники з карто́плею.
Він не лю́бить пампушки́ й голубці́. З напо́їв він лю́бить ка́ву
з молоко́м.

i   Що ви́бере Васи́ль із заку́сок?

ii Що він замо́вить із пе́рших страв?

iii Що Васи́ль візьме́ з дру́гих страв?

iv Що він бу́де пи́ти?

4 Greet a friend in Ukrainian:

You	Hi, I haven't seen you for ages (*for nearly a hundred years*)! What's new? What's happened over recent months?
X	Nothing much. I got married and bought a three-roomed flat in the centre of town.
You	I ought to have known! Your life is so quiet!

142

5 Order a meal in Ukrainian:

a What soups do you have? I don't like solyanka.

b You don't have any beer? Do you have a dry white wine?

c I don't eat fish. I would like fried steak with potatoes and salad.

d I'll have the prawns (but without mayonnaise, please), stuffed cabbage leaves and juice of some sort – orange, if you've got it. I don't want a first course.

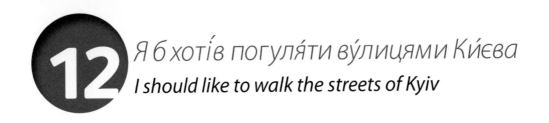

12 Я б хотів погуляти вулицями Києва
I should like to walk the streets of Kyiv

In this unit you will learn:

▶ *Something of Kyiv and its history*
▶ *More about verbs, adverbs and prepositions denoting directions*
▶ *How to be late in Ukrainian*

Діалог 1

TR 13, 00:08

A meeting by the Opera and Ballet Theatre (11.20am).

Стівен	Добрий день, Соломіє. Вибачте, будь ласка, що я запізнився. Я сів не на той тролейбус. Шкода, що Вам довелося чекати.
Соломія	Нічого, не хвилюйтеся. З кожним може статися. То куди Ви заїхали?
Стівен	Я сьогодні виїхав вчасно, сів на двадцятий тролейбус і доїхав до Хрещатика. Там я вийшов на кінцевій зупинці й запитав дорогу до Оперного театру в перехожого. Я йшов швидко, але, на жаль, запізнився на двадцять хвилин.
Соломія	Дарма. Все гаразд. Отже, куди ми сьогодні підемо?
Стівен	Я не знаю . . . Я б хотів погуляти вулицями Києва. Сьогодні такий теплий день. У мене є карта, можна скласти маршрут подорожі . . .
Соломія	Чудово. (*They sit on a bench and open the map*)

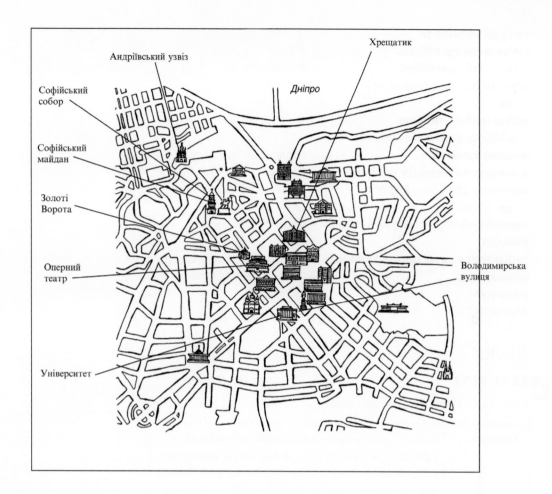

V	
запізни́тися (pf.)	*to be late*
тролéйбус	*trolleybus*
сíсти на тролéйбус	*to get on a trolleybus*
не той тролéйбус	*the wrong trolleybus* (lit.
	not that trolleybus (the trolleybus I needed))
я сів не на той тролéйбус	*I got on the wrong trolleybus*
шкодá	(here:) *it's a pity*
шкодá, що Вам довело́ся чекáти	*it's a pity that you had to wait*
нічо́го!	*it's nothing, it doesn't matter!*
хвилювáтися (-ю́юся, -ю́єшся) (impf.)	*to worry*
стáтися (third-person **стáнеться**) (pf.)	*to happen*
з кóжним мóже стáтися	*it can happen to anyone*
заї́хати (заї́ду, заї́деш) (pf.)	*to get somewhere*

то куди́ Ви заї́хали	so where did you end up?
ви́їхати (ви́їду, ви́їдеш) (pf.)	to leave
двадця́тий троле́йбус	trolleybus no. 20
дої́хати (дої́ду, дої́деш) (pf.) (до + gen.)	to reach, go as far as
ви́йти (ви́йду, ви́йдеш; past tense ви́йшов, ви́йшла, ви́йшли)	(here:) to get out
кінце́ва зупи́нка	terminus (lit. final stop)
я ви́йшов *на* кінце́вій зупи́нці	I got out at the terminus
запита́ти (у/в + gen.) доро́гу (до + gen.)	to ask (someone) the way (to)
перехо́жий (adj. functioning as noun)	passer-by
шви́дко	quickly
запізни́тися *на* два́дцять хвили́н	to be twenty minutes late
дарма́	(here:) it doesn't matter
маршру́т	route
по́дорож (f)	journey

Діало́г 2

 TR 13, 01:17

Solomiia and Stephen start their walk.

Соломі́я	Так. Ми пі́демо гуля́ти по найдавні́шій части́ні мі́ста – Старокиї́вській горі́. Ми за́раз на ву́лиці Володи́мирській. Ми пі́демо ціє́ю ву́лицею повз О́перний теа́тр до Золоти́х ворі́т, що коли́сь служи́ли головно́ю бра́мою – в'ї́здом до Ки́єва. Золоті́ воро́та бу́дуть ось там, ліво́руч. До ре́чі, бі́ля Золоти́х ворі́т за́раз є ста́нція метро́ з тако́ю ж на́звою, ду́же га́рна й нова́. Ви ще її́ не ба́чили?
Сті́вен	Ні. Я вже́ ї́здив на метро́, але́ небага́то.
Соломі́я	Пі́сля Золоти́х ворі́т ми продо́вжимо йти цим же бо́ком ву́лиці, поки́ ді́йдемо до Софі́йського майда́ну. Там ми поди́вимося прекра́сну па́м'ятку архітекту́ри та культу́ри на́шого наро́ду – Софі́йський собо́р.
Сті́вен	Мені́ так ціка́во Вас слу́хати. Ви чудо́во зна́єте істо́рію!
Соломі́я	Я про́сто ду́же люблю́ Ки́їв. Я тут народи́лася і не уявля́ю себе́ без ньо́го у майбу́тньому.
Сті́вен	А ми пі́демо на Андрії́вський узві́з? Мої́ знайо́мі бага́то зга́дували про ньо́го. Я давно́ хо́чу його́ поба́чити.
Соломі́я	Я са́ме туди́ хоті́ла Вас повести́ пі́сля відві́дання Софі́ї.

V **найдавні́ший**	*oldest, most ancient*
части́на	*part*
Старокиї́вська гора́	*Old Kyiv Hill*
повз (+ acc.)	*by, past*
золоти́й	*golden*
воро́та (n pl.: gen.: **ворі́т**)	*gates* (alt **i/o**)
Золоті́ воро́та	*the Golden Gates*
коли́сь	*in former times*
служи́ти (impf.)	*to serve*
головни́й	*main, chief*
бра́ма	*city gate*
ми пі́демо ціє́ю ву́лицею . . .	*we'll go **along** this street to the*
до Золоти́х ворі́т, що	*Golden Gates which served*
служи́ли головно́ю бра́мою	***as** the main gateway . . .*
в'ї́зд (**до** + gen.)	*entry (to)*
на́зва	*name*
з тако́ю ж на́звою	*with the same name*
я вже ї́здив на метро́	*I've already travelled on the metro*
продо́вжити (pf.)	*to continue*
іти́ цим же бо́ком ву́лиці	*to walk on the same side of the street*
по́ки (followed by a pf. verb)	*until*
дійти́ (дійду́, ді́йдеш) (past tense:	*to reach*
дійшо́в, дійшла́, дійшли́) (pf.)	
Софі́йський майда́н	*St Sophia's square*
па́м'ятка	*monument*
архітекту́ра	*architecture*
па́м'ятка архітекту́ри	*listed building* (lit. a monument of architecture)
культу́ра	*culture*
наро́д	*people, nation*
собо́р	*cathedral*
мені́ **так ціка́во Вас слу́хати**	*it is so interesting **for me** to listen to you*
про́сто	*simply*
народи́тися (pf.)	*to be born*
уявля́ти (impf.)	*to imagine, picture*
я не уявля́ю себе́ без ньо́го	*I cannot imagine myself without it [Kyiv]*
майбу́тнє (n. soft adj.)	*the future*

Андрі́ївський узві́з (gen.: **узво́зу**)
зга́дувати (impf.)
**я са́ме туди́ хоті́ла вас повести́
пі́сля відві́дання Софі́ї**

St Andrew's uzviz (alt. **i/o**) (lit. hill, rise)
to recall, mention
*that's **precisely** where I wanted to take you
after visiting St Sophia*

a Пра́вда чи непра́вда?

1 Стівен прийшо́в на зу́стріч вча́сно.

2 Соломі́я та Стівен почина́ють прогу́лянку на Софі́йському майда́ні.

3 У Ки́єві є ста́нція метро́ "Золоті́ воро́та".

4 Стівен хо́че поба́чити Андрі́ївський узві́з.

b Да́йте ві́дповіді на ці запита́ння англі́йською мо́вою

1 How late was Stephen for his meeting?

2 Did Stephen go to his meeting by metro?

3 On what side of Volodymyrs'ka Street will Stephen see the Golden Gates?

4 Why does Solomiia know Kyiv so well?

Як функціону́є мо́ва

1 PRONOUNS

Demonstrative pronouns – цей (*this*), той (*that*)

Here are the declensions in full:

a Masculine and neuter singular

Nom.	Acc.		Gen.	Dat./loc.	Inst.
цей (m)	(inanimate) цей/це		цього́	цьому́	цим
це (n)	(animate) цього́			(у/в, на) цьо́му	
той (m)	(inanimate) той/те		того́	тому́	тим
те (n)	(animate) того́			(у/в, на) то́му	

b Feminine singular

Nom.	Acc.	Gen.	Dat./loc.	Inst.
ця	цю	ціє́ї	цій	ціє́ю
			(у/в, на) цій	
та	ту	тіє́ї	тій	тіє́ю
			(у/в, на) тій	

c Plural (all genders)

Nom.	Acc.	Gen.	Dat.	Loc.	Inst.
ці	ці/цих/ (inanimate) ці, ті	цих	(у/в, на) цих	цим	ци́ми
ті	ті/тих/ (animate) цих, тих	тих	(у/в, на) тих	тим	ти́ми

The demonstrative pronoun **таки́й** (*such, what a ...!* followed by an adjective with exclamation) declines exactly like an adjective:

цей (же) (са́мий)/той (же) (са́мий) – *the same*

таки́й же/таки́й са́мий – *similar*

The pronoun comprises the demonstrative **цей** or **той** together with **же** and **са́мий**. **Цей, той** and **са́мий** decline and change gender according to the case and gender of the noun with which they stand. The pronoun can take any one of three forms:

▶ цей/той же са́мий
▶ цей/той же
▶ цей/той са́мий

They all mean the same thing. But what do we mean by 'same'? If your friend has a pen that looks in all respects identical to your own, you can say: 'You have the same pen as I do.' In Ukrainian, this would be:

У те́бе **така́ са́ма/така́ ж** ру́чка, ак у ме́не.

Таки́й са́мий/таки́й же means 'similar' whereas **цей/той са́мий** means 'selfsame'.

The emphatic pronoun **сам** means '(one)self' and it declines like an adjective, i.e. its nominative feminine, neuter and plural forms are **сама́, само́, самі́:**

Сті́вен *сам* ро́бить пере́клади з украї́нської мо́ви.	Stephen **himself** makes translations from Ukrainian.
Ві́ра *сама́* при́йде.	Vira **herself** will come.

This pronoun always refers to animate beings.

It can also have the meaning 'alone':

Сті́вен живе́ сам.	Stephen lives alone.

And it can form an expression meaning 'one-to-one':

Я бу́ду говори́ти з ним сам на сам.	I will talk to him one-to-one.

The adverbial form **са́ме** means 'namely, exactly, precisely' and emphasizes the word that follows.

Са́мий

> на **са́мому** поча́тку *at the very beginning, right at the beginning*

Са́мий emphasizes the noun that follows:

> Я стоя́в бі́ля са́мої стіни́. *I was standing right by the wall.*

Не той . . . (the wrong . . .)

> Я сів не на **той** троле́йбус. *I got on the wrong trolleybus.*

'Wrong' here means 'not the one that is required'. The Ukrainian equivalent is the demonstrative pronoun **той** preceded by **не**.

2 ADJECTIVES INTO NOUNS

You have already seen some adjectives being used as nouns. Now is a good time for some revision!

Remember: some adjectives are used as nouns. They decline like adjectives and, if they denote human beings, change gender according to the sex of the person signified.

So far you have seen:

перехо́жий	*passer-by* (a female passer-by would be a **перехо́жа**)
знайо́мий	*acquaintance* (a female acquaintance would be a **знайо́ма**)
лю́тий	*February* (**у лю́тому** – *in February*)
майбу́тнє	*the future* (**у майбу́тньому** – *in the future*)
мину́ле	*the past* (**у мину́лому** – *in the past*)
на́бережна	*embankment* (**на на́бережній** – *on the embankment*)
шампа́нське	*champagne* (**нема́є шампа́нського** – *there's no champagne*)

---

3 ALTERNATION OF VOWELS

There have been several words marked in the wordlists with (alt. **i/o**), (alt. **i/e**). Some more revision!

Most of the words you have already seen are nouns and many of them have **i** (**ї**) in the nominative case and **o** (**e/є**) in all the other cases. Here are some examples from previous units:

стіл	**на столі́**	**біль**	**бо́лю** (gen.)
Львів	**у Льво́ві**	**гість**	**го́стя** (gen.)
схід	**на схо́ді**	**бік**	**бо́ку** (gen.)
за́хід	**на за́ході**	**приє́мність**	**приє́мності** (gen.)
пі́вніч	**на пі́вночі**	**річ**	**ре́чі** (gen.)

In some words, the alternation takes place in the genitive plural:

Nom. s.	*Nom. pl.*	*Gen. pl.*
доро́га	**доро́ги**	**дорі́г**
село́	**се́ла**	**сіл**
—	**воро́та**	**ворі́т**

The alternation also takes place in verbs:

стоя́ти	*imperative:*	**стій!**
вести́	*past tense:*	**вів, вела́, вело́, вели́**

The necessary information about the words is given in the vocabulary at the back of the book.

4 ALTERNATION OF CONSONANTS

We have already seen (in Units 6 and 7) how the consonants **г**, **к**, **х** change to ('alternate with') **з**, **ц**, **с** in certain case endings. These notes will help revise and draw your attention to other alternations and the places in which they occur.

There are different sets of alternation.

In verbs

▶ throughout the present tense and related forms of certain first-conjugation verbs, e.g.:

бі́**г**ти – бі**ж**у́	*imperative*	бі**ж**и́, бі**ж**і́ть (alternation **г-ж**)
пла́**к**ати – пла́**ч**у	*imperative*	пла**ч**, пла́**ч**те (*to cry*) (alternation **к-ч**)
пи**с**а́ти – пи**ш**у́	*imperative*	пи**ш**и́, пи**ш**і́ть (alternation **с-ш**)
рі́**з**ати – рі́**ж**у	*imperative*	рі**ж**, рі́**ж**те (*to cut*) (alternation **з-ж**)
хо**т**і́ти – хо́**ч**у		(alternation **т-ч**)

▶ in the first-person singular of second-conjugation verbs, e.g.:

платити – плачу́ – пла́тиш   (alternation **т-ч**)

води́ти – воджу́ – во́диш   (alternation **д-дж**)

проси́ти – прошу́ – про́сиш   (alternation **с-ш**)

вози́ти – вожу́ – во́зиш   (alternation **з-ж**)

і́здити – і́жджу – і́здиш   (alternation **зд-ждж**)

with certain consonants the alternation also takes in the third-person plural, e.g.:

спати – сплю, спиш, сплять (*to sleep*)   (alternation **п-пл**)

люби́ти – люблю́, лю́биш, лю́блять   (alternation **б-бл**)

подиви́тися – подивлю́ся, поди́вишся, поди́вляться (alternation **в-вл**)

▶ in imperfective infinitives formed from perfective ones, e.g.:

запроси́ти – запро́шувати   (alternation **с-ш**)

замо́вити – замовля́ти   (alternation **в-вл**)

In making adjectives, other nouns and verbs from nouns

рі́к – рі́чни́й   (alternation **к-ч**)

друг – дру́жній – дружи́ти   (alternation **г-ж**)

доро́га – по́дорож   (alternation **г-ж**)

проха́ння – проси́ти   (alternation **х-с**; not very common!)

рі́чни́й   *annual*

дру́жній   *amicable, friendly*

проха́ння (n)   *request*

In forming diminutives

рука́ – ру́чка   (alternation **к-ч**)

кві́тка – кві́точка   (alternation **к-ч**)

нога́ – ні́жка   (alternation **г-ж**)

му́ха – му́шка   (alternation **х-ш**)

Alternations also happen in English, although not so obviously because they are not reflected in the spelling. Start with the verb 'sculpt' and add 'or' to get 'sculptor'. Now add 'ure' instead. Do you still pronounce the 't'? Unless you are being incredibly careful, the 't' becomes 'ch', i.e. like the Ukrainian alternation **т-ч**!

5 I'M SORRY I'M LATE

Contrast the tenses: English has a present tense, I am late, whereas in Dialogue 1, Stephen uses the perfective past tense: **я запізнився.** (The imperfective form of **запізнитися** is **запі́знюватися**.)

Compare:

Я поспіша́ю, тому́ що запізнююся **на** по́їзд.	*I am in a hurry because I am late for the train. (i.e. there isn't much time left, but I might still catch it)*
Я запізни́вся **на** по́їзд.	*I missed the train.*

> **LANGUAGE TIP**
> **запі́знюватися (ююся, -юєшся)** (impf.) *to be late*

6 GETTING AROUND

There are no conductors on some buses, trolleybuses and trams in Kyiv. You should buy your tickets (**квитки́** or **тало́ни**) in advance from kiosks on the street. Once on board, you put your **тало́н** into one of the little machines fixed on the sides and push the button. The ticket is valid for a journey of any length on the bus (or trolleybus or tram) on which it was punched. If the bus is packed and you cannot easily get to a punching machine, say: **переда́йте, будь ла́ска, на компо́стер** (*please pass [my ticket] to be punched*) – don't worry, you will get your ticket back! If you fail to show a valid ticket on demand, you will be liable to pay a fine (**штраф**). Ticket inspectors (**контроле́ри**) do not wear uniforms. Most of your fellow passengers will not, in fact, punch a ticket. This is because they have a one-month **проїзни́й** (**квито́к**).

The **метро́** system in Kyiv is new and still expanding. In order to use it, you first have to buy a token (**жето́н**). You insert the token into the slot of one of the automatic barriers and pass through. It is also possible to buy a **магні́тна ка́ртка** (*magnetic swipe card*) for use on the metro.

There are taxis, both state and private (**таксі́**). Always check the fare on the meter (**лічи́льник**). One special form of taxi is the **маршру́тне таксі́**, minibuses that operate on fixed routes but which can be hailed anywhere, not simply at bus stops. You pay the driver when you get on board.

7 ASKING THE WAY

тра́нспорт	*transport (specifically 'public transport')*
авто́бус	*bus*
троле́йбус	*trolleybus*
трамва́й	*tram*
зупи́нка	*stop*

Here are some useful phrases:

Як дістáтися до вýлиці . . .	How can I get to . . . street?
Як доїхати до плóщі . . .	How can I get to . . . square?
Ви мóжете їхати автóбусом нóмер 17.	You can go by a number 17 bus.
Мóжна їхати сімнáдцятим тролéйбусом.	You can go by trolleybus number 17.
Трéба їхати тролéйбусом 19.	You need a number 19 trolleybus.
Трéба/мóжна сíсти на трамвáй нóмер 20.	You can/need to get on a number twenty tram.
Як дійтú до університéту?	How can I get to the university?
Де знахóдиться ресторáн "Дніпрó"?	Where is the Dnipro restaurant?
Ідíть прямо одúн квартáл до магазúну "Квíти", поверніть правóруч і зрáзу побáчите вхід до ресторáну.	Go straight on for one block as far as the florist's shop, turn right and straight away you'll see the entrance to the restaurant.

Note: **Як** + infinitive form **дістáтися/дійтú** (on foot)/**доїхати** (by transport) is the normal way of asking how to get somewhere.

 дістáтися (дістáнуся, дістáнешся) (pf.) (**до** + gen.)   *to get (somewhere)*

повернýти (повернý, повéрнеш) (pf.) imperative: **повернíть!**   *to turn*

On the bus, trolleybus or tram

Де трéба зробúти пересáдку на автóбус нóмер 62?	Where can I change on to a number 62 bus?
Вам трéба пересíсти на зупúнці бíля річковóго вокзáлу.	You need to change at the stop by the river boat station.

 пересíсти (has the same form as **сíсти**) (pf.) **пересідáти** (impf.)   *to change*

(e.g. **з автóбуса на метрó, з тролéйбуса 20 на автóбус 15**)

Public transport is frequently very crowded and you might find yourself a long way from the doors. You are permitted to push your way through by politely asking your fellow passengers:

Ви зáраз вихóдите?	Are you getting off now?
Ви бýдете вихóдити?	Will you be getting off [at the next stop]?
Дозвóльте, будь лáска, пройти́.	Please let me through.

Announcements on the metro

 TR 13, 02:50

Стáнція "Дніпрó". Ви́хід на прáву платфóрму	This is Dnipro station. Exit to the right.
Обережно, двéрі зачиня́ються. Настýпна стáнція "Гідропáрк".	Be careful, the doors are closing. The next station is Hydropark.
Стáнція "Плóща Льва Толстóго". Перехід на стáнцію "Палáц спóрту". Настýпна стáнція "Республікáнський стадіóн".	This is Lev Tolstoy Square station. Change to Palace of Sport station. The next station is Republic Stadium.

стáнція	station
(*Note:* **вокзáл** is a large main-line station)	
ви́хід (gen.: **ви́ходу**)	exit (alt. **i/o**)
прáвий	right
лíвий	left
платфóрма	platform
обережний	careful
зачиня́ти (impf.)	to close (transitive)
зачиня́тися (impf.)	to close (intransitive)
перехід (gen.: **перехóду**)	transfer, crossing (alt. **i/o**)

? Test yourself: Впра́ви

1 Read through the announcements that you will hear on the metro in section 7. Now look at the map of Kyiv underground system and write down what announcements might be made on the section of route that runs between "Вокза́льна" and "Арсена́льна" stations. At all stations on this section, passengers leave the carriages on the left-hand side; at "Хреща́тик" station you can transfer to "Майда́н Незале́жності" station and at "Театра́льна" station you can transfer to "Золоті́ воро́та" station:

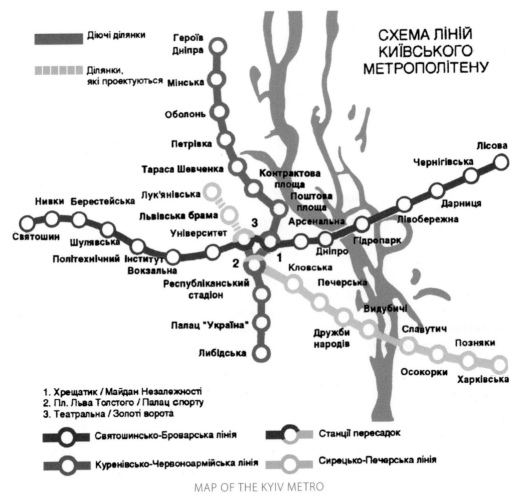

Діючі ділянки

Ділянки, які проектуються

СХЕМА ЛІНІЙ КИЇВСЬКОГО МЕТРОПОЛІТЕНУ

Героїв Дніпра
Мінська
Оболонь
Петрівка
Тараса Шевченка
Лук'янівська
Львівська брама
Університет
Нивки Берестейська
Святошин
Шулявська
Політехнічний інститут
Вокзальна
Республіканський стадіон
Палац "Україна"
Либідська

Контрактова площа
Поштова площа
Арсенальна
Дніпро
Кловська
Печерська
Дружби народів

Лісова
Чернігівська
Дарниця
Лівобережна
Гідропарк
Видубичі
Славутич
Познякі
Осокорки
Харківська

1. Хрещатик / Майдан Незалежності
2. Пл. Льва Толстого / Палац спорту
3. Театральна / Золоті ворота

Святошинсько-Броварська лінія

Куренівсько-Червоноармійська лінія

Станції пересадок

Сирецько-Печерська лінія

MAP OF THE KYIV METRO

2 Answer the following questions, using the possessive pronoun in brackets in the necessary case:

Приклад: Чиїм автомобілем ми поїдемо в гості (Мій)

Ми поїдемо в гості моїм автомобілем.

a Чию́ соба́ку звуть Ро́за? (наш)

b Чиїй до́ньці 12 ро́ків? (моя́)

c Чий телеві́зор учо́ра зіпсува́вся? (її)

3 Put the word in brackets into the required case – don't forget vowel alternation!

a Ба́тько живе́ на (схід) Украї́ни.

b Літа́к лети́ть пря́мо на (за́хід).

c У Карпа́тах бага́то (гора́).

d Моє́му си́нові ві́сім (рік).

4 Put the verbs in brackets into the required forms of the present tense:

a Мико́ла (хоті́ти) леті́ти до Пра́ги літако́м, а я за́вжди (ї́здити) по́їздом.

b Я не (могти́) купи́ти словни́к, бо я ніко́ли не (носи́ти) вели́кі кни́ги в рука́х.

c Я (проси́ти) тебе́ замо́вити дороге́ вино́, я сього́дні (плати́ти).

d Він за́раз (писа́ти) лист дружи́ні, що не (могти́) приї́хати в се́рпні.

5 Stephen and Solomiia continue their walk through old Kyiv by going down the street called *Andriyivs'ky uzviz*.

Приміт́ка: **Андрі́ївський узві́з** could be translated as St Andrew's Hill, but strictly speaking the word **узві́з** refers to the road by which goods were transported (**віз**, related to **вози́ти**) up (the meaning of the prefix **уз-**) the hill from Podil on the river Dnipro:

Стівен	Соломіє, Андрі́ївська це́рква – там?
Соломія	Так. Ми перейдемо́ че́рез пло́щу й за де́сять хвили́н бу́демо бі́ля Андрі́ївської це́ркви, яка́ стоі́ть на па́горбі, на са́мому поча́тку Андрі́ївського узво́зу. На узво́зі є бага́то карти́нних галере́й та худо́жніх сало́нів.
Стівен	Але́ сього́дні – вихідни́й день. Худо́жні сало́ни сього́дні працю́ють?
Соломія	Там бу́де бага́то худо́жників, що продаю́ть свої́ карти́ни. Ціє́ю га́рною ву́лицею ми спу́стимося на По́діл – стари́й і ду́же ціка́вий райо́н мі́ста. Там по́руч Дніпро́ і на́бережна.
Стівен	А мо́жна по́тім підня́тися фунікуле́ром на Володи́мирську гі́рку?
Соломія	Ми так і зро́бимо. Володи́мирська гі́рка – це чудо́ве мі́сце для прогу́лянок. Чи́сте пові́тря, густа́ зе́лень, га́рні але́ї, прекра́сний вид на рíку́.

V за де́сять хвили́н		*in ten minutes*
па́горб		*hill*
на са́мому поча́тку		*at the very beginning*
карти́нна галере́я		*picture gallery*
худо́жній сало́н		*artist's salon*
спусти́тися (спущу́ся, спу́стишся) (pf.) (**на** + acc.)		*to descend, go down (to)*
Поді́л (gen.: **Подо́лу**)		*Podil (the low town)* (alt. **i/o**)
райо́н		*district*
Дніпро́		*Dnipro (the river on which Kyiv stands)*
на́бережна (f adj.)		*embankment*
підня́тися (підніму́ся, підні́мешся) (pf.) (**на** + acc.)		*to ascend, go up (to)*
гі́рка		*hill, small mountain*
Володи́мирська гі́рка		*St Volodymyr's hill*
чи́стий		*pure, clean*
пові́тря (n)		*air*
густи́й		*thick*
але́я		*avenue*
вид (**на** + acc.)		*view (of)*

INDEPENDENCE SQUARE, KYIV.

13 Я привíз пропозúції щóдо ствóрення спíльного підприємства

I have brought proposals for the creation of a joint venture

In this unit you will learn:
▸ *About the conditional forms of verbs*
▸ *About the comparative and superlative degrees of adjectives*
▸ *Something about conducting business talks and going shopping for clothes*

Діалóг 1

 TR 14, 00:10

(*Note*: the style of these dialogues is intentionally much more formal than in previous texts. Stephen is therefore referred to as **Тéйлор**.)

In Solomiia Maliarchuk's office.

Малярчýк	Я мáю приéмність привітáти Вас в óфісі нáшої фíрми. Мóжемо відрáзу розпочáти робóту. Я вжé підготувáла пакéт докумéнтів, які мóжуть полéгшити нáшу прáцю. Íгоре Івáновічу, покажíть, будь лáска, нáшому гóстю підготóвлені папéри.
Тéйлор	Дякую за гостúнний прийóм.
Стáхів	Це пропозúції нáшого фінáнсового віддíлу, перéлік фáбрик, які мóжна включúти до нáшого проéкту. Це розрахýнки кóштів, потрíбних для модернізáції фáбрик і закупíвлі облáднання. Ось дáні про мерéжу магазúнів в Украíні та íнших краíнах, які могли б бýти зацікáвлені у співробітництві з нáми.
Тéйлор	Це дýже важлúва інформáція. На жáль, я не мóжу зáраз глúбше ознайóмитися з розрахýнками чéрез брак чáсу. Я вúсловлю своí міркувáння під час нáших настýпних зýстрічей, коли детáльно вúвчу ці матеріáли. Я такóж привíз письмóві пропозúції щóдо ствóрення спíльного підприємства і можлúвих джерéл фінансувáння проéкту. Ось для Вáшого рóзгляду плáни капіталовклáдень і можлúвості одéржати пóзику в бáнках дéяких краíн Європéйського Сою́зу.

160

V **пропози́ція** (**що́до** + gen.)	proposal (for)
честь (f.)	honour
привіта́ти (pf.)	to welcome
відра́зу	at once
розпоча́ти (**розпочну́**, **розпочне́ш**) (pf.)	to begin
підготува́ти (-**у́ю**, -**у́єш**) (pf.)	to prepare
полéгшити (pf.)	to make easier
пра́ця	work
підгото́влений	prepared
підгото́влені папéри	the papers that have been prepared
гости́нний	hospitable
прийо́м	reception
фіна́нсовий	financial
фіна́нсовий ві́дділ	finance department
перéлік	list
фа́брика	factory
включи́ти (pf.) (до + gen.)	to include (in)
проéкт	project
перéлік фа́брик, які́ мо́жна включи́ти до на́шого проéкту	a list of factories that can be included in our project
розраху́нок (gen.: **розраху́нку**)	calculation
кошт	cost, expense
потрі́бний (**для** + gen.)	necessary (for)
модерніза́ція	modernization
закупі́вля	(bulk) purchase
обла́днання (n)	equipment
да́ні (pl. adj.)	data
мерéжа	net, network
магази́н	shop
зацікáвити (**зацікáвлю**, **зацікáвиш**, **зацікáвлять**) (у/в + loc.) (pf.)	to interest [someone] (in)
співробі́тництво	collaboration
магази́ни, які́ могли́ бу́ти зацікáвлені у співробі́тництві	shops that might be interested in collaboration
важли́вий	important
на жа́ль	unfortunately
гли́бше	more deeply
ознайо́митися (з + inst.)	to familiarize oneself (with)
чéрез (+ acc.)	(here:) because of
брак	shortage
чéрез брак ча́су	because of a shortage of time

ви́словити (ви́словлю, ви́словиш, ви́словлять) (pf.)	to express
міркува́ння (n)	consideration
дета́льно	in detail
ви́вчити (pf.)	to study
коли́ я ви́вчу ці матеріа́ли	when I have studied these materials
письмо́вий	written
можли́вий	possible
джерело́	source
фінансува́ння (n)	financing
ро́згляд	scrutiny, inspection
капіталовкла́дення (n)	capital investment
можли́вість (gen.: **можли́вості**) (f)	possibility (alt. **i/o**)
по́зика	loan
можли́вість оде́ржати по́зику	the possibilty of receiving a loan
європе́йський	European
сою́з	union

Як функціону́є мо́ва

1 VERBS

More on aspect

Stephen is going to put forward his views when he has studied the proposals:

> Стı́вен **ви́словить** свої́
> міркува́ння, коли́ він
> **ви́вчить** пропози́ції.
>
> (lit. when he **will have studied**)

In English, a type of past tense is used after 'when'; Ukrainian uses the **perfective future** to denote the idea of completion of one action in the future before the next action – expressing his opinion – can begin.

Conditional

The conditional forms of verbs express:

▶ the **possibility** or **probability** of something happening if certain conditions are fulfilled, e.g.:

> Я б прийшо́в, якби́ я мав час.
> *I would come, if I had the time.*

▶ a **very polite form** of making requests, e.g.:

> Я б хотı́в ... Ви могли́ б ...?
> *I should like ... Would you please ...?*
>
> Чи не мо́жна було́ б ...?
> *Would it (not) be possible ...?*

The conditional mood is formed by adding the particle **би/б** as a separate word to the forms of the past tense, e.g.:

```
┌─────────────────────────────────────────────────────────────────┐
│  хотíти                                                           │
│                                                                   │
│  я хотíв би/хотíла б            ми хотíли б                        │
│  ти хотíв би/хотíла б           ви хотíли б                        │
│  він хотíв би                                                      │
│  вона хотíла б                  вони хотíли б                      │
│  воно хотíло б                                                     │
└─────────────────────────────────────────────────────────────────┘
```

Just as in the past tense, a verb in the conditional mood changes for gender and number, but not person. The particle **би/б** can stand either after or before the verb form, e.g.:

> Вонá хотíла **б**
>
> Вонá **б** хотíла

The form of the particle – **би** or **б** – depends on the preceding sound. If it is a consonant, use **би**; if it is a vowel, use **б**, e.g.:

> Я замóвив **би**
>
> Я **б** замóвив

▶ if

'If' is a very important word for conditional sentences.

a In Unit 4, you met one Ukrainian equivalent: **якщó**. **Якщó** is used to denote a condition that may well be fulfilled, e.g.:

Якщó Стíвен мáтиме час,	*If Stephen has the time, he*
він пої́де до Львóва.	*will go to L'viv.*
Якщó бýде дощ, я не прийдý.	*If it rains, I won't come.*

Note: compare the tense of the verbs after 'if' (present) and **якщó** (future).

Якщó is sometimes reduced to **як** in speech:

Як бýдеш у Лóндоні,	*If you're in London,*
зателефонýй.	*phone me.*

b There are some conditions that are unlikely to be fulfilled, e.g.:

> *If Stephen had the time, he would go to Turin.* (with the implication that he won't have the time).
>
> *If it had rained, I would not have come.* (but it didn't, so I came).

In such sentences, we need a different word for 'if' in Ukrainian: **якби.** This word consists of two elements, **як + би**; the presence of the conditional particle **би** means that the verb automatically goes into the past tense:

> Якби Стíвен **мав** час, він би пої́хав до Турина.
> Якби **був** дощ, я б не прийшóв/прийшлá.

► in order to

The phrase **щоб нала́годити виробни́цтво** (*in order to arrange production*) occurs in Dialogue 2. Here **щоб** (**що** + **б**) is followed by an infinitive. There are times, however, when it will be followed by the **past tense** of a verb:

Я б хоті́в, щоб Ви зателефонува́ли мені́.	*I would like you to phone me.* (lit. I would like that you should phone me)
Соломі́я сказа́ла Ігореві Іва́новичу, щоб він **замо́вив** два но́мери в готе́лі.	*Solomiia told Ihor Ivanovych to book two rooms in the hotel.* (lit. that he should book)

Note that the subjects in the two parts of each of these sentences are different.

2 ADJECTIVES

Degrees of comparison

There are three degrees of comparison:

(1) The **positive** degree, which serves simply to describe the noun to which it refers (the big house):

вели́кий буди́нок

(2) The **comparative** degree, which is used to make a comparison between two objects, e.g.:

Цей буди́нок **бі́льший**, **ніж** той.	*This building is **bigger** than that one.*

(3) The **superlative** degree, used to make a comparison between several objects on the basis on one criterion, e.g.:

Цей буди́нок – **найбі́льший** у мі́сті.	*This building is the **biggest** in town.*

Formation of the comparative and superlative degrees of comparison

Comparative Degree

The comparative degree is formed by inserting the suffix **-іш-** or **-ш-** before the adjectival ending, e.g.:

до́брий	добр**і**ший	*kinder**
приє́мний	приє́мн**і**ший	*more pleasant*
прости́й	прост**і**ший	*simpler*
деше́вий	деше́**в**ший	*cheaper*
молоди́й	моло́д**ш**ий	*younger, junior*
стари́й	ста́р**ш**ий	*older, elder, senior*

---

* The adjective **до́брий** was introduced in Unit 1 meaning 'good'; it also means 'kind' and in this meaning only the comparative is **добрі́ший**. (See below for the comparative form of **до́брий** (*good*).)

In some adjectives, the addition of the comparative suffix causes certain changes, e.g.:

важки́й	ва́жчий	*heavier, more difficult*
висо́кий	ви́щий	*higher, taller*
вузьки́й	ву́жчий	*narrower*
глибо́кий	гли́бший	*deeper*
дале́кий	да́льший	*more distant, further off*
до́вгий	до́вший	*longer*
дороги́й	доро́жчий	*dearer*
коро́ткий	коро́тший	*shorter*
легки́й	ле́гший	*lighter, easier*
низьки́й	ни́жчий	*lower*
швидки́й	шви́дший	*quicker*
широ́кий	ши́рший	*wider, broader*

глибо́кий	*deep*
дале́кий	*distant*
швидки́й	*quick*

Other useful comparatives:

бага́то	*a lot of*	бі́льше (+ gen.)	*more*
ма́ло	*a little, few*	ме́нше (+ gen.)	*fewer, less*

The word **ніж** is used between the items being compared; it is exactly equivalent to English 'than'. Another way is to use the preposition **від** and the genitive case, or the preposition **за** and the accusative case, e.g.:

Брат ста́рший від ме́не.	*My brother is older than I am.*
Дніпро́ ши́рший за Те́мзу. (Те́мза)	*The Dnipro is wider than the Thames.*

(*Note*: the Dnipro, despite appearances, is masculine.)

The comparative form can be emphasized in English by the addition of 'much', 'far', 'considerably', 'yet' or 'even', e.g. my car is much faster/that film was even better. The equivalent words in Ukrainian are:

дале́ко, бага́то/набага́то	*much*
куди́	*far*
зна́чно	*considerably*
ще	*yet*
на́віть	*even*

Цей фільм **ще цікаві́ший**.   *This film is even more interesting.*

Ріка́ Дніпро́ **зна́чно гли́бша**,   *The river Dnipro is far deeper*
   ніж Те́мза.   *than the Thames.*

> **LANGUAGE TIP**
> The comma after the comparative form and before **ніж** is compulsory in written Ukrainian.

Superlative degree

The superlative degree is formed by adding the prefix **най-** to the form of the comparative degree, e.g.:

до́брий	добрі́ший	**най**добрі́ший	*kindest*
приє́мний	приє́мні́ший	**най**приє́мніший	*pleasantest*
молоди́й	моло́дший	**най**моло́дший	*youngest*

Some comparative and superlative forms are quite different from their corresponding positive forms (compare in English: good – better – best; bad – worse – worst):

вели́кий	бі́льший	найбі́льший	*bigger*	*biggest*
до́брий (*good*)	кра́щий	найкра́щий	*better*	*best*
мале́нький	ме́нший	найме́нший	*smaller*	*smallest*
пога́ний	гі́рший	найгі́рший	*worse*	*worst*

> **LANGUAGE TIP**
> **пога́ний** *bad*

The superlative degree can also be formed by using **найбі́льш** before the positive form of the adjective, e.g.:

Ця кни́га найбі́льш ціка́ва.   *This book is the most interesting one.*

Of course, the book could be the least interesting one:

Ця кни́га **найме́нш** ціка́ва.

Діалóг 2

 TR 14, 01:53

Малярчýк	Пропонýю перейти до конкрéтних аспéктів нáшого контрáкту. Напри́клад, скі́льки, на Вáшу дýмку, трéба бýло б модернізувáти фáбрик в Украї́ні, щоб налáгодити виробни́цтво óдягу за вáшими технолóгіями?
Тéйлор	Я вважáю, що потрі́бно бýде дві фáбрики для виробни́цтва жінóчого óдягу, однá – що спеціалі-зýється на пошитті́ чоловíчого óдягу, і однé підприє́мство, якé виробля́є аксесуáри. Я такóж хотíв би включи́ти до нáшого проéкту тексти́льну фáбрику, щоб одéржувати я́кісні ткани́ни.
Малярчýк	Ми не пови́нні забувáти про ви́трати на транспортувáння і рекламý нáшої продýкції, а такóж на електроенéргію і страхувáння.
Тéйлор	Я візьмý на сéбе переговóри з можли́вими інвéсторами. Сподівáюся полáгодити ці питáння найбли́жчим чáсом.
Малярчýк	Ми мóжемо продóвжити цю розмóву пíсля Вáшої пої́здки до Львóва, де Ви познайóмитеся з генерáльним дирéктором однiєї з фáбрик.

конкрéтний	*concrete*
аспéкт	*aspect*
контрáкт	*contract*
напри́клад	*for example*
дýмка	*thought, opinion*
на Вáшу дýмку	*in your opinion*
модернізувáти (-ýю, -ýєш) (impf.)	*to modernize*
скíльки трéба бýло б модернізувáти фáбрик?	*how many factories should be modernized?* (lit. . . .would it be necessary to modernize)
налáгодити (налáгоджу, налáгодиш) (pf.)	*to arrange*
за (preposition followed by instr.)	(here:) *by means of*
технолóгія	*technology*
спеціалізувáтися (-ýюся, -ýєшся) (на + loc.) (impf.)	*to specialize (in)*
пошиття́ (n)	*sewing*
виробля́ти (impf.)	*to produce*
аксесуáри	*accessories*
тексти́льний	*textile (adj.)*
тексти́льна фáбрика	*textile factory*
щоб	*in order to*

одéржувати (-ую, -уєш) (impf.)	to obtain, receive
я́кісний	high quality
ткани́на	cloth
ви́трата (на + acc.)	expenditure (on)
транспортува́ння (n)	transportation
рекла́ма	advertising, advertisement
електроенéргія	electrical energy
страхува́ння (n)	insurance
я візьму́ на сéбе . . .	I shall take upon myself
інвéстор	investor
сподіва́тися	to hope
пола́годити (пола́годжу, пола́годиш) (pf.)	to settle
найбли́жчим ча́сом	in the very near future

a Пра́вда чи непра́вда?

1 Ста́хів пока́зує Сті́венові пропози́ції що́до ство́рення страхово́ї компа́нії.

2 Сті́вен привíз папéри стосóвно можли́вості одéржати пóзику у ба́нках.

3 Майбу́тнє спíльне підприємство бу́де виробля́ти óдяг за суча́сними зарубíжними технолóгіями.

4 Організа́тори спíльного підприємства не пови́нні забува́ти про рекла́му.

b Да́йте відповіді на ці запита́ння англíйською мóвою

1 What did Solomiia prepare for the business meeting?

2 How many factories will produce women's clothes?

3 Does Stephen suggest that the joint enterprise should buy good-quality cloth or make its own?

4 Who is going to conduct the negotiations with potential investors?

3 PRONOUNS

The reflexive pronoun себé

The case forms of this pronoun are very similar to those of the second-person singular pronoun **ти**, except that it has no nominative case:

Nom.		—
Acc.		себé
Gen.		себé
Dat.		собі́
Loc.	(на)	собі́
Instr.		собóю

Reflexive pronouns in English look like this:

I can see **myself** in the mirror.

You look pleased with **yourself/yourselves.**

She locked **herself** out of the house.

In Ukrainian, there is only the one reflexive pronoun, **себе́**: it always derives its meaning from the subject of the sentence in which it occurs, e.g.:

Я візьму́ на *себе цю робо́ту.	*I'll take this job upon **myself**.*
Сті́вен ві́зьме на *себе цю робо́ту.	*Stephen will take this job upon* ***himself***.
Я приві́з із собо́ю пропози́ції.	*I've brought the proposals with **me**.*
Сті́вен приві́з із собо́ю пропози́ції.	*Stephen brought the proposals with **him**.*

---

* *Note:* stress change.

❓ Test yourself: Впра́ви

(Check any unfamiliar words in the vocabulary at the back of the book.)

1 You are out shopping. Say what you want to buy by removing the brackets and making any necessary grammatical changes:

Example: Я хо́чу (сі́рий, пальто́) = Я хо́чу сі́ре пальто́.

Я хо́чу купи́ти сі́ре пальто́.

Я ма́ю купи́ти сі́ре пальто́.

Мені́ тре́ба купи́ти сі́ре пальто́.

Я хо́чу	(чо́рний	пла́ття)
Я хо́чу	(кори́чневий	штани́)
Я хо́чу	(зеле́ний	дже́мпер)
Я хо́чу купи́ти	(бі́лий/жо́втий	футбо́лка)
Я хо́чу купи́ти	(си́ній	пла́вки)
Я хо́чу купи́ти	(чо́рний	колго́ти)
Я хо́чу купи́ти	(сі́рий	костю́м)
Я ма́ю купи́ти	(ора́нжевий	шо́рти)
Я ма́ю купи́ти	(вели́кий	светр)
Я ма́ю купи́ти	(мале́нький	парасо́лька)
Мені́ тре́ба купи́ти	(мали́новий	спідни́ця)
Мені́ тре́ба купи́ти	(блаки́тний	плащ)
Мені́ тре́ба купи́ти	(фіоле́товий	су́мка)

2 Say what you would like to exchange, try on or buy by removing the brackets and making any necessary grammatical changes:

Example: Де я мо́жу поміня́ти (гро́ші)? = Де я мо́жу поміня́ти гро́ші?

поміня́ти

a

Де я мо́жу поміня́ти (до́лари)?

Де я мо́жу поміня́ти (су́кня)?

Де я мо́жу поміня́ти (костю́м)?

Де я мо́жу поміня́ти (крава́тка)?

помі́ряти

b

Де я мо́жу помі́ряти (плащ)?

Де я мо́жу помі́ряти (соро́чка)?

Де я мо́жу помі́ряти (ку́ртка)?

Де я мо́жу помі́ряти (окуля́ри)?

купи́ти

c

Де я мо́жу купи́ти (бі́лий папі́р)?

Де я мо́жу купи́ти (чо́рний ру́чка)?

Де я мо́жу купи́ти (вели́кий портфе́ль)?

Де я мо́жу купи́ти (черво́ний олівець)?

Де я мо́жу купи́ти (мале́нький магнітофо́н)?

Де я мо́жу купи́ти (па́ра шкарпе́тки)?

3 Now say what you like or dislike wearing:

Я (не) ношу́   (кори́чневий), (зеле́ний)   ко́лір

Я (не) люблю́   (бі́лий), (мали́новий)

Я (не) одяга́ю   (си́ній), (фіоле́товий)

Мені́ (не) подо́бається   (ора́нжевий), (жо́втий)

                        (блакти́тний), (сі́рий)

4 **Situations in which you can practise your Ukrainian:**

   a   Tell your colleague that because of illness you have not brought with you the papers on the setting up of a new company.

   b   You are in a bookshop in Kyiv. You say that you would like to buy a book about Ukraine for your wife/husband.

   c   Your Ukrainian friend asks you to go with him/her to buy clothes. Ask him/her about sizes and colours.

5 **Practise the comparative and superlative forms of adjectives. Put the following sentences into Ukrainian:**

   a   I need a cheaper room.

   b   There isn't a cheaper one. You're already living in the cheapest room in the hotel.

   c   I would like to change this blouse (**блу́зка**). It is too small for my wife – she needs a bigger one.

   d   What is the name of the deepest lake (**о́зеро**) in Ukraine?

   e   Ukrainian is a lot simpler than I thought!

6 **Make the following sentences conditional. Check which word for 'if' is being used:**

   Example: (Я подорожу́ю із сім'є́ю), якби́ я мав час.

   Я подорожува́в би із сім'є́ю, якби́ я мав час.

   a   (Оле́на ди́виться телеві́зор), якщо́ вона́ ма́тиме час.

   b   (Оле́г пока́же нам мі́сто), якщо́ бу́де мати час.

   c   (Сусі́д працю́є такси́стом), якби́ мав права́ (here: *drivers' licence*).

   d   (Ону́чка допомага́є бабу́сі), якби бабу́ся жила́ не так дале́ко.

7 **Rephrase the following sentences by replacing the underlined word(s) with Я хоті́в би (*I would like*), making any other changes that are necessary:**

   a   <u>Мо́жемо</u> відра́зу розпоча́ти робо́ту.

   b   <u>Я</u> ви́словлю свої́ міркува́ння під час на́ших насту́пних зу́стрічей.

   c   <u>Пропону́ю</u> перейти́ до конкре́тних аспе́ктів на́шого контра́кту.

   d   <u>Я</u> візьму́ на се́бе перегово́ри з можли́вими інве́сторами.

   e   <u>Ми мо́жемо</u> продо́вжити цю розмо́ву пі́сля Ва́шої пої́здки. Insight

The comma after the comparative form and before **ніж** is compulsory in written Ukrainian.

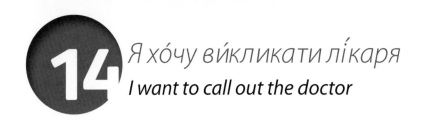

14 Я хо́чу ви́кликати лі́каря
I want to call out the doctor

In this unit you will learn:

▸ *How to describe common ailments*
▸ *Something about the medical service in Ukraine*
▸ *About impersonal verbs*
▸ *How to form the comparative and superlative degrees of adverbs*

Діало́г 1

 TR 15, 00:07

Conversation on the telephone.

О́льга	Алло́, це полікли́ніка? Я хо́чу ви́кликати лі́каря.
Чергова́ в реєстрату́рі	Прі́звище хво́рого.
О́льга	Ста́хів.
Чергова́ в реєстрату́рі	Ім'я́ та по-ба́тькові . . .
О́льга	Íгор Іва́нович.
Чергова́ в реєстрату́рі	Рік наро́дження . . .
О́льга	1951-й.
Чергова́ в реєстрату́рі	На що ска́ржиться?
О́льга	Температу́ра 38,5, боли́ть го́рло, ва́жко ковта́ти, не́жить, зага́льна сла́бість, його́ лихома́нить.
Чергова́ в реєстрату́рі	Ваш ви́клик прийня́то. Чека́йте лі́каря у пе́ршій полови́ні дня. По́ки що дава́йте хво́рому бага́то пи́ти.

полікли́ніка	*health centre*
ви́кликати (pf.)	*to call out*
лі́кар (gen.: **лі́каря**)	*doctor*
черговий	*successive, next*
	(as noun:) *person on duty*
чергова́	*female duty receptionist*
реєстрату́ра	*registration*
хво́рий	*sick; patient* (noun)
ска́ржитися (impf.) (**на** + acc.)	*to complain (of)*

174

болі́ти (impf.) (third-person singular: **боли́ть**; pl. **боля́ть**)	*to hurt*	
го́рло	*throat*	
боли́ть го́рло	*[his] throat hurts, i.e. he has a sore throat*	
ва́жко	*[it is] difficult*	
ковта́ти (impf.)	*to swallow*	
ва́жко ковта́ти	*[it is] difficult [for him] to swallow, swallowing is difficult*	
не́жить (m)	*cold (in the head)*	
зага́льний	*general*	
слабість (gen.: **слабості**) (f)	*weakness* (alt. **і/о**)	
лихома́нити (impf.) (impersonal verb)	*to feel feverish*	
його́ лихома́нить	*he feels feverish*	
ви́клик	*call*	
прийня́ти (**прийму́, при́ймеш**) (pf.)	*to receive, accept, take*	
ваш ви́клик при́йнято	*your call has been accepted*	
по́ки що	*for the time being*	

Як функціону́є мо́ва

1 NOUNS

More on declension – лі́кар

You can see from the title of the dialogue that the accusative/genitive of the noun **лі́кар** is **лі́каря**, as if the consonant **р** were soft. Just treat the word as a bit of grammatical oddity. Here are all the forms of the singular and plural:

	S.	Pl.
Nom.	лі́кар	лікарі́
Acc.	лі́каря	лікарі́в
Gen.	лі́каря	лікарі́в
Dat.	лі́кареві, лі́карю	лікаря́м
Loc.	(на) лі́кареві, лі́карі	лікаря́х
Inst.	лі́карем	лікаря́ми

Another noun that declines like this is **кобза́р** (gen.: **кобзаря́**), a singer who accompanies himself (they are always men!) on the traditional Ukrainian stringed instrument, the **ко́бза**. Shevchenko's first book of poetry, published in 1840, was entitled *Кобза́р*.

Ihor's name also changes in this way: **Я ба́чу Íгоря**. Not all nouns that end in **-р** decline in this way; check the vocabulary at the back of the book.

2 WHO HAS THE SORE THROAT?

Боли́ть гóрло – [his] throat hurts

It is clear from the context that it is Stakhiv who has the sore throat. If you need to be more precise you can say:

У мéне боли́ть гóрло.	*I have a sore throat.*
У тéбе боли́ть головá?	*Do you have a headache?*
У Соломíї боли́ть гóрло.	*Solomiia has a sore throat.*
У ньóго боля́ть зýби.	*He has toothache.*

Note the word order: it is usual for the verb **боли́ть/боля́ть** to stand before the part of the body that hurts.

Діалóг 2

In the chemist's shop after the doctor's visit.

Остáп	Я хóчу замóвити лíки на сьогóдні. Ось рецéпт.
Жíнка-фармацéвт	Так . . . Мікстýра бýде готóва о четвéртій годи́ні, а таблéтки мóжете одéржати відрáзу.
Остáп	Скíльки плати́ти?
Жíнка-фармацéвт	Платíть до кáси. Ось сýма.
(Ostap goes over to the cashier, pays and returns with a receipt)	
Остáп	Прóшу. *(Hands over the receipt)*
Жíнка-фармацéвт	Ось таблéтки, а це Вáша квитáнція на мікстýру. Лíки мóжна одéржати з четвéртої до сьóмої.
Остáп	Дя́кую.

рецéпт	*prescription*
фармацéвт	*pharmacist*
мікстýра	*liquid medicine, mixture*
таблéтка	*tablet*
плати́ти до кáси (кáса)	*to pay at the cash desk*

Діало́г 3

TR 15, 00:57

A conversation that evening.

Óльга	Як ти за́раз себé почува́єш?
Íгор	Дя́кую, тро́хи кра́ще, алé менé чому́сь моро́зить . . .
Óльга	Ти ви́пив лі́ки?
Íгор	Так, ужé дві́чі. О́лю, ну чому́ менí так не щасти́ть? Коли́ бага́то робо́ти і важли́во бу́ти в до́брій фо́рмі, я ра́птом захворі́в . . . Я ще вчо́ра відчува́в, що менé ну́дить, і голова́ була́ гаря́ча. Мені́ здава́лося, що я про́сто сто́млений.
Óльга	Ти про́сто підхопи́в ві́рус. Нічо́го, все ско́ро бу́де гара́зд. Тобі́ тре́ба відпочи́ти. Ужé смерка́є. Постара́йся поспа́ти.
Íгор	Мені́ не спи́ться, го́рло боли́ть.
Óльга	Тоді́ про́сто поле́ж, відпочи́нь. Твоя́ робо́та тебé почека́є.

почува́ти себé	*to feel (well, ill, etc.)*
як ти за́раз себé почува́єш?	*how do you feel now?*
чому́сь	*for some reason*
моро́зити (impf.)	*to chill (here used impersonally)*
менé моро́зить	*I feel chilled*
дві́чі	*twice*
щасти́ти (impf.) (impersonal verb)	*to be fortunate*
чому́ менí так не щасти́ть?	*why am I so unlucky?*
фо́рма	*form, condition*
важли́во бу́ти у до́брій фо́рмі	*it is important to be in good shape*
ра́птом	*suddenly*
захворі́ти (захворі́ю, захворі́єш) (pf.)	*to fall ill*
відчува́ти (impf.)	*to feel, be aware*
ну́дити (impf.) (here used impersonally)	*to feel sick*
менé ну́дить	*I feel sick*
гаря́чий	*hot*
підхопи́ти (підхоплю́, підхо́пиш), (pf.)	*to pick up*
ві́рус	*virus*
нічо́го	(here:) *never mind*
ско́ро	*soon*
відпочи́ти (відпочи́ну, відпочи́неш) (pf.) (second person singular imperative: **відпочи́нь**)	*to have a rest*

смерка́ти (impf.) (impersonal verb)	*to get dark*
постара́тися (pf.) (second person singular imperative: **постара́йся**)	*to try*
поспа́ти (посплю́, поспи́ш, . . . поспля́ть) (pf.)	*to get some sleep, take a nap*
мені́ не спи́ться	*I can't get to sleep*
тоді́	*then, in that case*
почека́ти (pf.)	*to wait for a bit*

a Пра́вда чи непра́вда?

1 В Íгоря боли́ть зуб.

2 Оста́п замовля́є лі́ки в апте́ці.

3 Лі́ки мо́жна оде́ржати за́втра.

4 Íгореві не спи́ться.

b Да́йте ві́дповіді на ці запита́ння англі́йською мо́вою

1 When will the doctor come to visit Stakhiv?

2 What kind of medicine was prescribed for Stakhiv?

3 Why does Ostap have to return to the chemist's shop?

4 Who advises Stakhiv to drink a lot of water?

3 VERBS

More on tense

Я ще вчо́ра відчува́в, що мене́ ну́дить.	*Yesterday, I already felt that I was sick.*

Contrast the tense forms in the English and Ukrainian sentences. There are two verbs in both: **я відчува́в** (*I felt*) and **мене́ ну́дить** (*I felt sick*). The second verb is in the present tense in Ukrainian, but it is in the past tense in English. Ukrainian preserves the tense at the actual moment of feeling. 'What was I feeling? – I feel sick.' It would also be possible to say: **Я ще вчо́ра відчува́в, що мене́ нуди́ло**.

More on aspect

The dialogue contains several examples of perfective verbs with the prefix **по-**, all of which denote performing the action for a little while:

поспа́ти	*to have a sleep, nap*
поле́жати	*to lie down for a bit, to have a lie down*
почека́ти	*to wait for a little while*

The prefix **за-** in **захворі́ти** denotes the beginning of the action (*to fall ill*).

Impersonal verbs

There have been examples of sentences containing verbs where the performer of the action is not clearly expressed, e.g.:

мені здає́ться   *it seems to me*

There are similar phrases denoting sickness or state of mind, e.g.:

його́ лихома́нить

мене́ моро́зить

її́ ну́дить

or good fortune, e.g.:

мені́ талани́ть   *I am lucky, successful*

їй щасти́ть

> **LANGUAGE TIP**
>
> **талани́ти** (impersonal verb) (impf.) *to be lucky, successful*

Other impersonal verbs denoting natural phenomena or processes, e.g.:

дощи́ть   *it is raining* (infinitive: дощи́ти (impf.))

смерка́є   *it is getting dark* (infinitive: смерка́ти (impf.))

мрячи́ть   *it is drizzling* (infinitive: мрячи́ти (impf.))

вечорі́є   *evening is coming on* (infinitive: вечорі́ти (impf.))

and also:

не вистача́є *there is not enough of* . . . (infinitive: вистача́ти (impf.))

браку́є   *there is a lack of* . . . (infinitive: бракува́ти (impf.))

> **LANGUAGE TIP**
>
> These verbs are called 'impersonal' because there is no personal subject. A similar situation arises in English in phrases like 'it is raining' or 'it seems to me', where the pronoun 'it' certainly fulfils the grammatical function of subject, but does not obviously fulfil any other function usually associated with pronouns, e.g. it does refer to any previously mentioned noun.

Impersonal verbs in Ukrainian share certain grammatical features:

▶ they have an infinitive, and forms for the past, present and future tenses
▶ they have endings only for the third-person singular in the present and future tenses, and the **neuter singular** form in the past tense
▶ they can have the suffix **-ся**. Indeed, some impersonal verbs never occur without it, e.g. **мені́ не спи́ться**.

Those impersonal verbs that relate to human beings take an object in the:

a   Accusative   Стівена лихома́нить

Тара́са ну́дило (*past*)

мене́ моро́зитиме (*future*)

b   Dative   Стівену щасти́ть

Тара́су талани́ть

c   Dative + genitive   Стівену не вистача́є гроше́й.
Stephen doesn't have enough money.

Тара́су браку́є ча́су.
Taras is short of time.

4 COMPARATIVE AND SUPERLATIVE DEGREE OF ADVERBS

Adverbs form their comparative and superlative degrees in exactly the same way as adjectives, except that the adjectival ending is replaced by the adverbial ending **-ше/-іше** (or occasionally **-ш/іш**):

до́бре	кра́ще	найкра́ще
пога́но	гі́рше	найгі́рше
ра́но	ранíше	найранíше
пізно	пізнíше	найпізнíше
бага́то	бíльше	найбíльше
ма́ло	ме́нше	найме́нше

Стівен **до́бре** розмовля́є
українською мо́вою, Тара́с
ще **кра́ще** зна́є її́, але́
найкра́ще не́ю гово́рить
Соломíя.

*Stephen speaks Ukrainian
well, Taras knows the
language even better, but
it is Solomiia who speaks
it best.*

Сього́дні я почува́ю себе́
пога́но, але́ за́втра бу́ду
почува́ти себе́ ще **гíрше**.

*I feel awful today but I shall
feel even worse tomorrow.*

Like the adjectives, the comparative degree of adverbs can be modified with words like **зна́чно** (*considerably*), **дале́ко**, **куди́** (*far*), **ще** (*even*), **тро́хи** (*a little*). The superlative degree of adverbs can be intensified by the addition of the prefixes **що-** or **як-**.

An important use of the comparative adverb in Ukrainian is in the phrase structure that corresponds to the English 'as ... as possible', e.g.:

якомо́га шви́дше   *as quickly as possible*

якомо́га деше́вше   *as cheaply as possible*

5 JOINING SENTENCES TOGETHER

Here are some of the words that are used to join different sentences together to form one whole sentence. Such words are called conjunctions:

▶ **що** (*that*) explains what comes earlier. You have seen sentences like this:

Добре, що Ви сказали про це.

Я бачу, що Ви читаєте українську газету.

Мені пощастило, що я Вас зустрів.

Мені здається, що нам слід відвідати не лише Київ та Львів.

Я ще вчора відчував, що мене нудить, і голова була гаряча.

Мені здавалося, що я просто стомлений.

▶ **щоб (для того, щоб)** (*in order to*) – used to denote purpose (see Unit 13):

Скільки . . . треба було б модернізувати фабрик в Україні, щоб налагодити виробництво одягу . . ?

▶ **якщо, якби** (*if*) – used to denote a condition (see Unit 13):

Телефонуйте мені, якщо маєте вільний час.

▶ **тому** (*therefore*) – denotes the result:

Стівен ніколи не був у Києві, тому через годину ми підемо гуляти вулицями міста.

У мене квитка не було, тому я заплатив контролерові штраф.

▶ **бо, тому що** (*because*) – denotes the cause:

Ми не заперечували, бо були дуже стомлені й голодні.

Стівен має кілька словників, тому що робить переклади.

Я збираюся їхати туди, тому що я маю комерційні інтереси.

You will notice that in each case the part of the sentence introduced by one of these words is separated off from the rest by a comma.

6 HEALTH MATTERS

Just in case!

Швидка допомога The first point of contact for someone suddenly taken ill in Ukraine is likely to be the **швидка допомога**, 'fast aid'.

Поліклініка The translation of **поліклініка** as 'health centre' is of necessity approximate. A typical **поліклініка** has facilities that may not always be found in a health centre in other countries, e.g. physiotherapy and X-ray equipment.

Температура 38,5 In Ukraine, body temperature is measured not in the mouth but under the armpit, where the normal temperature is 36.6.

Note that, in Ukrainian, a comma is used instead of a full stop to denote a decimal figure. Such figures are actually read: **тридцять вісім і п'ять; тридцять шість і шість**.

Ти ви́пив лі́ки? *Have you drunk your medicine?* In ordinary speech, medicines are **drunk**. Hence the phrases: **ви́пити лі́ки**, **табле́тку**, **порошо́к**, **мікстýру**.

In more official speech, medicines are taken, e.g. **прийня́ти лі́ки**, **табле́тку**, **порошо́к**, **мікстýру**.

 порошо́к (gen.: **порошкý**)   *powder*

Tablets for a headache This becomes tablets 'from' a headache in Ukrainian: **табле́тки від головно́го бо́лю**. Similarly with cough mixture: **мікстýра від ка́шлю**.

біль (gen.: **бо́лю**) (m)   *pain*
головни́й біль   *headache*
ка́шель (gen.: **ка́шлю**)   *cough*

Westerners may be surprised by the widespread use of traditional methods of healing in Ukraine. These include:

зеле́нка   *a green antiseptic liquid*
йод   *iodine*
пере́кис   *peroxide*
гірчи́чник   *mustard poultice*
тра́ви   *herbs*

Test yourself : Впра́ви

1 **Read the Ukrainian words in the left-hand column and find their English equivalents on the right:**

алергі́я	*injection*
бронхі́т	*massage*
діабе́т	*pulse*
антибіо́тик	*infection*
пневмоні́я	*bronchitis*
ін'є́кція	*analysis*
опера́ція	*diabetes*
інфе́кція	*pneumonia*
пульс	*antibiotics*
табле́тка	*thermometer*
ана́ліз	*mixture*
термо́метр	*vitamin*
маса́ж	*tablet*
міксту́ра	*allergy*
вітамі́н	*vitamin*

2 **Read the following text and answer the questions in English:**

Учо́ра мені́ подзвони́ла моя́ по́друга Окса́на. Вона́ сказа́ла, що її́ чолові́к захворі́в. У ньо́го висо́ка температу́ра, головни́й біль, ка́шель, не́жить. Окса́на ви́кликала лі́каря. Лі́кар прийшо́в, огля́нув хво́рого і сказа́в, що у ньо́го грип. Він ви́писав реце́пт і пояснив, як прийма́ти лі́ки. Окса́на побі́гла до апте́ки. Там вона́ оде́ржала табле́тки, кра́плі й мікстуру.

 поясни́ти (pf.)   *to explain*
кра́плі (pl.; sg.: кра́пля)   *drops*

– Who is Oksana and what did she do yesterday?

– What was her husband suffering from?

– What did the doctor say was wrong with him?

– What did the doctor explain?

– What did Oksana get at the chemist's?

3 Choose the right course of action in each instance:

a У хво́рого боли́ть го́рло:

Він   (i)   їсть моро́зиво.

        (ii)   прийма́є лі́ки.

        (iii) бі́гає.

b Тетя́на захворі́ла:

Вона   (i)   ска́ржиться дру́зям.

        (ii)   іде́ до рестора́ну.

        (iii) виклика́є лі́каря.

c О́льзі потрі́бні лі́ки:

Вона́   (i)   замовля́є їх в апте́ці.

        (ii)   йде́ до магази́ну.

        (iii) купу́є їх на ри́нку.

d Íгор хво́рий. Йому́ потрі́бно:

        (i)   йти́ у кінотеа́тр.

        (ii)   лежа́ти в лі́жку.

        (iii) порозмовля́ти із сім'є́ю.

4 Construct sentences that answer the question:

Example: Що ви ро́бите вве́чері? (диви́тися телеві́зор)

        – Уве́чері я дивлю́ся (ми ди́вимося) телеві́зор.

a Що лю́ди ро́блять на стадіо́ні?

(гра́ти у футбо́л/диви́тися матч/займа́тися спо́ртом)

b Чому́ Окса́на чита́є підру́чник? (учи́тися в університе́ті)

c Чому́ Оста́п сміє́ться? (чита́ти смішну́ кни́гу/диви́тися фільм/друг (розповіда́ти смішну́ істо́рію))

5 Situations in which you can practise your Ukrainian. Try writing sample dialogues and checking with the model answers in the Key:

a Complain to your Ukrainian friend that you:

– have a headache

– have no time to run to the chemist's shop to buy tablets for a headache

– have a sore throat and can't swallow

– feel feverish and will have to stay at home for a few days.

b   Your Ukrainian friend says that he/she is too ill to go to the health centre to make an appointment with a doctor (use a 'therefore' or a 'because'!). He/she asks you to phone the health centre to get a doctor to come out as soon as possible. You do so, and are told by the receptionist that the doctor will call tomorrow, in the second half of the day, and that your friend should stay (lie) in bed. He apologizes that he cannot come sooner, but he is very busy – there are more patients than doctors in the health centre. You tell your friend what the receptionist told you.

Як ви уявля́єте собі́ ідеа́льну дружи́ну?

What's your idea of the perfect wife?

In this unit you will learn:

▶ *How to form and use verbal adverbs*
▶ *How to describe the character and external appearance of other people*
▶ *How to ask politely for assistance*
▶ *How to change the subject*

Діало́г 1

On a visit to Ursula – the friend of Ihor and Ol'ha – in her flat on the Khreshchatyk.

Óльга	(*ди́влячись на екра́н телеві́зора – looking at the TV screen*) Як мені́ подо́бається Кларк Ґейбл! У ньо́го таке́ вродли́ве обли́ччя.
Ýрсула	У дити́нстві я ду́же люби́ла диви́тися фі́льми, в яки́х він зніма́вся. У ньо́го ду́же своєрі́дні, га́рні о́чі.
Íгор	О́лю, тобі́ не здає́ться, що я чи́мось на ньо́го схо́жий? Напе́вно, тому́ ти ви́йшла за ме́не за́між. Тобі́ сподо́балися мої́ о́чі . . .
Óльга	Бо́же мій, яке́ мо́же бу́ти порівня́ння! Я ма́ю на ува́зі, що ти в ме́не кра́щий за всіх зіро́к світово́го кіно́! Я до́сі так вважа́ю, на́віть пі́сля 20 [двадцяти́] ро́ків подру́жнього життя́.
Оста́п	Бра́во, дорогі́ батьки́! Ціну́ю ва́ше почуття́ гу́мору.
Íгор	Нія́ких жа́ртів! На́ша ма́ма за́вжди серйо́зна.
Оле́нка	Че́сно ка́жучи, мені́ все зрозумі́ло давно́. Вам про́сто пощасти́ло, що ви знайшли́ одне́ о́дного . . . Сті́вене, а от як Ви уявля́єте собі́ ідеа́льну дружи́ну? Зо́внішність, хара́ктер, профе́сія?
Тара́с	Типо́ве неви́нне дитя́че запита́ннячко . . .
Сті́вен	Я не ду́мав над цим, Оле́нко . . .
Оле́нка	Ну спра́вді, ду́же ціка́во . . .

фільм	*film*
екра́н	*screen*
зніма́тися (impf.)	(here:) *to be filmed*
своєрі́дний	*original, unique*
чи́мось (inst. of щось; something)	*in some way*
схо́жий (на + acc.)	*similar (to), like*

сподо́батися (pf.)	to please
тобі́ сподо́балися мої́ о́чі	you liked my eyes
порівня́ння (n)	comparison
ува́га	attention
ма́ти на ува́зі	to mean, have in mind
зі́рка	star
світови́й	(here:) world (adj.)
ти в ме́не кра́щий за всіх зіро́к світово́го кіно́	you're better than all the stars of world cinema, and you're mine!

(note that **зі́рка** is treated as an animate noun because it refers to human beings!)

до́сі	till now, so far
подру́жній	married
подру́жнє життя́	married life
цінува́ти (цінУ́ю, цінУ́єш) (impf.)	to appreciate
почуття́ (n)	feeling
гУ́мор	humour
почуття́ гУ́мору	sense of humour
жарт	joke
нія́ких жа́ртів!	no kidding!
чесний	honest
чЕ́сно ка́жучи	quite frankly (lit. honestly speaking)
мені́ все зрозумі́ло давно́	I understood everything perfectly a long time ago
одне́ о́дного	each other (m + f)
ідеа́льний	ideal (adj.)
хара́ктер	character
типо́вий	typical
неви́нний	innocent
запита́ннячко (colloquial, expressive)	tricky little question
дУ́мати (impf.)	to think

(When this verb is followed by the preposition **над** and inst. it has the meaning 'to consider, ponder'.)

Як функціонУ́є мо́ва

1 VERBAL ADVERBS
ди́влячись на екра́н телеві́зора (*looking at the TV screen*)

Ди́влячись is an example of a present-tense **verbal adverb**; it is formed from **диви́тися**. There are other examples of present-tense verbal adverbs in the dialogues in this unit: **ка́жучи** from **каза́ти**, **бУ́дучи** from **бУ́ти**, **працю́ючи** from **працюва́ти**. **Описа́вши** (from **описа́ти**) and **зашарі́вшись** (from **зашарі́тися**) are examples of past-tense verbal adverbs.

Like adverbs, they do not change their form and, like verbs, they have tense. Verbal adverbs frequently correspond to English verb forms in -ing. Look at the following examples:

Ідучи́ ву́лицею, я поба́чив старо́го знайо́мого.	*Walking along the street I saw an old acquaintance.*

The sentence could be changed to: **Коли́ я йшо́в ву́лицею** . . . (*As I walked along the street . . .*).

Гово́рячи про ідеа́льну дружи́ну, Сті́вен зашарі́вся.	*Speaking about his ideal wife, Stephen blushed.*

Here, too, we could make a change: **Коли́ Сті́вен говори́в про ідеа́льну дружи́ну** . . . (*When Stephen was talking about his ideal wife . . .*).

In both sentences, the action of walking along the street or speaking about an ideal wife is carried on **at the same time** as the action in the other part of the sentence: meeting the old acquaintance and blushing.

In the following examples, there is a different relationship between the actions:

Увійшо́вши до кімна́ти, Ігор помі́тив, що там нема́є дружи́ни.	*Entering the room, Ihor noticed that his wife wasn't there.*
Прочита́вши газе́ту, я пішов на робо́ту.	*Having read the newspaper I went to work.*

One action has to be completed before the other action can be started. The -ing forms in the first two examples correspond exactly to Ukrainian present-tense verbal adverbs. In the third, the -ing form is slightly misleading – Ihor cannot have noticed the absence of his wife until he was already in the room. This and the 'having . . .' construction in the fourth correspond to past-tense verbal adverbs.

Formation of verbal adverbs

▶ **Present-tense** verbal adverbs are formed from the third-person plural by removing the ending **-ть** and replacing it with the suffix **-чи**. The reflexive particle **-ся** becomes **-сь**:

Infinitive	3rd pers. pl.	Verbal adverb
чита́-ти	чита́ю-ть	чита́ю-**чи**
писа́-ти	пи́шу-ть	пи́шу-**чи**
і-ти́	іду́-ть	іду-**чи́** (note stress!)
працюва́-ти	працю́ю-ть	працю́ю-**чи**
смія́-ти-ся	смію́-ть-ся	смію́-**чи-сь**
диви́-ти-ся	ди́вля-ть-ся	ди́вля-**чи-сь**

The verbal adverb **бу́дучи** is a slight exception, it is formed from the third-person plural future tense (**бу́ду-ть**) of the verb **бу́ти**.

▶ **Past-tense** verbal adverbs are formed by adding the suffix **-ши** to the masculine singular past-tense form of mainly perfective verbs. Here again **-ся** becomes **-сь**:

Masc. sg. past tense	Past-tense verbal adverb
сказа́в	сказа́в-**ши**
увійшо́в	увійшо́в-**ши**
приніс	приніс-**ши***
засмі́яв-ся	засмі́яв-**ши-сь**

Use of verbal adverbs

Like verbs, verbal adverbs can also have objects (examples 1 and 2):

Ди́влячись фільм без Кла́рка Ге́йбла, О́льга засну́ла.	*[While] watching a film without [not starring] Clark Gable, Ol'ha fell asleep.*
Ви́пивши ка́ву, я пішо́в на робо́ту.	*After I had drunk (lit. having drunk) [my] coffee, I left for work.*
Ми розмовля́ли, си́дячи за столо́м.	*We chatted sitting at the table.*
Захворі́вши, Ста́хів не міг працюва́ти.	*After he fell ill (lit. having fallen ill), Stakhiv was unable to work.*

Note: The doer of the action is the same in both parts of the sentence and the part of the sentence containing the verbal adverb is set off in writing from the rest by a comma.

Verbal adverbs often occur in set expressions such as:

че́сно ка́жучи, щи́ро ка́жучи	*quite honestly*

When preceded by the negative word **не**, Ukrainian verbal adverbs translate English 'without' + the *-ing* form of the verb, e.g.:

М не бу́дучи нудно́ю	*without being boring*
М и йшли́ ву́лицею не поспіша́ючи.	*We walked along the street without hurrying.*

2 THE RECIPROCAL PRONOUN – ONE ANOTHER/EACH OTHER

Вам пощасти́ло, що ви знайшли́ одне́ о́дного.	*You were lucky to have found one another (each other).*

---

* The combination of letters **-сш-** is pronounced as a long 'sh' sound.

The forms of this compound pronoun are:

оди́н о́дного for (m + m) **одна́ о́дну** for (f + f)

одне́ (neuter!) **о́дного** for (m + f)

The case of the first part always stays the same (n); the second half can change according to its function in the sentence. Any preposition comes before the second part, e.g.:

Вони розмовляли оди́н з о́дним (m + m)/одна́ з о́дною (f + f)/
    одне́ з о́дним (m + f)

They were talking to (lit. with) *each other.*

3 MORE ON IMPERSONAL SENTENCES

You have seen several sentences where the verb is in the third-person plural form without a subject. Let's follow this up.

The phrase **у нас так ка́жуть** (*that's what people say here/that's what is said around here*) occurs in the next dialogue of this unit. The verb is in the third-person plural form with no subject (**вони́**); in the past tense the verb is in the plural form:

Сті́венові сказа́ли, що . . .   *Stephen was told that . . .*

У газе́тах пи́шуть, що . . .   *The papers are saying that . . .*

                 (lit. it is written in the papers)

You might see a notice in a restaurant or office saying:

У НАС НЕ КУ́РЯТЬ   NO SMOKING

Діало́г 2

The debate continues.

Сті́вен	Щи́ро ка́жучи, я вважа́ю, що суча́сна жі́нка ма́є бу́ти самості́йною, незале́жною, акти́вною. Стосо́вно ж дружи́ни . . . Напе́вно, якби́ я нава́жився одружи́тися, то ви́брав би жі́нку, яка́ ма́є прести́жну профе́сію, можли́во, свій бі́знес . . . Вона́ пови́нна бу́ти розу́мною, споко́йною, розсу́дливою, ане не нудно́ю. З весе́лим хара́ктером, із гу́мором.
Ігор	"Се́рце з пе́рцем" . . .
Сті́вен	Що?
Ігор	У нас так ка́жуть.
Ольга	Ще ка́жуть "чорт у спідни́ці" . . .
Ігор	Це про те́бе.
Оста́п	Ну го́ді вам!
Оле́нка	А портре́т?
Сті́вен	Я ще не ви́значився.
Оле́нка	Ну всé-таки . . . Яко́го ко́льору о́чі? Чо́рні? Си́ні?

Стíвен	Ні, менí подóбаються зелéні.
Олéнка	А волóсся?
Остáп	Якщó вонá обіймáє керівнý посáду, працюючи цíлими днями, то, мáбуть, сúве.

(They all laugh)

Стíвен	Волóсся тéмне. Я дýмаю, вонá булá б шатéнка.
Тарáс	Я, здаéться, знáю однý дýже незалéжну й розýмну жíнку, якá відповідáє цьомý óписові. Описáвши її портрéт, ти ще забýв сказáти, що вонá невисóка й одягáється дýже елегáнтно, бо за фáхом – худóжник-модельéр.
Стíвен	(зашарíвшись – *blushing*): Я не мав нікóго на увáзі конкрéтно.
Тарáс	Це менí здалóся.

V

сучáсний	*contemporary*
самостíйний	*self-reliant*
незалéжний	*independent*
актúвний	*active*
стосóвно (+ gen.)	*as for …*
навáжитися (pf.)	*to dare, resolve*
престúжний	*prestigious*
розýмний	*intelligent, clever*
спокíйний	*calm*
розсýдливий	*prudent, sensible*
нуднúй	*boring*
весéлий	*merry*
сéрце з пéрцем	(lit. a heart with pepper)
чорт	*devil*
чорт у спіднúці	(lit. a devil in a skirt)
гóді!	*enough!*
ну гóді вам	*come on, that's enough from you!*
вúзначитися (pf.)	*to be clear (about something)*
óко (pl.: **óчі;** gen. pl.: **очéй;** inst. pl.: **очúма**)	*eye*
волóсся (n)	*hair*
керівнúй	*leading*
посáда	*position*
обіймáти керівнý посáду	*to occupy a top job*
працюючи цíлими днями	*working for days on end*
шатéнка	*woman with chestnut hair*
óпис	*description*
описáти (опишý, опúшеш) (pf.)	*to describe*

описа́вши її портре́т	*having described her portrait*
невисо́кий	*short, not tall*
елега́нтний	*elegant*
бо	*because*
худо́жник	*artist*
худо́жник-модельє́р	*fashion designer*
зашарі́тися (pf.)	*to blush*
зашарі́вшись	*blushing* (lit. having blushed)
ніко́го (acc. and gen. of **ніхто́**)	*no one*

a Правда чи непра́вда?

1 У́рсула лю́бить фі́льми, в яки́х зніма́вся Кларк Ґейбл.

2 О́льга вважа́є свого́ чолові́ка кра́щим за всіх зіро́к світово́го кіно́.

3 Суча́сна жі́нка ма́є бу́ти самості́йною, незале́жною, акти́вною.

4 Сті́вен вважа́є га́рними зеле́ні о́чі.

b Да́йте ві́дповідь на запита́ння англі́йською мо́вою

1 Who is always serious?

2 Who asks Stephen to describe his ideal wife?

3 What is Stephen's idea of his future wife's character?

4 What does he say about her profession?

4 STOP IT! THAT'S ENOUGH!

For the moment when you cannot stand it any more!

One way of getting someone to stop doing something is to say **Ну го́ді вам!** The **ну** at the beginning means that the message is friendly – 'Oh, come on now, that's enough!'

If things are getting out of hand, you can also say:

До́сить!	*That's enough!*
Зупині́ться!	*Stop!*
Припині́ть!	*Stop [doing whatever it is you're doing]!*

Note: both **зупині́ться** and **припині́ть** are second-person plural imperatives, from **зупини́тися** and **припини́ти**, respectively.

5 WAYS OF GETTING INFORMATION OUT OF PEOPLE

When Stephen hesitates, Olenka tries to wheedle information out of him with:

Ну спра́вді!	*Oh, but it really is [very interesting]!*
Ну все́-таки . . .	*But all the same . . .*

with a suitably pleading tone on the **ну**.

In more everyday conversations, you can seek a reaction with:

Тобі́/Вам не здає́ться?	*Doesn't it seem to you?*
	Don't you think?
Ти не помі́тив/	*Have you noticed by any chance . . .?*
Ви не помі́тили?	
Чи ти не зна́єш/	*You don't happen to know,*
Чи ви не зна́єте?	*do you?*

Seeking information by asking a negative question is very polite in Ukrainian. When asking the way, begin your question with **Ви не ска́жете . . .?**, e.g.

Ви не ска́жете, як доі́хати	*Could you please tell me how to*
до університе́ту?	*get to the university?*

With an extra degree of deference:

Ви не могли́ б сказа́ти . . .?	*You couldn't by any chance*
	tell me . . . ?

6 EXCLAMATIONS

An obvious expression of surprise is **Бо́же мій!** (*my God!*). Depending on intonation and context **ах!** and **ох!** can express surprise or fear (*oh!, ah!*) or sorrow (*alas, oh dear*).

Ой is another useful exclamation of surprise, particularly when used with another word:

ой не́не!	(*related to* не́ня, *a familiar word for mother*)
ой ма́мо моя́!	
ой ли́шенько!	(*oh, how awful!* (ли́шенько is a diminutive form of ли́хо (*woe, misfortune*))
овва́!	(expressing amazement: *you don't say!*)

Бра́во! is used as an expression of approval, either genuine or ironic, in the same way as English 'bravo!'.

The much used **ну** can represent a variety of emotions, again depending on intonation and context. In the previous unit, Ihor used it to give vent to his frustration: **ну чому́ мені́ так не щасти́ть?** (*just why am I so unlucky?*). **Ну** can also be used as encouragement – 'come on!', 'get on with it'.

7 CHANGING THE SUBJECT

Apart from having had enough, or getting emotional, you may wish to change the direction of the conversation.

Note how Olenka shifts from her parents – 'you were fortunate in finding each other' – to directing a very personal question at Stephen: **А от як Ви уявля́єте собі́ ідеа́льну дружи́ну?** (*Now just how do **you** picture to yourself your ideal wife?*). **От** is a 'pointing' word like **ось** (*here is*), but is more frequent in phrases like this one, or in exclamations:

от тобі й на!	*well, I never!*
от тобі!	*take that!*
от як?!	*really?! You don't say?!*

8 ТИПО́ВЕ НЕВИ́ННЕ ДИТЯ́ЧЕ ЗАПИТА́ННЯЧКО (A TYPICAL INNOCENT CHILDISH LITTLE QUESTION)

There is irony here. The question is, of course, not innocent; the speaker's intentions are shown by the ending on **запита́ннячко**.

> **LANGUAGE TIP**
>
> The normal Ukrainian word for question is **запита́ння**. The ending gives the word the flavour of 'tricky little question'. This is part of the process by which Ukrainians can change words in an emotional sense, more often to signify endearment than in an ironical sense.

There is very little scope for doing this in English, with just a few words like 'mummy', 'daddy', 'mumsy', 'granny' and so on. It is certainly not possible to produce whole chains of derivatives from personal names. Olenka is so called because she is the young daughter of the family and the form is affectionate; she could also be addressed as **Оле́ночка**, **Оле́ся** or **Ля́ля**. Every family has its own traditions. Even the businesslady **Соломі́я** may, in the right circumstances, find herself become **Соломі́єчка**, **Солю́ня**, **Со́ля**, **Мі́я** or **І́я**.

There is even scope for emotion in adjectives. 'Chubby' in Ukrainian is **пухки́й**. A baby, however, may well be 'all nice and chubby' – **пухке́нький**. If the baby is 'all nice and clean' as well, he could be described as **чисте́нький** or **чисті́сінький** rather than plain **чи́стий** (*clean*). Emotion does not have to be involved. **Га́рний** when applied to human beings can mean either 'beautiful' or 'handsome'; **гарне́нький** will almost always be used with reference to women in the meaning 'pretty'.

9 ANOTHER LITTLE WORD – Ж

| Стосо́вно ж дружи́ни | *Now as far as a wife is concerned …* |

The single letter **ж** is called an **emphatic particle**, i.e. it puts a lot of emphasis on the word that it follows. Like **от** earlier, it can also be used to change the direction of a sentence.

Some more examples:

| Що ж вона́ сказа́ла на це? | *So just what did she say to that?* |
| Іди́ ж геть зві́дси! | *Oh do clear off out of here!* |

❓ Test yourself: Впра́ви

1 Practise describing appearances.

Here are some phrases for you to practise. Use the vocabulary at the back of the book:

Як він вигляда́є?

У ньо́го те́мне воло́сся. Він га́рний, ма́є прями́й ніс, сі́рі о́чі, чо́рні бро́ви, невели́ку те́мну бо́роду й ву́са. Я ду́маю, що в ньо́го ду́же га́рні ві́ї, темні й до́вгі. І ще мені́ подо́бається його́ смагля́ва шкі́ра й тонки́й про́філь.

Опиші́ть її зо́внішність

Вона́ гарне́нька. У не́ї відкри́те, прива́бливе обли́ччя. Вона́ ма́є хвиля́сте біля́ве воло́сся й сві́тлу шкі́ру. О́чі в не́ї ка́рі й вели́кі, ніс мале́нький. Що́ки й гу́би в не́ї рожо́ві, і всім подо́бається її чарівна́ по́смішка.

▷ Facial features

У ньо́го/не́ї:

сі́рі (ка́рі) о́чі

прями́й (кирпа́тий) ніс

до́вгі (густі́, руді́) ві́ї

рум'я́ні (бліді́) що́ки

пухкі́ (тонкі́, по́вні) гу́би

бліде́/рум'я́не обли́ччя

У ньо́го/не́ї на обли́ччі змо́ршки, ластови́ння.

Чи Сті́вен но́сить окуля́ри?

Чи Соломі́я но́сить сере́жки?

▷ Hair

Він лу́сий.	У ньо́го/не́ї пряме́/хвиля́сте/ кучеря́ве воло́сся.
Він ма́є зали́сину.	У ньо́го те́мна борода́/сві́тлі/ руді́ ву́са.

▷ Height

Мій та́то висо́кого зро́сту. (**зріст**: gen.: **зро́сту**) (alt. **і/о**)

Моя́ ма́ма сере́днього зро́сту.   Мій брат нивисокий на зріст.

2 Look at the portraits of our old acquaintances that follow. Taras, Solomiia, Stephen, Vira, Ihor and Ol'ha are among them. Try to guess who is who, using the information that follows:

Тара́с	Висо́кий, солі́дний, по́вний. Воло́сся сві́тле. Ма́є га́рні ву́са. Но́сить окуля́ри.
Соломі́я	Вродли́ва, невисо́ка, смагля́ва. О́чі вели́кі, воло́сся те́мне, хвиля́сте, до́вге.
Стівен	Елега́нтний, висо́кий, в окуля́рах. Блонди́н, о́чі невели́кі, серйо́зні.
Ві́ра	Воло́сся кучеря́ве. Обли́ччя по́вне, ніс мале́нький, кирпа́тий, на но́сі – ластови́ння. Но́сить вели́кі серéжки.
Íгор	Міцни́й, невисо́кого зро́сту. Лоб висо́кий, із залиси́нами, те́мне воло́сся і невели́ка борода́. Ніс вели́кий.
О́льга	Шате́нка, воло́сся коро́тке, пряме́. О́чі вели́кі, по́вні гу́би, весе́ле, га́рне обли́ччя.

3 Parts of the body are listed in the left-hand column; there are descriptive adjectives in the column on the right. Put each adjective with the most suitable noun, changing the form wherever necessary:

лоб	кирпа́тий
воло́сся	смагля́вий
о́чі	біля́вий
обли́ччя	висо́кий
ніс	ка́рий

4 Write out the following sentences in full in Ukrainian, translating the English phrases wherever necessary. Put the Ukrainian words in brackets into the correct case form:

a Я запроси́в її́ в кіно́, тому́ що (*I liked her eyes*).

b (*Have you thought about*) (на́ша пропози́ція) пообі́дати за́втра ра́зом в (рестора́н)?

c Я люблю́, коли́ моя́ дружи́на (*dresses very elegantly*).

d У ме́не га́рна маши́на, але́ в (мій друг) (*an even better one*).

e Чи твоя́ сестра́ (*is like your father*)?

16 Поїзд прибуває на першу колію

The train arriving on track number one . . .

In this unit you will learn:
▶ *About train travel in Ukraine*
▶ *About indefinite and negative words*
▶ *About participles and passive sentences*

Діалог 1

Taras, Stephen and Andrew are on Kyiv railway station, listening intently to the announcements.

Швидкий потяг номер 11 сполученням "Київ – Сімферополь" прибуває на першу колію. Нумерація вагонів з голови поїзда.

Тарас	Ви чули? Це наш потяг.
Стівен	Яка платформа?
Ендрю	Здається, перша, так?
Тарас	Так. Це дуже зручно.
(One hour later in a compartment of the Kyiv-Simferopol express)	
Провідниця	Будь ласка, ваші квитки. І приготуйте гроші на постіль.
Тарас	Ось, прошу, квитки.
Стівен	Скажіть, будь ласка, о котрій годині ми будемо в Сімферополі?
Провідниця	За розкладом ми прибуваємо завтра о десятій сорок ранку.
Ендрю	Можна попросити чаю?
Провідниця	Так. Вам зараз принести?
Тарас	Мені не треба, дуже спекотно. Хочеться чого-небудь холодного. Я буду пити воду, яку ми купили в дорогу . . .
Стівен	А я б випив чаю з великим задоволенням.
Ендрю	Будь ласка, дві склянки.
Провідниця	Добре. *(She leaves)*

колія	track, (here:) *platform*
швидкий потяг	express (lit.: fast train)
поїзд	train (means exactly the same as **потяг**)
сполучення (n)	connection
сполученням (inst. sg.)	(here:) on the route

нумера́ція ваго́нів з голови́ по́їзда	the carriages are numbered from the head/front of the train
приготува́ти (-у́ю, -у́єш) (impf.)	to prepare, get ready
по́стіль (gen.: посте́лі) (f.)	bedding (alt. **i/e**)
ро́зклад	timetable
за ро́зкладом	according to the timetable
вам за́раз принести́?	Do you want me to bring it right away?
[мені́] хо́четься чого́-небудь холо́дного	I feel like something cold
я бу́ду пи́ти во́ду, яку́ ми купи́ли в доро́гу	I'll drink the water that we bought **for the journey**
скля́нка	glass (for long drinks, incl. tea!)

Як функціону́є мо́ва

1 SOMETHING COLD – *ЩО-НЕ́БУДЬ ХОЛО́ДНЕ*

Taras wants something cold – in the genitive. It might be more accurate to say that he wants anything (**чого́-небудь**) cold – it doesn't matter what. Andrew asks for tea – also in the genitive. Here we have more examples of the 'partitive' use of this case; Andrew is, in fact, asking for some tea.

2 INTERROGATIVE PRONOUNS *ХТО?* AND *ЩО?*

Here are the full declensions:

Nom.	хто	що
Acc.	кого́	що
Gen.	кого́	чого́
Dat.	кому́	чому́
Loc.	(на) ко́му	чо́му
Instr.	ким	чим

3 INDEFINITE PRONOUNS, ADJECTIVES AND ADVERBS

Examples of indefinite pronouns in English are 'someone', 'anything'; 'some' is an indefinite adjective; 'anywhere' is an indefinite adverb.

You already know **щось** (*something*). It changes its form exactly like the question word **що**, except that its instrumental is **чи́мось** (*in some way*). We can produce other indefinite words by adding **-сь** to the corresponding question words:

хто?	*who?*	хтось	*someone*
де?	*where?*	десь	*somewhere*
куди́?	*[to] where?*	куди́сь	*[to] somewhere*
яки́й?	*what kind of?*	яки́йсь	*some kind of*

чому́	*why?*	чому́сь	*for some reason (or other)*
коли́?	*when?*	коли́сь	*at some time (or other), sometime ago*

Other indefinite words can be formed by adding the prefix **де-**:

де́хто and **де́що** mean the same as **хтось** and **щось**, although **де́що** can be used before adjectives to mean 'a little', 'rather', e.g. **де́що бі́льше** (*a little more*). **Де́який** has the sense of 'a certain'.

In most instances, these Ukrainian words are associated with the English 'some'. To be more indefinite, English uses 'any'. The Ukrainian equivalents are:

хто-не́будь	*anyone*
що-не́будь	*anything*
де-не́будь	*anywhere*
коли́-не́будь	*at some unspecified time, at any time, ever (in the future or in questions, e.g. **Ти коли́-не́будь працю́єш удо́ма?** Do you ever work at home?)*

It is not always easy to determine when to use a word with **-сь** or **не́будь**. Perhaps the most useful distinction is that words with **-сь** will probably be associated with verbs in the past tense and those with **-не́будь** tend to occur in questions or with future tense or conditional verbs:

Чи ти знайшо́в що-не́будь ціка́ве в книга́рні?	*Did you find anything interesting in the bookshop?*
Так, я купи́в щось ду́же ціка́ве.	*Yes, I bought something very interesting.*
Чи ви були́ де-не́будь учо́ра?	*Did you go anywhere yesterday?*
Я десь його́ ба́чив, але́ не пам'ята́ю де.	*I've seen him somewhere, but can't remember where.*

Even more indefinite are the words prefixed with **будь-**:

будь-хто́	*anyone at all*
будь-яка́ фа́брика	*any old factory*
бу́дь-коли	*at any time, ever*
Будь-хто́ мо́же це зроби́ти.	*Absolutely anyone can do that.*
Я мо́жу це зроби́ти бу́дь-коли.	*I can do it at any time.*

There are other ways of making indefinite words in Ukrainian, but you need only to be able to recognize them, e.g. **абúхто** (*whoever, no matter who*), **абúяк** (*any old how*). The word **кázна** means 'the devil only knows!'.

> **LANGUAGE TIP**
> For those who really like to know why: **кázна** is most likely short for **кат знає** – *the hangman knows*.

4 MORE ON RELATIVE PRONOUNS

The relative pronouns ('who', 'which', 'that') in Ukrainian are **якúй**, **котрúй**, **що**. Remember that they take the gender of the noun to which they refer:

Я вúпив вóду, якá булá в холодúльнику.	*I drank the water that was in the fridge.*

> **LANGUAGE TIP**
> **Вódа** is the object of the verb **вúпив** and is therefore in the accusative case. **Якá** is feminine in gender because it refers to **вódа** but is in the nominative case because it is the subject of the verb **булá**.

Я вúпив вóду, якý купúв у дорóгу.	*I drank the water that I had bought for the journey.*

> **LANGUAGE TIP**
> Here **якý** is accusative as the object of the verb **купúв**.

Діалóг 2

The trio settle in for their long journey.

Тарáс	До рéчі, ви б не хотíли чогó-нéбудь поїсти? Як тíльки я сідáю в пóїзд, я відрáзу чомýсь дуже хóчу їсти.
Стíвен	Я мáю пéчиво, бутербрóди та яблука. І ще якíсь цукéрки.
Éндрю	Я теж зáвжди берý щось у дорóгу. У мéне повна сýмка продýктів.
Провіднúця	Ось ваш чай. З вас сóрок копíйок.
Стíвен	Дя́кую.
Éндрю	Вúбачте, будь лáска . . . Прибуття́ до Сімферóполя за рóзкладом?

Провідни́ця	Так. (*She leaves*)
Тара́с	Éндрю, ти не мо́жеш відчини́ти вікно́?
Éндрю	. . . Нічо́го не вихо́дить!
Тара́с	Тре́ба нати́снути на ру́чку і потягти́ дони́зу . . . О, тепе́р до́бре. Сві́же пові́тря!
Éндрю	Я сього́дні з задово́пенням спа́тиму на ве́рхній поли́ці, там прохоло́дніше, якщо́ відчи́нене вікно́.
Сті́вен	Як би там не було́, а мені́ ще тре́ба прочита́ти ці́лу те́ку папе́рів, у ме́не за́втра в Сімферо́полі напру́жений день, бага́то зу́стрічей з коле́гами.

V

як ті́льки	*as soon as*
сіда́ти в по́їзд	*to get on a train*
цуке́рка	*a sweet, candy*
по́вний	*full*
проду́кти (usually pl.)	*food*
нічо́го не вихо́дить!	*it's no good, nothing happens*
нати́снути (pf.) (**нати́сну, нати́снеш**) (**на** + acc.)	*to press* (on)
потягти́ (потягну́, потя́гнеш) (pf.)	*to pull*
дони́зу	*down*
задово́лення	*pleasure*
ве́рхній	*upper, higher*
ни́жній	*lower*
поли́ця	(here:) *berth*
відчи́нений	*open*
як би там не було́	*however that may be*
те́ка	*folder*

a Правда чи неправда?

1 Швидки́й по́їзд но́мер 11 прибува́є на четве́рту ко́лію.

2 Сті́вен узя́в у доро́гу котле́ти, сир і полуни́цю.

3 Прибуття́ до Сімферо́поля за ро́зкладом.

4 Éндрю спа́тиме в купе́ на ни́жній поли́ці.

b Да́йте ві́дповідь на ці запита́ння англі́йською мо́вою

1 What does Taras give the carriage attendant?

2 How much does a glass of tea cost?

3 How do you open the windows on a train in Ukraine?

4 What has Stephen taken to read on the journey?

5 NEGATIVE PRONOUNS, ADJECTIVES AND ADVERBS

Compare these words with the indefinite words given earlier:

ніхтó	*no one*
ніщó	*nothing*

(The second part of these two words declines in the usual way; the genitive case of **ніщó, нічóго**, often functions as the subject of the sentence.)

Here are some more useful words of the same kind:

нідé	*nowhere*
нікýди	*(to) nowhere*
нікóли	*never*
нія́к	*nohow*

To this list should be added:

жóден/жóдний	*no* (adj.) (ніякий *no* (kind of))

Here are some examples of usage:

Я ні з кúм не розмовля́в.	*I didn't speak to anyone.* (note that the preposition comes between **ні** and the following case form of **хто**)
Стíвен нікóли не був в Украї́ні.	*Stephen has never been to Ukraine.*
Вонú нікýди не пішлú.	*They haven't gone anywhere.*
Немáє нія́кого сýмніву . . .	*There is no doubt . . .*

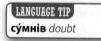

LANGUAGE TIP
сýмнів *doubt*

6 PARTICIPLES

Participles are adjectives formed from verbs; they can be used to replace a relative clause, i.e. part of a sentence introduced by one of the relative pronouns 'who', 'which', 'that':

The boy **running** (participle) along the street is my son.	*The boy **who is running*** (relative clause) . . .
I am reading a novel **written** (participle) by Dickens.	*. . . a novel **that was written*** (relative clause) . . .

As adjectives, participles in Ukrainian change according to the gender and case of the noun they accompany, but like verbs they can have tense and be either active (e.g. *running*) or passive (e.g. *written*). Only past-tense passive participles are in regular use. Many quite ordinary adjectives are historically active past participles, but you do not need to know this in order to be able to use the words concerned.

Passive past participles

The word **вдя́гнений** (*dressed*) is an example of a passive past participle. Some more examples: **зачи́нений** (*closed*), **відчи́нений** (*open*). These participles are formed only from verbs which are perfective – the few exceptions to this need not concern us here – and transitive (i.e. they have an object), by means of the adjectival suffix **-ний** (**-на, -не; -ні**) or **-тий** (**-та, -те; -ті**). Most verbs have **-ний**, but a number of important verbs take **-тий**.

Here are some of the most common verbs that form their passive past participles with **-тий**:

взя́ти/узя́ти	*to take*	взя́тий/узя́тий	*taken*
ви́пити	*to drink* (*up*)	ви́питий	*drunk* (not inebriated!)
забу́ти	*to forget*	забу́тий	*forgotten*
поча́ти	*to begin*	поча́тий	*begun*

Participles with **-ний**:

a first-conjugation verbs where a vowel precedes the indefinite suffix **-ти**:

написа́ти	*to write*	напи́саний	*written*
прочита́ти	*to read*	прочи́таний	*read*

b first-conjugation verbs with infinitives ending in **-увати**:

збудува́ти	*to build*	збудо́ваний	*built*
схвилюва́ти	*to move* (*emotionally*)	схвильо́ваний	*moved, touched*

c first-conjugation verbs with infinitives ending in **-нути**:

вдя́гнути	*to dress*	вдя́гнений	*dressed*

d first-conjugation verbs with a consonant preceding the infinitive suffix **-ти**:

привезти́	*to bring*	привезе́ (*3rd sg.*)	приве́зений *brought*

e second-conjugation verbs:

зроби́ти	*to do*	зроблю́ (*1st sg.*)	зро́блений *done*
пропусти́ти	*to miss*	пропущу́ (*1st sg.*)	пропу́щений *missed*

7 PASSIVE SENTENCES

In earlier units, you saw the following sentences:

Су́му **вка́зано** в деклара́ції. *The sum has been declared on the currency declaration form.*

Деклара́цію вже **запо́внено**. *The currency declaration form has already been completed.*

Ваш ви́клиик **при́йнято**. *Your call has been accepted.*

> **LANGUAGE TIP**
> No reference is made to the person who declared the currency on the form or who completed it or who took the call. The sentences simply state that the action has been/was performed.

A special form of the passive past participle is used, ending in **-но** or **-то**. By contrast to the English sentences, which have a grammatical subject (the sum, two rooms, your call) but no object, the Ukrainian construction does have an object (in the accusative case) but no subject.

Here are some more examples:

Йому́ не рекомендо́вано пи́ти ка́ву.	*He is advised not to drink coffee.*
Кни́гу вже прочи́тано?	*Has the book been read already?*
Листи́ вже напи́сано?	*Have the letters been written already?*
Матч уже зі́грано.	*The match has already been played.*
Усі́ ті́стечка вже́ з'ї́дено.	*All the cakes have already been eaten.*
Пої́здку заплано́вано на за́втра.	*The trip is planned for tomorrow.*
Бутербро́ди вже́ зро́блено, ка́ву нали́то.	*The sandwiches have already been made and the coffee poured out.*

8 THE WHOLE – A WHOLE

Я так хо́чу пи́ти, що ви́п'ю всю пля́шку.	*I am so thirsty that I shall drink the whole bottle.*
Я так хо́чу пи́ти, що зміг би ви́пити ці́лу пля́шку.	*I am so thirsty that I could drink a whole bottle.*

9 ALL

Here is the declension of **уве́сь/вве́сь** (*all*):

		S.		Pl.	
	M	F	N		
Nom.	уве́сь	уся́	усе́	усі́	
Acc.	(nom. or gen.)		усю́	усе́	(nom. or gen.)
Gen.	усього́	усіє́ї	усього́	усі́х	
Dat.	усьому́	усі́й	усьому́	усі́м	
Loc.	(на) усьо́му	усі́й	усьо́му	усі́х	
Inst.	усі́м	усіє́ю	усі́м	усіма́	

The neuter nominative singular form **усе** can mean 'everything': **все можли́ве** (*everything possible*). The plural form can mean 'everyone', e.g.:

Усі́ зна́ють (*plural verb form*) Тара́са.   *Everyone knows Taras.*

10 PRETEND YOU ARE ON KYIV RAILWAY STATION

TR 16, 00:08

Practise these phrases and make sure you understand them. They will be useful for the exercises that follow.

a Here are some more announcements

Ува́га! Швидки́й по́їзд но́мер 68 сполу́ченням "Берлі́н-Ки́їв" прибува́є на дру́гу ко́лію. Ви́хід до ваго́нів че́рез дру́гий по́верх вокза́лу. Нумера́ція ваго́нів з хвоста́ по́їзда.

Ува́га! Пасажи́рський по́їзд но́мер 189 сполу́ченням "Санкт-Петербу́рг-Ки́їв" запізню́ється на 20 хвили́н.

Ува́га! Швидки́й по́їзд но́мер 55 бу́де по́дано на четве́рту ко́лію. Нумера́ція ваго́нів з голови́ по́їзда.

Ува́га! Пасажи́рський по́їзд но́мер 604, "Ки́їв-Полта́ва" відправля́ється з п'я́тої ко́лії.

b You are booking tickets

You	Будь ла́ска, оди́н купе́йний на два́дцять четве́рте тра́вня до Оде́си.
X	Но́мер по́їзда?
You	П'ятдеся́т п'ять.
X	На два́дцять четве́рте купе́йних нема́є. Є плацка́рт.
You	А на яке́ число́ є купе́йні?
X	На два́дцять шо́сте.
You	До́бре. Я візьму́ на два́дцять шо́сте.
You	Про́шу, оди́н до Москви́ на во́сьме жо́втня, по́їзд но́мер 2, і на двана́дцяте наза́д, по́їзд но́мер 1.
X	На во́сьме до Москви́?
You	Так "СВ", будь ла́ска.
X	Є "СВ" на во́сьме. Зворо́тний на двана́дцяте?
You	Так, про́шу.
X	На двана́дцяте є купе́ й плацка́рт.
You	А на трина́дцяте?
X	На трина́дцяте є "СВ". Дава́ти? (*Shall I give it? i.e., do you want it?*)

Here are the names of some Ukrainian cities for the next exercise:

Терно́піль (*gen.*: Терно́поля)	*Ternopil* (alt. **і/о**)
Ха́рків (*gen.*: Ха́ркова)	*Kharkiv* (alt. **і/о**)
Чернівці́ (*gen*: Чернівці́в)	*Chernivtsi*
Іва́но-Франкі́вськ (*gen.*: Іва́но-Франкі́вська)	*Ivano-Frankivsk*
Черка́си (*gen.*:Черка́с)	*Cherkasy*
Кам'яне́ць-Поді́льський (*gen.*:Кам'янця́-Поді́льського)	*Kamianets-Podilskii*

c Train travel in Ukraine

At the railway station, the **пасажий** (*passenger*) joins the queue (**че́рга**) for the ticket office (**займа́ти че́ргу до ка́си**). When booking a ticket, you need to know, apart from where you want to go, the number of the train (**но́мер по́їзда**) by which you wish to travel. Your ticket will tell you the number of both your seat and the carriage in which you will be travelling. Announcements will tell you whether the carriages are numbered from the front (lit. *head*: **з голови́ по́їзда**) or from the rear (lit. *tail* (**хвіст**): **з хвоста́ по́їзда**). You should also know about different types of train and accommodation. The immediate vicinity of large towns is served by electric suburban train **електро́поїзд** (**електри́чка**). Long-distance trains are slow (**пасажи́рський по́їзд**) or fast (**швидки́й по́їзд**) and have different standards of accommodation:

спа́льний ваго́н (СВ)	*sleeping car (2 or 3 berths per compartment) (the best accommodation, but not available on all long-distance trains)*
купе́йний ваго́н	*carriage with separate compartments (4 berths per compartment (**купе**))*
плацка́ртний ваго́н	*open carriage with compulsory berth reservations*
загáльний (lit. common) ваго́н	*carriage with unreserved seats*

Each carriage on a long-distance train has a **провідни́к** (*steward, sleeping-car attendant*). It is from him or his female colleague, **провідни́ця**, that you buy tea and obtain your bed linen.

❓ Test yourself: Впра́ви

1 **Now include the cities from (10b) in the following enquiries and requests (in Ukrainian, of course!):**

a Can you please tell me when the train from Cherkasy arrives?

b When is the next train to Kharkiv, please?

c One first-class ticket please on the express train to Ivano-Frankivsk.

d I want to go by train (first class) to Odesa.

e I want to go by suburban electric train to Poltava on 19 August.

Try constructing sentences with requests for different types of accommmodation with other destinations: don't forget about the cities of Ukraine that you already know – **Ки́їв**, **Льві́в**, **Сімферо́поль**. You could add some international destinations apart from **Москва́**, **Санкт-Петербу́рг**, **Варша́ва**:

Мінськ	*Minsk* (the capital of Belarus – Білору́сь)
Бухаре́ст	*Bucharest* (the capital of Romania – Руму́нія)
Будапе́шт	*Budapest* (the capital of Hungary – Уго́рщина)
Ві́день (gen.: Ві́дня)	*Vienna*
Берлі́н	*Berlin*
Пра́га	*Prague*

2 **On board the train.**

Revise the expressions used to introduce yourself, say what your name is, what you do for a living and why you are in Ukraine. You may wish to say:

– *I am going to Odesa* (**на** + acc.) *for a conference* (**конфере́нція**).

– *I am going on holiday to Yalta for five days.*

– *I have spent* (say: I was) *two weeks in Luhans'k, I am going back to Kyiv and in two days I am flying home.*

– *I always feel very hungry when(ever) I get on a train. That's why* (**ось чому́**) *I have a large bag of food and several bottles of beer with me* (**із собо́ю**).

You will almost certainly have to say to the carriage steward:

– *Could I have a glass of tea, please? And how much do I owe you for the bed linen?*

3 Some more practice:

- *I'll wait here. I want you to buy the tickets.*
- *I was standing in the queue for (**за** + inst.) tickets, talking to a very interesting person.* (Remember what happens to **г** in the locative singular!)
- *The next train will arrive soon.*
- *Why are you an hour late?*

TR 16, 02:50

4 Translate your part in this dialogue into Ukrainian:

X	Який Вам квиток?
You	*One ticket to Zhytomyr and back.*
X	На коли?
You	*To Zhytomyr on 4 October, and back on 22.*
X	Вам купейний чи плацкартний?
You	*I'll take a compartment.*

(The English in the next two exercises may sound a little odd, but it is very close to the Ukrainian way of saying things.)

5 Practise the negative words. Translate into Ukrainian:

- **a** Nobody ever understands me.
- **b** I don't know anyone who knows how to make good coffee.
- **c** I haven't spoken Ukrainian to anyone for a long time.
- **d** I haven't brought any food for the journey with me.

6 Now practise the indefinite words:

- **a** I would drink something warm with great pleasure.
- **b** In my childhood I used to watch any kind of film.
- **c** Taras has gone off somewhere to buy food.
- **d** Let's meet some time!

17 За на́ших дороги́х госте́й!
Here's to the health of our dear guests!

In this unit you will learn:
- ▶ *About visiting Ukrainians as a guest*
- ▶ *About the major festivals celebrated in Ukraine*
- ▶ *More about the imperative*

Діало́г

Solomiia Maliarchuk celebrates her birthday at home in the company of her friends. Ol'ha, Ursula, Solomiia, Stephen, Taras, Andrew and Ihor are seated round the table.

Ігор	Я пропоную́ підня́ти тост за Соломі́ю!
Тара́с	Соломі́йко, за твоє́ здоро́в'я!
Ольга	Хай ща́стить!
Соломі́я	Дя́кую Вам усі́м, що прийшли́. Мені́ спра́вді ду́же приє́мно всіх вас ба́чити у се́бе сього́дні! І дя́кую вам за ці чудо́ві кві́ти й подару́нки!
Сті́вен	*(to Ursula)* В Украї́ні кві́ти дару́ють за́вжди чи лише́ на день наро́дження?
У́рсула	Тут існу́є тради́ція приноси́ти господи́ні кві́ти, якщо́ йдеш у го́сті. Це не обов'язко́во, але́ кві́там за́вжди ра́ді.
Соломі́я	*(to Stephen)* Сті́вене, Ви принесли́ чудо́ві кві́ти. Я ду́же люблю́ троя́нди ...
Сті́вен	Я ра́дий, що вони́ Вам сподо́балися.
Тара́с	Соломі́я вмі́є роби́ти чудо́ві буке́ти. І ще вона́ ро́бить компози́ції із сухи́х росли́н.
Є́ндрю	А ще мені́ подо́баються карти́ни, які́ вона́ малю́є.
Соломі́я	Я приготува́ла для вас сюрпри́з. *(Leaves the room)*
Ольга	А я зна́ю!
Ігор	Якщо́ ти ска́жеш, це вже́ бу́де не сюрпри́з!
(Solomiia enters the room bearing a large cake with candles already lit)	
Тара́с	Це ви́твір мисте́цтва! Шкода́ його́ рі́зати . . . Соломі́йко, пе́ред тим, як дмухну́ти й загаси́ти сві́чки, не забу́дь заду́мати бажа́ння!
У́рсула	Бажа́ємо тобі́, щоб усе́, про що ти поду́мала, збуло́ся!
Тара́с	Ви́пиймо за ща́стя!
Соломі́я	Я хо́чу ви́пити за госте́й. За вас, дру́зі!
Го́сті	Бу́дьмо!

V	пропонува́ти (-ýю, -ýєш) (impf.)	to propose
	підня́ти (підніму́, підні́меш) (pf.)	to raise
	підня́ти тост за (+ acc.)	to raise a toast (to)
	за твоє́ здоро́в'я	[here's] to your health
	хай щасти́ть!	good luck!
	мені́ приє́мно всіх вас ба́чити у се́бе	it is a pleasure for me to see you all here **in my place**
	подару́нок (gen.: **подару́нка**)	present, gift
	дарува́ти (-ýю, -ýєш) (impf.)	to give as a present
	на день наро́дження	on [someone's] birthday
	існува́ти (-ýю, -ýєш) (impf.)	to exist
	тради́ція	tradition
	господи́ня	mistress of the house
	обов'язко́вий	compulsory
	кві́там за́вжди ра́ді	[people are] always glad **of** flowers
	троя́нда	rose
	умі́ти (умі́ю, умі́єш) (impf.)	to be able (know how to)
	буке́т	bouquet
	компози́ція	composition
	сухи́й	dry
	карти́на	picture
	малюва́ти (-ю, -юєш) (impf.)	to paint, draw
	сві́чка	candle
	ви́твір (gen.: **ви́твору**)	product (alt. **i/o**)
	це ви́твір мисте́цтва!	it's a work of art!
	пе́ред тим, як	just before
	дмухну́ти (-ну́, -не́ш) (pf.)	to give a blow, puff
	загаси́ти (загашу́, зага́сиш) (pf.)	to put out, extinguish
	заду́мати бажа́ння	to make a wish
	збу́тися (збу́деться, збу́дуться) (pf.)	to come true
	ви́пиймо!	let's drink!
	ща́стя (n)	happiness
	бу́дьмо!	(lit.) let us be/may we all be [healthy, happy]!

a Правда чи неправда?

1 В Украї́ні кві́ти дару́ють, ко́ли йду́ть у го́сті.

2 Соломі́я малю́є га́рні карти́ни.

3 Тара́с вніс до кімна́ти торт.

4 У́рсула пропону́є тост за господи́ню.

b Да́йте ві́дповідь на ці запита́ння англі́йською мо́вою

   1 What toasts are proposed by Solomiia's guests?

   2 What are Solomiia's favourite flowers?

   3 What surprise did Solomiia prepare for her guests?

   4 What should she do before blowing out the candles?

Як функціону́є мо́ва

1 VISITING

> ● **INSIGHT**
>
> There is a tradition of taking flowers to the lady of the house when you go visiting – **якщо́ йдеш у го́сті**. In Unit 10, Taras told us that he and Stephen had been invited by Ihor Ivanovych to go visit him – **І고р Іва́нович запропонува́в** *поі́хати до ньо́го в го́сті*.

The phrase answers the questions **куди́?** (*where to?*) and **до ко́го?** (*to whom?*), i.e. there is motion involved:

Question: До ко́го (Куди́) Тара́с зі Сті́веном пої́хали/і́дуть/пої́дуть у го́сті?

Answer: Вони́ пої́хали в го́сті до І́горя.

2 CAN

You have already met the verbs **могти́** (*can, to be able*) and **умі́ти**, which could be translated in exactly the same way, but with a crucial difference in meaning:

могти́	*to have the physical ability to do something*
умі́ти/вмі́ти	*to have the necessary knowledge to do something*

Words related to these two verbs show the same difference:

мі́цний	*strong, robust*
міць (f)	*might*
умі́лий	*skilled*

3 *ЩЕ* AND *ВЖЕ*

Ще is normally translated in wordlists as 'still', 'yet' and **вже** as 'already'. It is important to see how these words have to be translated in quite a different way in English on a number of occasions:

i I ще вона́ ро́бить компози́ції із сухи́х росли́н.	*And she does dried flower arrangements **as well**.*
ii А ще мені́ подо́баються карти́ни.	*And I like the pictures **too** . . .*

iii Якщо́ ти ска́жеш, це вже́ бу́де не сюрпри́з.

*If you tell it won't be a surprise **any more**.*

iv Що ще?

*What **else** [do you want]?*

v Хо́чете ще ка́ви?

*Do you want **more** coffee?*

4 *ПЕ́РЕД ТИМ, ЯК . . .* MORE ON JOINING SENTENCES TOGETHER

This is an example of a compound conjunction – 'compound' because it consists of more than one element, 'conjunction' because it joins separate sentences together. Note that **пе́ред тим, як** is followed by an infinitive; the English equivalent is followed by an *-ing* form – 'just before blowing out the candles'. English frequently makes no distinction between prepositions and conjunctions, e.g.:

  i After (preposition) breakfast I went to work.

  ii After (conjunction) I had had breakfast, I went to work.

The Ukrainian equivalents are:

  iii Пі́сля (*preposition*) сніда́нку я пішо́в на робо́ту.

  iv Пі́сля то́го, як (*conjunction*) я посні́дав, я пішо́в на робо́ту.

Note: don't forget the verbal adverbs introduced in Unit 15! It would also be perfectly possible to say:

  v Посні́давши, я пішо́в на робо́ту.

> **LANGUAGE TIP**
> **посні́дати** (pf.) *to have breakfast*

5 THE IMPERATIVE

You have now seen many examples of second-person imperative forms, e.g.:

Infinitive	S.	Pl.
чита́ти	чита́й	чита́йте
телефонува́ти	телефону́й	телефону́йте
іти́	іди́	іді́ть
писа́ти	пиши́	пиші́ть
роби́ти	роби́	робі́ть
ви́бачити	ви́бач	ви́бачте

The picture is not quite as confusing as it looks at first sight. Everything depends on the **stress position** of the first-person singular and the **structure** of the second-person singular form of the present tense.

First conjugation

a If the second-person singular contains the sequence of letters **аєш** (i.e. **а + й + е**) or **ієш** (**і + й + е**), the singular imperative will end in **-й: читáєш – читáй**, to which **-те** is added to form the plural (or formal singular) – **читáйте**.

Also:

розумíти	розумíєш	розумíй	розумíйте

Note: important exception: давáти даéш **давáй** **давáйте**

b If the first-person singular has the stress on the ending (**берý, ідý, пишý**) and the second-person singular ends with a consonant + **еш**, the singular imperative will end in **-и**, the plural in **-íть**:

брáти	берéш	бери́	берíть
іти́	ідéш	іди́	ідíть
писáти	пи́шеш	пиши́	пишíть

c If the first-person has the stress on any other syllable (**рíжу**), the singular imperative has either no ending at all:

рíзати	рíжеш	ріж	рíжте

or a soft sign:

забýти	забýдеш	забýдь	забýдьте

Second conjugation

a If the second-person singular contains the sequence of letters vowel + **їш** (i.e. **й + і**) the singular ends in **-й:**

стоя́ти	стої́ш	стíй	стíйте

b If the first-person singular has the stress on the ending (**роблю́**) and the second-person singular consists of consonant + **иш**, the singular imperative will end in **-и**, the plural in **-íть:**

роби́ти	рóбиш	роби́	робíть

c If the first person has the stress on any other syllable (**ви́бачу**), the singular imperative has no ending at all:

ви́бачити	ви́бачиш	ви́бач	ви́бачте

Obviously these rules do not account for the irregular forms, e.g. **їж(те)** from **ї́сти**; such forms have to be noted separately.

The first-person plural imperative

Examples from this unit: **ви́пиймо** (*let's drink*); **бу́дьмо** (*let us be*).

The first-person plural imperative can be formed simply by replacing the ending **-те** with **-мо** or **-іть** with **-імо** (or sometimes **-м**), e.g. **чита́ймо**, **робі́м(о)**, **забу́дьмо**. An important oddity is the use of the past tense **пішли́** to mean 'let's go!'.

The third-person imperative

'Let him/her/it/them ...': this is formed by combining **хай** or **неха́й** with the third-person singular or plural form of the verb:

Хай (неха́й) Ігор зустрі́не   *Let Ihor meet Stephen!*
    Сті́вена!

Aspect and the imperative

The advice given in Unit 5 – note which aspect is used in the examples given in the dialogues and texts you will have read by the time you complete this course – still holds good. A perfective imperative tends to be used when the action is to be performed at the moment of speaking or refers to only one action, e.g. **Напиші́ть листі́вку**! (*Write a postcard!*). More general instructions are likely to be in the imperfective, e.g. **Пиші́ть мені́**! (*Write to me!*). One of the few clear-cut statements that can be made is that negated commands (**не** + imperative) are always in the imperfective aspect:

Не чита́йте цю кни́гу!   *Don't read this book!*
    Вона́ дуже пога́на!   *It's very bad!*

When the imperfective after **не** is in the perfective aspect, you are dealing with a warning:

Не забу́дь!   *(Mind you) don't forget!*

6 A NOTE ON NUMBER

These are nouns in Ukrainian that do not have both singular and plural forms. Some have only **singular** forms:

▶ words denoting objects that can exist only in the singular, e.g. geographical terms like **Іта́лія, Льві́в**
▶ words denoting substances and materials, e.g. **цу́кор, молоко́**
▶ abstract and collective terms, the names of branches of knowledge, e.g. **відпочи́нок** (*holiday*), **бі́знес, о́дяг, допомо́га, здоро́в'я, му́зика, торгі́вля, матема́тика, ціка́вість, ли́стя** (*foliage*).

Words of foreign origin like **фо́то, інтерв'ю́, ра́діо** form a special group. They have no case endings at all and therefore have the same form in both the singular and plural, e.g. **ва́ше інтерв'ю́, ва́ші інтерв'ю́**.

Other Ukrainian nouns occur only in the **plural**:

▸ nouns denoting objects that comprise two (*cf* English: scissors, shears, trousers, glasses), e.g. **окуля́ри**, **ме́блі**, **гро́ші**, **лі́ки**, **но́жиці** (*scissors*), **ша́хи** (*chess*). Also **імени́ни** (*nameday*), **кані́кули** (*holidays*)

▸ certain words denoting actions or feelings, e.g. **деба́ти** (*debate*), **ра́дощі** (*joy, happiness*), **за́здрощі** (*envy, jealousy*)

▸ certain geographical names (mountain ranges, cities), e.g. **Карпа́ти**, **Су́ми** (*Sumy* – city in Ukraine), **Афі́ни** (*Athens*).

7 VOWELS THAT DISAPPEAR AND REAPPEAR

> **LANGUAGE TIP**
>
> You have already seen that **o** and **e** can alternate with **i** under certain conditions and that they can also disappear entirely in declension (**вівто́рок**, gen.: **вівто́рка**). The vowels **o** and **e** can also be inserted between two consonants.

Inserted vowels

As you know, the genitive plural of most feminine and neuter nouns has no ending at all. If this would mean that two consonants come together at the end of the word, the vowel **o** is inserted between them to make pronunciation easier. This does not, of course, mean that Ukrainian words can never end in two consonants!

Nom. sg.	*Gen. pl.*
листі́вка	листі́**вок**
прогу́ля**нк**а	прогу́ля**нок**
ві**кн**о́	ві́**кон**

Something similar happens with masculine singular short-form adjectives, although here the inserted vowel is **e**, e.g.:

жо́дний, (m) жо́д**е**н, (f) жо́дна

Disappearing vowels

These are often known as 'fleeting vowels'. The vowel is present in the nominative singular but drops out in all the other case forms:

Nom. s.	*Gen. s.*
ві́т**е**р	ві́тру
ли́п**е**нь	ли́пня
се́рп**е**нь	се́рпня
ка́ш**е**ль	ка́шлю
д**е**нь	дня

O and **e** which alternate with **i** never drop out. A whole number of other words do not follow this pattern (e.g. **гýмор** (an obvious loan word), **жарт**, **аспéкт**, **рецéпт**, **контрáкт**, **харáктер**). If in doubt, check the vocabulary at the back of this book or a dictionary.

A hint: Ukrainian words ending in **-ець** or **-ок** all follow this pattern:

-ець:	украї́н**е**ць	украї́нця	украї́нці
	стіл**é**ць	стільця́	стільці́
	карбóван**е**ць	карбóванця	карбóванці

-ок:	буди́н**о**к	буди́нка	буди́нки
	рахýн**о**к	рахýнка	рахýнки
	подарýн**о**к	подарýнка	подарýнки
	спи́с**о**к	спи́ску	спи́ски
	розрахýн**о**к	розрахýнку	розрахýнки
	квит**ó**к	квитка́	квитки́

святкóвий стіл	*festive board*
скáтерка	*tablecloth*
прибóр	*item of cutlery*
ніж (gen.: **ножá**)	*knife* (alt. **i/o**)
видéлка	*fork*
лóжка	*spoon*
чáйна лóжка	*teaspoon*
сервíз	*service (of crockery)*
тарíлка	*plate*
чáшка	*cup*
блю́дечко	*saucer*
чáрка	*small glass (for spirits)*
кéлих/фужéр	*(wine) glass*
сервéтка	*serviette*

8 PRETEND YOU ARE CELEBRATING A GREAT OCCASION WITH YOUR UKRAINIAN FRIENDS

TR 17

a Greetings and congratulations

Вітáю тебé з (+ inst.) . . .	*Best wishes on . . .*
Вітáю Вас із (+ inst.) . . .	*(lit. I greet you with . . .)*

Now work out the occasion:

Вітáю тебé/Вас із Днем нарóдження!

Вітáю тебé/Вас із ювілéєм!

Вітáю тебé/Вас із річнúцею весíлля!

Вітáю тебé/Вас зі свя́том!

Щúро вітáю тебé з Різдвóм Христóвим і Новúм рóком!

Від усьóго сéрця вітáю Вас із нагóди Вáшого весíлля!

b Wishes

Бажáю Вам (dat.) (+ gen.)...   I wish you...

Бажáю тобí (dat.) (+ gen.)...

Приймíть моï найщирíші побажáння.

Бажáю Вам щáстя.

Бажáю тобí міцнóго здорóв'я.

Я хóчу побажáти тобí життéвих ýспіхів (*every success in life*).

Від усьóго сéрця бажáю тобí добрá й рáдості.

Нехáй цей день бýде для Вас світлим і рáдісним.

c Toasts

Toasts are a very important part of Ukrainian drinking culture. Everyone at a celebration dinner will be expected to take a turn at proposing one. Indeed, a toastmaster (**тамадá**) may be appointed to ensure that this happens! Here are some simple toasts, together with English translations:

Бýдьмо!	*Let's be/May we be!* (healthy, happy etc.) (i.e. cheers)
Я хóчу вúпити за твоé здорóв'я!	*I would like to drink to your health!*
Я пропонýю вúпити за щáстя й добрóбут ціéї сім'ï!	*I propose that we drink to the happiness and prosperity of this family!*

Різдвó Христóве	*Christmas*
від усьóго сéрця	*with all [my] heart*
іменúнник	*the person whose name day (or sometimes birthday) it is*
свя́то	*feast, festival*
святкувáти (-кýю, -кýєш) (impf.)	*to celebrate*
святкувáння (n)	*celebration*

218

ювіле́й	*jubilee*
річни́ця	*anniversary*
поздоро́влення (n)	*congratulations*
привіта́ння (n)	*greetings*
побажа́ння (n)	*wishes*
добро́бут	*prosperity*

d Holidays in Ukraine

The New Year (**Нови́й рік**) is observed by everyone; the parties begin on the evening of 31 December and continue throughout the next day. 1 January is a public holiday. Christmas (**Різдво́**) is observed according to the tradition of the Orthodox Church on 7 January. Some families also celebrate the Old New Year (**Стари́й нови́й рік**) on 14 January. Easter is a moveable feast, but it always falls in the spring. The dates of the Orthodox Easter rarely coincide with those of the Catholic festival. The holy days of Easter are collectively known as **Па́сха**. Easter Sunday is called **Вели́кдень**. It is customary to present bouquets of flowers to the ladies on 8 March – still known as **Міжнаро́дний жіно́чий день** (*International Women's Day*). 9 May marks the anniversary of the victory over Nazi Germany in the Second World War – **День Перемо́ги** (*Victory Day*). Ukrainian independence is celebrated on 24 August – **День Незале́жності Украї́ни**. These last two festivals are marked by public demonstrations, concerts and special open-air markets; the streets are decorated with flags and banners. Just as at New Year, people send congratulatory cards and telegrams to their friends.

? Test yourself: Впра́ви

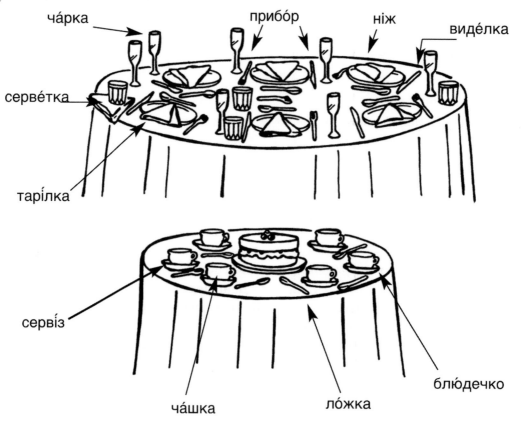

1 **Solomiia has prepared a list of all the items that have to be placed on the table for her guests. Check the pictures of the laid-up tables with the list that follows and say:**

   a what she has forgotten

   b what is superfluous on the table.

Спи́сок Соломі́ї (папіре́ць із бло́кнота) – *Solomiia's list (a page from her notebook)*

   ска́терка

   7 таріло́к для холо́дних заку́сок

   7 тарілочо́к для хлі́ба

   7 серве́ток

   7 ножі́в

   7 виде́лок

   7 ложо́к для десе́рту

   7 фуже́рів для шампа́нського

   7 ке́лихів для вина́

7 склянóк для води́

7 чарóк для коньякý

Приготувáти чáйний і кавóвий сервíзи: чашки́, блю́дечка, лóжечки

2 Now practise some written Ukrainian of your own!

Напиші́ть запрóшення свої́м дрýзям на святкувáння Новóго рóку у Вас вдóма. Запропонýйте їм приї́хати до Вас на 9.00 вéчора.

3 Some grammar revision.

Where possible, put the following nouns into the form of the nominative:

a plural: теáтр, здорóв'я, музéй, фóто, тост, поздорóвлення, подарýнок, щáстя, сервíз, джаз

b singular: сюрпри́зи, гóсті, штани́, сувенíри, шáхи, дебáти, концéрти, канíкули, вистáви, мéблі

4 Ol'ha, Ihor, Ursula and Andrew are walking in the Botanical Gardens after visiting an art exhibition. Read the dialogue and answer the questions that follow:

Óльга	Ви́ставка булá прóсто унікáльна. Я одéржала спрáвжнє задовóлення!
Íгор	Менí шкодá, що я не знавéць живóпису. Алé як дилетáнт, я дýже люблю́ диви́тися карти́ни й ходи́ти в музéї.
Ýрсула	Я такóж. Алé найбíльшу роль у моéму житті́ всé-таки відіграє́ мýзика. Менí дýже подóбається óпера, балéт і симфонíчна мýзика.
Éндрю	Я зáвжди дивувáвся, як люди́на, якá отримáла такý музи́чну освíту, як ти, мóже, пóряд із клáсикою, люби́ти рок, поп і джаз ... Я не мóжу цьогó збагнýти!
Óльга	Про смаки́ не сперечáються.
Ýрсула	Менí подóбається спрáвжня, таланов́ита мýзика, незалéжно від жáнру.
Éндрю	Що не кажíть, алé найпопулярнíший вид сучáсного мистéцтва – це кінó. Сьогóдні вíдео ди́вляться дорóслі й дíти. Я сам люблю́ кінофíльми.
Óльга	Я не мóжу ви́словитися прóти. Алé, якщó я мáю квитки́ до теáтру, я спокíйно пропущý будь-яки́й фільм.
Íгор	(*mysteriously*) Післязáвтра ти мáтимеш такý нагóду ...
Ýрсула	Я б такóж не відмóвилася піти́ до теáтру.
Éндрю	Ну, це невáжко. Ми з Тарáсом учóра купи́ли сім квиткíв до теáтру украї́нської дрáми на прем'є́ру. Ви не заперéчуєте?

a What is the most important art form in Ursula's life?

b What is it that Andrew finds difficult to understand?

c What art form does Andrew consider to be the most popular?

d What have Andrew and Taras bought?

ви́ставка	*exhibition*
знаве́ць (gen.: **знавця́**) (+ gen.)	*expert (on), connoisseur (of)*
живо́пис	*fine art paintings*
дилета́нт	*amateur*
роль (f)	*role*
відігравáти (third-person singular **відіграé**) (impf.) **роль**	*to play a role*
дивувáтися (у́юся, -у́єшся) (impf.)	*to be amazed*
освíта	*education*
пóряд із (+ inst.)	*alongside*
збагну́ти (-ну́, -не́ш) (pf.)	*to grasp, comprehend*
спереча́тися (impf.)	*to quarrel*
незалéжно від (+ gen.)	*independent(ly) of*
жанр	*genre*
що не кажíть, алé . . .	*whatever you say, . . .*
дорóслий	*adult (also used as noun, i.e.* **дорóслі**, *adults)*
я не мóжу ви́словитися прóти	*I can't say anything against it*
квитóк до теáтру	*ticket **for** the theatre*
відмóвитися (-мóвлюся, -мóвишся, -мóвляться (pf.)	*to refuse*

18

До побáчення, Украïно!
See you again, Ukraine!

In this unit you will learn:

▶ *About writing letters in Ukrainian*
▶ *Another way of denoting possession*
▶ *Some more negatives*
▶ *Something about wordbuilding*

Текст

TR 18, 00:07

On Stephen's last evening in Ukraine, Ostap and Natalka are asking him about his impressions of the country. Here is what he has to say while showing some slides. Read the text and answer the questions that follow.

Про прирóду Украïни менí дуже вáжко розповідáти . . . Я не знáю, як мóжна передáти словáми те, що я бáчив. Ось на цих слáйдах мóжна побáчити найкрасивíші місця́, якí я встиг сфотографувáти.

(1) Це Карпáти. Ярéмча. У мéне вийшóв чудóвий слайд біля водоспáду. Це скéля Дóвбуша, дýже гáрне мíсце.

(2) А ось, подивíться, якé незвичáйне фóто: це найбíльший гриб, якúй я бáчив у своéму життí! Я сам йогó знайшóв у лíсі.

(3) Це – Ялта, бíля морськóго пóрту. Я зміг зня́ти захід сóнця, мóре булó рожéвого кóльору, а кораблí – бíлі.

(4) Ще менí дýже сподóбалися ось ці місця́, недалéко від Запорíжжя. Я не мóжу забýти врáження, коли наш пóïзд ïхав по вузькíй смýжці сýші, якý отóчує з обóх бокíв водá. Подивíться, це – кáзка! З óдного бóку мáйже не вúдно бéрега, тíльки повéрхня водú, а з íншого бóку – хáти на зелéних пáгорбах, очерéт і вéрби над водóю, тúша і спóкій.

Я багáто читáв про красý украïнської прирóди, алé все однó словáми це не мóжна передáти. Украïна – рíзна на схóді й на зáході, на пíвночі й на пíвдні. І менí вáжко сказáти вам, де менí сподóбалося найбíльше.

Менí дýже шкодá, що ми з Тарáсом зáвтра від'ïжджáємо. Алé тепéр я знáю, що приïдý сюдú ще багáто разíв.

слайд	*(photographic) slide*
переда́ти слова́ми	*to put into words (lit. to put across with words)*
всти́гнути (-ну, -неш; past tense всти́г (m), всти́гла (f), всти́гли (pl.), (pf.)	*to manage*
сфотографува́ти (-у́ю, -у́єш) (pf.)	*to photograph*
у ме́не ви́йшов чудо́вий слайд	*I had a really good slide come out*
ске́ля	*rock, cliff*
незвича́йний	*unusual*
змогти́ (змо́жу, змо́жеш; past tense зміг (m), змогла́ (f), змогли́ (pl.)) (pf.)	*to manage, succeed*
зня́ти (зніму́, зні́меш) (pf.)	*(lit.) to take off (e.g. clothes), remove; (here): to take a photograph (of)*
сму́жка	*strip*
су́ша	*dry land*
ото́чувати (-ую, -уєш) (impf.)	*to surround*
з обо́х бокі́в	*on (lit. from) both sides*
ка́зка	*fairy story*
не ви́дно бе́рега	*the shore isn't visible*
пове́рхня	*surface*
очере́т	*reeds*
верба́	*willow*
спо́кій (gen.: спо́кою)	*calm peace* (alt. **i/o**)
все одно́	*all the same*
схід (gen.: схо́ду)	*east* (alt. **i/o**)
за́хід (gen.: за́ходу)	*west* (alt. **i/o**)
пі́вніч (gen.: пі́вночі) (f)	*north* (alt. **i/o**)
пі́вдень (gen.: пі́вдня) (m)	*south* (alt. **i/o**)
раз	*time (as in 'three times etc.')*
бага́то разі́в	*many times*

Запита́ння до те́ксту

a What is on slide no. 2?

b At what time of day was Stephen taking photographs in Yalta?

c What is so special about slide no. 4?

d What does Stephen find so difficult?

e Does Stephen think he will return to Ukraine?

Як функціону́є мо́ва

1 ANOTHER WAY OF DENOTING POSSESSION

Ukrainian has a set of commonly used adjectives, derived mainly from personal names, that denote possession. They are formed like this.

a with the suffix -ів, -їв:

Name	Adjective (m)	(f)	(n)	(pl.)
Сті́вен	Сті́венів	Сті́венова	Сті́венове	Сті́венові
Петро́	Петрі́в	Петро́ва	Петро́ве	Петро́ві
І́гор	І́горів	І́горева	І́гореве	І́гореві
Васи́ль	Васи́лів	Василе́ва	Василе́ве	Василе́ві
Сергі́й	Сергі́їв	Сергі́єва	Сергі́єве	Сергі́єві

Note the alternation of **i** in the suffix with **о**, **е** and **є**. As you can see from these examples this suffix is used with names of male human beings. It can also be tacked on to other nouns denoting males, e.g. **бра́тів/бра́това/бра́тове** (brother's); **ба́тьків/ба́тькова/ба́тькове** (father's); **учи́телів/учи́телева/учи́телеве** (teacher's).

b with the suffix -ин, -їн:

Name	Adjective (m)	(f)	(n)	(pl.)
Оле́на	Оле́нин	Оле́нина	Оле́нине	Оле́нині
О́льга	О́льжин	О́льжина	О́льжине	О́льжині
Марі́я	Марі́їн	Марі́їна	Марі́їне	Марі́їні
Мико́ла	Мико́лин	Мико́лина	Мико́лине	Мико́лині

This suffix is used with names of female human beings or with names of males (e.g. **Мико́ла** (Nicholas)) that decline like them. Note the change of **г** to **ж** in front of the suffix in the name **О́льга**. A similar change also occurs with **к**: **дочка́** has the possessive adjective **доччи́н** (daughter's). Other useful possessive adjectives are: **се́стрин** (sister's), **ма́терин** (mother's). This last word derives from **ма́ти**, a more formal word than **ма́ма**.

The masculine nominative singular ending of both suffixes is like that of short-form adjectives, i.e. it is without **-ий**.

Here are some examples of usage:

Сті́венові дру́зі	*Stephen's friends*
у бра́товій кварти́рі	*in [my] brother's flat*
ба́тькове крі́сло	*father's armchair*
Марі́їна маши́на	*Maria's car*

2 BUILDING UP NEW WORDS

a With prefixes

You have already seen several examples of verbs with prefixes. Let us look at one verb and see what meanings can be obtained by adding prefixes: **доста́вити**, formed by adding the prefix **до-** to the imperfective verb **ста́вити** (*to put, place*). This prefix has the same basic meaning as the preposition **до**, so with a little imagination we can see that **доста́вити** means 'to get/put something to a particular place', i.e. deliver. The corresponding imperfective is **доставля́ти**. Here are some more prefixes:

Prefix	Meaning	Verb (impf./pf.)	Meaning
ви	*out*	виставля́ти/ви́ставити	*to put/set out, exhibit*
		(виста́ва: *performance*: ви́ставка: *exhibition*)	
з(зі)	(here:) *with*	зіставля́ти/зіста́вити	*to put (s'thing) with (s'thing else), i.e. to compare*
у (в)	*into*	вставля́ти/вста́вити	*to insert*
пере	*across*	переставля́ти/переста́вити	*to move across, i.e. to transpose*

Sometimes the prefixes correspond to prepositions and have a similar meaning; in other instances (e.g. **пере**), there is no such relationship. Here are some more examples with the verb **роби́ти/зроби́ти**:

ви	виробля́ти/ви́робити	*to work out, produce, manufacture*
	(виробни́цтво: *manufacture, production*)	
до	доробля́ти/дороби́ти	*to finish making/doing*
за	заробля́ти/зароби́ти	*to gain by working, i.e.* to earn
	зароби́ти на хліб	*to earn one's livelihood*
	(заробі́ток (gen.: заробі́тку) *wages*)	
на	наробля́ти/нароби́ти	*to make/cause a lot of (especially unpleasant things)*
на (-ся)	наробля́тися/нароби́тися	*to overwork oneself*
пере	переробля́ти/перероби́ти	*to do over again, remake, transform*
про	проробля́ти/пророби́ти	*to spend time working*
	e.g. пророби́ти ввесь день	*to work the whole day*

18 *До поба́чення, Украї́но! See you again, Ukraine!* **227**

Of course, it is often impossible to predict exactly what a prefixed verb might mean, but these general guidelines may be of some assistance.

b With suffixes

Let us take as an example the verb **замовля́ти/замо́вити** (*to order*). By removing **-ляти** and **-ити**, and adding **-ник** to what is left, we obtain the word **замо́вник** (*someone who makes an order*); **-ник** denotes the doer of the action:

письме́нник	*someone who writes (professionally) = writer*
помічни́к	*someone who helps = assistant*
провідни́к	*someone who accompanies, 'leads through' = guide, train conductor/steward*
прово́дити	(impf.)/провести́ (pf.) *to escort, convey*
робітни́к	*someone who works = worker*

The equivalent form for women is **-ниця**.

Doers of action can also be denoted by **-тель, -ар, -яр**:

учи́тель/вчи́тель	*someone who teaches = teacher* (verb: учи́ти/вчи́ти)
лі́кар	*someone who heals = doctor* (лікува́ти)
маля́р	*someone who paints houses = painter and decorator* (малюва́ти: *to paint, draw a picture*)

-ість is a suffix that often forms feminine abstract nouns from adjectives; some such nouns correspond to English words ending in *-ness*:

гість *guest*	гости́нний *hospitable*	гости́нність *hospitality*
зло *evil*	злий *malicious*	злість *malice*
м'яки́й *soft*	м'яки́й *soft, tender*	м'якість *softness, tenderness*

A few more examples will be sufficient to show how words relate to each other:

рік *year*   річни́й *annual*   річни́ця *anniversary*

(This example also shows that suffixes do not always mean the same thing; **-ниця** in **річни́ця** obviously does not refer to doers of actions here!)

будува́ти *to build*   буди́нок/буді́вля *building*
    будіве́льний *building* (adj.)   будіве́льник *builder*
два/дво́є *two*   подві́йний *double*   подві́йність *duplicity*
    подво́їти *to (re)double*
    двозна́чний *ambiguous*   двоповерхо́вий *two-storeyed*

3 SOME MORE NEGATIVES

Negative pronouns, adjectives and adverbs were introduced in Unit 16. Some more words must now be listed in order to complete the picture. Compare these words with those given there:

ні́кого	*there is no one*
ні́чого	*there is nothing*
ні́де	*there is nowhere*
ні́куди	*there is nowhere* (motion)
ні́коли	*there is no time*

First, note the stress positions – the words in fact look the same as those in Unit 16, except for where the stress falls. These new negative words are used like this:

Мені́ ні́чого роби́ти.	*I have nothing to do.* (lit. there is nothing for me to do)
Нам ні́ з ким розмовля́ти украї́нською.	*There is no one for us to speak Ukrainian with.*
Йому́ ні́де сі́сти.	*He has nowhere to sit.* (lit. there is nowhere for him to sit)
Сті́венові ні́коли ду́мати про Соломі́ю.	*Stephen has no time to think about Solomiia.*

As you can see, these words are preceded by a noun or pronoun in the dative case. Now look at how the shift in stress position changes the meaning. Contrast these sentences:

Я тут ніко́го не зна́ю.	*I don't know anyone here.*
Мені́ ні́кого запита́ти про це.	*I have no one to ask about this.* (or: there is no one that I can ask about this)
Вона́ нічо́го не купи́ла.	*She didn't buy anything.*
Їй ні́чого сказа́ти.	*She has nothing to say.*
Він ніде́ не працю́є.	*He doesn't work anywhere.*
Йому́ ні́де жи́ти.	*He has nowhere to live.*
Ми ніку́ди не хо́димо вечора́ми.	*We don't go anywhere in the evenings.*
Нам ні́куди піти́.	*We have nowhere to go.*
Тебе́ ніко́ли нема́є вдо́ма.	*You're never at home.*
Тобі́ ні́коли відпочива́ти.	*You have no time to rest.*

Note that the negative words with the stress on the first syllable (**ні́кого, ні́чого, ні́де** etc.) require the dative case of the noun or pronoun and are followed by an infinitive.

4 BOTH

The numeral meaning 'both' has the following forms:

Nom.	обйдва (m) and (n) inanimate	обйдві (f)
Acc.	*as nom. or gen.*	
Gen.	обóх	
Dat.	обóм	
Loc.	(на) обóх	
Inst.	обомá	

There is also **обóє**, used to refer to a pair of human beings already mentioned (*the two of them*). It has the same case forms as **обйдва/обйдві**.

5 WRITING LETTERS

Solomiia and Stephen are obviously going to correspond, if only on business matters. Certain established principles have to be observed if the letter is to look really Ukrainian.

How to address letters

Addresses are written in the following way:

> Україна
>
> 252138 Київ
>
> бульвар Шевченка, 15, кв. 24
>
> Малярчук Соломії Миколаївні

The order is:

1 country (if writing from abroad)

2 postcode (**íндекс**) followed by the name of the town

3 street name, followed by house number, after which comes the number of the flat. The abbreviation **кв**. or **к**. stands for **квартúра**. Sometimes the abbreviation is omitted altogether: 15/24

4 addressee in the dative case, surname first, followed by first name and patronymic.

The letter itself begins with:

Дорогúй/Дорогá (followed by the name in the vocative case and an exclamation mark if you know the person quite well).

A greater degree of respect is shown by using **Шанóвний/Шанóвна** before the name and patronymic in the vocative or **пáне/пáні/пáнно** (*Mr/Ms* or *Mrs/Miss*) and the surname. Even more respect can be shown by starting the letter with the words **Вельмишанóвний добрóдію** (from **добрóдій**)! (*Dear Sir*) or **Вельмишанóвна добрóдійко** (from **добрóдійка**)! (*Dear Madam*).

It is customary to write these words in the middle of the line. The letter can be concluded with the words:

Із найкра́щими побажа́ннями	*With best wishes*
Ши́ро Ваш(а)	*Yours sincerely*
З пова́гою	*With respect*

These 'signing-off' words also go to the middle of the line. The date is written right at the end of the letter, on the left-hand side of the page; the signature is placed on the right-hand side. The first line of each pagaraph of a letter should begin some way into the line.

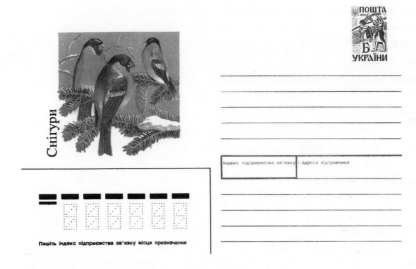

A UKRAINIAN ENVELOPE

Here are the standard abbreviations used in writing addresses:

вул.	ву́лиця	*street*
пл.	пло́ща	*square*
пров.	прову́лок	*lane*
просп.	проспе́кт	*avenue*
б-р	бульва́р	*boulevard*
буд.	буди́нок	*building*
корп.	ко́рпус	*block*
пов.	по́верх	*storey*
кв.	кварти́ра	*flat*
кімн.	кімна́та	*room*

Test yourself: Впрáви

1 Almost the last chance to test your comprehension! Read the following dialogue and text and answer the questions that follow:

🎧 TR 18, 02:43

Дзвінóк у двéрі Соломíїної квартúри *(a ring at the door of Solomiia's flat)*.

Соломíя	Хто там?
Гóлос	Я з фíрми "Конвáлія". Менí дорýчено достáвити замóвлення.
(Solomiia opens the door and sees a man standing there with an enormous bunch of flowers)	
Посúльний	Пáні Малярчýк?
Соломíя	Так.
Посúльний	Я із слýжби замóвлень. Це для Вас.
Соломíя	*(impressed)* А від кóго це? Хто зробúв замóвлення?
Посúльний	Ось квитáнція. Замóвлення зрóблено з Великобритáнії. Замóвник – пан С. Тéйлор. Ось йогó адрéса.
Соломíя	Дя́кую, не трéба, я знáю адрéсу. Дýже Вам вдя́чна.
Посúльний	До побáчення.

🇻 | | |
|---|---|
| **дзвінóк** (gen.: **дзвінкá**) | *ring* (of a bell) |
| **гóлос** | *voice* |
| **конвáлія** | *lily of the valley* [here used as the name of a florist's] |
| **доручúти** (pf.) | *to entrust* |
| **достáвити (достáвлю, достáвиш) (**pf.) | *to deliver* |
| **замóвлення** (n) | *order* |
| **менí дорýчено достáвити замóвлення** | *I have the job of delivering an order* |
| **посúльний** (adj. functioning as noun) | *delivery man* |

The letter from Stephen that arrived with the flowers

 TR 18, 03:25

Дорогá Соломíє!

Приймíть моí найщирíші поздорóвлення з Різдвóм Христóвим і Новим Рóком! Бажáю Вам щáстя, úспіхів і міцнóго здорóв'я. Сподівáюся, що у Вас все дóбре, Ви щасливі, Вáша робóта принóсить Вам рáдість.

Приймíть ці квíти на знак глибóкої повáги й щúрої симпáтії. Якщó коли-нéбудь Ви бýдете потребувáти моéї допомóги, я вважáтиму за честь зробити все можлиíве, щоб допомогти Вам.

Ще раз вітáю Вас зі свя́том і сподівáюся на продóвження нáшої спíльної робóти в новóму рóці.

Прошý Вас не вважáти себé зобов'язаною відповідáти на цей лист.

До побáчення,

Щúро Ваш,

Стíвен

знак	*sign*
приймíть ці квíти на знак глибóкої повáги	*accept these flowers as a sign of [my] deep respect*
потребувáти (+ gen.)	*to require, demand, need*
я вважáтиму за честь	*I shall consider [it] an honour*
зробити все можлиíве	*to do everything possible*
сподівáтися (на + асс.)	*to hope (for)*
продóвження (n)	*continuation*
зобов'язаний	*obliged*
прошý Вас не вважáти себé зобов'язаною	*please do not consider yourself obliged*

a Прáвда чи непрáвда?

1 Соломíя Малярчýк одéржала в подарýнок букéт квíтів.

2 Квíти булó надíслано чéрез фíрму "Роксолáна".

3 У своéму листí Стíвен попросив Соломíю про допомóгу.

4 Стíвен прóсить Соломíю обов'язкóво відповісти на йогó лист.

b Да́йте ві́дповідь на ці запита́ння англі́йською мо́вою

1 Who ordered the flowers?

2 Was the order placed in Kyiv?

3 What was the occasion for sending greetings to Solomiia?

4 What offer does Stephen make in the letter?

2 You take two telephone calls for Andrew in Ukrainian and have to leave the messages for him in English (i.e. who phoned and what the caller's message was):

1st call:

Алло́! Це телефону́є Олексі́й Гончаре́нко з компа́нії "Оме́га". Я вчо́ра прилеті́в із Ло́ндона. У ме́не є терміно́вий лист до Е́ндрю від його́ до́брого знайо́мого Ма́йкла Ро́бінсона. Майкл проси́в мене́ доста́вити цього́ листа́ до Ки́єва й одра́зу подзвони́ти Е́ндрю. Ось моя́ адре́са: ву́лиця Шовкови́чна, 38, кварти́ра 35. Телефо́н: 295 16 87. Я чека́тиму на дзвіно́к сього́дні вве́чері.

2nd call:

До́брий ве́чір! Це телефону́є О́льга. Я за́раз вдо́ма у Соломі́ї. З не́ю сього́дні ста́вся неща́сний ви́падок: у не́ї серйо́зна тра́вма колі́на. Ми подзвони́ли 03 і ви́кликали "швидку́ допомо́гу". Коли́ приї́хала маши́на, Соломі́ю забра́ли до травматологі́чного пу́нкту. Я пої́хала ра́зом із не́ю. У ліка́рні їй зроби́ли рентге́н, по́тім її огля́нув лі́кар. Перело́му нема́є, але́ тре́ба кі́лька днів поле́жати вдо́ма. Якщо́ змо́жеш, зателефону́й уве́чері. Па.

3 Your boss gives you some instructions in English to be passed by email to your partners in Kyiv in Ukrainian:

I want you to send birthday greetings to the manager (**нача́льник**) of Kyiv Railway Station Mr A V Pylypenko (*make sure you use all the phrases that Ukrainians like to include!*). Tell him that I hope our cooperation will continue in the future. Inform him that our company has sent him a packet with a catalogue (**катало́г**) of our latest products, and that we have booked tickets for a trip to Ukraine in February next year. We'll be phoning him next week. (*Don't forget to finish the fax properly!*)

4 Sort out the following phrases in such a way as to produce two separate messages. One is a postcard that you are going to send to a girlfriend while you are on holiday in Odesa, the other is a fax to your partners in Ukraine with information about your impending arrival.

Чека́тиму на твою́ ві́дповідь. Я приїжджа́ю на де́сять днів, щоб відві́дати ваш інститу́т. Ти ще не відпочива́ла цього́ ро́ку. Потрі́бно запроси́ти пре́су й телеба́чення на "кру́глий стіл", що відбу́деться 19 жо́втня. Поду́май про це, Ната́лочко. Хто доповіда́є на засіда́нні? Я купу́ю собі́ шашлики́, фру́кти, моро́зиво. Ваш помічни́к телефонува́в мені́ вчо́ра, і ми розроби́ли дета́льну програ́му візи́ту. Пишу́ тобі́ з Оде́си пе́ршу листівку. Шано́вний Володи́мире Миха́йловичу! Приві́т, моя́ кицю́ню! Чека́ю від вас дета́льної інформа́ції. У нас тут не ду́же жа́рко, як за́вжди буває́ у ве́ресні. Я тако́ж прошу́ мене́ повідо́мити про організа́цію засі́дання 21 числа́. Люблю́, цілу́ю, Андрі́й. Мо́жете телефонува́ти мені́ на робо́ту: я пе́ред від'ї́здом працю́ю до пі́знього ве́чора. Я відпочива́ю, вра́нці й уве́чері ходжу́ на пляж, ї́жджу на екску́рсії. Чи могли́ б Ви зустрі́ти мене́ о 9.20 ра́нку 13 жо́втня? Ду́же шко́да, що ти не пої́хала зі мно́ю. З пова́гою, Кули́к О. Р. Мо́ре ду́же те́пле. Тури́стів небага́то. Прошу́ тако́ж замо́вити мені́ го́тель на час мого́ відря́дження. Я б ду́же хоті́в, щоб ти могла́ при́їхати хоча́ б на ти́ждень до Оде́си, тут за́раз спра́вжній "оксами́товий сезо́н"!

LANGUAGE TIP

кицю́ня means 'kitten'; Ukrainians really do use the word to address people in very special circumstances!

Оксами́товий сезо́н (lit. 'velvet season'); try to imagine just how wonderful the weather is on the Black Sea coast in September!

---

5 How many words do you know that are directly related to the words in the following list? To what parts of speech do those words belong?

При́клад: лікува́ти (*verb*) ліки (*noun*)

лі́кар (*noun*)

ліка́рня (*noun*)

> матема́тика, украї́нський, спо́кій, до́брий, приє́мно, вдя́чний, нау́ка, замо́влення, по́їзд, щасли́вий, раху́нок, життє́вий, приготува́ти

6 a Make the following sentences negative by using the negative words from this unit and Unit 16:

i Я за́вжди їм бага́то фру́ктів.

ii Він ма́є бага́то дру́зів у рі́зних міста́х.

iii На́ша ма́ма за́вжди пі́зно прихо́дить з робо́ти.

b Translate the following sentences into Ukrainian:

i Stephen has no one to love but he cannot say that he never loved anyone!

ii I didn't go anywhere, because I didn't have anywhere to go.

iii I've never studied foreign languages, because I have no time to do it.

7 **Show that the nouns in the left-hand column belong to the persons in the right-hand column in two ways:**

    i by using the genitive case

    ii by using the possessive adjective forms

Приклад: рýчка   тíтка

                     рýчка тíтки, тíтчина рýчка

День нарóдження	Ýрсула
листíвка	Сергíй
адрéса	брат
телефóн	дирéктор

Key to the exercises

UNIT 1

(a) Пра́вда чи непра́вда: (п) *or* **(н)?** **1** (н) **2** (п) **3** (п) **4** (н) **(b)** **1** дя́кую, непога́но. **2** They are: Oksana, Taras' sister; Mykola, his brother; his mother Maria and his friend Andrew. **3** Mykola. **4** Mathematician.

Впра́ви **1** Maria is a mathematician, Andrew is a journalist, Mykola is an actor, Oksana is a musician. **2** Хто це? Це друг. Хто то? То учи́тель. Хто це? Це ма́ма. Хто то? То хло́пчик. Що це? Це ля́лька. Хто то? То чолові́к. Що це? Це ла́мпа. Що то? То де́рево. Хто це? Це ді́вчинка. Що то? То ґа́нок? Що це? Це мо́ре. **3** **(a)** Так, це чолові́к. **(b)** Так, це кни́га. **(c)** Ні, то ля́лька. **(d)** Ні, то кущ. **(e)** Так, це хло́пчик. **(f)** Так, то це́рква. **(g)** Ні, це олівець. **4** **(a)** **(i)** A **(ii)** D **(iii)** B **(iv)** C

5

M	F	N
чолові́к	жі́нка	со́нце
ґа́нок	кві́тка	де́рево
кіт	ді́вчинка	не́бо
хло́пчик	ї́жа	мо́ре
кущ	кни́га	я́блуко
автомобі́ль	ру́чка	фо́то
буди́нок	це́рква	
юна́к	ша́пка	
друг	ля́лька	
олівець	ла́мпа	
папі́р	сестра́	
цирк		
журналі́ст		

6 **(a)** Брат висо́кий. **(b)** Кві́тка га́рна. **(c)** Ру́чка моя́. **(d)** Я́блуко зеле́не. **(e)** Село́ краси́ве. **7** **(a)** Це мале́ньке я́блуко. **(b)** Це краси́ва кві́тка. **(c)** Це те́пла ша́пка. **(d)** Це висо́ке де́рево. **(e)** Це ціка́ва кни́га. **8** **(a)** Чия́ це ля́лька? **(b)** Чий це олівець? **(c)** Чиє́ це я́блуко? **(d)** Чия́ це кни́га? **(e)** Чиє́ це фо́то? **(f)** Чий це кіт? **9** **(a)** – (vi); **(b)** – (i); **(c)** – (ii); **(d)** – (v); **(e)** – (iii); **(f)** – (iv) **10** **(a)** Як Вас звуть? Мене́ звуть . . . **(b)** Це Ваш брат? Ні, це не мій брат, це мій друг.

UNIT 2

(a) Пра́вда чи непра́вда: **1** (н) **2** (п) **3** (п) **4** (н) **(b)** **1** Познайо́мся: це мій друг Сті́вен. **2** The living room. **3** They are very tall. **4** It's chilly in the garden.

Впра́ви **1** **(a)** Ти сіда́єш. **(b)** Ви ма́єте сад? **(c)** Ти зна́єш Сті́вена? **(a)** Ви сіда́єте. **(b)** Ти ма́єш сад? **(c)** Ви зна́єте Сті́вена?

2

Visitor:	Яка́ там кімна́та?
Host:	*It's the living room.*
Visitor:	Ду́же за́тишна кімна́та!
Host:	*Yes, we have soft comfortable furniture here.*
Visitor:	Чи це Ваш сад? Він вели́кий!
Host:	*Yes, it's my garden. It's very beautiful.*

3 (**a**) ма́ю (**b**) сіда́є (**c**) запро́шуємо (**d**) зна́єш **4** (**a**) Це мій друг. (**b**) Вона́ англі́йка. (**c**) Він ма́є вели́кий буди́нок. (**d**) Запро́шуємо до віта́льні. (**e**) Марі́я – кана́дка. **5** (**a**) Так, це віта́льня. (**b**) Ні, це Окса́на. (**c**) Ні, тут мале́нькі ві́кна. (**d**) Ні, це мій друг Е́ндрю. **6** (**a**) ні́мець; (**b**) італі́йка; (**c**) іспа́нець; (**d**) росія́нин/росія́нка; (**e**) украї́нець/украї́нка; (**f**) австралі́йка. **7** Приві́т! Заходь, будь ла́ска. Дя́кую, до́бре. А ти? Про́шу сіда́ти. **8** життя́; норма́льно; жахли́во; це моя́ дружи́на; друг; ду́же; з ва́ми; перепро́шую; ім'я́; Про́шу сіда́ти; Дя́кую; моя́ ма́ма украї́нка; Ваш буди́нок ду́же га́рний; за́тишно; Так; ду́же стари́й; зру́чний; Ми ма́ємо; кімна́ти; сад.

UNIT 3

(**a**) **Пра́вда чи непра́вда:** **1** (п) **2** (н) **3** (н) **4** (н) (**b**) **1** Coffee. **2** No. **3** Chernihiv. **4** At nine o'clock.

Впра́ви 1 (**a**) – (i); (**b**) – (ii); (**c**) – (ii); (**d**) – (i); (**e**) – (ii); (**f**) – (i) **2** (**a**) їсть (*or* бере́) (**b**) п'єш (**c**) живе́ (**d**) п'ємо́ **3** ді́вчину; кни́гу; мі́сто; англі́йця; украї́нця **4** (**a**) Ка́ву, будь ла́ска; Так, про́шу (будь ла́ска); Ні, дя́кую; Ду́же дя́кую, я люблю́ ті́стечка; Дя́кую, ду́же сма́чно; Так, про́шу. Ка́ва ду́же до́бра. (**b**) Перепро́шую, котра́ годи́на? Дя́кую; Так, я ду́же поспіша́ю. Я ма́ю йти додо́му; Ду́же дя́кую за гости́нність. До поба́чення. **5** (**a**) вокза́л/мо́ре/ робо́ту (**b**) бі́знес/життя́/сім'ю́ (**c**) Ки́їв/ мі́сто/Украї́ну (**d**) автомобі́ль/я́блуко/кни́гу (**e**) дя́дька/ті́тку **6** (**a**) У ме́не є дві сестри́ та (оди́н) брат. (**b**) У ме́не є три ону́ки. (**c**) У ме́не є чолові́к/жі́нка. (дружи́на). (**d**) Я ма́ю чолові́ка/жі́нку. (дружи́ну). (**e**) Я ма́ю ону́ка. (**f**) Я ма́ю батькі́в у Шотла́ндії.

UNIT 4

(**a**) **Пра́вда чи непра́вда:** **1** (н) **2** (п) **3** (н) **4** (п) (**b**) **1** Solomiia Maliarchuk (director of the 'Moda' clothing firm in Kyiv). **2** No. **3** Yes. **4** By air.

(**a**) **1** (н) **2** (п) **3** (н) **4** (н) (**b**) **1** One. **2** Because he often has to translate from English into Ukrainian. **3** From a friend in Kyiv. **4** A large calendar from Ukraine.

Впра́ви 1 до бра́та/мі́ста/ Аме́рики; з вокза́лу/ мі́ста/робо́ти; після обі́ду/ прі́звища/розмо́ви; без цу́кру/ вікна́/сестри́; для дру́га/ міністе́рства/маши́ни; бі́ля ба́нку/де́рева/ла́мпи; буди́нок парла́менту/міністе́рства/фі́рми; ча́шка ча́ю/молока́/ка́ви; бага́то словникі́в/озе́р/справ **2** (**a**) і (**b**) й (**c**) та **3** (**a**) пі́сля, до (**b**) без (**c**) в (**d**) до (**e**) від (**f**) для **4** Я живу́ в Ло́ндоні. Ось мій кабіне́т. Кабіне́т вели́кий та сві́тлий, там ду́же зру́чні ме́блі. Я дире́ктор вели́кої компа́нії. Я хо́чу відві́дати Ки́їв та і́нші міста́ Украї́ни. Я вже замо́вив квито́к на Украї́нські авіалі́нії. Я неодру́жений (незамі́жня), але́ ма́ю вели́ку роди́ну. У ме́не є батьки́ в Шотла́ндії, п'ять брати́в і чоти́ри сестри́. У ме́не тако́ж є бага́то дру́зів. **5** До́брий день. Це Вас турбу́є . . . [Це гово́рить . . .] Одну́ хвили́ночку, будь ла́ска. Перепро́шую, як Ва́ше прі́звище?

UNIT 5

(a) Пра́вда чи непра́вда: 1 (п) **2** (н) **3** (н) **4** (н) **(b) 1** Thursday. **2** Two. **3** Two. **4** Information about how to pay for goods in Ukraine and the current exchange rate.

Впра́ви 1 оди́н до́лар, одна́ гри́вня/ти́сяча; чоти́ри гри́вні/до́лари/ти́сячі; п'ять гри́вень/до́ларів/ти́сяч; два́дцять два до́лари; два́цять дві гри́вні/ти́сячі; 78 гри́вень/до́ларів/ти́сяч; 200 гри́вень/до́ларів/ти́сяч; 312 гри́вень/до́ларів/ти́сяч; 645 гри́вень/до́ларів/ти́сяч; бага́то гро́шей/валю́ти/гри́вень/до́ларів/ти́сяч; ма́ло гро́шей/валю́ти/гри́вень/до́ларів/ти́сяч; тро́хи гро́шей/валю́ти/гри́вень/до́ларів. **2** (**a**) Я не ма́ю маши́ни. (**b**) У ме́не є сад. (**c**) Ві́ра не ма́є ті́стечка. (**d**) У дире́ктора є помічни́к. (**e**) Фі́рма не ма́є літака́. (**f**) Чи у те́бе є квито́к? **3** (**a**) Ти не ма́єш кни́ги? У те́бе нема́є кни́ги? (**b**) Вони́ не ма́ють паспорті́в. У них нема́є паспорті́в. (**c**) Я не ма́ю са́ду. У ме́не нема́є са́ду. (**d**) Чи Ви не ма́єте словника́? Чи у Вас нема́є словника́? (**e**) Ві́ра не ма́є сестри́. У Ві́ри нема́є сестри́. (**f**) Се́стри не ма́ють гро́шей. У сесте́р нема́є гро́шей. (**g**) Сті́вен іще́ не ма́є ві́зи. У Сті́вена ще нема́є ві́зи. **4** Я ма́ю ([Мені́] тре́ба) замо́вити но́мер. На сього́дні. На двох. На чоти́ри (дні). **5** Де? — там, ось, тут; Зві́дки? — зві́дти, спе́реду, зві́дси; Куди́? — впере́д, сюди́, наза́д, туди́. **6** (**a**) (**i**) Я хо́чу но́мер на двох. (**ii**) На ти́ждень, мабу́ть, на два (ти́жні). (**iii**) Я не ма́ю гро́шей/У ме́не ма́ло гро́шей. (**iv**) Тре́ба/Я ма́ю поміня́ти до́лари на украї́нські гро́ші. (**b**) (**i**) Ході́мо до рестора́ну. Я ду́же хо́чу ї́сти, але́: (**ii**) Я не ма́ю/У ме́не нема́є украї́нських гро́шей. (**c**) (**i**) Он там пункт о́бміну (валю́ти). Скі́льки ти хо́чеш помі́ня ти? (**ii**) До́ларів два́дцять п'ять.

UNIT 6

(a) Пра́вда чи непра́вда: 1 (н) **2** (п) **3** (н) **4** (н) **(b) 1** Two years. **2** His business card. **3** He is a lawyer. **4** No.

Впра́ви 1 (**a**) (**i**) true (**ii**) false (**iii**) false (**iv**) false (**v**) true (**vi**) false (**b**) (**i**) Олексі́єві Дми́тровичу три́дцять чоти́ри ро́ки. (**ii**) Людми́лі Андрі́ївні два́дцять оди́н рік. (**iii**) Петро́ві Іва́новичу со́рок ві́сім ро́ків. (**iv**) Мико́лі Григо́ровичу п'ятдеся́т шість ро́ків. (**v**) Окса́ні Миха́йлівні два́дцять ві́сім ро́ків. **2** (**a**) Джо́ну/Джо́нові (**b**) дружи́ні (**c**) дире́ктору/дире́кторові/до дире́ктора (**d**) учи́тельці (**e**) Оле́гу/Оле́гові (**f**) Тетя́ні (**g**) Андрі́ю/Андрі́єві (**h**) Катери́ні (**i**) Вади́му/Вади́мові (**j**) Їй **3** (**a**) Студе́нт пи́ше листи́ учителя́м (**b**) Мико́ла пи́ше кни́гу. (**c**) Я пишу́ і́м'я. (**d**) Ми пи́шемо прі́звища. (**e**) Вони́ пи́шуть факс партне́рам. **4** (**a**) (iv) (**b**) (i) (**c**) (ii) (**d**) (iii) **5** (**a**) Нам тре́ба/Ми ма́ємо замо́вити но́мер. (**b**) Я плану́ю відві́дати Фра́нцію. (**c**) Нам тре́ба два но́мери "люкс". (**d**) Я бізнесме́н і ча́сто буваю́ в Украї́ні. (**e**) Я не ма́ю/У ме́не нема́є інформа́ції щодо фіна́нсів. (**f**) Мій друг чита́в украї́нську газе́ту. (**g**) Ми вже́ бува́ли в Украї́ні. (**h**) На́ша фі́рма ро́бить маши́ни/автомобі́лі. **6** (**a**) 5(f); (**b**) 5(h); (**c**) 5(b); (**d**) 5(d) **7** (**a**) autumn (**b**) 8 hours 37 minutes (**c**) during the day (**d**) +3 - +8

UNIT 7

(a) Пра́вда чи непра́вда: 1 (п) **2** (н) **3** (п) **4** (п) **(b) 1** The National Bank of Ukraine. **2** In order to understand his colleagues in Kyiv and L'viv without an interpreter. **3** A Ukrainian friend. **4** Good-looking fashionable clothes.

Впра́ви 1 (**a**) кореспонде́нтові (**b**) Націона́льному ба́нку (**c**) Ло́ндоні (**d**) Льво́ві (**e**) гіта́рі **2** (**a**) кни́зі (**b**) по́друга (**c**) жі́нці (**d**) ля́лька (**e**) ка́ртка (**f**) поі́здці (**g**) му́сі (**h**) ру́чка **3** (**a**) У, в (**b**) в (**c**) в (**d**) у (**e**) у (**f**) У (**g**) в **4** (**a**) ї́здити (**b**) ката́тися (**c**) чита́ти (**d**) ї́сти (**e**) танцюва́ти (**f**) гра́ти **5** (**a**) телефону́є до Ки́єва (**b**) телефону́є до Ки́єва (**c**) чита́в, учора́ (**d**) чита́ла, щодня́ **6** Some possible answers: (**a**) Мені́ три́дцять три ро́ки/шістдеся́т оди́н рік.

(**b**) Я народи́вся/народи́лася в ти́сяча сімдеся́т пе́ршому ро́ці. (**c**) Я народи́вся/народи́лася в сі́чні/листопа́ді. (**d**) Я народи́вся/ народи́лася в А́нглії/Сполу́чених Шта́тах Аме́рики. (**e**) Я народи́вся/народи́лася в Лі́дсі/Нью-Йо́рку. (**f**) Я тепе́р живу́ в Ло́ндоні. (**g**) Ні, я ще не був/ була́ в Украї́ні.

UNIT 8

(**a**) **Пра́вда чи непра́вда: 1** (п) **2** (н) **3** (н) **4** (п) (**b**) **1** Yes. **2** He has never been there before. **3** Train, steamer, perhaps car. **4** Six o'clock.

Впра́ви 1 (**a**) не був (**b**) не літа́в (**c**) не говори́в (**d**) не відліта́в **2** бу́деш писа́ти, писа́тимеш; бу́де писа́ти, писа́тиме; бу́демо писа́ти, писа́тимемо; бу́дете писа́ти, писа́тимете; бу́дуть писа́ти, писа́тимуть **3** бу́ду леті́ти/ леті́тиму; бу́деш працюва́ти/ працюва́тимеш; бу́де займа́тися/ займа́тиметься; бу́демо жи́ти/жи́тимемо; бу́дете міня́ти/міня́тимете; бу́дуть чека́ти/чека́тимуть **4** Я лечу́ літако́м. Ти ї́деш авто́бусом. Він гуля́є ву́лицею. Ми летимо́ літака́ми. Вони́ ї́дуть авто́бусами. Ви гуля́єте ву́лицями. **5** (**a**) помічнико́м дире́ктора (**b**) матема́тиком (**c**) жі́нкою Джо́на, три ро́ки (**d**) з англі́йськими бізнесме́нами **6** (**a**) A lawyer. (**b**) Don't forget the documents! (**c**) At the factory. (**d**) Thursday 29 July. (**e**) Tickets. (**f**) Pay her telephone bill, play tennis. (**g**) She is going to phone Ursula about a concert. (**h**) Stephen is arriving on Thursday 29 July at 10pm.

UNIT 9

(**a**) **Пра́вда чи непра́вда: 1** (н) **2** (п) **3** (н) **4** (п) (**b**) **1** They go through passport and customs control. **2** His passport. **3** Weapons, drugs. **4** US dollars

Впра́ви 1 nom., acc., gen., loc., dat., inst. **2** блаки́тне не́бо; зеле́на трава́; жо́втий лимо́н; си́льний чоловí́к; важки́й ка́мінь; до́вга доро́га **3** (**a**) хо́дить (**b**) іде́ (**c**) ї́де (**d**) ї́здить **4** (**a**) прийду́, принесу́ (**b**) прийшла́, принесла́ (**c**) приї́жджає, привезла́ (**d**) приї́хав, привíз **5** Ось мій па́спорт, квито́к і ми́тна деклара́ція. Я приї́хав/приї́хала на відпочи́нок. Я не зна́ю, що заборо́нене/які́ предме́ти заборо́нені. Дві́сті америка́нських до́ларів, сто три́дцять п'ять фу́нтів. Ні, у ме́не нема́є/я не ма́ю украї́нських гро́шей.

UNIT 10

(**a**) **Пра́вда чи непра́вда: 1** (п) **2** (н) **3** (н) **4** (п) (**b**) **1** Ihor's wife, Ol'ha. **2** Two. **3** They went for a walk to the river, sat down by the water and chatted. Stephen, Ihor and Ostap had a swim. **4** Very late.

Впра́ви 1 (**a**) Я мо́жу розмовля́ти францу́зькою мо́вою. Я хо́чу розмовля́ти німе́цькою мо́вою. Я мо́жу розумі́ти цей текст. Я хо́чу зна́ти це сло́во. (**b**) Він мо́же розмовля́ти францу́зькою мо́вою. Він хо́че розмовля́ти німе́цькою мо́вою. Вона́ мо́же розумі́ти цей текст. Вона́ хо́че зна́ти це сло́во. Ви мо́жете розмовля́ти францу́зькою мо́вою. Ми хо́чемо розмовля́ти німе́цькою мо́вою. Ви мо́жете розумі́ти цей текст. Ми хо́чемо зна́ти це сло́во. (**c**) Мені́ тре́ба розмовля́ти францу́зькою мо́вою. Тобí тре́ба розмовля́ти німе́цькою мо́вою. Нам тре́ба розумі́ти цей текст. Вам тре́ба зна́ти це сло́во. (**d**) Яки́ми мо́вами Ви володі́єте? Я зна́ю німе́цьку мо́ву, та́кож володі́ю украї́нською (мо́вою). **2** Іва́не – п'ятна́дцятого – тра́вня – ро́ку – двадця́того – ли́пня – се́реду – я – Украї́ни – Чо́рному мо́рі – я – но́мер – га́рному готе́лі – дружи́ни – готеля́ – чудо́вий парк – готе́лем – мо́ре – готе́лем – го́ри – наш но́мер – тре́тьому по́версі – телеві́зором – холоди́льником – телефо́ном – ду́шем – план – я – дружи́ною – їй – він – вона́ – по́їздом – Ки́єва – квитки́ – ми – літако́м – квитки́ – Ки́єва – Оде́си – по́їздом – годи́н – одна́ ніч – оди́н ра́нок – ми – комфо́ртом – моя́ дружи́на

– по́їздом – купе́ – чай – вікно́ – кни́гу – робо́ту – усі спра́ви – Ки́єві – ми – переса́дку – Оде́сі – електри́чку – мі́сця відпочи́нку – Оде́си – мо́ря – Оде́сі – ми – но́мер – готе́лі – двох – два – ти́жні – Оде́си – дру́га – він – Херсо́ні – я – лист – дру́га – він – мене́ – ми – дружи́ною – два ти́жні – Херсо́на – тридця́того ли́пня – днів – вам – на́ші пла́ни – лі́то – зу́стрічі.

3

N	стіле́ць	підло́га	лі́жко	коридо́ри	поли́ці	дзерка́ла	
A	стіле́ць	підло́гу	лі́жко	коридо́ри	поли́ці	дзерка́ла	
G	стільця́	підло́ги	лі́жка	коридо́рів	поли́ць	дзерка́л	
D	стільцю́	підло́зі	лі́жку	коридо́рам	поли́цям	дзерка́лам	
L	стільці́	підло́зі	лі́жку	коридо́рах	поли́цях	дзерка́лах	(на-у/в)
I	стільце́м	підло́гою	лі́жком	коридо́рами	поли́цями	дзерка́лами	

4 (**a**) п'ю, п'єш, п'є, п'ємо́, п'єте́, п'ють; бу́ду пи́ти, бу́деш пи́ти, бу́де пи́ти, бу́демо пи́ти, бу́дете пи́ти, бу́дуть пи́ти; пи́тиму, пи́тимеш, пи́тиме, пи́тимемо, пи́тимете, пи́тимуть (**b**) пишу́, пи́шеш, пи́ше, пи́шемо, пи́шете, пи́шуть; бу́ду писа́ти, бу́деш писа́ти, бу́де писа́ти, бу́демо писа́ти, бу́дете писа́ти, бу́дуть писа́ти; писа́тиму, писа́тимеш, писа́тиме, писа́тимемо, писа́тимете, писа́тимуть (**c**) їм, їси́, їсть, їмо́, їсте́, їдя́ть: бу́ду ї́сти, бу́деш ї́сти, бу́де ї́сти, бу́демо ї́сти, бу́дете ї́сти, бу́дуть ї́сти; ї́стиму, ї́стимеш, ї́стиме, ї́стимемо, ї́стимете, ї́стимуть **5** (**a**) чита́в, чита́ла, чита́ло, чита́ли (**b**) ішо́в, ішла́, ішло́, ішли́ (**c**) летів, летı́ла, летı́ло, летı́ли **6** (**a**) лежа́ло, столі́; ньо́му, лежа́ла (**b**) п'єте́; п'ю, ка́ву, її́ (**c**) ким, розмовля́ли; розмовля́в/ розмовля́ла, нови́м дире́ктором, зна́єте, його́ **7** (**a**) living room (**b**) kitchen (**c**) study **8** flat no. 4

UNIT 11

(**a**) Пра́вда чи непра́вда: **1** (п) **2** (п) **3** (н) **4** (н) (**b**) **1** Vegetable salad. **2** No. **3** Vira is writing a dissertation, works in libraries a lot. **4** No, Taras did.

Впра́ви 1 ча́шка зі сто́лу; две́рі з кімна́ти; стіле́ць із ку́хні; дзвони́ти з кабіне́ту

2

заку́ски	пе́рші стра́ви	дру́гі стра́ви	напо́ї
гриби́ марино́вані	борщ украї́нський з пампушка́ми,	голубці́ овоче́ві	горı́лка украї́нська з пе́рцем, коньяк "Ай-Пе́трі"
ковбаса́	ю́шка грибна́,	варе́ники з м'я́сом	шампа́нське напівсухе́
	соля́нка осетро́ва		ка́ва з молоко́м
		омле́т із трьох яє́ць	

3 (**i**) гриби́ марино́вані (**ii**) юшку грибну́ або́ соля́нку осетро́ву (**iii**) варе́ники з карто́плею (**iv**) ка́ву з молоко́м **4** Приві́т! Я не ба́чив (-ла) тебе́ ма́йже сто ро́ків. Що (в те́бе) ново́го? Що відбуло́ся за оста́нні мі́сяці? Нови́н ма́ло. Я одружи́вся (ви́йшла за́між) і купи́в(-ла) трикімна́тну кварти́ру в це́нтрі мі́ста. Мені́ тре́ба було́ зна́ти! У те́бе таке́ ти́хе (споко́йне) життя́! **5** (**a**) Які́ у Вас є супи́? Я не люблю́ соля́нку. (**b**) Чи Ви не ма́єте пи́ва? У Вас є сухе́ бі́ле вино́? (**c**) Я не їм ри́би. Я б хоті́в(-ла) сма́жений біфште́кс з карто́плею та сала́том. (**d**) Я беру́ (Я візьму́) креве́ток (але́ без майоне́зу, будь ла́ска), голубці́ овоче́ві та яки́йсь сік – апельси́новий, якщо́ є. Я не хо́чу пе́ршого (пе́ршої стра́ви).

UNIT 12

(a) Пра́вда чи непра́вда: 1 (н) **2** (н) **3** (п) **4** (п) **(b) 1** He was twenty minutes late. **2** No. **3** On the left-hand side. **4** She was born in Kyiv and loves it very much.

Впра́ви 1 Ста́нція "Вокза́льна". Обере́жно, две́рі зачиня́ються. Насту́пна ста́нція "Університе́т". / Ста́нція "Університе́т". Обере́жно, две́рі зачиня́ються. Насту́пна ста́нція "Театра́льна". / Ста́нція "Театра́льна". Перехі́д на ста́нцію "Золоті́ воро́та". Обере́жно, две́рі зачиня́ються. Насту́пна ста́нція "Хреща́тик". / Ста́нція "Хреща́тик". Перехі́д на ста́нцію "Майда́н Незале́жності". Обере́жно, две́рі зачиня́ються. Насту́пна ста́нція "Арсена́льна"./Ста́нція "Арсена́льна". Обере́жно, две́рі зачиня́ються. Насту́пна ста́нція "Дніпро́". **2** (**a**) на́шу (**b**) мої́й (**c**) її́ **3** (**a**) Ба́тько живе́ на схо́ді Украї́ни. (**b**) Літа́к лети́ть пря́мо на за́хід. (**c**) У Карпа́тах бага́то гір. (**d**) Моє́му си́нові ві́сім ро́ків. **4** (**a**) Мико́ла хо́че леті́ти до Пра́ги літако́м, а я за́вжди їжджу по́їздом. (**b**) Я не мо́жу купи́ти словни́к, бо я ніко́ли не ношу́ вели́кі кни́ги в рука́х. (**c**) Я прошу́ тебе́ замо́вити дороге́ вино́, я сього́дні плачу́. (**d**) Він за́раз пи́ше лист дружи́ні, що не мо́же приї́хати у се́рпні.

UNIT 13

(a) Пра́вда чи непра́вда: 1 (н) **2** (п) **3** (п) **4** (п) **(b) 1** A set of documents. **2** Two. **3** It should make its own cloth. **4** Stephen.

Впра́ви 1 Я хо́чу чо́рне пла́ття. Я хо́чу кори́чневі штани́. Я хо́чу зеле́ний дже́мпер. Я хо́чу купи́ти бі́ло-жо́вту футбо́лку. Я хо́чу купи́ти си́ні пла́вки. Я хо́чу купи́ти чо́рні колго́ти. Я хо́чу купи́ти сі́рий костю́м. Я ма́ю купи́ти ора́нжеві шо́рти. Я ма́ю купи́ти вели́кий светр. Я ма́ю купи́ти мале́ньку парасо́льку. Мені́ тре́ба купи́ти мали́нову спідни́цю. Мені́ тре́ба купи́ти блаки́тний плащ. Мені́ тре́ба купи́ти фіоле́тову су́мку. **2** (**a**) Де я мо́жу поміня́ти до́лари? Де я мо́жу поміня́ти су́кню? Де я мо́жу поміня́ти костю́м? Де я мо́жу поміня́ти крава́тку? (**b**) Де я мо́жу помі́ряти плащ? Де я мо́жу помі́ряти соро́чку? Де я мо́жу помі́ряти ку́ртку? Де я мо́жу помі́ряти окуля́ри? (**c**) Де я мо́жу купи́ти бі́лий папі́р? Де я мо́жу купи́ти чо́рну ру́чку? Де я мо́жу купи́ти вели́кий портфе́ль? Де я мо́жу купи́ти черво́ний олі́вець? Де я мо́жу купи́ти мале́нький магнітофо́н? Де я мо́жу купи́ти па́ру шкарпе́ток? **3** Я ношу́ кори́чневий ко́лір. Я люблю́ зеле́ний ко́лір. Я одяга́ю бі́лий ко́лір. Мені́ подо́баються мали́новий та блаки́тний кольори́. Я не ношу́ си́нього ко́льору. Я не люблю́ фіоле́тового ко́льору. Я не одяга́ю ора́нжевого ко́льору. Мені́ не подо́баються жо́втий та сі́рий кольори́. **4** (**a**) Я не приві́з(-везла́) паке́т докуме́нтів щодо ство́рення ново́ї компа́нії, тому́ що я хворі́в (-і́ла)/че́рез хворо́бу. (**b**) Я б хоті́в(-і́ла) купи́ти кни́гу про Украї́ну для свое́ї дружи́ни/ для свого́ чолові́ка or Я б хоті́в (-і́ла) купи́ти дружи́ні/чолові́кові (dat.) кни́гу про Украї́ну. (**c**) Яко́го ко́льору ти хо́чеш купи́ти дже́мпер (пла́ття, костю́м, спідни́цю, светр, плащ, соро́чку)? **5** (**a**) Мені́ потрі́бен деше́вший но́мер. (**b**) Деше́вшого нема́є. Ви вже ме́шкаєте у найдеше́вшому но́мері у готе́лі. (**c**) Я б хоті́ла обміня́ти цю блу́зку. Вона́ зана́дто мала́ для мое́ї дружи́ни – їй потрі́бна бі́льша. (**d**) Як назива́ється найгли́бше о́зеро в Украї́ні? (**e**) Украї́нська мо́ва значно прості́ша, ніж я ду́мав (-ла)! **6** (**a**) Оле́на диви́тиметься телеві́зор, якщо́ вона́ ма́тиме час. (**b**) Оле́г пока́же нам місто, якщо буде мати час. (**c**) Сусід працював би таксистом, якби він мав права. (**d**) Онучка допомагала б бабусі, якби бабуся жила не так далеко. **7** (**a**) Я б хотів відразу розпочати роботу. (**b**) Я б хотів висловити свої міркування під час наших наступних зустрічей. (**c**) Я б хотів перейти до конкретних аспектів нашого контракту (**d**) Я б хотів узяти на себе переговори з можливими інвесторами. (**e**) Я б хотів продовжити цю розмову після Вашої поїздки.

UNIT 14

(**a**) **Правда чи неправда: 1** (н) **2** (п) **3** (н) **4** (п) (**b**) **1** In the first part of the day. **2** A mixture and pills. **3** In order to collect the medicine after 4pm. **4** The duty receptionist.

Вправи 1 алергія – allergy; бронхіт – bronchitis; діабет – diabetes; антибіотик – antiobiotics; пневмонія – pneumonia; ін'єкція – injection; операція – operation; інфекція – infection; пульс – pulse; таблетка – tablet; аналіз – analysis; термометр – thermometer; масаж – massage; мікстура – mixture; вітамін – vitamin **2** She is a friend, and she called yesterday to say that her husband was ill. He has a high temperature, a headache, a cough and a headcold. The doctor said he has the flu. The doctor explained how to take the medicine. She got tablets, drops and mixture. **3** (**a**) Він приймає ліки. (**b**) Вона викликає лікаря. (**c**) Вона замовляє їх в аптеці. (**d**) Йому потрібно лежати в ліжку. **4** (**a**) На стадіоні люди грають у футбол. На стадіоні люди дивляться матч. На стадіоні люди займаються спортом. (**b**) Оксана читає підручник, тому що вона вчиться в університеті. (**c**) Остап сміється, тому що він читає книгу. Остап сміється, тому що він дивиться фільм. Остап сміється, тому що друг розповідає йому смішну історію. **5** (**a**) У мене болить голова. У мене немає часу піти до аптеки й купити ліки від головного болю. У мене болить горло, я не можу ковтати. У мене висока температура/Мене лихоманить і мені треба полежати вдома кілька днів. (**b**) – Я не можу піти в поліклініку до лікаря, тому що я дуже хворий (хвора). Дуже прошу тебе подзвонити до поліклініки й викликати лікаря якомога скоріше. – Я зателефонував (-ала) до поліклініки. Черговий (Чергова) в реєстратурі сказав (сказала), що лікар прийде завтра у другій половині дня. Він перепрошує, що не може прийти раніше, але каже, що у поліклініці більше хворих, ніж лікарів. Тобі треба полежати.

UNIT 15

(**a**) **Правда чи неправда: 1** (п) **2** (п) **3** (п) **4** (п) (**b**) **1** Ol'ha. **2** Olenka. **3** She has to be intelligent, calm, sensible, but not boring, with a merry character and a sense of humour. **4** She should have a profession, perhaps her own business.

Вправи 1 (for reading practice) **2** Taras – (iii); Solomiia – (i); Vira – (vi); Stephen – (v); Ihor – (ii) **3** Високий лоб, біляве волосся, карі очі, смагляве обличчя, кирпатий ніс. **4** (**a**) Я запросив її до кіно, тому що мені сподобалися її очі. (**b**) Ти подумав про нашу пропозицію пообідати завтра разом у ресторані? (**c**) Я люблю, коли моя дружина одягається дуже елегантно. (**d**) У мене гарна машина, але в мого друга – ще краща. (**e**) Чи твоя сестра схожа на твого батька?

UNIT 16

(**a**) **Правда чи неправда: 1** (н) **2** (н) **3** (п) **4** (н) (**b**) **1** The train tickets. **2** 20 copecks (he ordered two!) **3** You push down on them. **4** A folder with documents.

Вправи 1 (**a**) Скажіть, будь ласка, коли прибуває поїзд із Черкас? (**b**) Будь ласка, коли наступний поїзд до Харкова? (**c**) Один купейний квиток на швидкий поїзд до Іва́но-

Франкі́вська. (**d**) Я хо́чу їхати по́їздом (у купе́йному ваго́ні) до Оде́си (**e**) Я б хоті́в/-ла пої́хати електри́чкою до Полта́ви 19 се́рпня. **2** Я ї́ду до Оде́си на конфере́нцію. Я ї́ду на відпочи́нок до Я́лти на п'ять днів. Я був/-ла́ два ти́жні в Луга́нську, я ї́ду до Ки́єва, а че́рез два дні я лечу́ додо́му. Я за́вжди ду́же хо́чу ї́сти, коли сіда́ю в по́їзд. Ось чому́ я ма́ю вели́ку су́мку ї́жі (проду́ктів) та кі́лька пляшо́к пи́ва із собо́ю. Мо́жна попроси́ти скля́нку ча́ю? А скі́льки я ма́ю заплати́ти за по́стіль? **3** Я тут бу́ду чека́ти/чека́тиму/почека́ю. Я хо́чу, щоб Ти купи́в(и́ла)/Ви купи́ли квитки́./Я стоя́в(-я́ла) в че́рзі за квитка́ми й розмовля́в(-ла) із ду́же ціка́вою люди́ною. Незаба́ром приї́де/прийде́/прибу́де насту́пний по́їзд. /Чому́ Ви запізни́лися на годи́ну? **4** Оди́н квито́к до Жито́мира і наза́д. У Жито́мир на 4 жо́втня, а наза́д на 22. Я візьму́ купе́. **5** (**a**) Ніхто́ ніко́ли мене́ не розумі́є. (**b**) Я не зна́ю ніко́го, хто зна́є як/вмі́є роби́ти га́рну ка́ву. (**c**) Я до́вго не розмовля́в(-я́ла) ні з ки́м украї́нською мо́вою. (**d**) Я не прині́с(-несла́)/приві́з(-везла́) із собо́ю нія́кої ї́жі (нія́ких проду́ктів) для по́дорожі (в доро́гу). **6** (**a**) Я б ви́пив(-ила) чого́-не́будь/чого́сь те́плого з вели́ким задово́ленням. (**b**) У дити́нстві я диви́вся будь-які́ фі́льми. (**c**) Тара́с пішо́в куди́сь купи́ти ї́жі (проду́ктів). (**d**) Зустрі́ньмося коли́-не́будь/коли́сь.

UNIT 17

(**a**) **Пра́вда чи непра́вда: 1** (п) **2** (п) **3** (н) **4** (п) (**b**) **1** 'To Solomiia!', 'To Solomiia's health!', 'To happiness!' **2** Roses. **3** A large cake. **4** Make a wish.

Впра́ви 1 (**a**) хлі́бниця, 1 трі́лка, 7 таріло́чок для хлі́ба, 2 ножі́, 1 ло́жка для десе́рту, 7 ке́лихів для вина́, 7 склянок для води́, 3 ча́рки для коньяку́ (**b**) торт **2** (an example of a simple letter of invitation)

Ната́лко й Олексі́ю! Запро́шуємо Вас у го́сті на святкува́ння Ново́го ро́ку! Приїжджа́йте до нас на 9.00 годи́ну ве́чора. Чека́тимемо вас, Ю́рко й Тетя́на

3 (**a**) теа́три, музе́ї, то́сти, подару́нки, серві́зи (**b**) сюрпри́з, гість, сувені́р, конце́рт, виста́ва **4** (**a**) Music (**b**) Why she likes such different kinds of music. (**c**) Cinema (**d**) 7 tickets for a first night at the Ukrainian drama theatre.

UNIT 18

Запита́ння до те́ксту (**a**) A large mushroom. (**b**) At sunrise. (**c**) A strip of land surrounded by water – it's like a fairy story. (**d**) It's difficult for Stephen to find the words to describe the wonders of nature in Ukraine. (**e**) Yes, he does.

Впра́ви 1 (**a**) **Пра́вда чи непра́вда: 1** (п) **2** (н) **3** (н) **4** (н) (**b**) **1** Stephen. **2** No, in Great Britain. **3** Christmas and the New Year. **4** He offers his help to Solomiia, should she ever need it. **2** 1st call:

Mr Oleksiy Honcharenko called. He came yesterday from London and brought an urgent letter from Mr Robinson. He was asked to give you a ring just after his arrival in Kyiv. His address in Kyiv is: flat 35, 38 Shovkovychna St. Phone: 295 1687. He is expecting a phone call from you tonight.

2nd call:

Ol'ha phoned. She is at Solomiia's flat. Solomiia has had an accident: her knee was seriously hurt. An ambulance was called. Solomiia was taken to emergency. Ol'ha went there with her. After an X-ray, she was examined by a doctor. The bone was not broken, but she needs to stay in bed for a couple of days. Call them tonight.

3 Нача́льнику Ки́ївського залізни́чного вокза́лу па́нові М.А. Пилипе́нку.

Шано́вний па́не Пилипе́нко! Щи́ро віта́ю Вас із Днем наро́дження! Бажа́ю Вам ща́стя, у́спіху, міцно́го здоро́в'я! Сподіва́юся, що на́ша співпра́ця продо́вжиться у майбу́тньому. Незаба́ром ви оде́ржите катало́г на́шої найнові́шої проду́кції, яки́й на́ша компа́нія Вам надісла́ла. Ми тако́ж замо́вили квитки́ для пої́здки до Украї́ни в лю́тому. Ми зателефону́ємо Вам насту́пного ти́жня.

З найкра́щими побажа́ннями,

Щи́ро Ваш,

Ни́колас Де́йвіс

4 (**a**)

Приві́т, моя́ бі́лочко!

Пишу́ тобі́ з Оде́си пе́ршу листі́вку. У нас тут не ду́же жа́рко, як за́вжди буває́ у ве́ресні. Я відпочива́ю, вра́нці й увечері ходжу́ на пляж, ї́жджу на екску́рсії. Мо́ре ду́же те́пле. Тури́стів небага́то. Я купу́ю собі́ шашлики́, фру́кти, моро́зиво. Ду́же шкода́, що ти не поі́хала зі мно́ю. Ти ще ніде́ не відпочива́ла цього́ ро́ку. Я б ду́же хоті́в, щоб ти могла́ приі́хати хоча́ б на ти́ждень до Оде́си, тут за́раз спра́вжній "оксами́товий сезо́н"! подума́й про це, Ната́лочко. Чека́тиму твоє́ї ві́дповіді.

Люблю́, цілу́ю, Андрі́й.

(**b**)

Шано́вний Володи́мире Миха́йловичу!

Я приїжджа́ю на де́сять днів, щоб відві́дати ваш інститу́т. Ваш помічни́к телефонува́в мені́ вчо́ра, і ми розроби́ли дета́льну програ́му візи́ту. Потрі́бно запроси́ти пре́су й телеба́чення на "кру́глий стіл", що відбу́деться 19 жо́втня. Хто доповіда́є на засі́данні? Я тако́ж прошу́ мене́ повідо́мити про організа́цію засі́дання 21 числа́. Мо́жете телефонува́ти мені́ на робо́ту: я пе́ред від'ї́здом працю́ю до пі́знього ве́чора. Чи могли́ б Ви зустрі́ти мене́ о 9.20 ра́нку 13 жо́втня? Прошу́ тако́ж замо́вити мені́ го́тель на час мого́ відря́дження. Чека́ю від вас докла́дної інформа́ції.

З пова́гою,

Кули́к О.Р.

5 матема́тика (n), матема́тик (n), математи́чний (adj.); украї́нський (adj.), Украї́на (n), украї́нець (n), украї́нка (n); спо́кій (n), споко́йний (adj.); до́брий (adj.), добро́ (n); приє́мно (adv.), приє́мний (adj.); вдя́чний (adj.), дя́кувати (v), вдя́чність (n); нау́ка (n), науко́вий (adj.), науко́вець (n); замо́влення (n), замовля́ти (v), замо́вник (n); по́їзд (n), ї́здити (v), пої́здка (n); щасли́вий (adj.), ща́стя (n); раху́нок (n), рахува́ти (v); життє́вий (adj.), життя́ (n), жи́ти (v); приготува́ти (v), гото́вий (adj.), підгото́вка (n)

6 (**a**) (**i**) Я ніко́ли не їм бага́то фру́ктів. (**ii**) У ньо́го нема́є дру́зів ні в я́ких міста́х. (**iii**) На́ша ма́ма ніко́ли не прихо́дить пі́зно з робо́ти. (**b**) (**i**) Сті́вену ніко́го люби́ти, але́ він не мо́же сказа́ти, що він ніко́ли ніко́го не люби́в! (**ii**) Я нику́ди не ї́жджу, тому́ що мені́ ні́куди ї́здити./Я нику́ди не ходжу́, тому́ що мені́ ні́куди ходи́ти. (**iii**) Я ніко́ли не вивча́в(-ла) інозе́мні мо́ви, тому́ що в ме́не нема́є ча́су (мені́ ні́коли) це роби́ти. **7** (**i**) День наро́дження У́рсули, листі́вка Сергі́я, адре́са бра́та, телефо́н дире́ктора; (**ii**) У́рсулин День наро́дження, Сергі́єва листі́вка, бра́това адре́са, дире́кторів телефо́н

Ukrainian–English Vocabulary

The information presented in this vocabulary is derived from the most recent orthographical dictionary published in Kyiv, Орфографічний словник української мови, 1994.

Nouns: *the ending of the genitive singular is given for all declinable nouns, followed where necessary by the forms for other cases which cannot easily be derived from the nominative singular. The gender of each noun is also indicated.*

Adjectives: *the nominative endings for feminine, neuter and plural are also given. Where an adjective functions as a noun (e.g. лютий, перехожий) this is stated.*

Verbs: *the conjugation pattern for each verb (1 or 2) is given, followed by a note on aspect (impf. or pf.). The first- and second- persons singular of the present (impf.) or future (pf.) are given whenever they cannot directly be derived from the form of the infinitive (as is the form of the third-person plural where the letter -л- is inserted). Imperative (imp.) and past tense masculine and feminine singular forms are also added whenever guidance is required.*

а   *and, but*

абúхто, indef. pron.   *whoever, no matter who*

абó   *or*

абó ..., абó   *either ..., or ...*

абсолютно   *absolutely*

авіаконвéрт, -а, m.   *airmail envelope*

авіалінія, -ї, f.   *airline*

австралíєць, -íйця, m.   *Australian*

австралíйка, -и, dat. and loc. s. -йці, gen. pl. -йок   *Australian*

Австрáлія, -ї, f.   *Australia*

австрíйський, -а, -е; -і, adj.   *Austrian*

автóбус, -а, m.   *bus*

автомобíль, -я, m.   *car*

автовідповідáч, -á, m.   *answering machine*

аджé   *after all*

адрéса, -и, f.   *address*

адресáт, -а, m.   *addressee*

аеропóрт, -у, loc. в аеропортý, m.   *airport*

аксесуáри, -ів, pl.   *accessories*

актúвний, -а, -е; -і, adj.   *active*

актóр, -а, m.   *actor*

алé   *but*

алергíя, -ї, f.   *allergy*

алéя, -ї, f.   *avenue*

алкогóльний, -а, -е; -і, adj.   *alcoholic*

аллó!   *hello!* (telephone word)

Амéрика, -и dat. and loc. sg. -иці, f.   *America*

американéць, -нця, m.   *American*

американка, -ки, dat. and loc. s. -нці, gen. pl. -нок, f.   *American*

анáліз, -у, m.   *analysis*

англíєць, -íйця, m.   *Englishman*

англíйка, -и, dat. and loc. s. -йці, gen. pl. -йок, f.   *Englishwoman*

Áнглія, -ї, f.   *England, Great Britain*

анí ..., анí   *neither ..., nor*

антибіóтик, -а, m.   *antibiotic*

апельсúн, -а, m.   *orange*

апельси́новий, -а, -е; -і, adj. *orange*

апте́ка, -и, dat. and loc. s.-еці, f. *chemist's shop*

архітекту́ра, -и, f. *architecture*

ас, -а, m. *ace*

аспе́кт, -у, m. *aspect*

ассорті́, n. indecl. *assortment*

бабу́ся, -і, f. *granny*

бага́ж, -у, m. *luggage, baggage*

бага́то (+ gen.) *much, a lot of*

бажа́ння, -я, n. *wish*

бажа́ти, 1, vb. impf. (+ gen.) *wish*

балко́н, -а, m. *balcony*

бана́н, -а, m. *banana*

банк, -у, m. *bank*

бар, -у, m. *bar*

баскетбо́л, -у, m. *basketball*

ба́тько, -а, m. *father*

батьки́, -і́в, pl. *parents*

ба́чити, 2, vb. impf. *see*

без, prep. (+ gen.) *without*

безці́нний, -а, -е; -і, adj. *invaluable*

бе́рег, -а, m. *shore*

бере́за, -и, gen. pl. -рі́з, f. *birch tree*

бе́резень, -зня, m. *March*

бібліоте́ка, -и, dat. and loc. sg. -еці, f. *library*

бі́гати, 1, vb. impf. *run*

бі́гти, 2, vb. impf., біжу́, біжи́ш; past tense біг, бі́гла *run*

бізнесме́н, -а, m. *businessman*

бік, бо́ку, loc. s. (на) бо́ці *or* боку́ *side*

бі́лий, -а, -е; -і, adj. *white*

бі́лка, -и, dat. and loc. sg. -лці, gen. pl. -лок, f. *squirrel*

бі́ля, prep. (+ gen.) *by, next to*

біля́вий, -а, е; -і, adj. *blond*

біль, бо́лю, m. *pain*

бі́льший, -а, -е; -і, comp. adj. *bigger*

бі́ржа, -і, f. *stock exchange*

біфште́кс, -а, m. *beefsteak*

блаки́тний, -а, -е; -і, adj. *blue, light blue*

бланк, -а, m. *form*

бли́зько *near*

бліди́й, -а́; é; і́, adj. *pale*

блокно́т, -а, m. *notebook*

блонди́н, -а, m. *blond (person)*

блю́дечко, -а, gen. pl. -чок, n. *saucer*

бо *because*

бог, -а, voc. Бо́же!, m. *God*

болга́рський, -а, -е; -і, adj. *Bulgarian*

болі́ти, 2, vb. impf., 3rd s. боли́ть, 3rd pl. боля́ть *hurt*

борода́, -и, gen. pl. -рі́д, f. *beard*

борщ, -у, m. *borshch (beetroot soup)*

брак, -у, m. *shortage*

бракува́ти, 1, vb. impf. 3rd s. -у́є (impers. + dat.) *be short (of)* мені́ браку́є гро́шей *I am short of money*

бра́ма, -и, f. *city gate*

брат, -а, m. *brother*

бра́ти, 1, vb. impf., беру́, бере́ш; imp. бери́! бері́ть! *take*

брова́, -и́, gen. pl. брів, f. *eyebrow*

бронхі́т, -у, m. *bronchitis*

бува́ти, 1, vb. impf. *visit, spend time in*

бува́й(те)! *bye for now!*

буди́нок, -нку, m. *building, house*

будіве́льний, -а, -е; -і, adj. *building*

будіве́льник, -а, m. *builder*

будíвля, -i, gen. pl. -вель, f. *building*

будувáти, 1, vb. impf., -ýю, -ýєш *build*

будь-коли, indef. adv. *at any time*

будь лáска *please*

бýдьмо! *cheers!* (as a drinking toast)

бýдь-хтó, indef. pron. *anyone at all*

бýдь-якúй, -á, -é; -í, adj. *any kind of*

букéт, -а, m. *bouquet*

бульвáр, -у, m. *boulevard*

бутербрóд, -а, m. *sandwich*

бýти, vb., present tense є; future tense бýду, бýдеш; imp. будь! бýдьте! *be*

вагóн, -а, m. *(railway) carriage*

важкúй, -á, -é; -í, adj. *heavy, difficult*

вáжко *it is difficult*

важлúвий, -а, -е; -i, adj. *important*

важлúво *it is important*

вáжчий, -а, -е; -i, comp. adj. *heavier, more difficult*

валíза, -и, f. *suitcase*

валюта, -и, f. *currency*

вáнна кімнáта *bathroom*

варéник; -а, m. *varenyk*

ваш, -а, -е; -i, poss. pron. *your* (s. polite/pl.)

вбігáти, 1, vb. impf. *run into*

ввéзення, -я, n. *import*

вдя́гнений, -а, -е; -i, adj. *dressed*

вдя́чний, -а, -е; -i, adj. *grateful*

везтú, 1, vb. impf., -зý, -зéш; past tense віз, везлá *take, lead* (by transport)

Велúкдень, -кóдня, m. *Easter Sunday*

Великóдні свя́та *Easter festival*

велúкий, -а, -е; -i, adj. *big, great, large*

вельмишанóвний, -а, е; -i, adj. *highly esteemed*

вербá, -й, f. *willow*

вéресень, -сня, m. *September*

вермішéль, -i, f. *vermicelli*

вéрхній, -я, -є; -i, adj. *upper*

весéлий, -а, -е; -i, adj. *merry*

весíлля, -я, n. *wedding*

веснá, -й, f. *spring*

вестú, 1, vb. impf. ведý, ведéш; past tense вів, велá *take, lead* (on foot)

вечéря, -i, f. *supper*

вéчір, -чора, m. *evening*

вечíрній, -я, -є; -i, adj. *evening*

вечорíти, 1, vb. impf., 3rd s. -íє (impers) *decline towards evening*

взя́ти, 1, vb. pf., візьмý, вíзьмеш; imp. візьмú! візьмíть! *take*

ви, pers. pron., acc. gen. and voc. вас, dat. вам, inst. вáми *you* (s. polite/plural)

вúбачити, 2, vb. pf., -чу, -чиш, -чать; imp. вúбач(те)! (+ dat.) *excuse, forgive*

вúбрати, 1, vb. pf., -беру, -береш *choose*

вивчáти, 1, vb. impf. *learn*

вúвчити, 2, vb. pf. *learn (completely)*

вигляда́ти, 1, vb. impf. *look (like)*

вид, -у, loc. sg. на видý, m. (на + acc) *view (of)*

видéлка, -и, dat. and loc. s. -лці, gen. pl. -лок, f. *fork*

вúдний, -а, -е; -i, adj. *visible*

вúзначитися, 2, vb. pf. *be clear (about something)*

вúїхати, 1, vb. pf., -їду, -їдеш *leave, drive out (of somewhere)*

вúйти, 1, vb. pf., -йду, -йдеш; past tense -йшов, -йшла *leave, go out, get off*

вúйти зáміж (за + acc.) *marry (woman to a man)*

ви́клик, -у, m.   *call*

виклика́ти, 1, vb. impf.   *call out*

ви́кликати, 1, vb. pf., ичу, -ичеш   *call out*

ви́конати, 1, vb. pf.,   *fulfil, carry out*

ви́нний, -а, -е; -і, adj.   *guilty*

вино́, -á, n.   *wine*

ви́падок, -дку, m.   *chance, occurrence, incident*

неща́сний ви́падок   *accident*

ви́писати, 1, vb. pf., -ишу, -ишеш   *write out*

ви́пити, 1, vb. pf., -п'ю, -п'єш; imp. -пий(те)!   *drink up*

ви́пиймо!   *let's drink!*

ви́раз, -у, m.   *phrase, expression*

ви́рішити, 2, vb. pf.   *decide*

ви́робити, 2, vb. pf., -блю, -бимо, -блять   *produce, manufacture*

виробля́ти, 1, vb. impf.   *produce, manufacture*

виробни́цтво, -а, n.   *production*

ви́сіти, 2, vb. impf., -ишу́, -иси́ш   *hang* (intrans.)

ви́словити, 2, vb. pf., -влю, -виш, -влять   *express*

ви́словитися, 2, vb. pf., -влюся, -вишся, -вляться   *express oneself*

висо́кий, -а, -е; -і, adj.   *high, tall*

ви́соко   *high*

виста́ва, -и, f.   *performance*

ви́ставити, 2, vb. pf., -влю, -виш, -влять   *put out, exhibit*

ви́ставка, -и, dat. and loc. s. -вці, gen. pl. -вок, f.   *exhibition*

виставля́ти, 1, vb. impf.   *put out, exhibit*

вистача́ти, 1, vb. impf. (impers. + dat.)   *be sufficient*

ви́твір, -вору, m.   *work, creation*

ви́трата, -и, f. (на + acc)   *expenditure (on)*

ви́хід, -ходу, m.   *exit*

вихідни́й день   *day off*

вихо́дити, 2, vb. impf., -джу, -диш   *leave, go out*

ви́щий, -а, -е; -і, comp. adj.   *higher, taller*

вівто́рок, -рка, m.   *Tuesday*

від, prep. (+ gen.)   *from*

відбивна́, -о́ї, f. adj. functioning as noun   *chop*

відбува́тися, 1, vb. impf.   *happen, take place*

відбу́тися, 1, vb. pf., 3rd s. відбу́деться   *happen, take place*

відварни́й, -á, -é; -í, adj.   *boiled*

відвезти́, 1, vb. pf., -зу́, -зе́ш, past tense -віз, -везла́   *take (someone somewhere)*

відве́ртість, -тості, inst. s. -тістю, f.   *frankness, sincerity*

відві́дання, -я, n.   *visit*

відві́дати, 1, vb. pf.   *visit*

відві́дувати, 1, vb. impf., -ую, -уєш   *visit*

відві́дувач, -а, m.   *visitor*

відді́л, -у, m.   *department*

відігра́вати, 1, vb. impf., -аю, -аєш   *play (a part, role)*

від'ї́зд, -у, m.   *departure*

відкри́ти, 1, vb. pf., -ию, -иєш   *reveal, open*

відкри́тий, -а, -е; -і, adj.   *open; sincere, frank, candid*

відлеті́ти, 2, vb. pf., -ечу́, -ети́ш   *leave, depart (by air)*

відліта́ти, 1, vb. impf.   *leave, depart (by air)*

відмо́витися, 2, vb. pf., -влюся, -вишся, -вляться   *refuse*

відо́мий, -а, -е; -і, adj.   *known, renowned*

відповідь, -i, inst. s. -ддю, gen. pl. -дей, f. *answer*

відповісти́, vb. pf, -ві́м, -ві́си, -ві́сть; -вімо́, -вісте́, даду́ть ві́дповідь *answer*

відпочива́ти, 1, vb. impf. *rest, relax, have a holiday*

відпочи́нок, -нку m. *holiday*

відпочи́ти, 2, vb. pf., -йну, -йнеш; impf. -чи́нь(те)! *have a rest*

відпра́вник, -a, m. *sender*

відпу́стка, -и, dat. and loc. sg. -тці, gen. pl., -ток, f. *holiday*

відра́зу (одра́зу) *at once*

відрекомендува́тися, 1, vb. pf., -у́юся, -у́єшся *introduce oneself*

відря́дження, -я, n. *business trip*

відчи́нений, -а, -е; -i, adj. *open*

відчини́ти, 2, vb. pf. *open*

відчува́ти, 1, vb. impf. *feel, be aware*

ві́за, -и, f. *visa*

візи́т, -у м. *visit*

візи́тна ка́ртка *business card*

вікно́, -á, gen. pl. кон, n. *window*

ві́льний,-a, -е; -i, adj. *free*

ві́льно *fluently, freely*

він, pers. pron., acc. and gen. його́ (ньóго), dat. йому́, inst. ним, loc. ньóму *he, it* (referring to inanimate m. nouns)

ві́рус, -y, m. *virus*

ві́русний, -a, -е; -i adj. *viral*

ві́сім, card. num. *eight*

вісімдеся́т, card. num. *eighty*

вісімдеся́тий, -a, -е; -i, ord. num. *eightieth*

вісімна́дцятий, -a, -е; -i, ord. num. *eighteenth*

вісімна́дцять, card. num. *eighteen*

вісімсо́т, card. num. *eight hundred*

віта́льня, -i, gen. pl. -лень, f. *reception room, parlour*

вітамі́н, -y, m. *vitamin*

віта́ти, 1, vb. impf. (з + inst.) *welcome; congratulate* (on)

ві́тер, -тру, m. *wind*

ві́шалка,-и, dat. and loc. s. -лці, gen. pl. -лок, f. (clothes) *hanger*

ві́я, -ï, f. *eyelash*

в'їжджа́ти, 1, vb. impf. *enter, drive into*

в'їзд (до + gen.) *entry* (to)

в'ї́здити, vb. impf. ї́жджа́ю̆, -ї́здиш *enter, drive into*

в'ї́хати, 1, vb. pf., -ї́ду, -ї́деш *enter, drive into*

вла́сне *precisely, exactly*

влеті́ти, 2, vb. pf., -ечу́, -ети́ш *fly into*

вліта́ти, 1, vb. impf. *fly into*

води́ти, 2, vb. impf., -джу́, -диш *take, lead* (on foot)

воді́й, -я́, m. *driver*

водно́час *at the same time*

вози́ти, 2, vb. impf., -ожу́, -о́зиш *take, lead* (by transport)

вокза́л, -y, m. *station*

волейбо́л, -y, m. *volleyball*

володі́ти, 1, vb. impf., -і́ю, -і́єш (+ inst.) *possess*

воло́сся, -я, n. (always s.) *hair*

вона́, pers. pron., acc., й (gen. ï ḯ, нéï), dat. їй, inst. нéю, loc. ній *she, it* (referring to f. inanimate nouns)

вони́, pers. pron., acc. and gen. їх (них), dat. їм, inst. ни́ми, loc. них *they*

воно́, pers. pron., acc. and gen. його́ (ньóго), dat. йому́, inst. ним, loc. нім/ ньóму *it* ворóта, -рíт, pl.   *gates*

восени́   *in autumn*

вóсьмеро, coll. num.   *eight*

вóсьмий, -а, -е; -і, ord. num.   *eighth*

восьмисóтий, -а, -е; -і, ord. num.   *eight hundredth*

впере́д   *forwards, to the front*

впізнáти, 1, vb. pf.   *recognize*

впли́нути, 1, vb. pf., -ну, -неш (на + асc.)   *have an influence (on)*

впрáва, -и, f.   *exercise*

вродли́вий, -а, -е; -і, adj.   *beautiful, handsome*

все óдно   *all the same*

все-таки́   *all the same*

всесвíтній, -я, -є; -і, adj.   *universal*

всесвíтньо відóмий   *world renowned*

ву́жчий, -а, -е; -і, comp. adj.   *narrower*

вузьки́й, -á, -é; -і, adj.   *narrow*

ву́лиця, -і, f.   *street*

вус, -а, nom. pl. ву́са m.   *moustache*

ву́хо, -а, n.   *ear*

вхід, вхóду, m.   *entrance*

вхóдити, 2, vb. impf., -джу, -диш   *enter, go into*

вчáсно   *on time*

в'язáти, 1, vb. impf., -яжу́, -я́жеш   *knit*

гадáти, 1, vb. impf.   *think, imagine*

газе́та, -и, f.   *newspaper*

гáзовий, -а, -е; -і, adj.   *gas (adj.)*

гай, гáю, m.   *grove of trees*

галере́я, -ї, f.   *gallery*

гарáж, -á, m.   *garage*

гарáзд,   *fine, OK*

гарне́нький, -а, -е; -і, adj.   *pretty*

гáрний, -а, -е; -і, adj.   *beautiful*

гарнíр, -у, m.   *garnish*

гаря́чий, -а, -е; -і, adj.   *hot*

гідрометце́нтр, -у, m.   *meteorological centre*

гíрка, -и, dat. and loc. sg. -рці, gen. pl. -рок, f.   *hill*

гірчи́чник, -а, m.   *mustard poultice*

гíрший, -а, -е; -і, comp. adj.   *worse*

гість, гóстя, m.   *guest*

іти́/ї́хати в гóсті (до + gen.)   *to visit (someone)*

гітáра, -и, f.   *guitar*

глибóкий, -а, -е; -і, adj.   *deep*

гли́бше, comp. adv.   *more deeply*

гли́бший, -а, -е; -і, comp. adj.   *deeper*

гнíватися, 1, vb. impf. (на + асc.)   *be angry (with)*

говори́ти, 2, vb. impf.   *speak*

годи́на, -и, f.   *hour*

годи́нник, -а, m.   *watch, clock*

гóді!   *that's enough!*

головá, -и, f., gen. pl. голíв   *head*

головни́й, -á, -é; -í, adj.   *main, chief*

голóдний, -а, -е; -і, adj.   *hungry*

гóлос, -у, m.   *voice*

гóлосно   *loudly*

голубе́ць, -бця́, m.   *cabbage roll, stuffed cabbage*

голуби́й, -á, -é; -í, adj.   *blue, light blue*

гольф, -а, m.   *golf*

горá, -и́, gen. pl. гір, f.   *mountain, hill*

горíлка, -и, dat. and loc. sg. -ці, f.   *vodka*

горíх, -а, m.   *nut(s)*

гóрло, -а, n.   *throat*

госпóдар, -я, m.   *host, master of the house*

господи́ня, -і, f.   *hostess, mistress of the house*

гости́нний, -а, -е; -i, adj.   *hospitable*

гости́нність, -ності, inst. s., -ністю,
    f.   *hospitality*

готе́ль, -ю, m.   *hotel*

готі́вка, -и, dat. and   loc. sg. -вці, f.   *cash,
    ready money*

гото́вий,-а, -е; -i, adj.   *ready, prepared*

готува́ти, 1, vb. impf.,-ýю, -ýєш   *cook*

гра́дус, -а, m.   *degree*

гра́ти, 1, vb. impf.   *play*

гриб, -а, m.   *mushroom*

грибни́й, -á, -é; -í, adj.   *mushroom (adj)*

гри́вня, -i, gen. pl. -вень, f.   *hryvnia*

грип. -у, m.   *flu*

гро́ші, -шей, pl.   *money*

гру́день, -дня, m.   *December*

губа́, -и́, f.   *lip*

гуля́ти, 1, vb. impf.   *walk*

гу́мор, -у, m.   *humour*

густи́й, -á, -é; -í, adj.   *thick, bushy*

ґа́нок, -нку, m.   *porch*

дава́ти, 1, vb. impf., даю́, даéш; imp.
    дава́й(те)!   *give*

давно́   *for a long time*

дале́кий, -а, -е; -i, adj.   *distant*

дале́ко   *far off*

дале́ко (+ comp. adj.)   *far*

да́лі   *further, and so on*

да́льший, -а, -е; -i, comp. adj.   *further off,
    more distant*

да́ні, -них, pl. adj.   *data*

дарма́   *it doesn't matter!*

дарува́ти, 1, vb. impf., -ýю, -ýєш   *give (as a
    gift)*

да́ти, vb. pf., дам, даси́, дасть; дамó, дастé,
    даду́ть; imp. да́й(те)!   *give*

дах, -у, loc. s. на даху́, m.   *roof*

да́ча, -i, f.   *summer house, dacha*

два, m. and n.; дві, f., card. num.   *two*

двадця́тий, -а, -е; -i, ord. num.   *twentieth*

два́дцять, card. num.   *twenty*

двана́дцятий, -а, -е; i, ord. num.   *twelfth*

двана́дцять, card. num.   *twelve*

две́рі, -éй, inst. -рми́ or -ри́ма, pl.   *door*

дві́сті, card. num.   *two hundred*

дві́чі   *twice*

дво́є, coll. num.   *two*

двозна́чний, -а, -е; -i, adj.   *ambiguous*

двокімна́тний, -а, -е; -i, adj.   *two-roomed*

двоповерхо́вий, -а, -е; -i, adj.   *two-storey*

двохсо́тий, -а -е; -i, ord. num.   *two
    hundredth*

де?   *where?*

деба́ти, -ів, pl.   *debate*

дев'яно́стий, -а, -е; -i, ord. num.   *ninetieth*

дев'яно́сто, card. num.   *ninety*

де́в'ятеро, coll. num.   *nine*

дев'я́тий, -а, -е; -i, ord. num.   *ninth*

дев'ятисо́тий, -а, -е; -i, ord. num.   *nine
    hundredth*

дев'ятна́дцятий, -а, -е; -i, ord.
    num.   *nineteenth*

дев'ятна́дцять, card. num.   *nineteen*

дев'ятсо́т, card. num.   *nine hundred*

де́в'ять, card. num.   *nine*

де́кілька (+ gen.)   *several, a few*

деклара́ція, -ї, f.   *customs declaration form*

де-не́будь, indef. adv.   *anywhere,
    somewhere*

день, дня, m.   *day*

день наро́дження   *birthday*

де́рево, -а, n.   *tree*

дерев'я́ний, -а, -е; -і, adj.   *wooden*

деру́н, á, m.   *potato pancake*

десе́рт, -у, m.   *dessert*

де́сятеро, coll. num.   *ten*

деся́тий, -а, -е; -і, ord. num.   *tenth*

де́сять, card. num.   *ten*

десь, indef. adv.   *somewhere*

дета́льний, -а, -е; -і, adj.   *detailed*

дета́льно   *in detail*

де́хто, indef. pron.   *someone*

де́що, indef. pron.   *something; (followed by comp. adj. or adv.) a little (more)*

де́який, -а, -е;-і, indef. adj.   *certain*

дже́мпер, -а, m.   *jumper*

джерело́, á, n.   *source*

дзвіно́к, -нкá, m.   *(telephone) call, ring (at the door)*

дзе́ркало, -а, n.   *mirror*

диви́тися, 2, vb. impf., -влю́ся, -вишся   *look; watch (film, TV)*

дивови́жний, -а, -е; -і,   adj.   *strange, amazing*

дивува́ти, 1, vb. impf., -у́ю, -у́єш   *surprise*

дивува́тися, 1, vb. impf., -у́юся, -у́єшся (+ dat.)   *be amazed*

дилета́нт, -а, m.   *amateur*

дире́ктор, -а, m.   *director*

дискéта, -и, f.   *floppy disk*

дити́нство, -а, n.   *childhood*

дитя́чий, -а, -е; -і, adj.   *children's*

діабе́т, -у, m.   *diabetes*

діало́г, -у, m.   *dialogue*

ді́вчина, -и, f.   *girl*

ді́вчинка, -и, dat. and loc. s. -нці, gen. pl. -áток, f.   *little girl*

діду́сь, -уся́, m.   *granddad*

дізна́тися, 1, vb. pf.   *find out*

дійти́, 1, vb. pf., -йду́, -йдеш; past tense -йшо́в, -йшлá   *reach, get to* (on foot)

ділови́й, -á, -é; -і, adj.   *business (adj.)*

діста́тися, 1, vb. pf., -áнуся, -áнешся   *get (somewhere)*

ді́ти, -éй, inst. ді́тьми, pl.   *children*

ді́я, -ї, f.   *act (of a play)*

для, prep. (+ gen.)   *for*

дмухну́ти, 1, vb. pf., -ну́, -нéш   *puff*

Дніпро́, -á, m.   *Dnipro*

до, prep. (+ gen.)   *to*

до поба́чення!   *goodbye*

до рéчі   *by the way, incidentally*

доба́, -и́, f., gen. pl. діб   *twenty-four hours*

до́бре!   *fine!*

до́брий, -а, -е;-і, adj.   *good, kind*

добри́день!   *hello!*

до́брий день!   *hello!*

добро́, -á, n.   *good*

добро́бут, -у, m.   *prosperity*

добро́дій, -я, voc. s. -ію!, m.   *sir*

добро́дійка, -и, voc. s. -ко!, gen. pl. -йок, f.   *madam*

до́вгий, -а, -е; -і, adj.   *long*

до́вго   *long, for a long time*

довести́ся, 1, vb. pf., 3rd s. доведе́ться; past tense довело́ся (impers. + dat.)   *have to*

до́вший, -а, -е; -і, comp. adj.   *longer*

додо́му   *home(wards)*

дозво́лити, 2, vb. pf. (+ dat.)   *permit*

дозвóльте! *let me/us, allow me/us . . .*

доïхати, 1, vb. pf., -ïду, -ïдеш *reach, get as far as*

доклáдний, -а, -е; -i, adj. *exact, precise*

докумéнт, -а, m. *document*

долетíти, vb. pf., -ечý, -етúш *arrive* (by air)

дóля, -i, f. *fate*

домáшнiй, -я, -є; -i, adj. *domestic*

домóвитися, 2, vb. pf., -влюся, -вишся, -вляться (з + inst.) *agree, arrange* (with)

дóнька, -и, dat. and loc. sg. -нцi, gen. pl. -ньок, f. *daughter*

доповiдáти, 1, vb. impf. *report*

допомагáти, 1, vb. impf. (+ dat.) *help*

допомóга, -и, dat. and loc. s. -озi, f. *help, assistance*

допомогтú, 1, vb. pf., -можý, -мóжеш, past tense, -мíг, -моглá (+ dat.) *help*

доробúти, 2, vb. pf., -блю, -биш, -блять *finish making/doing*

дороблáти, vb. impf. *finish making/doing*

дорóга, -и, dat. and loc. s. -озi, gen. pl. -рíг, f. *road, journey, way*

дорогúй, -á, -é; í, adj. *dear, expensive*

дóрого *it is expensive*

дорóжчий, -а, -е;-i, comp. adj. *dearer*

дорóслий, -а, -е; -i, adj. and noun *adult*

доручúти, 2, vb. pf. *entrust*

дóсить! *that's enough!*

дóсi *till now, so far*

достáвити, 2, vb. pf., -влю, -виш, -влять *deliver*

дощ, -у, m. *rain*

дощúти, 2, vb. impf. (impers.) *be raining*

дрiбнúця, -i, f. *trifle, small matter*

друг, -а, nom. pl. дрýзi, m. *friend*

дрýгий, -а, -е; -i, ord. num. *second*

дружúна, -и, f. *wife*

дружúти, 2, vb. impf. *be good friends*

дрýжнiй, -я, -є; -i, adj. *friendly, amicable*

дублáнка, -и, dat. and loc. s. -нцi, gen. pl. -нок, f. *leather overcoat*

дýже *very*

дýмати, 1, vb. impf. (над + inst.) *think; ponder on*

дýмка, -и, dat. and loc. s. -мцi, gen. pl. -мóк, f. *idea, thought*

дýрень, -рня, m. *fool*

дурнúй,-á, -é; -i, adj. *stupid*

душ, -у, m. *shower*

душéвний, -а -е; -i, adj. *spiritual*

дáдько, -а, m. *uncle*

дáкувати, 1, vb. impf., -ую, -уєш, (+ dat.) *thank*

дáкую! *thank you!*

еконóмiка, -и, dat. and loc. sg. -цi, f. *economics*

екрáн, -а, m. *screen*

екскýрсiя, -ï, f. *excursion*

експрéс-пóшта, -и, f. *express post*

елегáнтний, -а, -е; -i, adj. *elegant*

елегáнтно *elegantly*

елéктрика, -и, dat. and loc. s. -цi, f. *electricity*

електрúчка, -и, dat. and loc. s. -цi, gen. pl. -чок, f. *electric suburban train*

електроенéргiя, -ï, f. *electricity*

емóцiя, -ï, f. *emotion*

Єврóпа, -и, f. *Europe*

європéйський, -а, -е; -i adj. *European*

жанр, -у, m.   *genre*

жáрко   *it is hot*

жарт, -у, m.   *joke*

жахлúвий, -а, -е; -і, adj.   *terrible*

жахлúво!   *awful!*

жетóн, -а, m.   *token*

живóпис, -у, m.   *painting* (genre)

жúти, 1, vb. impf., живý, живéш   *live*

житлó, -á, n.   *dwelling*

життéвий, -а, -е; -і, adj.   *life*

життя́, -я́, n.   *life*

жíнка, -и, dat. and loc. s. -нці, f., gen. pl.
   -нóк   *woman, wife*

жінóчий, -а, -е; -і, adj.   *female*

жóвтень, -вня, m.   *October*

жóвтий, -а, -е; -і, adj.   *yellow*

жóден, short-form adj., -дна, -дне; -дні   *none,
   no* (kind of)

журнáл, -у, m.   *journal*

журналíст, -а, m.   *journalist*

з (із, зі), prep. (+ gen.)   *from*

з (із, зі), prep. (+ inst.)   *with*

за, prep. (+ acc.)   *for; during, over* (in
   time expressions); *beyond; than* (after
   comparatives)

за, prep. (+ inst.)   *behind, beyond, on the
   other side of; according to*

за Цéльсієм   *centigrade*

заблукáти, 1, vb. pf.   *get lost*

заборóнений, -а, -е; -і, adj.   *forbidden*

забрáти, 1, vb. pf., -берý, берéш   *take*
   (someone off somewhere)

забувáти, 1, vb. impf.   *forget*

забýти, 1, vb. pf., -ýду, -ýдеш; imp.
   -бýдь(те)!   *forget*

завдавáти, 1, vb. impf., -даю, -даєш   *cause*

зáвжди   *always*

зáвтра   *tomorrow*

загáльний, -а, -е; -і, adj.   *general*

загасúти, 2, vb., д., -ашý, -áсиш   *extinguish,
   put out*

задовóлення, -я, n.   *satisfaction*

задýмати, 1, vb. pf.   *think up*

зáздрощі, -ів, pl.   *envy, jealousy*

заїхати, 1, vb. pf., -їду, -їдеш   *get somewhere*
   (a long way off)

займáтися, 1, vb. impf. (+ inst.)   *deal with, be
   busy with, go in for*

зáйнятий, -а, -е; -і, adj.   *busy*

зайтú, 1, vb. pf., зайдý, зáйдеш; past tense
   -йшóв, -йшлá (по + acc.)   *call* (for); *set* (of
   the sun)

закупíвля, -і, f.   *purchase in bulk*

закýска, -и, dat. and loc. s. -сці, gen. pl. -сок,
   f.   *hors d'oeuvre*

залúсина, -и, f.   *bald patch*

залишáтися, 1, vb. impf.   *remain*

залишúтися, 2, vb. pf.   *remain*

замóвити, 2, vb. f., -влю, -виш, -влять   *order,
   reserve, book*

замóвлення, -я, n.   *order*

замовля́ти, 1, vb. impf.   *order, reserve, book*

замóвник, -а, m.   *person who places an order*

замóк, -мкá, m.   *lock*

занáдто   *excessively*

заперéчувати, 1, vb. impf., -ую, -уєш   *object*

запéчений, -а, -е; -і, adj.   *baked*

запитáння, -я, n.   *question*

запитáти, 1, vb. pf.   *ask* (a question)

запізнúтися, 2, vb. pf. (на + acc.)   *be late*
   (for)

запі́знюватися, 1, vb. impf., -ююся, -юєшся (на + acc.) *be late (for)*

запланований, a, -e; -i, adj. *planned*

запланува́ти, 1, vb. pf., -у́ю, -у́єш, *plan*

запо́внити, 2, vb. pf. *complete, fill in*

запропонува́ти, 1, vb. pf., -у́ю, -у́єш *propose, suggest*

запроси́ти, 2, vb. pf., -ошу́, -о́сиш *invite*

запро́шення, -я, n. *invitation*

запро́шувати, 1, vb. impf., -ую, -уєш *invite*

за́раз *now, at any moment*

зарази́тися, 2, vb. pf., -ажу́ся, -а́зишся *get infected*

зароби́ти, 2, vb. pf.,-блю́, -биш, -блять *earn*

заробі́тна платня́ *wage, salary*

заробі́ток, -тку, m. *wage, salary*

заробля́ти, 1, vb. impf. *earn*

засі́дання, -я, n. *meeting*

засмія́тися, 1, vb. pf., -ію́ся, -іє́шся *burst out laughing*

засну́ти, 1, vb, pf., -ну́, -не́ш *fall asleep*

зателефонува́ти, 1, vb. pf.,-у́ю, -у́єш *phone*

за́тишний, -á, -e; -i, adj. *quiet, peaceful, cosy*

за́тишно *it is cosy*

затри́муватися, 1, vb. impf.,-уся, -уєшся *be held up, stay*

захворі́ти, 1, vb. pf., -і́ю, -і́єш *fall ill*

захво́рювання, -я, n. *ailment*

за́хід, -ходу, m. *west*

за́хідний, -a, -e; -i, adj. *western*

захо́дити , 2, vb. impf., -джу, -диш *come in, enter*

захопи́ти, 2, vb. д., -плю́, -пиш, -плять *catch*

зацікáвити, 2, vb. pf., -влю, -виш, -влять (у/в + loc.) *interest (someone in something)*

зачиня́ти, 1, vb. impf. *close (transitive)*

зачиня́тися, 1, vb. impf. *close (intransitive)*

зашарі́тися, 1, vb. pf.,-і́юся, -і́єшся *blush*

збагну́ти, 1, vb. pf., -ну́, -не́ш *grasp, comprehend*

зберегти́, 1, vb. pf., -ежу́, -ежéш; past tense -рíг, реглá *preserve*

збирáтися, 1, vb. impf. plan, *get ready*

зби́тий, -a, -e; -i, adj. *whipped*

збíгати, 1, vb. pf. *run down, pop down*

збро́я, -ї, f. (always s.) *weapons*

збудува́ти, 1, vb. pf., -у́ю, -у́єш *build*

збу́тися, 1, vb. pf., 3rd s. -у́деться *come true*

зважáти, 1, vb. impf. (на + acc) *pay attention (to)*

звáти, 1, vb. impf., зву, звеш *call*

звертáтися, 1, vb. pf., (до + gen.) *apply (to)*

зви́кнути, 1, vb. pf., -ну, -неш; past tense звик, зви́кла *get used (to)*

звичáйний, -a, -e; -i, adj. *usual*

звичáйно! *of course!*

звíдки? *where from? whence?*

звíдси *from here, hence*

звíдти *from there, thence*

зворо́тний, -a, -e; i, adj. *return*

згáдувати, 1, vb. impf., -ую, -уєш *mention, recall*

згóда, -и, f. *agreement*

згóда! *that's agreed!*

згóден, short-form adj., -дна, -дне; -дні *in agreement*

я згóден/згóдна з Вáми *I agree with you*

здавáти, 1, vb. impf., -даю́, -даéш *let (property)*

здавáтися, 1, vb. impf. (impers. + dat.), 3rd s. здаéться *seem* зда́ти, 1, vb. pf., -да́м, -даси́, -да́сть, -дамо́, -дасте́, -даду́ть   let (property)

здогада́тися, 1, vb. pf.   guess

здо́му   from home

здоро́вий, -а, -е; -і, adj.   healthy

здоро́в'я, -я, n.   health

зеле́ний, -а, -е; -і, adj.   green

зеле́нка, -и, dat. and loc. s. -нці, f.   zelenka (a green antiseptic liquid)

зе́лень, -і, inst. s. -нню, f. greenery

земля́, -і́, f.   ground

Земля́, -і́, f.   Earth

зерни́стий, -а, -е; -і, adj.   granular

зза́ду   from behind

зима́, -и́, f.   winter

зи́чити, 2, vb. impf.   wish

зігра́ти, 1, vb. pf.   play

зійти́, 1, vb. pf., зійду́, зі́йдеш; past tense -йшо́в, -йшла́   ascend, go up; rise (of the sun)

зі́рка, -и, dat. and loc. s. -рці, gen. pl. зіро́к, f.   star

зіста́вити, 2, vb. pf., -влю, -виш, -влять   compare

зіставля́ти, 1, vb. impf.   compare

з'ї́здити, 2, vb. pf, -ї́жджу, -ї́здиш   make a trip

з'ї́сти, vb. pf., їм, -ї́си, -ї́сть; -ї́мо́, -їсте́, -їдя́ть; imp. -ї́ж(те)!; past tense -ів, -ї́ла   eat (up)

зло, -а, gen. pl. зол, n.   evil

злий, -а, -е; -і, adj.   evil, malicious

злість, зло́сті, inst. s. злі́стю, f.   malice

змі́шувати, 1, vb. impf., -ую, -уєш   mix

змогти́, 1, vb. pf., -о́жу, -о́жеш; past tense зміг, змогла́   be able; manage, succeed

змо́ршка, -и, dat. and loc. s. -шці, gen. pl. -шок, f. wrinkle

знаве́ць, -вця́, m. (+ gen.)   expert (on)

знайо́мий, -а, -е; -і, adj. familiar; (as noun) acquaintance

знайти́, 1, vb. pf., -йду́, -йдеш; past tense -йшо́в, -йшла́   find

знак, -а, m.   sign

зна́ти, 1, vb. impf.   know

знахо́дитися, 1, vb. impf., -джуся, -дишся   be situated

зна́чно (+ comp. adj.)   considerably

знена́цька   unawares

знима́тися, 1, vb. impf.   be filmed

зня́ти, 1, vb. pf., зніму́, зні́меш   take off (clothes), remove; take a photograph of

зо́внішність, -ності, inst. s. -ністю, f.   external appearance

золоти́й, -а́, -е́; -і, adj.   golden

зріст, -ро́сту, m.   size

зроби́ти, 2, vb. pf., -блю́, -биш, -блять   do, make

зрозумі́лий, -а, -е; -і, adj.   intelligible

зрозумі́ти, 1, vb. pf., -і́ю, -і́єш   understand

зру́чний, а, -е; -і, adj.   comfortable

зру́чно   it is convenient

зуб, -а, m.   tooth

зупини́тися, 2, vb. pf.   stay, stop

зупи́нка, -и, dat. and loc. sg. -нці, f.   stopкінце́ва зупи́нка   terminus

зустрі́ти, 1, vb. pf., -і́ну, -і́неш; imp. -і́нь(те)   meet

зустрі́тися, 1, vb. pf., -і́нуся, -і́нешся   meet each otherзустрі́ньмося!   let's meet!

зу́стріч, -і, inst. -ччю, gen. pl. -чей, f.   meeting

зустрічáти, 1, vb. impf.   *meet*

зустрічáтися, 1, vb. impf.   *meet with each other*

з'ясóвувати, 1, vb. impf., -ую, -ує   *clarify*

і   *and*

Івáно-Франкíвськ, -а, m.   *Ivano-Frankivsk*

ідеáльний, -а, -е; -і, adj.   *ideal*

ідéя, -ї, f.   *idea*

ікрá, -и́, f.   *caviare*

імени́ни, -ни́н, pl.   *nameday*

іменни́к, -а, m.   *person celebrating nameday*

імпонувáти, 1, vb. impf., -у́ю, -у́єш (+ dat.)   *inspire respect (in)*

і́мпортний, -а, -е; -і, adj.   *imported*

ім'я́, і́мени, n.   *name, first name* ім'я́ по бáтькові   *patronymic*

інвéстор, -а, m.   *investor*

і́ндекс, -у, m.   *postcode*

інозéмний, -а, -е; -і adj.   *foreign*

інститу́т, -у, m.   *institute*

інтелігéнтний, -а, -е; -і, adj.   *cultured, polite*

інтерв'ю́, n. indecl.   *interview*

інтерéс, -у, m.   *interest*

інфéкція, f.   *infection*

інформáція, -ї, f.   *information*

і́нший, -а, -е; -і, adj.   *other*

існувáти, 1, vb. impf., -у́ю, -у́єш   *exist*

іспáнець, -ця, m.   *Spaniard*

Іспáнія, -ї, f.   *Spain*

іспáнка, -и, dat. and loc. sg. -нці, gen. pl. -нок   *Spaniard*

і́спит, -у, m.   *examination*

італíєць, -і́йця, m.   *Italian*

італíйка, -и, dat. and loc. sg. -йці, gen. pl. -йок   *Italian*

Італíя, -ї, f.   *Italy*

іти́, 1, vb. impf., іду́, іде́ш; imp. іди́! ідíть!; past tense ішóв, ішлá   *go (on foot)*

їдáльня, -і, gen. pl. -лень, f.   *dining room*

ї́жа, -і, f.   *food*

ї́здити, 2, vb. impf., ї́жджу, ї́здиш   *go, travel, ride*

ї́ї, poss. pron. indecl.   *her, its (referring to inanimate f. nouns)*

ї́сти, vb. impf., їм, їси, їсть; їмó, їстé, їдять; imp. їж(те)!; past tense їв, ї́ла   *eat*

ї́х, poss. pron. indecl.   *their*

ї́хати, 1, vb. impf. ї́ду, ї́деш   *go, travel*

й   *and*

йогó, poss. adj., indecl.   *his, its (with reference to m. nouns)*

йод, -у, m.   *iodine*

кабачóк, -чкá, m.   *marrow*

кабінéт, -у, m.   *office, study*

кáва, -и, f.   *coffee*

казáти, 1, vb. impf., -ажу́, -а́жеш   *say*

кáзка, -и, dat. and loc. s. -зці, gen. pl. -зóк, f.   *fairy story*

календáр, -я́, m.   *calendar*

калькуля́тор, а, m.   *calculator*

кáмінь, -меня, m.   stone

Канáда, -и, f.   *Canada*

канадíєць, -і́йця, m.   *Canadian*

канáдка, -и, dat and loc. s. -ці, gen. pl. -ок, f.   *Canadian*

канáпа, -и, f.   *divan*

канíкули, -ул, pl.   *holidays*

капіталовкла́днення, -я, n. *capital investment*

карбо́ванець, -нця, m. *karbovanets* (former currency of Ukraine)

ка́рий, -а, -е; -і, adj. *hazel* (colour of eyes)

Карпа́ти, gen. -а́т, pl. *the Carpathian mountains*

карти́на, -и, f. *picture*

карти́нний, -а, -е; -і, adj. *picture*

ка́ртка, -и, dat. and loc. s. -тці, gen. pl. -ток, f. *card*

карто́пля, -і, f. *potato(es)*

ка́са, -и, f. *cash desk*

каси́р, -а, m. *cashier*

катало́г, -у, m. *catalogue*

ка́шель, -шлю, m. *cough*

квадра́тний, -а, -е; -і, adj. *square*

кварти́ра, -и, f. *flat*

квита́нція, -ї, f. *receipt*

квито́к, -тка́, m. (до + gen.) *ticket (for)*

кві́тень, -тня, m. *April*

кві́тка, -и, dat. and loc. sg. -тці, nom. pl. кві́ти *flower*

ке́лих, -а, m. *(wine) glass*

керівни́й, -а́, -е́; -і́, adj. *leading*

керівни́цтво, -а, n. *management*

керува́ти, 1, vb. impf., -у́ю, -у́єш (+ inst.) *manage, rule*

Ки́їв, Ки́єва, m. *Kyiv*

ки́лим, -а, m. *carpet, rug*

кирпа́тий, -а, -е; -і, adj. *snub-nosed*

ки́ця, -і, f. *kitten*

кі́лька (+ gen.) *several, a few*

кіт, кота́, m. *cat*

клі́мат, -у, m. *climate*

кни́га, -и, dat. and loc. sg. -и́зі, f. *book*

книга́рня, -і, gen. pl. -рень, f. *bookshop*

кни́жка, -и, dat. and loc. s. -жці, gen. pl. -жок, f. *book*

ко́бза, -и, f. *kobza*

кобза́р, -я́, m. *kobza player*

ковбаса́, -и́, f. *salami, sausage*

ковта́ти, 1, vb. impf. *swallow*

код, -у, m. *code*

ко́жний, -а, -е; -і (also short m. form ко́жен), adj. *each, every, anyone*

колго́ти, -го́т, pl. *tights*

коле́га, -и, dat. and loc. s. -зі, m. or f. *colleague*

коли́? *when?*

коли́-не́будь, indef. adv. *anytime, ever, some time (or other)*

коли́сь, indef. adv. *some time ago, at one time*

колі́но, -а, n. *knee*

ко́лір, -льору, m. *colour*

ко́лія, -ї, f. *track, platform*

комерці́йний, -а, -е; -і, adj. *commercial*

коме́рція, -ї, f. *commerce*

комо́ра, -и, f. *pantry, storeroom*

компа́нія, -ї, f. *company*

компози́тор, -а, m. *composer*

компози́ція, -ї, f. *composition*

комп'ю́тер, -а, m. *computer*

комфо́рт, -у, m. *comfort*

конва́лія, -ї, f. *lily of the valley*

конве́рт, -а, m. *envelope*

конкре́тний, -а, -е; -і, adj. *concrete*

ко́нсул, -а, m. *consul*

ко́нсульский, -а, -е; -і, adj. *consular*

контра́кт, -у, m. *contract*

контроле́р, -а, m. *inspector*

контро́ль, -ю, m.   *control*

коньяќ, -у́, m.   *cognac*

копі́йка, -и, gen. pl. -йо́к, f.   *kopiyka (100th part of a hryvnia)* (NB: nom. pl. копі́йки, but дві копі́йки; п'ять копі́йок)

коре́ктний, -а, -е; -і, adj.   *correct*

кореспонде́нт, -а, m.   *correspondent*

коридо́р, -у, m.   *corridor*

кори́чневий, -а, -е; -і, adj.   *brown*

коро́ткий, -а, -е; -і, adj.   *short*

коро́тший, -а, -е; -і, comp. adj.   *shorter*

ко́рпус, -а, m.   *block*

костю́м, -а, m.   *suit*

котле́та, -и, f.   *cutlet*

котри́й, -а́, -é; -і́   *which?*

коха́ний, -а, -е; -і, adj. functioning as noun   *beloved*

коха́ння, -я, n.   *love*

коха́ти, 1, vb. impf.   *love*

кошт, -у, m.   *cost, expense*

ко́штувати, 1, vb. pf., 3rd s. ко́штує   *cost*

краб, -а, m.   *crab*

крава́тка, -и, dat. and loc. s. -тці, gen pl. -ток, f.   *tie*

краї́на, -и, f.   *country*

кра́пля, -і, gen. pl. -пель, f.   *drop*

краса́, -и́, f.   *beauty*

краси́вий, -а, -е; -і, adj.   *beautiful, handsome*

кра́щий, -а, -е; -і, adj.   *better*

креве́тка, -и, dat. and loc. s. -тці, gen. pl. -ток, f.   *prawn*

креди́т, -у, m.   *credit*

креди́тна ка́ртка   *credit card*

креме́зний, -а, -е; -і, adj.   *robust, sturdy*

Крим, -у, loc. s. у Криму́, m.   *Crimea*

кри́мський, -а, -е; -і, adj.   *Crimean*

крім, prep. (+ gen.)   *apart from*

крі́плений, -а, -е; -і, adj.   *fortified*

крі́сло, -а, gen. pl. -сел, n.   *armchair*

кру́глий, -а, -е; -і, adj.   *round*

куди́?   *where to? whither?*

куди́ (+ comp. adj.)   *far*

куди́сь, indef. adv.   *somewhere (to)*

культу́ра, -и, f.   *culture*

купе́, n. indecl.   *compartment*

купи́ти, 2, vb. pf., -плю́, -пиш, -плять   *buy*

купо́н, -а, m.   *coupon (also karbovanets)*

купува́ти, 1, vb. impf., -у́ю, -у́єш   *buy*

куро́рт, -у, m.   *resort*

курс, -у, m.   *exchange rate*

ку́ртка, -и, dat. and loc. s. -тці gen. pl. -ток, f.   *jacket*

ку́хня, -і, gen. pl. -хонь, f.   *kitchen*

кучеря́вий, -а, -е; -і, adj.   *curly*

кущ, -а, m.   *bush*

ла́мпа, -и, f.   *lamp*

ластови́ння, -я, n. (always s.)   *freckles*

легки́й, -а́, -é; -і́, adj.   *light, easy*

ле́гко   *easily, it it easy*

легкова́жний, -а, е; -і, adj.   *frivolous*

ле́гший, -а, -е; -і, comp. adj.   *lighter, easier*

лежа́ти, 2, vb. impf., -жу́, -жи́ш   *lie*

леті́ти, 2, vb. impf,. -ечу́, -ети́ш   *fly*

лимо́н, -а, m.   *lemon*

ли́пень, -пня, m.   *July*

ли́сий, -а, -е; -і, adj.   *bald*

лист, -а́, m.   (до + gen.)   *letter (to/for)*

листі́вка, -и, dat. and loc. s. -вці, gen. pl. -вок, f.   *postcard*

листопа́д, -а, m.   *November*

ли́стя, -я, n.   *foliage*

лихома́нити, 2, vb. impf. (impers. +
   dat.)   *feel feverish*

лише́   *only, just*

лі́вий,-а, -е; -i, adj.   *left*

ліво́руч   *on the left, to the left*

лі́жко, -а, loc. s. у лі́жку, gen. pl. -жок,
   n.   *bed*

лі́кар, -я, m.   *doctor*

ліка́рня, -i, gen. pl. -рень, f.   *hospital*

лі́ки, -iв, pl.   *medicine*

лікува́ти, 1, vb. impf., -ýю, -ýєш   *heal*

лiс, -у, m.   *forest*

літа́к, -á, m.   *plane*

літа́ти, 1, vb. impf.   *fly*

лі́то, -а, n.   *summer*

лiфт, -а, m.   *lift*

лічи́льник, -а, m.   *meter*

ло́жа, -i, f.   *box* (in a theatre)

ло́жа бенуа́р   *grand circle* (in a theatre)

ло́жечка, -и, dat. and loc. s. -чці, gen. pl. -чóк,
   f.   *small spoon, teaspoon*

ло́жка, -и, dat. and loc. s. -жці, gen. pl. -жóк,
   f.   *spoon*

Луга́нськ, -а, m.   *Luhansk*

Львів, Льво́ва, m.   *Lviv*

люби́ти, 2, vb. impf., -блю́, -биш,
   -блять   *love, like*

любо́в, -i, inst. s. -óв'ю, f.   *love*

лю́ди, -дéй, inst. -дьми́, pl.   *people*

лю́стра, -и, f.   *chandelier*

лю́тий, -ого, m. adj. functioning as
   noun   *February*

ля́лька, -и, dat. and loc. s. -льці, gen. pl.
   -льóк, f.   *doll*

мабу́ть   *perhaps, maybe*

магази́н, -у, m.   *shop*

магнітофо́н, -а, m.   *tape recorder*

маде́ра, -и, f.   *Madeira* (wine)

майбу́тнє, -нього, n. adj. functioning as
   noun   *the future*

майбу́тній, -я, -є; -i, adj.   *future*

майда́н, -у, m.   *square*

ма́йже   *almost, nearly*

майоне́з, -у, m.   *mayonnaise*

мале́нький, -а, -е; -i, adj.   *little, small*

мали́й, -á, -é -i, adj.   *little, small*

мали́новий, -а, -е; -i, adj.   *crimson*

ма́ло (+ gen.)   *few, little*

малюва́ти, 1, vb. impf., -ю́ю, -ю́єш   *paint*

маля́р, -á, m.   *painter* (house)

ма́ма, -и, f.   *mother, mummy*

мане́ра, -и, f.   *manner*

марино́ваний, -а, -е; -i, adj.   *marinated*

ма́рка, -и, dat. and loc. s. -рці, gen. pl. -рок,
   f.   *postage stamp*

маршру́т, -у, m.   *route*

маса́ж, -у, m.   *massage*

ма́сло, -а, n.   *butter*

матема́тик, -а, m.   *mathematician*

матема́тика, -и, dat. and loc. s. -ици,
   f.   *mathematics*

ма́ти, 1, vb. impf.   *have*

ма́ти ра́цію   *be right*

матч, -у, m.   *match* (sporting)

маши́на, -и, f. (coll.)   *car*

ме́блі, -iв, pl.   *furniture*

мед, -у, loc. s. на меду́, m.   *honey*

ме́нше (+ gen.)   *fewer, less*

ме́нший, -а, -е; -і, comp. adj.   *smaller*

меню́, n. indecl.   *menu*

мере́жа, -і, f.   *net(work)*

мета́, -и́, f.   *aim, purpose*

метр, -а, m.   *metre*

метро́, n. indecl.   *underground railway*

ме́шкати, 1, vb. impf.   *live, dwell*

ми, pers. pron., acc., gen. and loc. нас, dat.
   нам, inst. на́ми   *we*

мину́лий, -а, -е; -і, adj.   *last*

мисте́цтво, -а, n.   *art*

ми́тний, -а, -е; -і, adj.   *customs*

ми́тниця, -і, f.   *customs*

між, prep. (+ inst.)   *between*

міжнаро́дний, -а, -е; -і, adj.   *international*

мій, m., моя́, f., моє́, n.; мої́, pl., poss.
   pron.   *my, mine*

мікстура́, -и, f.   *liquid medicine, mixture*

мілі́ція, -ї, f.   *police*

мільйо́н, -а, m., card, num.   *million*

мільйо́нний, -а, -е; -і, ord. num.   *millionth*

міністе́рство, -а, n.   *ministry*

міні́стр, -а, m.   *minister*

міркува́ння, -я, n.   *consideration*

мі́сто, -а, n.   *town, city*

мі́сце, -я, n.   *place; seat* (in a theatre)

місце́вий, -а, -е; -і, adj.   *local*

мі́сяць, -ця, m.   *month*

міцни́й, -а́, -є́; -і́, adj.   *powerful, strong*

міць, мо́ці, inst. s., мі́ццю, f.   *might, power*

мо́ва, -и, f.   *language*

могти́, 1, vb. impf., мо́жу, мо́жеш; past tense
   міг, могла́   *can, be able*

модерніза́ція, -ї, f.   *modernization*

модернізува́ти, 1, vb. impf., -ую,
   -у́єш   *modernize*

мо́дний, -а, -е; -і, adj.   *fashionable*

мо́же бу́ти   *maybe, perhaps*

можли́вий, -а, -е; -і, adj.   *possible*

можли́вість, -ості, inst. s. -істю, f.   *possibility*

можли́во   *possibly*

мо́жна   *it is possible*

молоди́й, -а́, -є́; -і́, adj.   *young*

моло́дший, -а, -е; -і, adj.   *youngest*

молоко́, -а́, n.   *milk*

мо́ре, -я, n.   *sea*

моро́з, -у, m.   *frost*

моро́зиво, -а, n.   *ice cream*

моро́зити, 2, vb. impf., -о́жу, -о́зиш   *chill*
   (also used as impers.)

мрячи́ти, 2, vb. impf. (impers.)   *drizzle*

му́зика, -и, dat. and loc. s. -ці, f.   *music*

музика́нт, -а, m.   *musician*

му́сити, 2, vb. impf., -у́шу, -у́сиш   *must,
   have to*

му́ха, -и, dat. and loc. s. -ci, f.   *fly*

м'яки́й, -а́, -є́; -і́, adj.   *soft*

м'я́кість, -кості, inst. s. -кістю, f.   *softness,
   tenderness*

м'ясни́й, -а́, -є́; -і́, adj.   *meat*

м'я́со, -а, n.   *meat*

на, prep.(+ acc.)   *то*на все до́бре!   *all
   the best!*на жаль   *unfortunately*на мою
   ду́мку   *in my opinion*

на, prep. (+ loc.)   *at*

набага́то (+ comp. adj.)   *much*

на́бережна, -ої, adj. functioning as f.
   noun   *embankment*

наважитися, 2, vb. pf.   *dare, resolve*

навесні   *in spring*

навіть   *even*

навколо, prep. (+ gen.)   *around*

навчитися, 2, vb. pf.   *learn*

нагода, -и, f.   *occasion*

нагорі   *upstairs*

над, prep. (+ inst.)   *over, above*

надавати, 1, vb. impf., -даю, -даєш (+ gen.)   *give (a lot of something)*

надалі   *in the future*надзвичайно   *extraordinarily*

надовго   *for long*

назад   *backwards, to the rear*

назва, -и, f.   *name*

наївний, -а, -е; -і, adj.   *naive*

найбільш (+ adj.)   *most*

найбільше   *most of all*

найбільший, -а, -е; -і, super. adj.   *biggest*

найближчим часом   *in the very near future*

найгірший, -а, -е; -і, super. adj.   *worst*

найдавніший, -а, -е; -і, super. adj.   *oldest, most ancient*

найкращий, -а, -е; -і, super. adj.   *best, very best*

наймати, 1, vb. impf.   *rent*

найменш (+ adj.)   *least*

найменший, -а, -е; -і, super. adj.   *smallest*

найняти, vb. pf., -йму, -ймеш   *rent*

налагодити, 2, vb. pf., -джу, -диш   *arrange*

налити, 1, vb. pf., -ллю, -ллєш   *pour (out)*

напевно   *probably, for sure*

написати, 1, vb. pf., -ишу, -ишеш   *write*

напій, -пою, m.   *beverage, drink*

наприклад   *for example*

напружений, -а, -е; -і, adj.   *busy*

наркотичний, -а, -е; -і, adj.   *narcotic*

наробити, 2, vb. pf., -блю, -биш, -блять   *make (a lot of)*

наробитися, 2, vb. pf., -блюся, -бишся, -бляться   *overwork oneself*

наробляти, 1, vb. impf.   *make (a lot of)*

нароблятися, 1, vb. impf.   *overwork oneself*

народ, -у, m.   *people, nation*

народження, -я, n.   *birth*

народити, 2, vb. pf., -джу, -диш   *give birth to*

народитися, 2, vb. pf., джуся, -дишся   *be born*

наскільки   *as far as*

настільки   *to such an extent*

настільний, -а, -е; -і, adj.   *table*

настрій, -рою, m.   *mood*

наступний, -а, -е; -і, adj.   *next*

натиснути, 1, vb. pf., -ну, -неш (на + асс.)   *press (on)*

натуральний, -а, -е; -і, adj.   *natural*

наука, -и, f.   *science*

науковець, -вця, m.   *scientist*

науковий, -а, -е; -і, adj.   *scientific*

національний, -а, -е; -і, adj.   *national*

начальник, -а, m.   *manager, head*

наш, -а, -е; -і, poss. pron.   *our, ours*

не   *not*не видно (+ gen.)   *. . . is/are not visible*не той, . . .   *wrong*

небо, -а, nom. pl. небеса, gen. pl. небес, n.   *sky*

невже?   *is it really possible?*

невинний, -а, -е; -і, adj.   *innocent*

невисокий, -а, -е; -і, adj.   *short*

недалеко (від)   *not far (from)*

неділя, -і, f.   *Sunday*

не́жить, -ю, m.   *cold (in the head)*

незаба́ром   *soon*

незале́жний, -а, -е; -і, adj.   *independent*

незале́жно від (+ gen.)   *independently of*

незвича́йний, -а, -е; -і, adj.   *unusual*

незмі́нний, -а, -е; -і, adj.   *unchanged*

неодмі́нно   *without fail*

неодру́жений, -а, -е; -і, adj.   *unmarried*

непога́но   *not bad*

непра́вда, -и, f.   *falsehood*

несподі́ваний, -а, -е; -і, adj.   *unexpected*

нести́, 1, vb. impf., -су́, -се́ш; past tense ніс,
    несла́   *carry*

неха́й . . .   *may . . .*

нещасли́вий, -а, -е; -і, adj.   *unlucky*

неща́сний, -а, -е; -і, adj.   *unhappy*

неща́сний ви́падок   *accident*

нещода́вно   *recently*

ни́жній, -я, -є; -і, adj.   *lower*

ни́жчий, -а, -е; -і, comp. adj.   *lower*

низьки́й, -á, -é, -í, adj.   *low*

ни́зько   *low*

ні   *no*

ніде́, neg. adv.   *nowhere*

ні́де, neg. adv.   *there is nowhere*

ніж   *than (after comparatives)*

ніж, ножа́, m.   *knife*

ні́кого, neg. pron.   *there is no one*

ніко́ли, neg. adv.   *never*

ні́коли, neg. adv.   *there is no time*

ніку́ди, neg. adv.   *nowhere (to)*

ні́куди, neg. adv.   *there is nowhere* (motion)

ні́мець, -мця, m.   *German*

Німе́ччина, -и, f.   *Germany*

німке́ня, -і, f.   *German*

ніс, но́са, m.   *nose*

ніхто́, neg. pron.   *no one, nobody*

ні́чого, neg. pron.   *there is nothing*

нічо́го!   *it doesn't matter!*

ніщо́, neg. pron.   *nothing*

нія́кий, -а, -е; -і, neg. adj.   *no (kind of)*

нови́й, -á, -é; -í, adj.   *new*

новина́, -и́, f.   *news*

нога́, -и, dat. and loc. s. -озі́, gen. pl. ніг,
    f.   *leg, foot*

но́жиці, -иць, pl.   *scissors*

но́мер, -а, m.   *room (in a hotel)*

норма́льно!   *OK!*

носи́ти, 2, vb. impf., -ошу́, -о́сиш   *carry, wear*

нуди́ти, 2, vb. impf. (impers. + acc.)   *feel sick*

нудни́й, -á, -é; -í, adj.   *boring*

о (об), prep. (+ loc.)   *at (in clock time
    phrases)*

обере́жний, -а, -е; -і, adj.   *careful*

оби́два, m. and n.; оби́дві, f.   *both*

обі́д, -у, m.   *lunch*

обі́дати, 1, vb. impf.   *have lunch*

обла́днання, -я, n.   *equipment*

обли́ччя, -я, n.   *face*

о́бмін, -у, m.   *exchange*

обов'язко́вий, -а, -е; -і, adj.   *compulsory*

обов'язко́во   *it is compulsory*

обража́тися, vb. impf.   *be offended*

овва́!   *you don't say!*

овоче́вий, -а, -е; -і, adj.   *vegetable*

огіро́к, -рка́, m.   *cucumber*

огля́нути, 1, vb. pf., -ну, -неш   *examine,
    look over*

оголоси́ти, 2, vb. pf., -ошу́,
    -о́сиш   *announce*

оголо́шення, -я, n.   advertisement, small ad

одержати, 2, vb. pf., -жу, -жиш   get, obtain

оде́ржувати, 1, vb. impf., -ую, -уєш   get, obtain

Оде́са, -и, f.   Odesa

оди́н, m.; одна́, f.; одне́, n., card. num.   one

оди́н о́дного (m. + m.); одна́ о́дну (f. + f.); одне́ о́дного (m. + f.)   one another

одина́дцятий, -а, -е; -і, ord. num.   eleventh

одина́дцять, card. num.   eleven

одна́к   however

однокімна́тний, -а, -е; -і, adj.   one-roomed

одра́зу (відразу)   at once

одру́жений, -а, -е; -і, adj.   married

одружи́тися, 2, vb. pf.,   get married (man to a woman)

одужання, -я, n.   recovery

о́дяг, -у, m.   clothing

одяга́ти, 1, vb. impf.   dress (someone)

одяга́тися, 1, vb. impf.   dress onself, get dressed

о́зеро, -а, n.   lake

ознайо́митися, 2, vb. pf., -млюся, -мишся, -мляться (з + inst.)   familiarize oneself (with)

о́ко, -а, nom. pl. о́чі, gen. pl. -че́й, inst. pl. -чи́ма   eye

окре́мий, -а, -е; -і, adj.   separate

оксами́товий, -а, -е; -і, adj.   velvet

окуля́ри, -ів, pl.   glasses

олівець, -вця́, m.   pencil

омле́т, -у, m.   omelette

он   over there (is/are)

ону́к, -а, m.   grandson

ону́чка, -и, dat. and loc. sg. -чці, gen. pl. -чок, f.   granddaughter

опера́ція, -ї, f.   operation

описа́ти, 1, vb. pf., -ишу́, -и́шеш   describe

ора́нжевий, -а, -е; -і, adj.   orange (colour)

осві́та, -и, f.   education

оселе́дець, -дця, m.   herring

осетри́на, -и, f.   sturgeon

осетро́вий, -а, -е; -і, adj.   sturgeon

о́сінь, о́сені, inst. s. о́сінню, f.   autumn

особли́вий, -а, -е; -і, adj.   special

оста́нній, -я, -є; -і, adj.   last, final

ось   here is

от   here, there, behold! look!

о́тже   so, well then!

офіціа́нт, -а, m.   waiter

офіціа́нтка, -и, dat. and loc. s. -тці, gen. pl. -ток, f.   waitress

офіці́йний, -а, -е; -і, adj.   official

офо́рмити, 2, vb. pf., -млю, -миш, -млять   obtain (a visa)

охолоди́ти, 2, vb. pf., -джу́, -диш   cool down

очере́т, -у, m.   reeds

па!   bye-bye!

па́горб, -а, m.   hill

пальто́, -а́, n.   overcoat

пампу́шка, -и, dat. and loc. s. -шці, gen. pl. -шо́к, f.   garlic bun

пам'ята́ти, 1, vb. impf.   remember

па́м'ятка, -и, dat. and loc. s. -тці, f.   monument

па́м'ятка архітекту́ри   listed building

пан, -а, voc. па́не!, m.   Mr

па́ні, f. indecl.   Mrs

папі́р, -пе́ра, m.   paper (document)

папі́р, -пе́ру, m.   paper (material)

папіре́ць, -рця́, m.   sheet of paper

па́пка, -и, dat. and loc. s. -пці, gen. pl. -пок, f.   file, folder

па́ра, -и, f.   pair

парасо́лька, -и dat. and loc. s. -льці, gen. pl.
-льок, f.   *umbrella*

парла́мент, -у, m.   *parliament*

паропла́в, -а, m.   *steamer*

партер, -у, m.   *stalls* (in a theatre)

партне́р, -а, m.   *partner*

пасажи́р, -а, m.   *passenger*

па́спорт, -а, m.   *passport*

па́спортний, -а, -е; -і, adj.   *passport*

Па́сха, -и, f.   *Easter*

па́хнути, 1, vb. impf., 3rd s. па́хне (+
inst.)   *smell* па́хне горі́лкою!   *there's a
smell of vodka!*

пе́вен, short m. form, -вна, -вне; -вні
adj.   *certain, sure*

пенсіоне́р, -а, m.   *pensioner*

пенсіоне́рка, -и, dat. and loc. s. -рці, gen. pl.
-рок, f.   *pensioner*

перебі́льшувати, 1, vb. impf., -ую,
-уєш   *exaggerate*

перевести́, 1, vb. pf., -еду́, -еде́ш; past tense
-ві́в, -вела́   *transfer*

переговори, -ів, pl.   *talks*

передава́ти, vb. impf., -даю́, -дає́ш   *hand
over, pass*

переда́ти, vb. pf., -дам, -даси́, -дасть; -дамо́,
-дасте́, -даду́ть   *hand over, pass*

переда́ти слова́ми   *put into words*

передпоко́й, -кою, m.   *vestibule*

перейти́, 1, vb. pf., -йду́, -йдеш, past tense
-йшо́в, -йшла́   *cross, go across*

пере́кис, -у, m.   *peroxide*

пере́клад, -у, m.   *translation*

переклада́ч, -а́, m.   *interpreter, translator*

перекла́сти, 1, vb. pf., -аду́, -аде́ш; past tense
-а́в, -а́ла   *translate*

переко́наний, -а, -е; -і, adj. (у/в +
loc.)   *convinced* (of something)

переконати, 1, vb. pf. (у/в + loc.)   *convince*
(someone of something)

перелі́к, -у, m.   *list*

перело́м, -у, m.   *fracture*

перемо́га, -и, dat. and loc. s. -о́зі, f.   *victory*

перепро́шувати, 1, vb. impf., -ую,
-уєш   *apologize, beg pardon*

перепро́шую!   *I'm sorry!*

переробити, 2, vb. pf., -блю, -биш,
-блять   *do over again, remake, transform*

переробля́ти, vb. impf.   *do over again, remake,
transform*

переса́дка, -и, dat. and loc. s. -дці, gen. pl.
-док, f.   *change* (of transport)

пересіда́ти, 1, vb. impf.   *change* (means of
transport)

пересі́сти, 1, vb. pf., -ся́ду, -ся́деш   *change*
(means of transport)

переста́вити, 2, vb. pf., -влю, -виш,
-влять   *move across, transpose*

переставля́ти, 1, vb. impf.   *move across,
transpose*

перехі́д, -хо́ду, m.   *transfer, crossing*

переходити, 2, vb. impf., -джу́, -диш   *cross,
go across*

перехо́жий, -а; -і, adj. functioning as
noun   *passer-by*

пе́рець, -рцю, m.   *pepper, paprika*

пе́рший, -а, -е; -і, ord. num.   *first*

печери́ця, -і, f.   *champignon*

пе́чиво, -а, n. (always s.)   *biscuits*

печі́нка, -и, dat. and loc. s. -нці, f.   *liver*

пи́во, -а, n.   *beer*

писа́ти, 1, vb. impf., пишу́, пи́шеш   *write*

письме́нник, -а, m.   *writer*

письмо́вий, -а, -е; -і, adj.   *writing; written*

пита́ння, -я, n.   *question*

пита́ти, 1, vb. impf.,   *ask*

пити, 1, vb. impf., п'ю, п'єш; imp.
   пий(те)!   *drink*

пів   *half*

пі́вдень, -дня, m.   *south*

пі́вніч, -ночі, inst. sg. -ніччю, f.   *north*

під, prep. (+ inst.)   *under, below*

під час (+ gen.)   *during*

підвечі́рок, -рку, m.   *tea (meal)*

підво́зити, 2, vb. impf., -о́жу, -о́зиш   *give
   someone a lift*

підгото́вка, -и, dat. and loc. s. -вці, gen. pl.
   -вок, f.   *preparation*

підгото́влений, -а, -е; -і, adj.   *prepared*

підготува́ти, 1, vb. pf., -у́ю, -у́єш   *prepare*

піджа́к, -а́, m.   *jacket*

підійти́, 1, vb. pf., -йду́, -йдеш, past tense
   -йшо́в, -йшла́   *approach, come/go up to*

під'їзд, -у, m.   *main entrance door to a block
   of flats*

підло́га, -и, dat. and loc. s. -о́зі, f.   *floor*

підня́ти, 1, vb. pf., -німу́, -німеш   *raise*

підня́тися, 1, vb. pf., -німу́ся,
   -німешся   *ascend, go up*

підприє́мство, -а, n.   *enterprise*

підру́чник, -а, m.   *textbook*

підхо́дити, 2, vb. impf., -джу́,
   -диш   *approach, come/go up to*

підхопи́ти, 2, vb. pf., -плю́, -пиш,
   -плять   *pick up, catch*

пі́зній, -я, -є; -і, adj.   *late*

пі́зно   *it is late*

пі́сля, prep. (+ gen.)   *after*

післяза́втра   *the day after tomorrow*

піти́, 1, vb. pf., піду́, пі́деш; past tense пішо́в,
   пішла́   *go, set off*

піч, пе́чі, inst. s. пі́ччю, gen. pl., пече́й,
   f.   *oven, stove*

пла́вки, -вок, pl.   *swimming costume*

пла́кати, 1, vb. impf., -а́чу, -а́чеш   *cry*

план, -у, m.   *plan; town map*

планува́ти, 1, vb. impf., -у́ю, -у́єш   *to plan*

плати́ти, 2, vb. impf., -ачу́, -а́тиш   *pay*

пла́ття, -я, n.   *dress*

платфо́рма, -и, f.   *platform*

плащ, -а́, m.   *raincoat*

племі́нник, -а, m   *nephew*

племі́нниця, -і, f.   *niece*

плита́, -и́, f.   *cooker*

пло́ща, -і, f.   *square*

плюс   *plus (in temperatures)*

пляж, -у, m.   *beach*

пля́шка, -и, dat. and loc. s. -шці, gen. pl. -шо́к,
   f.   *bottle*

пневмоні́я, -ї, f.   *pneumonia*

по, prep. (+ loc.)   *through*по-
   ки́ївськи   *Kyiv-style, à la Kyiv*

побажа́ння, -я, n.   *wish*

поба́чити, 2, vb. pf.   *see*

поба́читися, 2, vb. pf.   *see one another*

побі́гти, 2, vb. pf., -іжу́, -іжи́ш; past tense -бі́г,
   -бі́гла   *run*

побу́ти, 1, vb. pf., -у́ду, -у́деш   *spend a little
   time*

пова́га, -и, dat. and loc. sg. -а́зі, f.   *respect*

поважа́ний, -а, -е; -і, adj.   *respected*

поважа́ти, 1, vb. pf.   *respect*

повернути, 1, vb. pf., -ну́, -неш   *turn*

повернутися, 1, vb. pf., -ну́ся,
   -нешся   *return*

по́верх, -у, dat. and loc. s. -рсі, m.   *storey*

повести́, 1, vb. pf., -еду́, -еде́ш; past tense
   -ві́в, -вела́   *take (someone somewhere
   on foot)*

повече́ряти, 1, vb. pf.   *have supper*

повз, prep. (+ acc.)   *by, past*

пови́нен, short form m. -нна, -нне; -нні,
   adj.   *obliged*

повідо́мити, 2, vb. pf., -млю, -миш, -млять;
   imp. -до́м(те)!   *inform*

пові́льно   *slowly*

пові́тря, -я, n.   *air*

по́вний, -а, -е; -і, adj.   *full*

повтори́ти, 2, vb. pf.   *repeat*

пога́ний, -а, -е; -і, adj.   *bad*

пога́но!   *bad!, rotten!*

поговори́ти, 2, vb. pf.   *have a talk*

пого́да, -и, f.   *weather*

погоди́тися, 2, vb. pf., -джуся,
   -дишся   *agree*

погуля́ти, 1, vb. pf.   *go for a walk, have a
   walk*

пода́лі   *a bit further off*

подару́нок, -нка, -m.   *present, gift*

подві́йний, -а, -е; -і, adj.   *double*

подві́йність, -ності, inst. s. -ністю,
   f.   *duplicity*

подво́їти, 2, vb. impf., -о́ю, -о́їш   *redouble*

подзвони́ти, 2, vb. pf.   *give a phone call*

подиви́тися, 2, vb. impf., -влюся, -вишся,
   -вляться   *have a look*

поді́бний, -а, -е; -і, adj.   *similar*

подо́батися, 1, vb. impf. (+ dat.)   *please*

по́дорож, -і, inst. sg. -жжю, gen. pl. -жей,
   f.   *journey*

подорожува́ти, 1, vb. impf., -ую, -у́єш   *travel*

по́друга, -и, dat. and loc. s. -узі, f.   *friend
   (female)*

подру́жній, -я, -є; -і, adj.   *married*

поду́мати, 1, vb. pf.   *think (for a bit)*

позавчо́ра   *the day before yesterday*

поза́ду   *behind*

поздоро́влення, -я, n.   *congratulations*

по́зика, -и, dat. and loc. s. -иці, f.   *loan*

познайо́мити, 2, vb. pf., -млю, -миш,
   -млять (з + inst.)   *introduce (someone to
   someone)*

познайо́митися, 2, vb. pf., -млюся, -мишся,
   -мляться (з + inst.)   *become acquainted
   (with)*

по́їзд, -а, m.   *train*

по́їздка, -и, dat. and loc. s. -дці, f.   *trip*

пої́сти, vb. pf., -ї́м, -їси, -і́сть; -їмо́, -їсте́,
   -їдя́ть; imp. -ї́ж(те)!; past tense -ї́в,
   -ї́ла   *have a bite to eat*

пої́хати, 1, vb. pf., -ї́ду, -ї́деш   *set off, make
   a trip*

показа́ти, 1, vb. pf., -ажу́, -а́жеш   *show*

по́ки   *while*

по́ки не (+ pf. verb)   *until*

по́ки що   *for the time being*

поклада́ти, 1, vb. impf.   *put, place*

покла́сти, 1, vb. pf., -аду́, -аде́ш; past tense -а́в,
   -а́ла   *put, place*

пола́годити, 2, vb. pf., -джу, -диш   *settle*

полама́тися, 1, vb. pf.   *break down*

по́ле, -я, n.   *field*

полегши́ти, 2, vb. pf.   *make easier*

полежа́ти, 2, vb. pf., -жу, -жиш: imp.
   -ле́ж(те)!   *have a lie down*

полиця, -і, f.   *shelf; berth*

поліклініка, -и, dat. and loc. sg. -ці, f.   *health centre*

полуниця, -і, f.   *strawberry*

полюбити, 2, vb. pf., -блю, -биш, -блять   *become fond of*

поляк, -а, m.   *Pole*

Польща, -і, f.   *Poland*

помідор -а, m.   *tomato*

поміняти, 1, vb. pf.   *change*

поміряти, 1, vb. pf.   *try on* (clothing)

помітити, 2, vb. pf., -ічу, -ітиш   *notice*

помічник, -á, m.   *assistant, helper*

понеділок, -лка, m.   *Monday*

пообідати, 1, vb. pf.   *have some lunch*

попереду   *in front*

поплавати, 1, vb. pf.   *have a swim*

попросити, 2, vb. pf., -ошу́, -óсиш   *ask for, request; ask* (somebody to do something)

порá, -й, f.   *proper time* порá рóку   *season*

порівняння, -я, n.   *comparison*

порошóк, -шкý, m.   *powder*

портвéйн, -у, m.   *port* (drink)

пóруч   *close by*

пóряд із (+ inst.)   *alongside*

посáда, -и, f.   *position*

посáдка, -и, dat. and loc. s. -дці, f.   *landing* (of an aircraft)

поселитися, 2, vb. pf.,   *settle in* (e.g. in a hotel room)

посередині   *in the middle*

посерéдник, -а, m.   *agent*

посильний, -а; -і, adj. functioning as noun   *delivery person*

пóслуга, -и, dat. and loc. s. -узі, f.   *service, favour*

пóсмішка, -и, dat. and loc. s. -шці, gen. pl. -шок, f.   *smile*

поснідати, 1, vb. pf.   *have breakfast*

посóльство, -а, n.   *embassy*

поспáти, 2, vb. pf., -плю́, -пиш, -плять   *get some sleep*

поспішáти, 1, vb. impf.   *hurry, be in a hurry*

постáвити, 2, vb. pf., -влю, -виш, -влять; imp. -стáв(те)!   *place, put*

постáвка, -и, dat. and loc. s. -вці, gen. pl. -вок, f.   *delivery*

постарáтися, vb. pf.   *try*

пóстіль, -тéлі, inst. s. постíллю *or* постéлею, f.   *bedding*

пóсуд, -у, m.   *crockery*

пóтім   *then, later*

потребувáти, 1, vb. pf., -ýю, -ýєш (+ gen.)   *demand, need*

потрíбний, -а, -е; -і, adj. (для + gen.) (also short m. form потрíбен)   *necessary (for)*

пóтяг, -а, m.   *train*

потягти, 1, vb. pf., -гнý, -гнеш   *pull*

почáти, 1, vb. pf., -чнý, -чнéш   *begin*

почáток, -тку, m.   *beginning*

почекáти, 1, vb. pf.   *wait for a bit*

починáтися, 1, vb. impf.   *begin* (intrans.)

почувáти, 1, vb. impf. себé   *feel*

почуття, -я, n,   *feeling*

пошиття, -я, n.   *sewing*

пóшта, -и, f.   *post*

пощастити, 2, vb. pf. (impers. + dat.)   *be lucky* мені пощастило   *I had a stroke of luck*

пояснити, 2, vb. pf.   *explain*

прáвда, -и, f.   *truth*

прáвий, -а, -е; -і, adj.   *right*

пра́во, -а, n. (на + acc.) *right (to)*

право́руч *on the right, to the right*

пра́пор, -а, m. *flag*

працівни́ця, -і, f. *official (f.)*

працюва́ти, 1, vb. impf., -юю, -юєш *work*

пра́ця, -і, f. *work*

предме́т, -а, m. *item, object*

предста́вити, 2, vb. pf., -влю, -виш, -влять *introduce (someone)*

представни́к, -а́, m. *representative*

прем'є́ра, -и, f. *first night of a play*

пре́са, -и, f. *press*

прибіга́ти, 1, vb. impf. *come running*

прибі́гти, 2, vb. pf., -іжу́, -іжи́ш; past tense -бі́г, -бі́гла *come running*

прибува́ти, 1, vb. impf. *arrive*

прива́бливий, -а, -е; -і, adj. *attractive*

прива́тний, -а, -е; -і, adj. *private*

привезти́, 1, vb. pf., -зу́, -зе́ш; past tense -ві́з, -везла́ *bring (by transport)*

приві́т! *hi!*

привіта́ння, -я, n. *greetings*

привіта́ти, 1, vb. pf. (з + inst.) *welcome; congratulate (on)*

приво́зити, 2, vb. impf., -о́жу, -о́зиш *bring (by transport)*

приголо́мшити, 2, vb. pf. *stun, amaze*

приготува́ти, 1, vb. pf., -у́ю, -у́єш *prepare, get ready*

пригоща́тися, 1, vb. impf. *help oneself*

приє́мний, -а, -е; -і, adj. *pleasant, nice*

приє́мність, -ності, inst. s. -ністю, f. *pleasure*

приє́мно *it is nice*

приземле́ння, -я, n. *landing*

приїжджа́ти, 1, vb. impf. *come, arrive (by transport)*

приї́зд, -у, m. *arrival*

приїзди́ти, 2, vb. impf., -їжджу́, -їзди́ш *come, arrive (by transport)*

приї́хати, 1, vb. pf., -і́ду, -і́деш *come, arrive*

прийня́ти, 1, vb. pf., -йму́, -ймеш *receive, accept, take*

прийом, -у, m. *reception*

прийти́, 1, vb. pf., -йду́, -йдеш past tense -йшо́в, -йшла́ *come, arrive (on foot)*

при́клад, -у, m. *example*

прикордо́нник, -а, m. *frontier guard*

прикра́са, -и, f. *ornament*

прилеті́ти, 2, vb. pf., -ечу́, -ети́ш *come, arrive (by air)*

приліта́ти, 1, vb. impf. *come, arrive (by air)*

принести́, 1, vb. pf., -су́, -сеш' past tense -ніс, -несла́ *bring (on foot)*

прино́сити, 2, vb. impf., -о́шу, -о́сиш *bring (on foot)*

припини́ти, 2, vb. pf. *stop (doing something)*

приро́да, -и, f. *nature*

прихо́дити, 2, vb. impf., -джу, -диш *come, arrive (on foot)*

при́ятель, -я, m. *friend*

при́ятелька, -и, dat. and loc. s. -льці, gen. pl. -льок, f. *friend (female)*

приятелюва́ти, 1, vb. impf., -юю, -юєш *be friends*

прі́звище, -а, n. *surname*

про, prep. (+ acc.) *about*

проаналізува́ти, 1, vb. pf., -у́ю, -у́єш *analyse*

проба́чити, 2, vb. pf., imp. -ба́ч(те)! *forgive, excuse*

пробіга́ти, 1 vb. impf. *run past*

пробі́гти, 2, vb. pf., -іжу́, -іжи́ш; past tense -бі́г, -бі́гла *run past*

проблéма, -и, f. *problem*

пробýти, 1, vb. pf., -ýду, -ýдеш *spend time*

провестѝ, 1, vb. pf., -едý, -едéш; past tense -вíв, -велá *escort, convey*

провіднѝк, -á, m. *sleeping-car attendant*

провіднѝця, -і, -f. *sleeping-car attendant*

провóдити, 2, vb. impf., -джу, -диш *escort, convey*

провýлок, -лка, m. *lane*

прогрáма, -и, f. *programme*

прогýлянка, -и, dat. and loc. sg. -ці, gen. pl. -нок, f. *walk*

продавáти, 1, vb. impf., -аю́, -аéш *sell*

прóдаж, -у, loc. sg. (в) прóдажу, m. *sale*

продáти, vb. pf., -дáм, -дасѝ, -дáсть; -дамó, -дастé, -дадýть *sell*

продóвження, -я, n. *continuation*

продóвжити, 2, vb. pf. *continue*

продýкти, -ів, pl. *food*

проéкт, -у, m. *project*

проїжджáти, 1, vb. impf. *drive past/through*

проїздити, 2, vb. impf., -їжджý, -їздиш *drive past/through*

проїзнѝй квитóк *travel pass*

проїхати, 1, vb. pf., -їду, -їдеш *drive past/through*

пройтѝ, 1, vb. pf., -йдý, -йдеш, past tense -йшóв, -йшлá *pass (through)*

пролетíти, 2, vb. pf., -ечý, -етиш *fly past/through*

пролітáти, 1, vb. impf. *fly past/through*

пропозѝція, -ї, f. *proposal*

пропонувáти, 1, vb. impf., -ýю, -ýєш *propose*

пропустѝти, 2, vb. pf., -ущý, -ýстиш *miss*

проробѝти, 2, vb. pf., -блю́, -биш, -блять *spend time working*

проробля́ти, 1, vb. impf. *spend time working*

просѝти, 2, vb. impf. -ошý, -óсиш *ask for, request*

проспéкт, -у, m. *avenue*

прóсто *simply*

протé *however*

прóти, prep. (+ gen.) *against*

профéсор, -а, voc. -ре!, m. *professor*

прóфіль, -ю, m. *profile*

прохáння, -я, n. *request*

прохóдити, 2, vb. impf,. -джу, -диш *pass, go through*

прохолóдний, -а, -е; -і, adj. *cool*

прохолóдно *it is cool*

прочитáти, 1, vb. pf. *read (through)*

проя́снення, -я, n. *clear period*

прямѝй, -á, -é; -í, adj. *straight, direct*

пря́мо *straight (ahead)*

пульс, -у, m. *pulse*

пункт, -у, m. *point, spot, place*

пункт óбміну *bureau de change*

пухкѝй, -á, -é; -í, adj. *chubby*

пшенѝця, -і, f. *wheat*

п'ятдеся́т, card. num. *fifty*

п'ятдеся́тий, -а, -е; -і, ord. num. *fiftieth*

п'я́теро, coll. num. *five*

п'я́тий, -а, -е; -і, ord. num. *fifth*

п'ятисóтий, -а, -е; -і, ord. num. *five hundredth*

п'ятнáдцятий, -а, -е; -і, ord. num. *fifteenth*

п'ятнáдцять, card. num. *fifteen*

п'я́тниця, -і, f. *Friday*

п'ятсо́т, card. num.   *five hundred*
п'ять, card. num.   *five*

ра́дий, -а, -е; -і, adj. (+ dat.)   *glad*
ра́дісний, -а, -е; -і, adj.   *joyful*
ра́дість, -дості, inst. s. -дістю, f.   *joy*
раді́ти, 1, vb. impf., -ію, -ієш   *be pleased*
ра́дощі, -ів, pl.   *joy, happiness*
раз, -у, m.   *time*
ра́зом із (+ gen.)   *together with*
райо́н, -у, m.   *district*
ра́на, -ни, f.   *wound*
ра́нок, -нку, m.   *morning*ра́птом   *suddenly*
раху́нок, -нка, m.   *bill*
реєстрату́ра, -и, f.   *registration*
рейс, -у, m.   *journey, flight*
рекла́ма, -и, f.   *advertising, advertisement*
рентге́н, -у, m.   *X-ray*
рестора́н, -у, m.   *restaurant*
реце́пт, -а, m.   *prescription*
речовина́, -и́, f.   *substance*
ри́ба, -и, f.   *fish*
ри́бний, -а, -е; -і, adj.   *fish (adj.)*
риболо́вля, -і, f.   *fishing*
ри́нок, -нку, loc. s. -нку, m.   *market*
рис, -у, m.   *rice*
рі́дкісний, -а, -е; -і, adj.   *rare, unusual*
рі́зати, 1, vb. impf., рі́жу, рі́жеш   *cut*
Різдво́, -а (Різдво́ Христо́ве), n.   *Christmas*
рік, ро́ку, m.   *year*
ріка́, -и́, dat. and loc. s. ріці́, f.   *river*
річ, ре́чі, inst. s. рі́ччю, gen. pl. рече́й, f.   *thing*
до ре́чі   *by the way*

рі́чка, -и, dat. and loc. s. -чці, gen. pl. -чо́к, f.   *river, stream*
річкови́й вокза́л   *landing stage*
річни́й, -а́, -е́; -і́, adj.   *annual*
річни́ця, -і, f.   *anniversary*
роби́ти, 2, vb. impf., -блю́, -биш, -блять   *do, make*
робітни́к, -а́, m.   *worker*
робо́та, -и, f.   *work*
роди́на, -и, f.   *(extended) family*
роже́вий, -а, -е; -і, adj.   *rosy, pink*
розва́жливий, -а, -е; -і, adj.   *thoughtful, careful*
розвива́ти, 1, vb. impf.   *develop*
ро́згляд, -у, m.   *inspection, scrutiny*
розібра́тися, 1, vb. pf., -зберу́ся, -збере́шся (в + loc.)   *make sense (of), understand*
розказа́ти, 1, vb. pf., -ажу́, -а́жеш; imp. -кажи́!, -кажі́ть!   *tell*
ро́зклад, -у, m.   *timetable*
розлучи́тися, 2, vb. pf., (з + inst.)   *get divorced (from)*
розмо́ва, -и, f.   *conversation*
розмовля́ти, 1, vb. impf.   *speak, converse*
розповіда́ти, 1, vb. impf.   *tell, relate, narrate*
ро́зповідь, -і, inst s. -ддю, f.   *account (of events)*
розпоча́ти, 1, vb. pf., -чну́, -чне́ш   *begin*
розрахо́вувати, 1, vb. impf., -ую, -уєш   *reckon*
розрахо́вуватися, 1, vb. impf., -уюся, -уєшся   *pay, settle up*
розраху́нок, -нку, m.   *calculation*
розроби́ти, 2, vb. pf., -блю́, -биш, -блять   *work out, draw up*
розсу́дливий, -а, -е; -і, adj.   *prudent, sensible*

ро́зум, -у, m.   *reason, mind*

розумі́ти, vb. impf., -і́ю, -і́єш   *understand*

розу́мний, -а, -е; -і, adj.   *intelligent, clever*

роль, -і, inst. s. ро́ллю, f.   *role*

романти́чний, -а, -е; -і, adj.   *romantic*

Росі́я, -ї, f.   *Russia*

росія́нин, -а, nom. pl. росія́ни, gen. pl.
    росія́н, m.   *Russian*

росія́нка, -и, dat. and loc. s. -ці, gen. pl. -нок,
    f.   *Russian*

росли́на, -и, f.   *plant*

руди́й, -а́, -е́; -і́, adj.   *red (of hair)*

рука́, -и́, dat. and loc. s. руці́, f.   *hand, arm*

Руму́нія, -ї, f.   *Romania*

рум'я́ний, -а, -е; -і, adj.   *ruddy*

ру́чка, -и, dat. and loc. s. -чці, gen. pl. -чок,
    f.   *pen*

ряд, -у, loc. sg. (у)ряду́/ря́ді, m.   *row*

сад, -у, loc. у саду́, m.   *garden*

сала́т, -у, m.   *salad*

сало́н, -у, m.   *salon*

сам, emphatic pron.   *(one)self*

са́ме   *precisely*

са́мий, -а, -е; -і, emphatic adj.   *very*

самості́йний, -а, -е; -і, adj.   *self-reliant*

светр, -а, m.   *sweater*

свини́на, -и, f.   *pork*

сві́дчення, -я, n.   *evidence*

сві́жий, -а, -е; -і, adj.   *fresh*

свій, m.; своя́, f.; своє́, n.; свої́, pl.   *my, your,
    his, her, our, their (own)*

світ, -у, m.   *world*

світови́й, -а́, -е́, -і́, adj.   *world*

сві́тлий, -а, -е; -і, adj.   *bright, light*

сві́чка, -и, dat. and loc. s. -чці, gen. pl. -чок,
    f.   *candle*

своєрі́дний, -а, -е; -і, adj.   *original, unique*

свя́то, -а, n.   *festival*

святко́вий, -а, -е; -і, adj.   *festive*

святкува́ння, -я, n.   *celebration*

святкува́ти, 1, vb. impf., -у́ю, -у́єш   *celebrate*

себе́, reflexive pron., no nom., acc. and gen.
    себе́, dat. and loc. собі́, inst. собо́ю   *self*

сезо́н, -у, m.   *season*

секре́т, -у, m.   *secret*

секрета́р, -я́, m.   *secretary*

секу́нда, -и, f.   *second*

село́, -а, gen. pl. сіл, n.   *village*

се́меро, coll. num.   *seven*

семисо́тий, -а, -е; -і, ord. num.   *seven
    hundredth*

серве́тка, -и dat. and loc. s. -тці, gen. pl. -ток,
    f.   *serviette*

серві́з, -у, m.   *service (of crockery)*

се́рдитися, vb. impf., -джуся, -дишся (на +
    acc.)   *be angry (with)*

середа́, -и́, f.   *Wednesday*

сере́дній, -я, -є; -і, adj.   *middle, medium*

сере́жка, -и dat. and loc. s. -ці, gen. pl. -жок,
    f.   *earring*

серйо́зний, -а, -е; -і, adj.   *serious*

се́рпень, -пня, m.   *August*

се́рце, -я, gen. pl. серде́ць, n.   *heart*

сестра́, -и́, gen. pl. сесте́р, f.   *sister*

сигаре́та, -и, f.   *cigarette*

си́льний, -а, -е; -і, adj.   *strong*

син, -а, m.   *son*

си́ній, -я, -є; -і, adj.   *blue, dark blue*

сир, -у, m.   *cheese*

сіда́ти, 1, vb. impf.   *sit down*

сік, со́ку, loc. sg. у соку́, m.   *juice*

сім, card. num.   *seven*

сімдеся́т, card. num.   *seventy*

сімдеся́тий, -а, -е; -і, ord. num.   *seventieth*

сімна́дцятий, -а, -е; -і, ord. num.   *seventeenth*

сімна́дцять, card. num.   *seventeen*

сімсо́т, card. num.   *seven hundred*

Сімферо́поль, -я, m.   *Simferopol*

сім'я́, -ї́, f.   *family*

сі́рий, -а, -е; -і, adj.   *grey*

сі́сти, 1, vb. pf., ся́ду, ся́деш   *sit down*

сі́сти на (+ acc.)   *get on* (means of transport)

сі́чень, -чня, m.   *January*

ска́ржитися, 2, vb. impf. (на + acc.)   *complain (of)*

ска́терка, -и, dat. and loc. s. -рці, gen. pl. -рок, f.   *tablecloth*

скеля, -і, f.   *rock, cliff*

скі́льки?   *how many?*

скла́сти, 1, vb. pf., -аду́, -аде́ш, past tense -ав, -а́ла   *put together, form*

скля́нка, -и, dat. and loc. sg. -нці, gen. pl. -но́к, f.   *(drinking) glass*

ско́ро   *soon*

ску́чити, 2, vb. pf., (за + inst.)   *miss, long for*

сла́бість, -бості, inst. s. -бістю, f.   *weakness*

слайд, -а, m.   *(photographic) slide*

слід (+ dat.)   *ought, should*

словни́к, -а́, m.   *dictionary*

сло́во, -а, gen. pl. слів, n.   *word*

службо́вий, -а, -е; -і, adj.   *official*

служи́ти, 2, vb. impf.   *serve*

слу́хати, 1, vb. impf.   *listen*

слу́шний, -а, -е; -і, adj.   *proper, reasonable*

слю́сар, -я, m.   *plumber*

смагля́вий, -а, -е; -і, adj.   *swarthy, tanned*

сма́жений, -а, -е; -і, adj.   *fried*

смак, -у, m.   *taste*

смачни́й, -а́, -е́; -і́, adj.   *tasty*

сма́чно   *it is tasty*

смерка́ти, 1, vb. impf. (impers.)   *get dark*

смета́на, -и, f.   *sour cream*

сміятися, 1, vb. impf., -ію́ся, -іє́шся   *laugh*

сму́жка, -и, dat. and loc. s. -жці, gen. pl. -жок, f.   *strip*

сніг, -у, loc. s. у снігу́, m.   *snow*

сніда́нок, -нку, m.   *breakfast*

собо́р, -у, m.   *cathedral*

солі́дний, -а, -е; -і, adj.   *solid*

соло́дкий, -а, -е; -і, adj.   *sweet*

соля́нка, -и, dat. and loc. s. -нці, f.   *solyanka (a kind of soup)*

со́нце, -я, n.   *sun*

со́рок, card. num.   *forty*

соро́ко́вий, -а, -е; -і, ord. num.   *fortieth*

соро́чка, -и, dat. and loc. s. -чці, gen. pl. -чо́к, f.   *shirt*

соси́ска, -и, dat. and loc. sg. -ці, gen. pl. -сок, f.   *(Frankfurter) sausage*

со́тий, -а, -е; -і, ord. num.   *hundredth*

со́ус, -у, m.   *(culinary) sauce*

сою́з, -у, m.   *union*

спа́льний ваго́н   *sleeping car*

спа́льня, -і, gen. pl. -лень, f.   *bedroom*

спа́ти, 2, vb. impf., сплю, спиш, сплять   *sleep*

спеко́тний, -а, -е, -і, adj.   *hot (of weather)*

спекотно   *it is hot*

спе́реду   *from the front*

спереча́тися, 1, vb. impf.   *quarrel*

спеціалізува́тися, 1, vb. impf., -у́юся, -у́єшся (на + loc.) *specialize (in)*

спини́ти, 2, vb. pf., *stop* (transitive)

спини́тися, 2, vb. pf. *stop* (intransitive)

спита́ти, 1, vb. pf. *ask*

співпрацюва́ти, 1, vb. impf., -юю, -юєш *collaborate*

співпра́ця, -і, f. *collaboration*

співчува́ти, 1, vb. impf. (+ dat.) *sympathize (with)*

спідни́ця, -і, f. *skirt*

спі́льний, -а, -е; -і, adj. *joint*

сподіва́тися, 1, vb. impf. (на + acc.) *hope (for)*

сподо́батися, 1, vb. pf. (+ dat.) *please*

спо́кій, -кою, m. *calm, peace*

споко́йний, -а, -е; -і, adj. *calm*

спорт, -у, m. *sport*

спра́ва, -и, f. *affair, business, matter*

спра́вді *really, truly*

справжні́й, -я, -є; -і, adj. *real, genuine*

спусти́тися, 2, vb. pf., -ущу́ся, -у́стишся *descend, go down*

става́ти, 1, vb. impf., стаю́, стає́ш (+ inst.) *become*

ста́вити, 2, vb. impf., -влю, -виш, -влять, imp. ста́в(те)! *put, ask (a question)*

ста́влення, -я, n. (до + gen.) *attitude (towards)*

ста́нція, -ї, f. *station*

стари́й, -а́, -е́; -і́, adj. *old*

ста́рший, -а, -е; -і, comp. and super. adj. *elder, eldest*

ста́тися, 1, vb. pf., 3rd s. ста́неться (з + inst.) *happen (to)*

створення, -я, n. *creation*

створи́ти, 2, vb. pf. *create*

сте́жити, 2, vb. impf. (за + inst.) *look after*

сте́ля, -і, f. *ceiling*

стіл, стола́, m. *table*

стіле́ць, -льця́, m. *chair*

стіна́, -й, f. *wall*

сто, card. num. *hundred*

столи́чний, -а, -е; -і, adj. *capital*

стоми́тися, 2, vb. pf., -млюся, -мишся, -мляться *get tired* я стоми́вся *I am tired*

сто́млений, -а, -е; -і, adj. *tired*

стосо́вно (+ gen.) *relating to, on the matter of*

стосу́нок, -нку, m. *relation, attitude*

стоя́ти, 1, vb. impf., -ою́, -ої́ш, imp. стій(те)! *stand*

стра́ва, -и, f. *dish, course*

страхова́ компа́нія *insurance company*

страхува́ння, -я, n. *insurance*

стра́шно *terribly*

стри́маність, -ності, inst. s. -ністю, f. *reserve*

субо́та, -и, f. *Saturday*

су́кня, -і, gen. pl. -конь, f. *dress*

су́ма, -и, f. *sum*

су́мка, -и, dat. and loc. s. -мці, gen. pl. -мок, f. *bag*

су́мнів, -у, m. *doubt*

сумни́й, -а́, -є́; -і́, adj. *sad*

сумува́ти, 1, vb. impf., -ю́ю, -у́єш *be sad*

суп, -у, m. *soup*

сусі́д, -а, m. *neighbour*

сусі́дка, -и, dat. and loc. s. -дці, gen. pl. -док, f. *neighbour*

сухи́й, -а́, -е́; -і́, adj. *dry*

суча́сний, -а, -е; -і, adj. *modern*

су́ша, -і, f. *dry land*

сфотографува́ти, 1, vb. pf., -у́ю, -у́єш *photograph*

схвилюва́ти, 1, vb. pf., -юю, -юєш *move (emotionally)*

схід, схо́ду, m. *east*

схі́дці, -ів, pl. *staircase*

схо́жий, -а, -е; -і, adj. (на + асс.) *like, similar (to)*

сього́дні *today*

сьо́мий, -а, -е; -і, ord. num. *seventh*

сюди́ *here, hither*

сюрпри́з, -у, m. *surprise*

та *and*

табле́тка, -и, dat. and loc. s. -тці, gen. pl. -ток, f. *tablet*

табли́чка, -и, dat. and loc. sg. -ччі, gen. pol. -чок, f. *noticeboard*

так *yes*

так і *just precisely*

так собі́! *so-so!*

таки́й же, . . . *same*

таки́й са́мий, . . . *similar*

таки́й, -á, -é; -í, adj. *such (a) (in exclamations followed by an adjective)*

тако́ж *also*

таксі́, n. indecl. *taxi*

талани́ти, 2, vb. impf. (impers. + dat.) *be lucky*

тало́н, -а, m. *ticket (urban transport)*

там *there*

тарі́лка, -и dat. and loc. s. -лці, gen. pl. -лóк, f. *plate*

тарі́лочка, -и, dat. and loc. s. -ччі, gen. pl. -чóк, f. *small plate*

та́то, -а, m. *daddy*

твій, m., твоя́, f., тво́є, n.; твої́, pl., poss. pron. *your (s. familiar)*

теж *also*

те́ка, -и, dat. and loc. s., те́ці, f. *file, folder*

тексти́льний, -а, -е; -і, adj. *textile*

телеба́чення, -я, n. *television*

телеві́зор, -а, m. *television (set)*

телегра́ма, -и, f. *telegram*

телефо́н, -у, m. *telephone, telephone number*

телефонува́ти, 1, vb. impf., -ýю, -ýєш *phone*

те́мний, -а, -е; -і, adj. *dark*

те́ніс, -у, m. *tennis*

те́плий, -а, -е; -і, adj. *warm*

термінó́вий, -а, -е; -і, adj. *urgent*

термінó́во *urgently*

термо́метр, -а, m. *thermometer*

техноло́гія, -ї, f. *technology*

ти, pers. pron., acc. and gen. тебé, dat. and loc. тобі́, inst. тобóю *you (s. familiar)*

ти́ждень, -жня, m. *week*

типо́вий, -а, -е; -і, adj. *typical*

ти́сяча, -і, f., card. num. *thousand*

ти́сячний, -а, -е; -і, ord. num. *thousandth*

ти́хий, -а, -е; -і, adj. *quiet, peaceful*

ти́хо *it is quiet*

тісни́й, -á, -é; -í, adj. *narrow, tight*

ті́стечко, -а, n. *cake*

ті́тка, -и, dat. and loc. s. -ці, f. *aunt*

ткани́на, -и, f. *cloth, fabric, material*

то *that is, those are*

тóбто *in other words, i.e.*

това́р, -у, m. *goods*

товари́ство, -а, n. *club, society; folks*

това́риш, -а, m. *companion, workmate*

това́ришка, -и, dat. and loc. s. -шці, gen. pl. -шóк f. *companion* товаришува́ти, 1, vb. impf., -у́ю, -у́єш *be friends*

тоді́ *then, in that case*

той, m., та, f., те, n.; ті, pl., dem. pron. *that*

тому́ *therefore; ago* (in time phrases)

тому́ що *because*

тонки́й, -а́, -е́; -і́, adj. *slender, slim*

торгі́вля, -і, f. *trade*

тост, -у, m. *toast* (drinking)

то́чно *certainly*

то́що *and so on, etc.*

трава́, -и́, f. *grass, herb*

тра́вень, -вня, m. *May*

тра́вма, -и, f. *injury*

травматологі́чний пункт *accident & emergency department; A&E*

традиці́йний, -а, -е; -і, adj. *traditional*

тради́ція, -ї, f. *tradition*

трамва́й, -а́я, m. *tram*

тра́нспорт, -у, m. *transport*

транспорте́р, -а, m. *conveyor*

транспортува́ння, -я, n. *transportation*

тра́питися, 2, vb. pf., 3rd s. -питься, 3rd pl. -пляться *happen*

тре́ба *(it is) necessary*

тре́тій, -я, -є; -і, ord. num. *third*

три, card. num. *three*

трива́лість, -лості, inst. s. -лістю *length, duration*

тридця́тий, -а, -е; -і, ord. num. *thirtieth*

три́дцять, card. num. *thirty*

трикімна́тний, -а, -е; -і, adj. *three-roomed*

трина́дцятий, -а, -е; -і, ord. num. *thirteenth*

трина́дцять, card. num. *thirteen*

триста, card. num. *three hundred*

тріска́, -и́, dat. and loc. s. -сці́, f. *cod*

тріско́вий, -а, -е; -і, adj. *cod*

тро́є, coll. num. *three*

троле́йбус, -а, m. *trolleybus*

тропі́чний, -а, -е; -і, adj. *tropical*

тро́шки *a bit, a little*

троя́нда, -и, f. *rose*

трьохсо́тий, -а, -е; -і, ord. num. *three hundredth*

туале́т, -у, m. *toilet*

туди́ *there, thither*

турбо́та, -и, f. *trouble*

турбува́ти, 1, vb. impf., -у́ю, -у́єш *trouble, disturb*

турбува́тися, 1, vb. impf., -у́юся, -у́єшся *trouble oneself*

тури́ст, -а, m. *tourist*

тут *here*

у (в), prep. (+ асс.) *to, into*

у (в), prep. (+ loc.) *in*

убра́ний (вбра́ний), adj. *dressed*

ува́га, -и, dat. and loc. s. -зі, f. *attention*

уважа́ти (вважа́ти), 1, vb. impf. *consider*

уве́сь, m.; уся́, f.; усе́, n.; усі́, pl. (ввесь, вся, все; всі) *all*

уве́чері (вве́чері) *in the evening*

увійти́, 1, vb. pf., -йду́, -йде́ш, past tense -йшо́в, -йшла́ *enter, go into*

уго́рщина, -и, f. *Hungary*

удво́х (вдвох) *the two of us together*

уде́нь (вдень) *in the daytime*

удо́ма (вдо́ма) *at home*

удру́ге (вдру́ге) *for the second time*

уже́ (вже) *already*

узвíз, -вóзу, m.   *hill*

узи́мку (взи́мку)   *in winter*

указáти (вказáти), 1, vb. pf., -ажý,
   -áжеш   *indicate, point out*

уключи́ти (включи́ти), 2, vb. pf., (до +
   gen.)   *include (in)*

Украї́на, -и, f.   *Ukraine*

украї́нець, -нця, m.   *Ukrainian*

украї́нка, -и, dat. and loc. s. -ці, f.   *Ukrainian*

украї́нський, -а, -е; -і, adj.   *Ukrainian*

улíтку (влíтку)   *in summer*

умивáти (вмивáти), 1, vb. impf.   *wash*

умивáтися (вмивáтися), 1, vb. impf.   *wash
   oneself*

умíлий, -а, -е; -і, adj.   *skilled*

умíння, -я, n.   *ability*

умíти (вмíти), 1, vb. impf., -íю, -íєш   *be able,
   know how*

університéт, -у, m.   *university*

уночí (вночí)   *at night*

упéрше   *for the first time*

уражáти (вражáти), 1, vb. impf.   *amaze*

урáження, -я, (врáження) n.   *impression*

урáнці (врáнці)   *in the morning*

ýспіх, -у, m. (usually pl. ýспіхи, -ів)   *success*

устáвити (встáвити), 2, vb. pf., -влю, -виш,
   -влять   *insert*

уставля́ти (вставля́ти), 1, vb. impf.   *insert*

усти́гнути (всти́гнути), 1, vb. pf., -ну,
   -неш   *manage, succeed*

учи́тель (вчи́тель), -я, m.   *teacher*

учи́телька (вчи́телька), -и dat. and loc. s.
   -льці, gen. pl. -льок, f.   *teacher*

учóра (вчóра)   *yesterday*

уявля́ти, 1, vb. impf. (собí)   *imagine (to
   oneself)*

фáбрика, -и, dat. and loc. s. -иці, f.   *factory*

факс, -у, m.   *fax*

фарширóваний, -а, -е; -і, adj.   *stuffed*

фах, -у, m.   *profession*

фахівéць, -вця́, m.   *specialist*

філé, n. indecl.   *fillet*

фінáнси, -ів, pl.   *finances*

фінáнсовий, -а, -е; -і, adj.   *financial*

фінансувáння, -я, n.   *financing*

фіолéтовий, -а, -е; -і, adj.   *violet (colour)*

фірáнка, -и, dat. and loc. s. -нці, gen. pl. -нок,
   f.   *curtain, window blind*

фíрма, -и, f.   *firm*

фíрмовий, -а, -е; -і, adj.   *firm's*

фóрма, -и, f.   *form, condition*

фортепіáно, n. indecl.   *piano*

фóто, n. indecl.   *photograph*

фотомодéль, -і, inst. s. -дéеллю, f.   *model*

Фрáнція, -ї, f.   *France*

францýженка, -и, dat. and loc. s. -нці, gen. pl.
   -нок   *Frenchwoman*

францýз, -а, m.   *Frenchman*

фрукт, -а, m. (usually pl. – фрýкти, -ів)   *fruit*

фруктóвий, -а, -е; -і, adj.   *fruit*

фужéр, -а, m.   *(wine) glass*

фунікулéр, -а, m.   *funicular railway*

функціонувáти, 1, vb. impf., -ýю,
   -ýєш   *function*

футбóлка, -и, dat. and loc. s. лці, gen. pl. -лок,
   f.   *sports shirt*

хай . . .   *may . . .*

харáктер, -у, m.   *character*

хвили́на, -и, f.   *minute, moment*

хвилювáтися, 1, v. impf., -ююся,
   -юєшся   *worry* (intransitive), *be worried*

хвилястий, -а, -е; -і, adj.   *wavy*

хвіст, -воста, m.   *tail*

хворий, -а, -е; -і, adj.   *sick;* noun   *patient*

хворіти, vb. impf., -íю, -íєш   *be ill*

хéрес, -у, m.   *sherry*

хлóпчик, -а, m.   *boy*

хмáрно   *it is cloudy*

ходити, 2, vb. impf., -джý, -диш   *go* (on foot)

ходíмо!   *let's go!*

хол, -у, m.   *hall*

хóлод, -у, m.   *cold*

холóдний, -а, -е; -і, adj.   *cold*

хóлодно   *it is cold*

хотíти, 1, vb. impf., хóчу, хóчеш   *want*

хочá   *although*

хочá б   *even if only*

хто?, interrog. pron., acc. and gen. кого́, dat. кому́, inst. ким, loc. кому́   *who?*

хто-нéбудь, indef. pron.   *anyone, someone*

хтось, indef. pron. acc. and gen. когось, dat. комусь, inst. кимось, loc. комусь (кімось)   *someone*

худóжник, -а, m.   *artist*

худóжник-модельéр   *fashion designer*

худóжній, -я, -є; -і, adj.   *artistic, art*

це   *this is, there are*

цей, m., ця, f., це, n.; ці, pl., dem. pron.   *this*

цéрква, -и, gen. pl. -кóв, f.   *church*

цибýля, -і, f.   *onion*

цирк, -у, m.   *circus*

цікáвий, -а, -еп -і, adj.   *interesting*

цікáвити, 2, vb. impf., -влю, -виш, -влять   *interest*

цікáвитися, 2, vb. impf., -влюся, -вишся, -вляться   *be interested in, wonder*

цікáвість, -вості, inst. s. -вістю, f.   *curiosity*

цíлий, -а, -е; -і, adj.   *whole*

цілувáти, 1 vb. impf., -ýю, -ýєш   *kiss*

цінá, -й, f.   *price*

цінувáти, 1, vb. impf., -ýю, -ýєш   *appreciate*

цукéрка, -и, dat. and loc. s. -рці, gen. pl. -рок, f.   *sweet, candy*

цýкор, -кру, m.   *sugar*

чай, -ю, m.   *tea*

чáйна лóжка   *teaspoon*

чарівнúй, -á, -é; -í, adj.   *enchanting*

чáрка, -и, dat. and loc. s. -рці, gen. pl. -рóк, f.   *glass* (for spirits)

час, -у, m.   *time*

частúна, -и, f.   *part*

чáсто   *often*

чáшка, -и, dat. and loc. s. -шці, gen. pl. -шóк, f.   *cup*

чверть, -і, f.   *quarter*

чек, -а, m.   *cheque*

чекáти, 1, vb. impf. (на + acc.)   *expect, wait (for)*

чéрвень, -вня, m.   *June*

червóний, -а, -е; -і, adj.   *red*

чéрга, -и, dat. and loc. s. -рзі, f.   *queue*

черговúй, -á, -é; -í, adj. *successive, next;* noun   *person on duty*

чéрез, prep. (+ acc.)   *via, through, because of*

Чернівцí, -ів, pl.   *Czernowitz*

Чернíгів, -гова, m.   *Chernihiv*

чéсно   *honestly*

чéсний, -а -е; -і, adj.   *honest*

честь, -і, inst. s. -тю, f.   *honour*

четвéр, -ргá, m.   *Thursday*

чéтверо, coll. num.   *four*

четве́ртий, -а, -е; -і, ord. num. *fourth*

чи *or; whether* (word introducing a question)

чий, -я́, -є́; -ї́? interrog. pron. *whose?*

чи́мось *in some way*

число́, -а́, n. *number, date*

чи́стий, -а, -е; -і, adj. *clean*

чита́ти, 1, vb. impf. *read*

чо́вен, -вна, m. *boat*

чолові́к, -а, m. *man, husband*

чолові́чий, -а, -е; -і, adj. *male*

чому́? *why?*

чому́сь *for some reason*

чо́рний, -а, -е; -і, adj. *black*

чорно́слив, -у, m. *prunes*

чорт, -а, m. *devil*

чоти́ри, card. num. *four*

чотирна́дятий, -а, -е: -і ord. num. *fourteenth*

чотирна́дцять, card. num. *fourteen*

чоти́риста, card. num. *four hundred*

чотирьохсо́тий, -а, -е; -і, ord. num. *four hundredth*

чудо́вий, -а, -е; -і, adj. *wonderful*

чудо́во! *great! fine!*

чу́ти, 1, vb. impf. *hear*

шампа́нське, -ого, adj. functioning as n. noun *champagne*

шано́вний, -а, -е; -і, adj. *esteemed, respected*

ша́пка, -и, dat. and loc. s. -пці gen. pl. -пок, f. *hat*

шате́нка, -и dat. and loc. s. -ці, gen. pl. -нок, f. *woman with chestnut hair*

ша́фа, -и, f. *cupboard*

ша́хи, -ів, pl. *chess*

шашли́к, -у́, m. *kebab*

швидки́й, -а́, -е́; -і́, adj. *quick, fast*

шви́дко *quickly*

шви́дший, -а, -е; -і, comp. adj. *quicker, faster*

ше́стеро, coll. num. *six*

шестисо́тий, -а, -е; -і, ord. num. *six hundredth*

широ́кий, -а, -е; -і, adj. *wide, broad*

ши́рший, -а, -е; -і, comp. adj. *wider, broader*

ши́ти, 1, vb. impf. и́ю, -и́єш *sew*

шістдеся́т, card. num. *sixty*

шістдеся́тий, -а, -е; -і, ord. num. *sixtieth*

шістна́дцятий, -а, -е; -і, ord. num. *sixteenth*

шістна́дцять, card. num. *sixteen*

шістсо́т, card. num. *six hundred*

шість, card. num. *six*

шкарпе́тка, -и dat. and loc. s. -тці, gen. pl. -ток, f. *sock*

шкі́ра, -и f. *skin*

шкіряни́й, -а́, -е́; -і́, adj. *leather* (adj.)

шкода́! *it's a pity!*мені́ шкода́ *I'm sorry*

шокола́д, -у, m. *chocolate*

шо́рти, -ів, pl. *shorts*

шо́стий, -а, -е; -і, ord. num. *sixth*

Шотла́ндія, -ї, f. *Scotland*

шпро́ти, -ів, pl. *sprats*

штамп, -а, m. *cancellation stamp*

штани́, -і́в, pl. *trousers*

штраф, -у, m. *fine*

щасли́во! *cheerio!*

щасти́ти, 2, vb. impf. (impers. + dat.) *be lucky*

мені́ щасти́ть *I am in luck*

ща́стя, -я, n. *happiness*

ще *yet, still, also, as well*

щи́рий, -а, -е; -і, adj.   *sincere*

щи́ро   *sincerely*

що?, interr. pron., acc. що, gen. чого́, dat. чому́, inst. чим, loc. чому́   *what?*

що-не́будь, indef. pron.   *anything, something*

щоб   *in order to*

щодня́   *every day*

щодо prep. + gen.   *as for, as to*

щойно   *just*

щока́, -и, dat. and loc. s -щоці́, gen. pl. щік, f.   *cheek*

щопра́вда   *indeed*

щось, indef. pron., acc. щось, gen. чого́сь, dat. чому́сь, inst. чи́мось, loc. чому́сь   *something*

ювелі́рний, -а, -е; -і, adj.   *jewellery*

юна́к, -а́, m.   *young man*

юри́ст, -а, m.   *lawyer*

ю́шка, -и, dat. and loc. s. -шці, f.   *yooshka (a kind of soup)*

я, pers. pron., acc. and gen. мене́, dat. and loc. мені́, inst. мно́ю   *I*

я́блуко, -а, n.   *apple*

я́блучний, -а, -е; -і, adj.   *apple*

я́года, -и, gen. pl. я́гід, f.   *berry*

язи́к, -а́, m.   *tongue*

яйце́, -я́, gen. pl. яє́ць, n.   *egg*

як?   *how?*

як ті́льки   *as soon as*

якби́   *if*

яки́й, -а́, -é; -і́, adj.   *how, what (a)!* (in exclamations, followed by adj.)

яки́й, -а́, -é; -і́, relative pron.   *which, that*

яки́й? interrogative adj.   *what kind of?*

яки́йсь, -а́сь, -е́сь; -і́сь, indef. adj.   *some kind of*

я́кісний, -а, -е; -і adj.   *high quality*

я́кість, -кості, inst. sg. -кістю, f.   *quality*

якомо́га (+ comparative adv.)   *as . . . as possible*

якщо́   *if*

я́ловичий, -а, -е; -і, adj.   *beef* (adj.)

Я́лта, -и, f.   *Yalta*

япо́нець, -ця, m.   *Japanese*

Япо́нія, -ї, f.   *Japan*

япо́нка, -и, -нці, dat. and loc. s. gen. pl. -нок f.   *Japanese*

яскра́вий, -а, -е; -і, adj.   *bright*

Grammatical index

The numbers in bold are the numbers of the units that include the material.